The Enemy in Italian Renaissance Epic

THE EARLY MODERN EXCHANGE

Series Editors

Gary Ferguson, University of Virginia; Meredith K. Ray, University of Delaware

Series Editorial Board

Frederick A. de Armas, University of Chicago; Valeria Finucci, Duke University; Barbara Fuchs, UCLA; Nicholas Hammond, University of Cambridge; Kathleen P. Long, Cornell University; Elissa B. Weaver, Emerita, University of Chicago

The Early Modern Exchange publishes studies of European literature and culture (c. 1450–1700) exploring connections across intellectual, geographical, social, and cultural boundaries: transnational, transregional engagements; networks and processes for the development and dissemination of knowledges and practices; gendered and sexual roles and hierarchies and the effects of their transgression; relations between different ethnic or religious groups; travel and migration; textual circulation/s. The series welcomes critical approaches to multiple disciplines (e.g., literature and law, philosophy, science, medicine, music, etc.) and objects (e.g., print and material culture, the visual arts, architecture), the reexamination of historiographical categories (such as medieval, early modern, modern), and the investigation of resonances across broad temporal spans.

Titles in the Series

Involuntary Confessions of the Flesh in Early Modern France, Nora Martin Peterson

The Enemy in Italian Renaissance Epic: Images of Hostility from Dante to Tasso, Andrea Moudarres

The Enemy in Italian Renaissance Epic

Images of Hostility from Dante to Tasso

Andrea Moudarres

UNIVERSITY OF DELAWARE PRESS
Newark
Distributed by the University of Virginia Press

University of Delaware Press
© 2019 by Andrea Moudarres
All rights reserved
Printed in the United States of America on acid-free paper

First published 2019

ISBN 978-1-64453-000-9 (cloth)
ISBN 978-1-64453-001-6 (paper)
ISBN 978-1-64453-002-3 (e-book)

1 3 5 7 9 8 6 4 2

Library of Congress Cataloging-in-Publication Data is available for this title.

Cover art: Detail from *David with the Head of Goliath*, Caravaggio, 1606.
(Galleria Borghese, Rome, Lazio, Italy/Bridgeman Images)

From you, O goddess, from you the winds flee away, the clouds of heaven from you and your coming; for you the wonder-working earth puts forth sweet flowers, for you the wide stretches of ocean laugh, and heaven grown peaceful glows with outpoured light.

—Lucretius, *De rerum natura*

Contents

Acknowledgments	ix
Introduction	1
1. Between Fathers and Sons: Sowers of Enmity in *Inferno* 28	15
2. The Enemy within the Walls: Treachery, Pride, and Civil Strife in Pulci's *Morgante*	43
3. The Enemy as the Self: Madness and Tyranny in Ariosto's *Orlando Furioso*	75
4. The Geography of the Enemy: Christian and Islamic Empires from the Fall of Constantinople to Tasso's *Gerusalemme Liberata*	105
Epilogue: The Mirror of the Friend?	143
Notes	147
Bibliography	203
Index	239

Acknowledgments

This book began as a doctoral dissertation at Yale University under the enlightening supervision of Giuseppe Mazzotta. His voracious intellectual curiosity has been—and always will be—a source of inspiration. Millicent Marcus and David Quint provided generous feedback and probing criticism that helped me rethink the structure of this project. Without Piero Boitani's encouragement and unflinching support over the last twenty years, I would not have crossed the Pillars of Hercules. His course on Ulysses at the University of Rome, "La Sapienza," ignited my passion for the study of literature. I am also indebted to my teachers, colleagues, and friends at the University of Notre Dame: Zyg Barański, Ted Cachey, Margaret Meserve, Christian Moevs, Colleen Ryan, Patrick Vivirito, and John Welle. They created a stimulating and welcoming atmosphere during the two years in which South Bend was my home.

My colleagues at the UCLA Department of Italian have fostered a supportive environment without which I would not have been able to complete this book: Massimo Ciavolella, Thomas Harrison, Lucia Re, Pete Stacey, Dominic Thomas, Elissa Tognozzi, and Stefania Tutino. I also wish to express my gratitude to other UCLA colleagues in neighboring departments: Carol Bakhos, Lia Brozgal, Jean-Claude Carron, Nina Eidsheim, Barbara Fuchs, Robert Gurval, David Kim, Efraín Kristal, Benjamin Madley, Kirstie McClure, Joseph Nagy, Anthony Pagden, Davide Panagia, David Schaberg, Giulia Sissa, Zrinka Stahuljak, Bronwen Wilson, and Maite Zubiaurre. Their wisdom and collegiality have made UCLA an ideal setting for me to learn, teach, and write. Among the colleagues whose suggestions and criticism over the last several years have improved this book I am particularly grateful to Albert Ascoli, Jo Ann Cavallo, Jim Coleman, Laura Giannetti, Toby Levers, David Lummus, Barry McCrea, Vittorio Montemaggi, Pina Palma, Gabriele Pedullà, Kristin Phillips-Court, Diego Pirillo, Alessandro Polcri, Guido

Ruggiero, Arielle Saiber, Justin Steinberg, Walter Stephens, Nora Stoppino, Francesca Trivellato, and Jane Tylus.

I am also grateful to the reviewers of this manuscript—their suggestions have significantly strengthened this project—and to Julia Oestreich, who has provided indispensable guidance throughout the publication process. I also owe a debt of gratitude to Valeria Finucci and Meredith Ray, who have supported the publication of this book in The Early Modern Exchange Series for the University of Delaware Press. Thanks to Julia Boss, who has extensively commented on the entire manuscript, and my research assistants at UCLA: Nina Bjekovic, Sarah Cantor, Allison Collins, Cristina Politano, and Joseph Tumolo, all of whom have provided much needed help at various stages of this project. Research for this book has been made possible by an ACLS New Faculty Fellowship and a UCLA Faculty Career Development Award.

Most of all, I am grateful to my loving family. Special thanks to my wife Christiana, who has read and seen this project develop since its inception. To my sister Laura I am especially grateful for her thoughtfulness and wit. I dedicate this book to my parents, Pina and Haisam, who have supported me all along.

An earlier version of a section of chapter 1 was published as a journal article, "Beheading the Son: Mohammed and Bertran de Born in *Inferno* 28," *California Italian Studies* 5:1 (2014): 550–65. Chapter 2 includes a short and much revised version of an essay published as, "The Giant's Heel: Pride and Treachery in Pulci's *Morgante*," *MLN* 127.1 (2012): 164–72; an earlier version of a section of chapter 4 was published as a journal article, "Crusade and Conversion: Islam as Schism in Pius II and Nicholas of Cusa," *MLN* 128.1 (2013): 40–52, © The Johns Hopkins University Press. Chapter 4 includes a revised section published as a book chapter, "The Geography of the Enemy: Old and New Empires between Humanistic Debates and Tasso's *Gerusalemme liberata*," in *New Worlds and the Italian Renaissance: Contributions to the History of European Intellectual Culture*, ed. Andrea Moudarres and Christiana Purdy Moudarres (Leiden: Brill, 2012), 291–332. My thanks to these publishers for their permission to reprint this material.

The Enemy in Italian Renaissance Epic

Introduction

IN THE OPENING LINES of his unfinished historical epic *Civil War*, the Roman poet Lucan deploys a graphic bodily metaphor of self-mutilation to introduce the subject of his poem. Writing at the time of Nero, in the first century CE, Lucan takes a strikingly anti-imperial and anti-Virgilian position on the political upheaval that led to the rise of the Augustan Principate. He depicts the Roman commonwealth as a body gutting itself by means of the internecine conflict between Julius Caesar and Pompey, his son-in-law. At the same time, since the city of Rome was *caput mundi* (literally, "head of the world," as Lucan writes in *Civil War* 2.655), a war that eviscerated Rome would, by extension, decapitate the world order that existed before the emergence of the Empire: "Of war I sing, war worse than civil, waged over the plains of Emathia, and of legality conferred on crime; I tell how an imperial people turned their victorious hands against their own vitals; how kindred fought against kindred; how, when the compact of tyranny was shattered, all the forces of the shaken world contended to make mankind guilty; how standards confronted hostile standards, eagles were matched against each other, and pilum threatened pilum" (*Civil War* 1.1–7).[1] The self-inflicted wound in Rome's political body vividly captures the institutional disintegration of the Republic: Lucan thus exposes the ugly truth about the war to which Virgil only briefly alludes in the *Aeneid*. In a well-known passage from book 6 of Virgil's work, Aeneas descends to Hades to encounter his father Anchises, who prophecies Rome's imperial future, issuing an *ex post facto* warning to his descendants ("*pueri*") Caesar and Pompey not to engage in civil—and fratricidal—combat. Using a corporeal image that Lucan would intensify to more poignant effect in the above-cited passage, Anchises states: "Steel not your hearts, my sons, to such wicked war nor vent violent valour in the vitals of your land" ["ne, pueri, ne tanta animis adsuescite bella / neu patriae validas in viscera vertite viris"] (*Aeneid* 6.832–33).[2] Of course, by the time Virgil's

Anchises delivers his rueful admonition, Caesar and Pompey have already slashed Rome's *viscera*, setting the stage for Augustus's rise to power and for the *Aeneid*'s apparent celebration of the emperor. In the proem of *Civil War*, Lucan adopts the bodily image of Anchises's warning with a significant modification, which underscores the self-destructive quality of this enmity: it is not just the conflict's two protagonists, but notably the Roman people ("populus"), who eviscerated the fatherland ("patria"). Lucan's emphasis in the subsequent lines on the city's symbols of power—the standards ("signa"), the eagles ("aquilas"), and the javelin ("pilum")—further highlights the mirror-like image of the enemies fighting each other for the rule of Rome.

The kindred-fighting-kindred leitmotiv runs through the entire poem, climaxing in the battle between Pompey's and Caesar's troops in book 7, where Lucan portrays the men ready to fight in the battle of Pharsalia, as the cosmic elements clash around them (*Civil War* 7.151–84). Pompey eventually flees the battlefield to seek refuge in Egypt, where he is in turn beheaded—a synecdoche for the global consequences of Rome's discord (9.123–24)—at the request of King Ptolemy XIII, who attempted to please Caesar with this treacherous feat (8.663–75). As we shall see in chapter 1, Dante's gruesome depiction of the schismatics in *Inferno* 28 evokes the gory spectacle of mutilated bodies in Lucan's *Civil War*, not only because of his decision to include Curio, Caesar's lieutenant, in this group of sinners, but more specifically because of the canto's emphasis on decapitation as an emblem of institutional breakdown. Through their words and deeds, Dante suggests, the Islamic prophet Muhammad and the Provençal poet Betran de Born, the most prominent characters in *Inferno* 28, beheaded the mystical body of the Church and the body politic of the state. By representing the Republic's dismemberment as a cataclysmic event with universal repercussions, Lucan ties together the individual, the polity, and the cosmos within an overarching narrative of internal strife, and Dante picks up on this point.

The Enemy in Italian Renaissance Epic follows the same narrative of internal strife, exploring enmity within the self, the state, and the world through the prism of prominent works of the Italian literary canon: Dante's *Commedia*, Luigi Pulci's *Morgante*, Ludovico Ariosto's *Orlando Furioso*, and Torquato Tasso's *Gerusalemme Liberata*. My central argument is that early modern Italian literature conceived of all forms of hostility—even those conventionally considered external, such as the conflicts between Christian and Islamic forces in the Middle Ages and Renaissance—as predominantly internal. In other words, these poems' often critical engagement with the political dynamics of their time shows enmity arising ultimately from *within* political or religious entities. This literary characterization of enmity as an endogenous disorder of the body politic is largely consistent with the historical realities of the Italian Peninsula between the thirteenth and sixteenth centuries. Indeed, my medico-political treatment of treachery and civic discord in Pulci's *Morgante* in chapter 3, for instance, will demonstrate how the nature of power relations in medieval and early modern Italian city-states, in which familial ties and political authority were deeply intertwined, renders futile any attempt to present an absolute separation between the private and public spheres, and therefore between personal and political foes.

Further, as we shall see, the epics examined in the present study typically portray the enemy as a distorted mirror-image of the protagonist: the giant Morgante slain by a tiny crab's cancer-inducing bite in Pulci's work; mad Orlando as his own nemesis in the *Furioso*; Christian and Islamic empires joined in matching universalist ambitions in the *Liberata*. My use of the mirror as a metaphor to illustrate the nature of enmity in Italian Renaissance epic adopts, by contrast, the trope with which Seneca opens the *De Clementia* (55 CE), his politico-pedagogical treatise on the virtue of princely mercy. Seneca offers his work as a mirror to his pupil Nero (who had recently ascended to power at the age of seventeen), initiating a genre—that of the *speculum principis*, or mirror of the prince—which was destined to have enormous influence during the Middle Ages and Renaissance. The mirror, Seneca tells the young emperor, will "reveal you to yourself" ["te tibi ostendere"] (*De Clementia* I, 1).[3] That ten years later a hardly merciful Nero would force Seneca and the above-mentioned Lucan, Seneca's nephew, to commit suicide suggests that the philosopher's mirror probably revealed a fiend rather than a model of virtue. Paraphrasing the Delphic maxim implicit in Seneca's use of the mirror trope, through my examination of hostility, I show that in Italian Renaissance epic to "know thyself" also means to "know thine enemy."[4]

The Concept of the Enemy

By showing that all forms of hostility as understood in Renaissance epic are fundamentally internal, I also aim to challenge some key assumptions in the influential theory of the enemy articulated by the twentieth-century jurist and political thinker Carl Schmitt. In *The Concept of the Political* (1932), Schmitt argues that the political enemy is "the other, the stranger; and it is sufficient for his nature that he is, in a specially intense way, existentially something different and alien."[5] This enemy is not, Schmitt adds, a "private adversary," but "solely the public enemy."[6] His distinction between private adversary and public enemy is rooted in the difference between the Latin words *inimicus* and *hostis* (and their Greek equivalents *echthros* and *polemios*). Citing as evidence passages from Plato's *Republic* and from the *Digest* by second-century Roman jurist Pomponius, Schmitt posits that *inimicus* defines a private opponent and *hostis* a public—that is, sovereign—antagonist, against whom a legitimate authority may declare war.[7]

On the surface, the linguistic distinction between these two terms, and the concepts they signify, is accurate and provides a useful instrument to demarcate the legal boundaries of warfare, especially for state authorities seeking to assert their exclusive prerogative to exercise political violence. An individual (or group of individuals) who operates outside these boundaries can thus be branded as an outlaw or a terrorist and deprived of the protections granted by the laws of war. Yet, as I will discuss shortly, classical and early modern uses of *hostis* and *inimicus* in both philosophical and poetic works demonstrate the impossibility of neatly differentiating between private and public enemies (and even between internal and external threats), especially in geographical areas and historical periods characterized by high political volatility of the kind seen in early modern Italy. Indeed, one might venture to suggest that medieval and Renaissance representations of conflicts may provide an effective paradigm to understand the fluid nature of enmity in modern times, as interstate hostilities often blend into civil strife, while internecine discord frequently morphs into open or proxy war among nation-states.[8] For Italy in World War II and Iraq during and after the 2003 Operation Iraqi Freedom, foreign intervention triggered civil war and/or sectarian struggle. Yet, the world is now witnessing a parallel blurring of *inimicus* and *hostis* in the ongoing fighting in Syria, where an anti-government insurrection that began in 2011 spiraled into a multi-sided conflict involving state and non-state actors from within and outside the neighboring region. In each case, the messy historical reality shows geopolitical opponents engaged in combat alongside or against armed factions within weak or failed states.

In order to clarify my foregoing claim that the authors considered in this book represented enmity chiefly as an endogenous phenomenon, in what remains of this Introduction I should like to address two central terminological and theoretical issues and their long-term implications. I will first sketch out a brief linguistic history of the enemy, drawing particular attention to the ambiguity between definitions of personal and public enmity, mainly in classical antiquity. I will then outline the theory of cosmopolitanism (or world citizenship) and the principle of concentric circles of affiliation (from self to humankind) developed by Stoic thinkers between the third century BCE and the second century CE. An analogous principle of concentric circles, a kind of "telescopic" perspective or worldview, has partly inspired the structure of this book.

Hostis versus Inimicus

As noted above, Schmitt attempts to support his distinction between private adversaries and political enemies by referring to Greco-Roman terminology: "The enemy is *hostis*, not *inimicus* in the broader sense; πολέμιος, not ἐχθρός."[9] To be sure, in book 5 of the *Republic*—a text that Schmitt cites in a footnote added to the 1932 revised edition of *The Concept of the Political*—Plato underscores the difference between an external war that pits Hellenes against Barbarians and an episode of internal discord among Hellenes (470). While here Plato terms the former type of conflict as *polemos*, he labels the latter as *stasis*. That being said, as Moreno Morani has shown in his study on the semantics of enmity, Plato's point in this passage is not demonstrative of a general paradigm in Greek antiquity.[10] Even Plato himself, in another dialogue, the *Mexenus* (243e), describes civil strife with a phrase, *oikeios polemos* (literally, "family war"), that would be theoretically absurd, since it is impossible for external war to emerge from within a family.[11] Moreover, the word that Homer used several centuries before Plato to define an enemy—public or private—is *dusmenh*, which appears in book 24 of the *Iliad* when Hermes urges Priam to leave the Achaean camp after retrieving the body of his son Hector (24.364–65), and in book 16 of the *Odyssey* in reference to the suitors, Odysseus's fellow citizens who sought to exploit his long absence from Ithaca in order to usurp his throne and marry his wife Penelope (16.121). The words *polemios* and *echthros* (purportedly used, according to Schmitt, to identify the two forms of hostility) eventually came to be used interchangeably, or even jointly for the purpose of emphasis, by numerous authors, including fifth-century tragedians Aeschylus and Sophocles.[12]

If we turn to the distinction between *hostis* and *inimicus* in Roman texts, we see a similar pattern. The clearest and most cogent distinction between the two terms can be found in Cicero's *De officiis*. Here, Cicero asserts that the word "*hostis*" originally meant "guest" or "pilgrim," and eventually came to designate a public foe: "And yet long lapse of time has given that word a harsher meaning: for it has lost its signification of 'stranger' and has taken on the technical connotation of 'an enemy under arms'" ["Quamquam id nomen durius effecit iam vetustas; a peregrino enim recessit et proprie in eo, qui arma contra ferret, remansit"] (*De officiis* I, xii, 37).[13] Cicero then notes that *hostes* wage wars (*bella*) for supremacy or glory, whereas *inimici* ("personal enemies") and *competitores* ("rivals") contend for honor or social position ["certamen honoris et dignitatis"] (38). Cicero's explanation of the *hostis-inimicus* relationship influenced legal thought for centuries to come—indeed, well into the eighteenth century with Immanuel Kant's discussion of international right.[14] Even Cicero, however, occasionally deviated from the paradigm he put forth in the *De officiis*. For instance, he wrote that a citizen who, like Mark Antony or Catiline, takes action or conspires against the state may be regarded as a "hostem patriae" ["enemy of his native land"] (*Philippics* II, I, 2).[15]

Numerous other Roman texts of the early imperial era similarly show great terminological fluidity. The use of *hostis*, in particular, seems to have been far broader than a narrow interpretation of Cicero's theory would suggest. Rather than apply the term strictly to political enemies, extremely influential authors such as Virgil and Seneca often used *hostis* to signify individual adversaries (mortals or deities) or abstract forces. At a crucial moment in book 12 of the *Aeneid*, for instance, Aeneas's enemy Turnus states that he only fears the gods, describing Jove as *hostis*: "it is the gods who daunt me, and the enmity of Jove" ["di me terrent et Iuppiter hostis"] (*Aeneid* 12.895). The example of Seneca's *Hercules Furens*, to which we shall return in chapter 3, is particularly poignant, since the Greek hero paradoxically describes himself as his own *hostis*, after awakening from the outburst of frenzy that has driven him to kill his wife and children: "my enemy is anyone who does not identify my enemy" ["hostis est quisquis mihi / non monstrat hostem"] (*Hercules Furens* 1167–68).[16] Even if Hercules were not the enemy he seeks in this dizzying hall of verbal mirrors, the slaughter of a single family would not meet the standard of lawful war as outlined by Cicero. Hercules's actual adversary—the tyrant Lycus, whom Hercules kills in the first part of Seneca's play—is in fact merely an illegitimate ruler. According to Cicero's terminology, Lycus should not be considered a *hostis* either, but he is labeled as such by Hercules: "and Alcides' final foe will be Lycus" ["fiatque summus hostis Alcidae Lycus"] (635). Subsequently, however, Hercules terms Lycus *inimicus* (987), thus illustrating that the difference between internal and external enmities remains ambiguous in early imperial Roman literature.

The blurring of the terms *hostis* and *inimicus* has not been limited to works of fiction. In most of his philosophical treatise *De beneficiis*, Seneca follows Cicero's conception of enmity fairly closely, but in several passages he diverges from it significantly. In the first book, Seneca portrays Hercules as a benefactor of humanity and "a foe of the wicked" ["malorum hostis"] (*De beneficiis* I, xiii, 3).[17] And in a later passage, the Stoic philosopher appears to use another word (*adversarius*) that signals hostility as a synonym of *hostis*: "Do you call that a prayer, in which a grateful friend and an enemy might equally share, and which, if the last part were unuttered, you would not doubt that an adversary and foe had made?" ["Votum tu istud vocas, quod inter gratum et *inimicum* potest dividi, quod non dubites *adversarium* et *hostem* fecisse, si extrema taceantur?"] (VI, xxvii, 3, emphasis mine). In Lucan's *Civil War*, the distinction collapses beginning with the poem's very first word, "bella," whose use should notionally be limited to military confrontations with external (non-Roman) enemies. Later in Book 1, a matron running frantically through the streets of Rome bewails the paradox of civil war, shouting "what madness is this that drives Romans to fight Romans; what war is this without a foe?" ["quo tela manusque / Romanae miscent acies, bellumque sine hoste est?"] (*Civil War* 1.681–82). The historical reality of the conflict has leveled the distinction between *inimicus* and *hostis* to a frenzied cry. In this conflict, as Lucan remarks when narrating Caesar's campaign in Spain, "he who had found no acquaintance among the foe was no true Roman" ["Nec Romanus erat, qui non agnoverat hostem"] (4.179).

Thirteen centuries later, in the midst of a philological revival of Classical Latin, leading Italian humanists such as Giovanni Boccaccio, Coluccio Salutati, and Leon Battista Alberti provided further examples of the linguistic pattern sketched out thus far. In his collection of short narratives *Famous Women*, for instance, Boccaccio calls Eros and Fortune *hostis* (XXIII, 9; XXXI, 11; and XXXIII, 4).[18] In his unfinished mythological encyclopedia *De laboribus Herculis*, Salutati characterizes Saturn as a *hostis* of human life (II, 14).[19] And in his political satire *Momus*, Alberti uses *inimicus* and *hostis* interchangeably, adopting the latter word to describe individual deities, especially Momus's own antagonist Hercules (I, 85 and I, 87).[20] It is also worth noting that of the two Latin words used to define the enemy, only *inimicus* was assimilated faithfully into the European vernaculars that took shape in the medieval period (as *nemico* in Italian, *ennemi* in French, *enemigo* in Spanish, and of course "enemy" in English). *Hostis* was instead adopted in a more abstract sense as "hostility" (or in the adjective form as "hostile"); hostility and its various cognates rendered the Latin *hostis* as a condition of opposition, rather than as a reference to those opposed.

Before turning to the theory of cosmopolitanism, I would like to make one last point stemming from Schmitt's appropriation of the difference between *inimicus* and *hostis*. In the above-mentioned passage of the *Concept of the Political*, the German jurist denies the political validity of Jesus's injunction to love one's enemies ("diligite inimicos vestros," according to the Vulgate translation of Matthew 5:44 and Luke 6:27), claiming that Jesus was only referring to private, not public, enemies.[21] To corroborate his assertion, Schmitt suggests that Christians, presumably during the medieval and early modern periods, would have never described their Muslim foes as *inimici*. The philological reality is, again, significantly more nuanced than Schmitt would have it. It is true that at the height of the confrontation between the Habsburg and Ottoman Empires, the sixteenth-century Spanish theologian Juan Ginés de Sepulveda—whom Schmitt praises in his *Glossarium* and whose role in the politico-theological debates of his time I will discuss in chapter 4—drew a distinction between personal offenses and political hostility, arguing that Jesus's exhortation against meeting violence with violence does not extend to Muslims.[22] Yet numerous other Christian authors between the twelfth and sixteenth centuries did, in fact, describe the Muslims as *inimici*. I shall return to this topic in chapters 1 and 4. For now, it suffices to mention the examples of two theologians, the abbot of Cluny Peter the Venerable (in the twelfth century) and Aeneas Silvius Piccolomini, then Pope Pius II (in the fifteenth century), both of whom branded the Saracens as "crucis inimicos" ("enemies of the Cross"), evoking one of the most salient points of contention between Islam and Christianity, namely the Muslim denial of the crucifixion of Christ.[23] It is also important to remember that for centuries Islam was considered a Christian sect that had divided the Catholic—that is, universal—body of the Church.[24] Despite its own universalist ambitions, Islam was understood by many medieval and early modern Christian authors to be a perfectly suitable internal enemy.

Cosmopolitanism

The earliest expression of Christian universalism is usually ascribed to Saint Paul's letters, especially those to the Galatians and the Colossians. In an oft-cited chapter of the Epistle to the Galatians, Paul states: "In thee shall all nations be blessed" and "There is neither Jew nor Greek: there is neither bond nor free: there is neither male nor female. For you are all one in Christ Jesus" (Galatians 3:8 and 3:28).[25] While a discussion of Christian universalism is beyond the limits of this study, it is worth noting that the belief that all humans are part of the body of Christ had enormous implications in the medieval and early modern eras, especially when its spiritual and eschatological roots were planted into the pre-existing myth of a universal Roman Empire. I will return to the issue of global empire shortly. What I should add to this preamble is that Saint Paul's own version of universalism might be traced back to Stoic cosmopolitanism. The historical and philosophical premises of cosmopolitanism have been at the center of academic debates for the last two decades, partly because the end of the Cold War prompted a rethinking of issues such as global citizenship and transnational imperialism. Martha Nussbaum has been at the forefront of these debates, publishing several essays since the mid-1990s proposing cosmopolitanism as an ideal pedagogical model in a globalized era.[26] Numerous other studies have effectively explored the evolution of cosmopolitanism across the ages, its relevance to the modern world, and its inherent risks.

The anecdote typically adduced as the beginning of cosmopolitanism is the claim attributed to fourth-century Cynic philosopher Diogenes that he was a *cosmopolites*, a citizen of the world.[27] Diogenes's offhand remark is only the prelude to a more complex understanding of an individual's relationship with the rest of humankind. As Katja Maria Vogt has argued in her work on the Stoic *cosmopolis*, Greek philosophers Zeno of Citium and Chrysippus of Soli (fourth- and third-century BCE) saw the cosmos as a city regulated by reason and law—specifically, the law of nature.[28] In their view, all human beings are citizens of this community. Zeno and Chrysippus's political theory had a significant influence on later authors, including Cicero and Seneca (and perhaps Lucan), as well as Emperor Marcus Aurelius. Indeed, in the *Meditations*, Aurelius wrote that the "Universe (*cosmos*) is a kind of Commonwealth (*polis*)."[29] One of the most thought-provoking developments in the history of Stoic cosmopolitanism was the idea presented by the Neo-Stoic Hierocles (second century CE), who in one of the few extant fragments of his works claimed, possibly inspired by Cicero's vision of human fellowship, that individual identities and affiliations can be envisioned as concentric circles surrounding the self: "each of us [...] is circumscribed as though by many circles [...]. The first and closest is that which each person draws around his own mind, as the center: in this circle is enclosed the body [...]. The furthest out and largest one, which surrounds all the circles, is that of the entire race of human beings."[30] As Nussbaum has noted, cosmopolitanism conceives humankind as a worldwide community, but this conception does not entail the abandonment of each individual's personal, familial, local, and national identities in the name of an indistinct globalism that does away with the spheres of difference and individuality that make up the human constellation.[31] However, as David Armitage has suggested, one of the less studied implications of cosmopolitanism is that every war in a *cosmopolis* is inevitably civil,[32] for even a confrontation between two states must still be regarded as a conflict within the larger concentric circle of humankind.

A cosmopolitan viewpoint of this kind helps conceptualize the idea of the enemy in the Middle Ages and the Renaissance more compellingly than does a strict adherence to the *inimicus-hostis* dichotomy, since the Stoic vision of a universal community of humankind better reflects the rhetoric of world monarchy that authors such as Dante and Ariosto revisited—with skepticism at times, as I will highlight—even as they experienced a deeply unstable and fragmented political environment. It is not coincidental that in the *Monarchia*, the exile Dante envisioned a global empire that would defend peace and justice for every human being, and that in the *De Vulgari Eloquentia*, he—a victim, like many of his compatriots, of Florence's political discord—described himself as a citizen of the world: "To me, however, the whole world is a homeland, like the sea to fish" ["Nos autem, [cui] mundus est patria velut piscibus equor"].[33] As we shall see in chapter 1, Dante's political program was grounded in the myth of a Roman Empire without end that Virgil had represented as a remedy to Rome's decades-long internal strife in the *Aeneid* (1.279), a cure that Lucan would deconstruct in vividly corporeal terms in the *Civil War*, as noted at the beginning of this Introduction. It is also significant that in his *Monarchia*, Dante framed the relationship between the individual and the whole of humankind, between microcosm and macrocosm, using a corporeal metaphor, wherein a progressive correspondence, akin to that of Hierocles's concentric circles, links together the various political entities that make up the world monarchy.

Circles of Enmity

The cosmopolitan image of concentric circles, and the potential for conflict inherent within each circle, underlies the structure of *The Enemy in Italian Renaissance Epic*. The first chapter, on Dante, serves as a corollary and exemplification of the telescopic perspective outlined in the Introduction. Each of the remaining three chapters examines a different form of enmity: within the self, as madness and tyranny; within the polity, as betrayal and sedition, and within the world, as Christianity's encounter with Islam. In the interest of presenting a historically coherent narrative, I have, however, organized the chapters chronologically. Thus, my examination of civic discord in Pulci's *Morgante* (chapter 2) precedes my discussion of Orlando's inward strife in Ariosto's *Furioso* (chapter 3). It is my hope that this two-pronged approach integrating theoretical and historical perspectives will help clarify the political trajectories reflected in the poems discussed in this book[34]: after delving into the taxonomy of war in *Inferno* 28 (chapter 1), I move from the confines of an ostensibly republican city-state, fifteenth-century Florence (chapter 2), to those of a sixteenth-century world arena in which multinational empires compete for hegemony across different continents (chapter 4). Within this historical development, chapter 3 plays a pivotal role by shifting the focus from the Italian communes and *signorie* to the (purportedly universal) Holy Roman Empire of Charles V.

I begin chapter 1, "Between Fathers and Sons: Sowers of Enmity in *Inferno* 28," with a section dedicated to the issue of peace in the *Monarchia*, in which Dante describes peace as the effect of the theological virtue of *charitas* (love) on every political entity, ranging from the individual to the world empire he envisages. In juxtaposition to the harmony depicted in *Monarchia*, I examine the horrors of *Inferno* 28, where Dante represents the effects of discord on the mystical body of the Church and the political body of the State by graphically portraying the punishment suffered by the sowers of discord, whose "bodies" are maimed by a sword-wielding devil. The first sinner whose suffering is described in this canto is the Prophet Muhammad, to whom I dedicate a significant portion of the chapter, emphasizing how Dante adapts the traditional view of the founder of Islam as a renegade Christian. I then turn to Dante's snapshot of the Roman general Curio, whom Lucan in the *Civil War* portrays exhorting Julius Caesar to advance southward after crossing the Rubicon, fueling the antagonism between Caesar and Pompey, and Dante's depiction of the Provençal poet Bertran de Born, who fostered enmity between King Henry II of England and his son Henry, also known as the Young King. In this chapter, I also argue that Dante represents these three sowers of discord as a foil to the role of poet and prophet of peace that he envisioned for himself. In the *Commedia* and the *Monarchia*, Dante develops a discourse whose key tenets—the role of Rome within the intellectual imaginary of the West, the destructive effects of internecine strife in early modern Italian city-states, and the representation of Islam in Europe—resurface in the works of Pulci, Ariosto, and Tasso.

In chapter 2, "The Enemy within the Walls: Treachery, Pride, and Civil Strife in Pulci's *Morgante*," I focus on enmity within a state, giving pride of place to two crucial episodes of Pulci's poem—the death of Morgante, killed by a small crab, and the death of Orlando, betrayed by the fellow Christian knight Ganelon—vis-à-vis the 1478 Pazzi conspiracy. Through the investigation of these episodes in relation to their literary, medical, and theological sources, I show that, because of treachery's corrupting effect, Pulci characterizes it as a cancerous disease that poses a fundamental threat to the body politic. By choosing to identify treachery as the gravest sin, moreover, Pulci follows in the footsteps of Dante, who had confined traitors to the lowest circle of Hell. Whereas the sowers of discord incite conflicts openly with their actions and words, Pulci's traitors hide their enmity behind a mask of friendship and trust.

Chapter 3, "The Enemy as the Self: Madness and Tyranny in Ariosto's *Orlando Furioso*," examines Orlando's madness in the *Furioso* in light of classical theories on the nature and symptoms of *furor*, with particular attention to the tripartition of the soul in Plato's *Phaedrus* and *Republic*. Subsequently, I consider the effects of Orlando's loss of reason, a loss that Ariosto characterizes as a metaphorical decapitation (*Furioso* 23.121), and compare the paladin's unrestrained brute force with the absolute power that epitomizes the rule of a tyrant, according to ancient and early modern political philosophy. Furthermore, by discussing the influence of Seneca's *Hercules Furens* on Ariosto's representation of Orlando's madness in the *Furioso*, I contend that in Ariosto's poem the fiercest enemy a hero must face lies within himself. Ariosto's reflection on absolute power is also, I argue, a critique of the Empire of Charles V, whose sway over the Italian Peninsula grew dramatically in the years preceding the publication of the third and last edition of the *Furioso* in 1532.

In chapter 4, "Christian and Islamic Empires: Global Enemies in Tasso's *Gerusalemme Liberata*," I investigate Tasso's epic in light of his particular take on two interrelated historical developments that reshaped the early modern world: on the one hand, the multifaceted religious conflicts both between Christian and Islamic forces after the fall of Constantinople in 1453, and within Western Christendom as a result of the Protestant Reformation initiated by Martin Luther in 1517; and, on the other hand, the European colonization of America in the first half of the sixteenth century and the ensuing politico-theological controversies regarding the status of indigenous American populations. This chapter will therefore focus on Tasso's depiction of Muslim enemies and of the journey beyond the Pillars of Hercules undertaken by two Christian soldiers to rescue Rinaldo, the hero destined to conquer Jerusalem, from the garden of Armida, the beautiful witch Rinaldo loved. Two key issues emerge from my discussion of the *Liberata*. First, two and a half centuries after Dante had categorized Muhammad among the sowers of discord in *Inferno* 28, Islam was still often viewed in Western Europe as a rebellious sect that had arisen from the universal body of the Catholic Church. Second, the traditional myth of Rome as the empire that purportedly pacified the whole world underlies the idea of unity envisioned in Tasso's poem. I will show that, despite enduring sectarianism within and on the borders of their respective dominions, both Habsburg and Ottoman rulers embraced the myth of a universal empire for their own purposes, thus creating a scenario in which Christian and Islamic enemies are mirror images of each other. My reading of the *Liberata*, however, challenges the common scholarly claim that the battle for Jerusalem depicted in Tasso's poem stands as a microcosm for a global clash of civilizations, in which Catholic European nations kill or convert all of humankind at sword-point. I argue instead that Tasso represents a rapidly changing world order, centered in Europe but ultimately irreducible to a single political or religious authority.

Epic and Enmity

By addressing the theme of enmity through a literary lens, *The Enemy in Italian Renaissance Epic* probes the representation of political power (and of this power's limitations) in Renaissance Italy. While the focus of my approach is specific in geographical terms, its scope is decisively comparative, integrating close intertextual reading of poetic works with an overarching assessment of the historical forces at play in those works. In terms of structure and methodology, then, this study follows on examinations of the epic genre by such critics as Michael Murrin, David Quint, Jo Ann Cavallo, Dennis Looney, and Tobias Gregory, all of whom have investigated historical and thematic patterns both within and outside the Renaissance epic canon.[35] Throughout the book, I consider early modern Italian authors' engagement with classical and biblical traditions in relation to the cultural, institutional, scientific, and religious turmoil they witnessed in the Italian peninsula and beyond. As we shall see, these poets' understanding of the political dynamics of their time was frequently critical, and their criticism was animated by a clear-eyed view of the instability inherent in the exercise of political power. From this standpoint, enmity is, in its various forms, a pervasive symptom of this instability and not, as Schmitt argued in *The Concept of the Political*, the animating feature of political life.[36]

Although several studies on early modern culture have engaged with Schmitt's thought, most of these have operated primarily from the perspective of political philosophy.[37] A few monographs published in the last fifteen years by such critics as Victoria Kahn, Jacques Lezra, Julia Reinhard Lupton, and Nichole Miller have also revealed the significant scholarly potential of revisiting pre-modern literature using twentieth- and twenty-first-century political theology as a lens of analysis.[38] These critics have enriched our knowledge of the early modern age by tackling a variety of issues ranging from citizenship and sovereignty to violence and subjectivity. They have productively put thinkers such as Hannah Arendt, Walter Benjamin, Jacques Derrida, and Carl

Schmitt (to name only a few) into dialogue with one another, as well as with early modern authors, especially playwrights such as Christopher Marlowe and William Shakespeare, and philosophers such as Jean Bodin, Thomas Hobbes, and Baruch Spinoza.[39] Whereas Lupton's *Citizen-Saints* is clearly (albeit not exclusively) centered on Elizabethan drama, in the majority of studies that follow this critical approach, the examination of literary texts seems to take an ancillary position to the reflection on theoretical questions. The focus of my book is instead squarely literary. I use the concept of the enemy as an interpretive key to the political aspects of the poems that, from the standpoint of this book, best allow us to gain a deeper insight into the human condition and, more specifically, into the historical and intellectual dynamics of Renaissance Italy. I analyze these poems in their historical milieu, connecting them with their classical and biblical antecedents, and, rather than engaging with Carl Schmitt—who referred to early modern writings with the main purpose of articulating his own vision of political theology—or with other modern theorists, I engage with the literary scholars who have most significantly informed my understanding of these poems and their authors.

Finally, I would add that most scholars who have considered the relationship between early modern literature and political theology have thus far explored literary territories distant from those I investigate in the following pages.[40] No study, in fact, has been conducted on the interplay between theories of enmity (ancient or modern) and Renaissance epic, a poetic genre that, given its political underpinnings, is particularly well suited to addressing theoretical issues related to power, conflict, and violence through the discourse of poetry. As I will suggest in the Epilogue—turning briefly to the reconciliation scene between Achilles and Priam in Book 24 of the *Iliad*, with Simone Weil's essay "The *Iliad*, or the Poem of Force" as a point of departure—I hope that the perspective I adopt here can be extended to poems well beyond the limits of the Italian Renaissance.

CHAPTER 1

Between Fathers and Sons
Sowers of Enmity in *Inferno* 28

IN A CRUCIAL PASSAGE of the *Monarchia*, Dante formulates a political analogy between the individual and humankind that encapsulates "the guiding principle" ["principium inquisitionis directivum"] (1.3.2) of his quest for the ideal world government:

> And in order to understand the subject of our inquiry clearly, we should be aware that nature produces the thumb for a definite end, that it makes the whole hand for another end, which is different from this, and the arm for yet another end, which is different from both of the others, and the whole man for still another end, which differs from all of the others. In just the same way, nature directs the individual man to one end, and the household to another, the neighborhood to another, and the city to another, and the kingdom to another. And, lastly, God eternal by his art, which is nature, brings into being the human race for an end, which is what is best for the whole (ibid.).[1]

In Dante's corporeal analogy, the differing purpose of each limb and organ, as compared to the role of the human body in its entirety, corresponds in turn to the end or goal of each political entity. Similarly different in purpose, these political entities (individual, household, neighborhood, city, kingdom) further combine to comprise the global empire. Thus, as the thumb is to the individual body, so the individual is to all humankind.

Aristotle outlined a similar progression from family to *polis* in book 1 of the *Politics*, where he asserts that "the first thing to arise is family" and the city-state "is the highest of all communities" (1252a).² But Dante expands Aristotle's perspective to include the individual and the human race in its entirety. Although he begins with the traditional *topos* of the body politic developed by such authors as the Roman historian Livy and twelfth-century proto-humanist John of Salisbury as a starting point,³ Dante extends the image possibly by incorporating the microcosm–macrocosm parallel set forth, among others, by two contemporaries of John of Salisbury, the Platonist philosophers Bernardus Silvestris and Alan of Lille.⁴ Dante might have also thought of Thomas Aquinas's reworking of similar ideas in the *Summa Theologiae*, where he states that "all men born of Adam may be considered as one man" and that "all who are members of one community are reputed as one body, and the whole community as one man" ["omnes homines qui nascuntur ex Adam, possunt considerari ut unus homo [...] omnes qui sunt unius communitatis, reputantur quasi unum corpus, et tota communitas quasi unus homo"] (*S. T.* I-II, q. 81, a. 1).⁵ As Dante knew well (and as I have noted in the Introduction), the idea of a "political community of the human race" ["universalis civilitatis humani generis"] (*Mn.* 1.2.8) ultimately traces its conceptual roots to the Stoic notion of cosmopolitanism and to early Christian theology, particularly Saint Paul's letters. Here, it suffices to mention an example Dante certainly knew: Cicero's use of the phrases "human society" and "common body of humanity" ["hominum communitate" and "humanitatis corpore"] (*De officiis* III, vi, 32).⁶

As he displays the analogy of disparate members operating in pursuit of their discrete goals, in *Monarchia* Dante further asserts that the human community should be governed by a single ruler, who would be called "monarch" or "emperor" (*Mn.* 1.5.4–10).⁷ The emperor's uncontested authority and his commitment to the virtues of justice and charity (*charitas*) would create the necessary conditions for universal peace.⁸ And only under monarchical rule could humanity resemble God, model of the unity principle that underlies Dante's politico-theological vision: "the human race is most like God when it is most nearly one. This is so because the true principle of unity exists only in him, for it is written, 'Hear, O Israel, the Lord thy God is one.'" ["genus humanum maxime Deo assimilatur quando maxime est unum: vera enim ratio unius in solo illo est; propter quod scriptum est: 'Audi, Israel, Dominus Deus tuus unus est.'"] (1.8.3).⁹ Until unified under a monarch or an emperor, however, humankind will find itself perpetually at war.

Dante offers the most vivid account of this state of affairs in *Inferno* 28, a canto in which, as Jane Chance has suggested, the sowers of discord, reduced to their dismembered bodies, represent an inversion of the unity principle theorized in the *Monarchia*.[10] These sinners (and their horrific punishments) exemplify how enmity can destroy any political or religious community. That *Inferno* 28 is not centered around one single protagonist, but rather portrays a series of variously famous figures with whom Virgil and the pilgrim interact, has led most scholars to neglect the overall structure of this canto and to focus on its individual characters, especially the Prophet Muhammad and the Provençal poet Bertran de Born. In this chapter, I will instead argue that the canto's cohesiveness resides precisely in its movement from macro- to micro-political structures. It is also noteworthy that most, if not all, of the characters depicted in *Inferno* 28 incited father-son conflicts. In particular, I will show that Muslim rejection of the dogma of the Trinity—the central source of doctrinal dissent between Islam and Christianity throughout the Middle Ages—allows us to establish a connection that runs through the whole canto, linking Muhammad to de Born. Both sinners, in Dante's presentation, broke the tie between father and son: in so doing, the former breached the principle on which the unity of the Catholic Church was founded, while the latter violated the norm of inheritance that undergirded the dynastic legitimacy of a temporal kingdom.

Notwithstanding the martial images in *Inferno* 28 and in several other cantos of the *Commedia*,[11] Giuseppe Mazzotta and, in his footsteps, Vittorio Montemaggi have eloquently described Dante as a poet of peace.[12] I hope to push their arguments one step further to address the following question: how does this understanding of Dante connect to his emphasis on the father-son relationship in *Inferno* 28? This chapter will argue that Dante's conception of war and peace revolves around the nexus of this central relationship. Indeed, Dante hints in book 1 of the *Convivio* that the bond between father and son epitomizes the most intimate form of human love: "Tanto è la cosa più prossima quanto, di tutte le cose del suo genere, altrui è più unita: onde di tutti li uomini lo figlio è più prossimo al padre [...] La sopra detta cagione, cioè d'essere più unito quello ch'è solo prima in tutta la mente, mosse la consuetudine della gente, che fanno li primogeniti succedere solamente, sì come [più] propinqui, e perché più propinqui più amati" ["A thing is nearest to the extent that of all things of its kind it is most closely related to another thing; thus of all men the son is nearest to the father (...) The cause mentioned above, namely that that is more closely related which first exists alone in all the mind, induced people to adopt the custom of making the first-born sole heirs, since they are the closest, and, because the closest, the most loved"] (1.12.4–7).[13]

I should like to add that I do not intend to undertake a general discussion of the Trinity or of the father figures in Dante's works, nor to reconstruct the poet's relationships with his own father or his children.[14] I specifically want to address the issue of father-son hostility in *Inferno* 28, as well as the larger intellectual framework underlying this canto. In my conclusion, I will briefly turn to the last chapter of the *Monarchia*—where Dante recommends that the emperor demonstrate toward the pope the same reverence a firstborn son should show toward his father (3.15)—to suggest that Dante saw himself as the poet and prophet of peace who could heal the rift between secular and spiritual authorities, a rift that he considered the main cause of the world's disorder. My analysis of *Inferno* 28 is comprised of three main sections reflecting the telescopic perspective that, as noted in the Introduction, helps inform the structure of this book. The first section addresses global conflict through Dante's depiction of Muhammad as a religious schismatic; the second focuses on strife within a commonwealth by analyzing Dante's portrait of Curio, one of Caesar's lieutenants in the Roman civil war; and the third revisits Dante's depiction of Bertran de Born and his dismembering punishment as an opportunity to probe the metaphorical political unit formed by a king and his firstborn son. In each of these sections we shall see that, as I argue throughout the book, enmity arises from within the body politic. In *Inferno* 28, enmity is mirrored in the dismemberment of each sinner's body.

Muhammad's Universal Schism

After leaving Guido da Montefeltro among the counselors of fraud in *Inferno* 27, Dante and Virgil move on to the ninth *bolgia* (ditch). Here, they come upon the sowers of discord, sinners whose words and deeds caused divisions within their political or religious institutions. The sowers of discord are punished by a sword-wielding devil who attacks them repeatedly, slashing their "bodies" whenever they near him. As the sinners roam through the *bolgia*, their injuries heal, preparing them for further sword attacks in an eternal cycle of carnage.[15] The sight of their punishment is so gruesome that the poet professes his inability to narrate adequately the horror of this *bolgia*, which more than any other resembles a chaotic battlefield. Not even the litany of wars evoked in the canto's opening tercets, Dante claims, could fully represent the wounds and mutilated limbs he witnessed among these sinners:

> Chi poria mai pur con parole sciolte
> dicer del sangue e de le piaghe a pieno

ch'i' ora vidi, per narrar più volte?
Ogne lingua per certo verria meno
per lo nostro sermone e per la mente
c'hanno a tanto comprender poco seno.
S'el s'aunasse ancor tutta la gente
che già, in su la fortunata terra
di Puglia, fu del suo sangue dolente
per li Troiani e per la lunga guerra
che de l'anella fé sì alte spoglie,
come Livïo scrive che non erra,
con quella che sentio di colpi doglie
per contrastare a Ruberto Guiscardo;
e l'altra il cui ossame ancor s'accoglie
a Ceperan, là dove fu bugiardo
ciascun Pugliese, e là da Tagliacozzo,
dove sanz'arme vinse il vecchio Alardo;
e qual forato suo membro e qual mozzo
mostrasse, d'aequar sarebbe nulla
il modo de la nona bolgia sozzo. (28.1–21)

[Who could ever, even with unbound words, tell in full of the blood and wounds that I now saw, though he should narrate them many times? Every tongue would surely fail, because our language and our memory have little capacity to comprehend so much. If one gathered together all the people who ever, on the travailed earth of Apulia, groaning poured forth their blood on account of the Trojans, and in the long war that took such heaped spoils of rings, as Livy writes, who does not err, and the people who suffered wounds when resisting Robert Guiscard, and the others whose bones are still being collected at Ceperano, where every Apulian was a liar, and at Tagliacozzo where old Elard won without arms; and this one showed his perforated, this one his truncated member, it would be nothing to equal the wretched mode of the ninth pocket.]

To reinforce his assertion that no author could successfully describe in words the violence of the ninth ditch, Dante fills his initial disclaimer (in rhetorical terms, the *praeteritio*) with literary allusions. He mirrors the accumulation of battles and body parts that characterizes the whole canto in a corresponding buildup of textual fragments from classical and medieval sources, including

Ovid's *Tristia*, Virgil's *Aeneid*, Livy's *Ab urbe condita*, Dante's own *Convivio*, and—most significantly, in light of the canto's conclusion—Bertran de Born's poem "Si tuit li dol."[16]

The pilgrim's first encounter in this *bolgia* is with the Prophet Muhammad, founder of Islam. The disturbing portrait of Muhammad in *Inferno* 28 has drawn increased scholarly attention in recent years for its resonance with the current political interest in the relationship between Islam and the West. The 2007 issue of *Dante Studies*, for example, was entirely dedicated to the topic of Dante and Islam. This recent scholarship has effectively highlighted important aspects of Dante's representation of the Prophet and has examined some of the sources that Dante might have considered in crafting the episode.[17] Yet Dante's scatological description of Muhammad has not been fully probed in relation to its theological background, particularly the Muslim rejection of the Trinitarian dogma. As I examine Dante's Muhammad in relation to this key point of dichotomy between Islam and Christian doctrine, I will focus especially on Peter the Venerable and Riccoldo da Montecroce, two leading anti-Islamic polemicists of the Middle Ages. Both writers adopted excremental imagery to describe Islam as a collection of ancient heresies. But before delving into the relevant passages of *Inferno* 28, let us first outline the doctrinal framework that underlies Dante's representation of Muhammad as a sower of discord.

As I have noted elsewhere,[18] Church Fathers such as Saint Jerome and Saint Augustine, and medieval encyclopedists such as Isidore of Seville, saw only a subtle difference between heresy and schism. While heresy is traditionally described as a sin against faith (a sin that perverts dogma), schism is defined as a sin against love, or *charitas* (a sin that indicates a rebellion against the Church). According to Isidore, the words "sect" and "heresy" had similar origins in the Latin and Greek verbs *secare* and *harein*, which can both be translated as "to cut off" (*Etymologies* 8.3). The close association between heresy and sect is such that, in the *Summa Theologiae*, Aquinas makes no distinction between the two (*S. T.* II-II, q. 11, a. 1).[19]

In a subsequent section of the *Summa*, Aquinas sets forth definitions of peace and of the vices that work against it. These definitions are critical to understanding the different forms of conflicts represented in *Inferno* 28.[20] Peace, he explains, is one of three effects resulting from the "principal act of charity which is love" ["actum caritatis principalem, qui est dilectio"] (*S. T.* II-II, q. 28). Aquinas describes peace as "the work of justice indirectly, in so far as justice removes the obstacle of peace: but it is the work of charity directly, since charity, according to its very nature, causes peace" ["pax est opus iustitiae indirecte, inquantum scilicet removet prohibens. Sed est opus caritatis directe, quia secundum propriam rationem caritas pacem causat"] (II-II, q. 29, a. 3). He also states that concord is not sufficient to define peace, because concord only "denotes union of appetites among various persons, while peace denotes, in addition to this union, the union of appetites even in one man" ["concordia importat unionem appetituum diversorum appetentium, pax autem, supra hanc unionem, importat etiam appetituum unius appetentis unionem"] (II-II, q. 29, a. 1).

He then identifies a nucleus of "sins contrary to peace" ["peccatis quae opponuntur paci"] (S. T. II-II, q. 37). Among these, the sin of discord is opposed to concord and charity in the broadest terms: "concord results from charity, in as much as charity directs many hearts together to one thing, which is chiefly the Divine good, secondarily, the good of our neighbor. Wherefore discord is a sin, in so far as it is opposed to this concord" ["Concordia autem (...) ex caritate causatur, inquantum scilicet caritas multorum corda coniungit in aliquid unum, quod est principaliter quidem bonum divinum, secundario autem bonum proximi. Discordia igitur ea ratione est peccatum, inquantum huiusmodi concordiae contrariatur"] (II-II, q. 37, a. 1). With respect to deeds, Aquinas indicates four vices against peace: schism, war, strife, and sedition, each of these corresponding to different forms of conflict. More specifically, schism, which he terms a "special sin," represents a fracture of spiritual and ecclesiastical unity: "the schismatic intends to sever himself from that unity which is the effect of charity: because charity unites not only one person to another with the bond of spiritual love, but also the whole Church in unity of spirit" ["(schismatis) intendit se ab unitate separare quam caritas facit. Quae non solum alteram personam alteri unit spirituali dilectionis vinculo, sed etiam totam Ecclesiam in unitate spiritus"] (II-II, q. 39, a. 1).

While Dante clearly embraces the traditional association of schism and heresy, he does part from Aquinas's view when he considers the relative gravity of heresy and schism. For the Dominican theologian, heresy, as a sin against faith, is more grievous than schism (S. T. II-II, q. 39, aa. 1–2). For Dante, the opposite is true. If charity is indeed the "root and foundation" of all virtues, as Aquinas argues in *Summa Theologiae* II-II, q. 23, a. 8, then Dante draws from this argument the conclusion that sins against charity should be considered more severe than those against other virtues.[21] Dante might have also considered here two well-known chapters of the first letter to the Corinthians in which Saint Paul describes the Church as the body of Christ (1 Corinthians 12:27) and also stresses the preeminence of charity over the other virtues ("And now there remain faith, hope, and charity, these three: but the greatest of these is charity," 1 Corinthians 13:13). The doctrinal premise of charity's preeminent importance, closely linked to Dante's concern over the institutional divisions caused by the schismatics within the Church, explains why in the *Commedia* he would place Muhammad among the sowers of discord rather than among the heretics, whom Dante labels as *"eresïarche"* ["chiefs of heresies"] (*Inf.* 9.127) and whose punishment he describes in Cantos 9–11 of *Inferno*. Thus, Dante's categorization both incorporates and, at key points, diverges from a traditional view of Muhammad as a heretic. As I will discuss below, this Christian view of Islam's prophet, which persisted throughout the Middle Ages and into the Renaissance, originated from several legends that portrayed Muhammad as a renegade Christian clergyman who turned against the Church.[22]

Peter the Venerable, the twelfth-century abbot of Cluny who played a key role in disseminating knowledge of the Qur'an in Europe, contributed significantly to the notion that Islam was a heretical sect. In a letter to Peter of Poitiers, one of the members of the team involved in translating the Qur'an into Latin, Peter the Venerable describes Muslims as "those enemies of the cross of Christ" ["illos vere inimicos crucis Christi"], because they deny that Christ died on the Cross.[23] In another epistle to Bernard of Clairvaux, who was then advocating for renewing the Crusades, the abbot defines Islam as an "impious sect" ["impiam sectam"].[24] Another passage from this letter deserves particular attention in relation to Dante's graphic portrayal of Muhammad. In it, Peter the Venerable explains why he commissioned a translation of the Qur'an: he describes the Muslim faith as a collection of heresies or, more bluntly, as "this sludge of all heresies" ["hac fece universarum heresum"].[25] Peter uses a similar coprological image—albeit focused on the chronological range, rather than on their geographical scope, of the heresies assimilated by Islam—in his *Summa totius haeresis Saracenorum*. Here, he presents Muhammad as drinking deeply of the devil's ancient heresies and the Qur'an as being the excremental product of Muhammad's intake: "almost all the sludge of the ancient heresies" ["omnes pene antiquarum heresum feces"].[26]

Peter the Venerable's unflattering definition seemed still to resonate a century and a half later, as a virtually identical image appears in another work that would significantly shape European views of Islam from the fourteenth to the sixteenth centuries. In his *Contra legem Sarracenorum*, Dominican friar Riccoldo da Montecroce, a contemporary and fellow citizen of Dante, again uses a fecal image: "You must know that the devil spewed into Muhammad the sludge of all ancient heretics that he (the devil) had previously sown hither and thither" ["Et sciendum quod omnium antiquorum hereticorum feces, quas diabolus in aliis sparsim seminauerat, simul in Machometum reuomuit"].[27] Riccoldo's description of Islam is especially intriguing because, after spending over ten years as a missionary in the Near East (including an extensive stay in Baghdad, where he learned Arabic and studied Islam), he had returned to his native city to work at Santa Maria Novella around the year 1300, certainly before Dante left Florence for the diplomatic mission to Rome in September or October 1301 that preceded his exile.[28] I know of no indisputable evidence that Dante ever met Riccoldo in Florence or that he later read Riccoldo's or Peter the Venerable's works, though neither event seems beyond the realm of possibility, given Dante's remarkably wide intellectual interests and reading habits. More important here is whether an echo, be it direct or mediated, of the earlier excremental definitions of Islam can be identified in Dante's poem.

The possible relevance of the graphic—and, by modern standards, utterly offensive—caricatures of Islam presented by Peter and Riccoldo becomes particularly suggestive as soon as Virgil and the pilgrim encounter the horribly disfigured image of Muhammad in *Inferno* 28. After the long introduction to the canto, Dante faces the sight of Muhammad with his trunk slashed and his entrails hanging between his legs:

Già veggia, per mezzul perdere o lulla,
com'io vidi un, così non si pertugia,
rotto dal mento infin dove si trulla.
Tra le gambe pendevan le minugia;
la corata pareva e 'l tristo sacco
che merda fa di quel che si trangugia.
Mentre che tutto in lui veder m'attacco,
guardommi e con le man s'aperse il petto,
dicendo: "Or vedi com'io mi dilacco!
vedi come storpiato è Mäometto!
Dinanzi a me sen va piangendo Alì,
fesso nel volto dal mento al ciuffetto." (28.22–36)

[Surely a barrel, losing centerpiece or half-moon, is not so broken as one I saw torn open from the chin to the farting-place. Between his legs dangled his intestines; the pluck was visible, and the wretched bag that makes shit of what is swallowed. While I was all absorbed in the sight of him, he, gazing back at me, with his hands opened up his breast, saying: "Now see how I spread myself! See how Mohammed is torn open! Ahead of me Ali goes weeping, his face cloven from chin to forelock."]

The repetition of the verb "vedere" emphasizes Dante's total absorption in the brutality of the scene. The scene's tension between historical witnessing and outright voyeurism betrays the fundamental risk of war poetry, a genre that, as we shall see below in my discussion of Bertran de Born's sin, may ultimately tempt the reader with an esthetics of violence. Indeed, at the beginning of the following canto, Dante describes his eyes as intoxicated ("inebrïate") by the grim sight of the ninth *bolgia* (29.1–3). Even by the standards of the *Commedia*, whose linguistic arsenal is formidably rich, the anatomical terminology in this arresting portrait of Muhammad is distinctive, given that "mezzul," "lulla," "pertugia," "trulla," "minugia," "corata," "trangugia," "dilacco," and "ciuffetto" are all words that appear nowhere else in the poem.

Dante's linguistic insistence on the prophet's body parts is consistent with the macabre spectacle of war introduced at the beginning of the canto, and his display of Muhammad's wound accentuates the intense physicality that characterizes both his punishment and the suffering of the canto's other sowers of discord. Among the terms conveying this impression of physicality, "merda" is perhaps the most conspicuous, although Dante employs similar scatological language in other passages of *Inferno*, especially in canto 18 (lines 116 and 131).[29] Most commentators of the *Commedia* have vaguely explained Dante's introduction of "merda" into *Inferno* 28 as belonging to the allegedly realistic style of the cantos dedicated to lower Hell, or as expressing a generally derogatory attitude toward Muhammad.[30] Yet this ghastly scene, which reaches its nadir in the excremental details of lines 26–27 and may well evoke a prior tradition of describing Islam in digestive terms, in fact makes a more specific argument about Islamic doctrine. I contend that Dante here suggests the following: as all of the heresies disrupting Church unity were expelled in the form of Islamic doctrine, so did Muhammad transform into feces the errors that he was fed by his dubious masters. By portraying the digestion of these teachings in crudely materialistic terms, Dante might further be dramatizing another common medieval assumption about Islam, namely that it unduly emphasizes earthly and corporeal pleasures or, along a different trajectory, that Muslims reject the spiritual nourishment offered by the body of Christ through the sacrament of the Eucharist.[31]

While exhibiting his wound to the pilgrim, Muhammad explains which category of sinners is punished in the ninth *bolgia*. He points out his cousin and son-in-law Alì, whose wound from forehead to chin complements the slash in Muhammad's trunk. The reference to Alì might indicate that Dante was in some limited way aware of the rift between Shia and Sunni sects of Islam, or we might interpret this image more simply, as a straightforward acknowledgment that Alì was a follower of Muhammad.³² Although it is unclear what, if anything, Dante knew about the conflict within Islam, he does place three Muslims—Avicenna, Averroës, and the Saladin—among the great spirits whom the pilgrim encounters in Limbo (*Inf.* 4.143–44 and 4.129), sheltered from the intense corporeal punishment suffered by the damned who are beyond the First Circle. This choice recognizes the extraordinary scientific and philosophical achievements in the Muslim world during the Middle Ages and the magnanimity of the Sultan of Egypt and Syria, who conquered Jerusalem in 1187. Conditional homage for exemplary Muslims notwithstanding, the medieval Christian perspective was that Muhammad himself embodied perfect enmity against the Catholic Church, to the point that he was often branded a satanic individual and a forerunner of the Antichrist. This characterization plays in part on the etymological meaning of Satan, which is "adversary," as Isidore of Seville explains in *Etymologies* 8.11.³³

In the eyes of medieval Christianity, Muhammad was guilty of tearing apart the universal *corpus mysticum* of the Church,³⁴ whose head is Christ. The *corpus mysticum* imagery, developed from Saint Paul's letters, articulated a hierarchical relationship between part and whole that, in many respects, dovetails with the socio-corporeal images discussed at the start of this chapter: "Now you are the body of Christ, and members of member" (1 Corinthians 12:27) or "For in one Spirit were we all baptized into one body, whether Jews or Gentiles, whether bond or free; and in one Spirit we have all been made to drink. For the body also is not one member, but many" (1 Corinthians 12:13–14). Seen from this perspective, the divisions that Muhammad forced upon the Church rent apart the mystical body of Christ. Thus, in the moral economy of Dante's *Inferno*, no *bolgia* fit him better than that of the schismatics, and no punishment better than one that slashes his body. Indeed, the conflation of heresies that Muhammad ingested and his role in hindering religious unity made him the very "prince of the schismatics," as he was defined in the *Ottimo Commento*: "in particulare tratta della qualità della pena d'uno principe di questi scismatici, cioè di Maumetto, il quale con la sua scisma hae più danno dato alla Chiesa di Dio, e alla fede cristiana, che nullo, o tra tutti gli altri incomparabilmente" ["It deals especially with the prince of these schismatics, Muhammad, who has damaged the Church of God with his schism incomparably more than any other sinner of this ditch"].³⁵

Dante's sowers of discord had during their lifetime caused religious and/or political divisions. They had also, as mentioned earlier in this chapter, divided fathers and sons. In Muhammad's case, Dante's contemporaries would have seen evidence of this particular sin in the chief point of doctrinal disagreement between Christianity and Islam: the Muslim refusal to regard Jesus Christ as the Son of God, consubstantial with the Father. Beginning as early as the eighth century, a vast number of Christian theologians addressed the threat, both doctrinal and political, posed by Islam. John of Damascus, who lived in Syria under the Omayyad dynasty (661–750), wrote a book titled *De Haeresibus* whose chapters 100 and 101 tackle the so-called "superstition of the Ishmaelites, the fore-runner of the Antichrist."[36] "Ishmaelites" was one of the epithets used to identify the Muslims, along with "Saracens" (derived from Abraham's wife Sarah, mother of Isaac) and "Hagarenes" (derived from Hagar, Abraham's slave and mother of Ishmael). All of these epithets arise from the episodes in Genesis 16 and 21 narrating the fractured kinship underlying the three monotheistic Abrahamic religions: Islam, Christianity, and Judaism. John's main accusation against the "Ishmaelites" involves the fundamental doctrine of the Trinity, as contrasted with Islam's belief in what might best be described as the absolute unity of God:

> Since you [Ishmaelite] say that Christ is Word and Spirit of God, how do you scold us as Associators? For the Word and the Spirit is inseparable each from the one in whom this has the origin; if, therefore, the Word is in God it is obvious that he is God as well. If, on the other hand, this is outside of God, then God, according to you, is without word and without spirit. Thus, trying to avoid making associates to God you have mutilated Him. For it would be better if you were saying that he has an associate than to mutilate him. [...] *Therefore, by accusing us falsely, you call us Associators; we, however, call you Mutilators of God.*[37]

In short, John calls Muhammad's followers "Mutilators," because they cut apart the body of the Church, denying the unity between God the Father and Christ.

A similar line of attack would continue to characterize anti-Islamic polemics for centuries to come. Influential authors such as Peter the Venerable, Thomas Aquinas, and Riccoldo da Montecroce reiterated that the main point of theological contention between Islam and Christianity consisted in the Muslims' refusal to accept the doctrines of Incarnation and Trinity, both of which had also been highly controversial in the early phases of Christianity. In the *Summa totius haeresis Saracenorum*, for instance, Peter the Venerable narrated the often-rehashed legend of Muhammad's religious education with the monk Sergius, a follower of Nestorianism and Arianism, heresies that called into question the divine nature of Christ.³⁸ Aquinas, who did not substantively address the question of Islam in the *Summa contra gentiles*, dedicated the first chapters of his short treatise *De rationibus fidei* to a rather detailed refutation of Islamic objections to the doctrines of Incarnation and Trinity, which together, he pointed out, constitute the foundation of the Christian faith.³⁹ Likewise, at the beginning of his *Contra legem Sarracenorum*, Riccoldo launches his critique of the Qur'an by outlining Islam's debt to early Christian heresies that denied the consubstantiality of Christ with the Father.⁴⁰ In the first and second letters of his *Epistole ad Ecclesiam triumphantem*, Riccoldo further states that by denying the divine nature of Christ, Muhammad sought to "remove" ("tollere") the Father from the Son.⁴¹ Elsewhere in the *Epistole* (letter 3), and again in the *Contra legem Sarracenorum*, Riccoldo expresses the same concept, using the word "scisma" to interpret the Qur'anic (Sura 23, verse 91) description of the risk that would exist if God had a son: "in the chapter titled *Elmuminim*, Muhammad says that, if God had a son, the whole world would be in danger, as there would be a schism between them" ["dicit Mahometus de deo in capitulo *Elmuminim* quod si haberet filium, quod totius mundus esset in periculo, esset enim inter eos scisma"].⁴²

Regardless of any specific influence from a single work, it is clear from a wide range of sources to which Dante might have had access that during the Middle Ages no tenet was considered a greater source of division between Islam and Christianity than the doctrine of the Trinity, with its affirmation of Christ's divinity. And as Saint Paul's first letter to the Corinthians describes Christ as the head of the *corpus mysticum* of the Church, so does that same epistle further elucidate the terms in which Muhammad's role could be framed as divider of father and son: "But I would have you know, that the head of every man is Christ; and the head of the woman is the man; and the head of Christ is God" (1 Corinthians 11:3).⁴³ If, in Saint Paul's footsteps, we assume that "the head of Christ is God," then by denying the Trinity, Muhammad and his followers figuratively behead the Son. It is in this context extremely significant that "scisma" is a *hapax*, appearing only once in the *Commedia*, and that the character who speaks the word is Muhammad, who serves as spokesman for the sowers of discord: "tutti li altri che tu vedi qui, / seminator di scandalo e di scisma / fuor vivi e però son fessi così" ["All the others you see here were sowers of scandal and schism while they were alive, and therefore are they cloven in this way"] (*Inf.* 28.34–36). Muhammad's performance in this role singularly mirrors that of Bertran de Born, who utters one of the numerous *hapax prolegomena* of this canto, "contrapasso" ("counter-suffering"), as the final word of *Inferno* 28. Also worth noting is the interpretive history of a passage from the Gospel of John that strikingly foreshadows the principle of kingly unity between father and son to which I shall return below: Christ's statement that "I and the Father are one" (John 10:30). Saint Augustine cites this verse in a section of his *De trinitate* dedicated to the rebuttal of the Arian heresy (*De trinitate* 5.3.4)—the heresy that Peter the Venerable and Riccoldo da Montecroce argued, and many of their contemporaries believed, was the forerunner of Islam.

Civil War

The pilgrim's encounter with Muhammad ends with the latter's prophecy of another religious conflict, this one involving a small sect (the *Apostolici*) headed by the renegade priest Dolcino Tonielli (*Inf.* 28.55–60). At this juncture, the canto's geographic focus shifts to conflicts within the Italian Peninsula.[44] In the short span of about fifty lines, the pilgrim and Virgil happen upon several sinners: Pier da Medicina, probably a little-known nobleman from the Romagna region whom Dante must have met (28.70–75);[45] Curio, a Roman tribune who joined Caesar's ranks during the civil war; and Mosca dei Lamberti, a member of a prominent Florentine family involved in Florence's strife in the early thirteenth century. Dante's attention to civil conflicts centers on the Romagna, a region that the poet described in the preceding canto as a place of perpetual strife (27.37–39), and on Ancient Rome and Florence. The regional focus is unsurprising, given Dante's direct involvement in Florentine politics, as well as the close kinship between Rome and Florence. Various Florentine chronicles relate that both cities were founded under the aegis of Mars.[46] Dante's native city, moreover, was the offspring of Roman colonists and Fiesolan settlers whose own town had been destroyed during the repression of Catiline's conspiracy. Thus, in his *Tresor*, Brunetto Latini, Dante's former teacher, notes that Florence was doomed to suffer war and discord because the city emerged from the union of two different communities in an area called "Campo di Marte" ("Field of Mars"): "the Florentines are constantly at war and in a state of discord" ["li Florentin son tozjors en guerre et en descort"].[47]

In *Inferno* 28, all three characters mentioned above—Pier da Medicina, Curio, and Mosca de' Lamberti—exemplify the dangers of enmity within kingdoms or cities. Yet Dante's depiction of Curio deserves particular attention, for it sheds poignant light on the role that Dante envisioned for himself amid the political unrest besetting the Italian Peninsula in the early fourteenth century. Risen to prominence as a tribune of the plebs, Curio was exiled from Rome as a supporter of Caesar, whom he then exhorted to march southward after crossing the Rubicon, thus triggering the civil war against Pompey. That Pompey was Caesar's son-in-law, and that he was decapitated at the behest of King Ptolemy XIII of Egypt (*Civil War* 8.663–75), is consistent with the canto's emphasis on the violent disruption of political family ties, particularly those between fathers and sons. In part because Curio is silenced in *Inferno* 28, he has also been rather neglected by Dante scholars, eclipsed in scholarship (as in the poem) by the loquacious Muhammad and Bertran de Born at the beginning and end of the canto. This juxtaposition of speaking and silent characters is not uncommon in Dante's Hell, where sinners such as Paolo Malatesta (*Inf.* 5), the Greek hero Diomedes (*Inf.* 26), and the Archbishop Ruggieri (*Inf.* 33) suffer silently while their notoriously garrulous companions (Francesca, Ulysses, and Count Ugolino) converse with the pilgrim and Virgil.

Two interrelated issues, however, make Dante's decision to condemn Curio as a sower of discord highly problematic. First, Caesar's victory in the civil war was crucial for the rise of the Roman Empire, an event that Dante considers providential, as he explains at length in book 2 of the *Monarchia*.[48] Why, then, would Dante condemn an individual whose words led to this event? This issue is easily resolved: most scholars agree that, although the rise of the Empire was indeed providential, Dante thought that the preceding civil war was nonetheless woeful; similar logic would recognize the Crucifixion as necessary for the salvation of humankind, yet simultaneously see that Judas's betrayal of Jesus was wholly sinful.[49] However, Curio's damnation is also problematic for reasons that involve Dante more personally and thus merit further scrutiny. In April 1311, perhaps only a year or two after writing *Inferno* 28, Dante addressed a letter to King Henry VII of Germany, the man who in 1312 would be crowned Holy Roman Emperor. Dante, hoping that Henry could usher in the resurgence of the Empire,[50] urged him in this 1311 letter to march on with his army through Northern Italy and seize Florence, using the same adage that Curio utters in Lucan's *Civil War* when exhorting Caesar to cross the Rubicon: "delay is ever fatal to those who are prepared" ["semper nocuit differre paratis"] (*Civil War* 1.281). Yet in *Inferno* 28, Dante paraphrases these same words to identify Curio as a sower of discord: "'l fornito / sempre con danno l'attender sofferse" ["one prepared always suffers from delay"] (*Inf.* 28.98–99).[51] The recurrence of Curio's words raises a number of questions: Is there a difference between Curio and Dante, or a difference in the circumstances in which they spoke out? Assuming that there is some difference between the two (i.e., that

Dante himself is not a sower of discord like Curio, and thus also a hypocrite), how does Dante's use of these words in his 1311 epistle to Henry align with the vision of politics rooted in the father-son relationship that characterizes *Inferno* 28?

As we shall see in the following pages, juxtaposing Dante's letter to Henry with Lucan's portrait of Curio in the *Civil War* suggests that the answer to the first question lies not in outcome, but in motives.[52] This crucial Dantean distinction between intention and outcome arises in other key passages of the *Commedia*. A typical example would be Dante's treatment of Emperor Constantine: although he was unwittingly responsible for the corruption of the Church through his alleged donation of the Western half of the Roman Empire to Pope Sylvester, Constantine is still counted among the blessed souls in the Heaven of Jupiter (cf. *Inf.* 19.115–17 and *Par.* 20.55–60). In his own case, Dante seems to consider his advice to Henry to be justified by his disinterested motivation. Scholars have long noted that Dante projects Henry's liberation of Italy onto a prophetic background. The frequent biblical references embedded in the letter cast the Emperor as a messiah, whose descent into Italy will bring peace and freedom to the suffering exiles of this new Babylon (*Epistles* 7.8).[53] In lending his voice to support Henry's providential task, Dante—an exile, like Curio—claims that he is not pursuing his own interests, but merely serving as the spokesman of all peace-seeking Tuscans (*Epistles* 7.1). Even a cursory glance at the Classical source that Dante uses in *Inferno* 28 suggests that Curio, by contrast, was eager to foment war for personal gain.

Book 1 of Lucan's *Civil War*, the anti-imperial poem on the conflict that led to the establishment of Caesar's rule and eventually of Augustus's Empire, is already widely understood to have been the main source for Dante's representation of Curio. My goal here, however, is not to revisit the topic of sources, but to look more closely at Dante's engagement with Lucan's depiction of Curio: in particular, to relate Curio's involvement in the Roman civil war to the pattern of father-son conflicts in *Inferno* 28, and to highlight Dante's aspiration to bridge the gap between Pope and Emperor via his letter to Henry VII. Toward this end, we must focus on Lucan's depiction of Curio's character and motivations. Introducing Curio's fateful speech to Caesar, Lucan labels the former tribune as brazen and greedy: "with them [the tribunes] came Curio of the reckless heart and venal tongue" ["audax venali comitatur Curio lingua"] (*Civil War* 1.269). Dante exploits this snapshot—the vivid physical detail of a "venal tongue"—in his caustic portrayal of Curio's punishment. In his Dantean afterlife, Curio appears stunned ("sbigottito"), with his tongue fittingly cut off:

"Questi è desso e non favella.
Questi, scacciato, il dubitar sommerse
in Cesare affermando che 'l fornito
sempre con danno l'attender sofferse."
Oh quanto mi pareva sbigottito
con la lingua tagliata ne la strozza
Curïo, ch'a dir fu così ardito! (*Inf.* 28.96–102)

["This is he, and he cannot speak. He, an exile, drowned Caesar's doubts, affirming that one prepared always suffers from delay." Oh how dismayed Curio seemed, with the tongue cut out of his throat, he who was so bold to speak!]

Dante captures with his usual pithiness the image of an overreaching, greedy Curio that emerges from the *Civil War*. The prominent rhyming of "sbigottito" with "ardito" powerfully underscores the contrast between Curio's boldness in book 1 of the *Civil War* and his helplessness as a damned soul in *Inferno* 28. Even the dieresis that splits his name, "Curïo," conveys his being divided— separated, in particular, from his tongue, the organ that most evidently defines his sin.

In another scathing passage from book 4 of the *Civil War*, Lucan sketches the young lieutenant's temperament, emphasizing the personal ambition and avarice that corrupted him and led him to join Caesar. For good measure, Lucan adds here that Curio harmed Rome more than the likes of Sulla, Marius, and Caesar, all of whom Lucan deeply loathed. While these others may have bought Rome, it was Curio who sold it:

Rome never bore a citizen of such high promise, nor one to whom the constitution owed more while he trod the right path. But then the corruption of the age proved fatal to the State, when ambition and luxury and the formidable power of wealth swept away with their cross-current the unstable principles of Curio; and, when he yielded to the booty of Gaul and Caesar's gold, his change turned the scale of history. Though powerful Sulla and bold Marius, like bloodstained Cinna and all the line of Caesar's house, secured the power to use the sword against our throats, yet to none of them was granted so high a privilege; for they all bought their country, but Curio sold it. (4.814–20)[54]

Since Dante, like Aristotle, considered greed to be the opposite of the cardinal virtue of justice (*Mn.* 1.11.11), we can appreciate his disdain for Curio. Indeed, what emerges from book 4 of Lucan's work is the image of Curio as a petty anti-hero, an ironic collage of heroes like Scipio, Aeneas, and Hercules, all of whom the Roman poet evokes in describing Curio's ill-fated mission in Africa, which led to his death and the near-total destruction of his army by the African King Juba (*Civil War* 4.581–798).[55] Perhaps even more noteworthy is Lucan's juxtaposition between Curio and Cato. Dante would famously extol the latter as an emblem of the four cardinal virtues and of liberty in canto 1 of *Purgatorio*: "Li raggi de le quattro luci sante / fregiavan sì la sua faccia di lume, / ch'i' 'l vedea come 'l sol fosse davante" and "libertà va cercando, ch'è sì cara / come sa chi per lei vita rifiuta" ["The rays of the four holy lights so adorned his face with brightness that I saw him as if the sun had been before him" and "he seeks freedom, which is so precious, as one knows who rejects life for her sake"] (*Purg.* 1.37–39, 71–72).[56] Much like Curio in book 4, in book 9 of the *Civil War*, Cato is the protagonist of a daunting mission in Africa. During this mission, Cato heroically leads the soldiers formerly under Pompey's command through the Libyan Desert.

On structural grounds alone, it is logical to treat Curio as Cato's antithesis in Lucan's poem. Although we cannot know for certain how many books the *Civil War* would have comprised had Lucan not committed suicide, it is plausible that, like Virgil's *Aeneid*, Lucan's work would have included twelve books.[57] A twelve-book structure would locate Curio's and Cato's African campaigns in symmetrical positions in the poem—fourth and fourth to the last, respectively. More substantively, Lucan's Cato embodies an austere version of Roman *virtus* and aims to defend Rome's unity irrespective of the political parties involved in the fight. A passage from book 9 of the *Civil War* further accentuates the contrast between Curio and Cato, in terms that Dante could have hardly missed. Here, Lucan praises the great Stoic as "the true father of his country, a man most worthy to be worshipped by the Romans" ["parens verus patriae, dignissimus aris"] (*Civil War* 9.601). This definition possibly inspired Dante's own description of Cato as "un veglio solo, / degno di tanta reverenza in vista, / che più non dee a padre alcun figliuolo" ["a solitary old man, worthy, by his appearance, of so much reverence that never son owed father more"] (*Purg.* 1.31–33). Thus, if Lucan's and Dante's poems present Curio as a greedy warmonger willing to sell his city to the highest bidder, then both also contrast him with Cato as Rome's ideal *pater patriae*.

Lucan's portrayal of a corrupt Curio thus helps us decipher the apparent contradiction between Dante's readiness to damn Curio among the sowers of discord in *Inferno* 28 and his willingness to use Curio's proverbial *sententia* in his letter to Henry VII. In the letter, after lamenting Henry's reluctance to liberate Tuscany from unjust rulers (*Epistles* 7.4), Dante cites the examples of Curio from the *Civil War* and Mercury from the *Aeneid*, in the latter case referring to a well-known episode from book 4 in which Mercury exhorts Aeneas to leave Africa and abandon his nascent affair with Dido, the Queen of Carthage (*Aeneid* 4.272–76). In his plea, Dante also mentions Henry's firstborn son and heir John, whom he compares to Aeneas's son Ascanius:

> Let the words of Curio to Caesar be heard again: "While your foes are in confusion and before they have gathered strength, make haste; delay is ever fatal to those who are prepared. The toil and danger are no greater than before, but the prize you seek is higher." And let the words of Anubis [Mercury], rebuking Aeneas, be heard again too: "If the glory of your great destiny is powerless to kindle your ardour, and if you will exert no effort to win fame for yourself, at least think of Ascanius, now growing up, and all that you hope from him as your heir, destined to rule in an Italy which shall become the Italy of Rome."
>
> For your royal firstborn, John, a king in his own right, to whom, once the sun has set on the day which is now dawning, the future generations will turn, is for us another Ascanius. (*Epistles* 7.4–5)[58]

The parallel between Henry and Aeneas partly offsets the anti-imperial ideology of the citation from Lucan's poem and introduces a series of parental images that inform the last part of Dante's letter. Dante describes the Emperor as "Ecclesie filius" and the Pope as "pater patrum" (*Ep.* 7.8 and 7.26, respectively). By advocating the return of the Emperor to Rome, in the *Epistola* 7 Dante aims to reestablish what he considers the proper relationship between the Pope and the Emperor in terms that, as we shall see shortly, anticipate the last chapter of the *Monarchia*. We should notice, too, that Dante describes Henry's son John as "rex." John did become king of Bohemia in 1310, but describing him as natural heir to the Empire is puzzling, insofar as Dante here conveniently neglects that Emperor was an elected, not hereditary, position. Dante's apparent "mistake" may have been designed to assert the principle of unity between a king, or in this case an emperor, and his firstborn son. In the *Commedia*, the violation of this principle finds its most dramatic visualization in the episode of Bertran de Born, the last among the sowers of discord in *Inferno* 28.

Two in One and One in Two

A brief intermission foreshadows the hallucinatory moment in which the Provençal poet takes the stage. After the encounter with Curio, Dante sees Mosca dei Lamberti, one of the men who initiated the internecine conflicts between Florence's Buondelmonti and Amidei clans. As Dante might have read in a chronicle erroneously attributed to Brunetto Latini, it was Mosca who gave the decisive advice to kill Buondelmonte during the family meeting that ensued from Buondelmonte's rupture of engagement with his Amidei fiancé.[59] His literally seminal act of violence—"mal seme de la gente tosca" ["the seed of evil for the Tuscans"] (*Inf.* 28.108)—eventually led to the struggle between the Guelphs and the Ghibellines. In *Inferno* 28, Mosca is portrayed as a badly mutilated figure, his hands cut off, who repeats the same four words he supposedly spoke during the fateful meeting with his relatives: "Capo ha cosa fatta" ["a thing done has a head"] (28.107; my translation).[60] In Mosca's logic of violence, only death could fully avenge Buondelmonte's violation of the Amidei family honor. Dante contemptuously responds by cursing Mosca's lineage, which would indeed be truncated by the same conflicts that Mosca had helped to initiate with his advice: "E io li aggiunsi: 'E morte di tua schiatta'" ["And I added: 'And the death of your clan'"] (28.109). In emphasizing that Mosca's words also led to the destruction of his own family, Dante shows that revenge is a reflexive act of violence that ultimately harms both victim and perpetrator.[61]

As Mosca abandons the scene as a "persona trista e matta" ["a person mad with sorrow"] (*Inf.* 28.111), Dante's confidence in the authority of his poetic voice is momentarily shaken by a grisly sight—a sight that, he claims, only the "asbergo" ["hauberk"] (28.117) of his conscience allows him to retell. The pilgrim sees a trunk without its head walking among the other sowers of discord, a sarcastic reversal of Mosca's assertion, a few lines earlier, that "a thing done has a head":

> Ma io rimasi a riguardar lo stuolo,
> e vidi cosa ch'io avrei paura,
> senza più prova, di contarla solo;
> se non che coscïenza m'assicura,
> la buona compagnia che l'uom francheggia
> sotto l'asbergo del sentirsi pura.
> Io vidi certo, e ancor par ch'io lo veggia,
> un busto senza capo andar sì come

andavan li altri de la trista greggia;
e 'l capo tronco tenea per le chiome,
pesol con mano a guisa di lanterna:
e quel mirava noi e diceva: "Oh me!"
Di sé facea a sé stesso lucerna,
ed eran due in uno e uno in due;
com'esser può, quei sa che sì governa. (28.112–26)

[But I remained to gaze at the host, and I saw something that I would fear, without more proof, even to retell, except that my conscience makes me confident, the good companion that frees a man, if it wears the hauberk of knowing itself pure. I surely saw, and it seems I still see it, a torso without a head walking like the others of the sorry flock; and his severed head he was holding by the hair, dangling it from his hand like a lantern, and the head was gazing at us, saying: "Oh me!" Of himself he made a lamp for himself, and they were two in one and one in two; how that can be, he knows who so disposes.]

Dante's appeal here to the purity of his conscience mirrors the rhetorical *praeteritio* with which he had earlier questioned his ability to adequately represent the horrors of the ninth *bolgia*. The repeated use of the verb "vedere," a constant throughout *Inferno* 28, is probably meant to corroborate the authenticity of Dante's experience (or the accuracy of his witnessing). At the same time, the martial term "asbergo," another *hapax* in the poem, aptly introduces the encounter with Bertran de Born and sharpens the irony of the word "greggia" ("sheepfold") that Dante uses to brand the war-loving sinners of this *bolgia*. In the *De Vulgari Eloquentia*, Bertran is the author Dante uses to illustrate war poetry in the Provençal tradition: "On these themes alone, if I remember rightly, we find that illustrious individuals have written poetry in the vernacular: Bertran de Born on arms, Arnaut Daniel on love, Giraut de Borneil on integrity; Cino da Pistoia on love, his friend on integrity" ["Circa que sola, si bene recolimus, illustres viros invenimus vulgariter poetasse; scilicet Bertramum de Bornio, arma; Arnaldum Danielem, amorem; Gerardum de Bornello, rectitudinem; Cinum Pistoriensem, amorem; amicum eius, rectitudinem"] (*DVE* 2.2.9).[62] Dante does not include any Italian war poet in his short catalog, noting only in passing that the martial genre fulfills the soul's lowest function, the vegetative, as opposed to the theme of rectitude—the noblest theme, of which Dante himself is Italy's chief exponent—which corresponds to the soul's highest faculty, the rational (2.2.8).

Some scholars have argued persuasively that a passage from Alan of Lille's *Anticlaudianus* may have served as a source for Dante's depiction of Bertran de Born's singular punishment in *Inferno* 28.⁶³ In Alan's allegorical epic, Discord is described as thirsty for war and more eager than any other vice to engage in battle against the virtues. After the New Man kills Discord, he beheads "her with his sword, he disjoins head from trunk. And it is fitting that the head should be discordant with the trunk of her through whom strife, hatred, madness, dissension, quarrel first arose, through whom conflict, wrath, primeval fear and the desire for war first came to be" ["Et merito caput a trunco discordat in illa / per quam lis odium rabies dissension rixa / prima fuit, per quam primo conflictus et irae / primaevique metus et belli prima cupido"] (*Anticlaudianus* 9.37–40).⁶⁴ This iconography complements Bertran's assertion in *Inferno* 28 that the retribution inflicted on him reenacts the breach he caused in the continuity of kingship from father to son. In his classic work *The King's Two Bodies*, Ernst Kantorowicz showed that the law of inheritance in Justinian's *Institutiones* and the gloss to it by the thirteenth-century jurist Accursius had established a symbol of indivisibility between the ruler and his successor. This symbol conferred perpetual value to the crown as symbol of the realm. With legalistic concision, these medieval texts affirm that a king and his son are one "according to the fiction of the Law" ["pater et filius unum fictione iuris sunt"].⁶⁵ Since he sowed discord between Henry II and his son, creating an unnatural separation between two components of a symbolic royal body, Bertran is condemned to carry his own head like a lantern (*Inf.* 28.122). Bertran is thus two in one and one in two (28.125). His punishment literalizes the crime of *lèse-majesté*—literally, "wounded majesty"—that he instigated by means of his counsel to the young Henry.⁶⁶

The image of Bertran lighting his way by carrying his own head as a lantern is not only visually haunting, but it also demonstrates Dante's understanding of the relationship between ethics and poetry that ultimately determines Bertran's inclusion among the sowers of discord.⁶⁷ To better appreciate the significance of this relationship, we might contrast the dramatic scene of *Inferno* 28 with a familiar episode of the *Commedia* that involves two other martial poets, Virgil and Statius, whose works Dante knew quite well. In *Purgatorio* 20, Dante and Virgil are stunned by an earthquake, which they will soon learn signals the absolution of a soul. The apparition of the atoned spirit in the following canto reenacts Christ's encounter with two of his disciples at Emmaus after His resurrection (Luke 24:13–15): "O frati miei, Dio vi dea pace" ["O my brothers, may God give you peace"] (*Purgatorio* 21.13). The reader eventually learns through elaborate periphrasis that this atoned character is Statius, author of the unfinished *Achilleid* and, more importantly, of the *Thebaid* (21.82–93). Thebes was traditionally considered the city of tragedy, and Dante often echoes this *topos* in *Inferno*, especially in the cantos dedicated to lower Hell.[68] In Statius's work, Thebes's deep-rooted internal enmity is perhaps most vividly illustrated in the image of Eteocles's and Polynices's corpses burning on a divided pyre in the last book of the *Thebaid*.[69] Once identified to the pilgrim, Statius explains in detail his debt to the *Aeneid*, prompting a comic exchange: Virgil discloses his identity, and Statius responds effusively (*Purg.* 21.121–36). Dante uses the cordial tenor of this scene to offset the dark themes—civil war, fratricide, parricide, and incest—that made Statius's poetry famous, and to initiate a sequence of cantos (*Purgatorio* 21–26) that openly celebrate friendship in conjunction with poetry.[70]

Later on, in canto 22, Statius acknowledges that, in addition to inspiring his poetry, Virgil had unwittingly moved him to become a Christian. He attributes his conversion to a well-known passage of *Eclogue* 4, Virgil's prophecy of an imminent new Golden Age under the sign of Justice (4.4–10), that was frequently misinterpreted in the Middle Ages as predicting the coming of Christ. In narrating Virgil's role in his conversion, Statius clearly evokes the spectacle of Bertran de Born's punishment:

Facesti come quei che va di notte,
che porta il lume dietro e sé non giova,
ma dopo sé fa le persone dotte,
quando dicesti: "Secol si rinova;
torna giustizia e primo tempo umano,
e progenie scende da ciel nova.
Per te poeta fui, per te cristiano." (*Purgatorio* 22.67–73)

[You did as one who walks at night, who carries the light behind him
and does not help himself, but instructs the persons coming after,
when you said, "The age begins anew; justice returns and the first
human time, and a new offspring comes down from heaven." Through
you I became a poet, through you a Christian.]

The contrast between this depiction of Virgil carrying a lamp behind himself and that of Bertran in *Inferno* 28 carrying his head like a lantern is striking. Although Virgil was a pagan and he is thus, in the *Commedia*, confined to Limbo, he is praised for his poetry that, however inadvertently, illuminated his readers' path to salvation. Bertran instead swings his head, making a lamp for himself—a bitter inversion of spiritual illumination—because he incited conflicts and took pleasure in the violence inherent in all wars.[71] Bertran sinned because he treated the wounds and suffering of battle as a source for boasting and exhilaration, whereas Virgil presented war as a grim but necessary reality. Aeneas must face the inevitable battles that come with the pursuit of his mission, as the Cumaean Sibyl foretells when she predicts the Trojan hero's future (*Aeneid* 6.86). And internecine conflicts are a self-inflicted wound on the body of the fatherland, as Anchises warns when he anticipates the enmity between Caesar and Pompey (6.830–35).

Among the many passages from Bertran's works that Dante echoes in *Inferno* 28 is—paradoxically—the *sirventes* (troubadour song) "Si tut il duol," in which Bertran bewails the demise of Henry, known as the Young King, whom the poet had encouraged to rebel against his father King Henry II of England. This was the event that caused young Henry's premature death and, in Dante's fiction, Bertran's own infernal damnation. Though Dante's interpretation of Bertran's role in the conflict between Henry II and his son might not have been historically accurate, his version of events was popular in the Middle Ages. Bertran's reputation as a warmonger was recorded in various *Vidas* (short biographies) of the Provençal poet that circulated in the late Middle Ages: "He was master whenever he so desired of King Henry of England and his son. But he always wanted a state of war to reign between father, son and brothers, turning each against the others. [. . .] And if they were at peace or truce, he at once strove and sought to break the peace by means of his sirventes, and to demonstrate how peace strips honor from everyone" (my translation).[72] The battle-thirsty quality that defines Bertran in the *Vidas* reappears now as the sin that condemns him to Dante's Hell. Of course, Dante also displays his own facility as a martial poet in *Inferno* 28. But while Bertran's poems celebrate the violent esthetics of combat, the horrid scenes of this canto indicate Dante's refusal to glorify war through poetic means. This is true not only in *Inferno* 28, but also in other similarly warlike cantos: *Inferno* 8–9, where Dante narrates the *viator*'s and Virgil's hard-won "conquest" of the City of Dis, and *Inferno* 21–22, describing the grotesque platoon of devils who escort the pilgrim and Virgil through the ditch of the barrators.[73] Dante's engagement with war poetry is thus instrumental to the ethical goal that he outlines in the *Epistle to Cangrande*: "the aim of the whole and of the part is to remove those living in this life from a state of misery, and to bring them to a state of happiness" ["finis totius et partis est removere viventes in hac vita de statu miserie et perducere ad statum felicitates"] (*Epist*. 13.15).[74]

Inferno 28 ends on a self-aggrandizing note from Bertran. In the final lines, he reveals his identity and peremptorily addresses the pilgrim with his wish that his infernal predicament be broadcasted to a wide audience:

> Quando diritto al piè del monte fue,
> levò 'l braccio alto con tutta la testa
> per appressarne le parole sue,
> che fuoro: "Or vedi la pena molesta,
> tu che, spirando, vai veggendo i morti:
> vedi s'alcuna è grande come questa.
> E perché tu di me novella porti,
> sappi ch'i' son Bertram dal Bornio, quelli
> che diedi al re giovane i ma' conforti.
> Io feci il padre e 'l figlio in sé ribelli;
> Achitofèl non fé più d'Absalone
> e di Davìd coi malvagi punzelli.
> Perch'io parti' così giunte persone,
> partito porto il mio cerebro, lasso!,
> dal suo principio ch'è in questo troncone.
> Così s'osserva in me lo contrapasso." (28.127–42)

[When he was directly at the foot of the bridge, he raised high his arm far up, head and all, to bring his words close to us, which were: "Now see my wretched punishment, you who go still breathing to view the dead: see if any is great as this. And that you may take back news of me, know that I am Bertran de Born, he who gave the young king the bad encouragements. I made father and son revolt against each other: Achitophel did no worse to Absalom and David with his evil proddings. Because I divided persons so joined, I carry my brain divided, alas, from its origin, which is in this trunk. Thus you observe in me the counter-suffering."]

In this passage, Bertran complains—or perhaps more correctly, he boasts—about his punishment, which he clearly considers to be exceptional. His use of the term "contrapasso" (which appears here for the first and only time in the *Commedia*) underlines the allegation of exceptionality regarding his treatment in Hell.[75] As Bertran further explains the cause of his damnation and the logic of his suffering, Dante takes the opportunity to emphasize the idea of unity between father and son that informs the structure of this canto. Bertran's phrases "così giunte persone" and "in sé ribelli," in particular, suggest the reflexive quality of the hostility between Henry II and the Young King. And when Bertran describes his own decapitation with a suggestion that the "principio" of his "cerebro" is in the trunk, he seems to invert the traditional order of power relations exemplified by the political body and grounded in the conceptualization of the king as the head of state. If the "principio" coincides with the father, as would seem logical here, then the "cerebro" presumably corresponds to the son. Dante's inversion may develop an alternative physiological metaphor of sovereignty, one rooted in the literal application of Aristotle's theory that the nervous system originates from the heart.[76] Or, as I think more likely, Dante implies that Bertran's reversal of the legitimate political hierarchy between king and prince partly explains the Provençal poet's condemnation in the depths of the ninth *bolgia*.

Poet and Prophet of Peace

In summary, then, Dante punishes the schismatics of *Inferno* 28 so harshly not only because they created religious and/or political divisions, but also because they severed what he regarded as the fundamental bond between fathers and their sons: Muhammad, in Dante's eyes, had decapitated the universal body of the Church and divided God the Father from the Son by denying the dogma of the Trinity; Curio had inflamed Rome's civil conflicts by fomenting war between Julius Caesar and his son-in-law Pompey; Bertran de Born had ruptured the continuity of hereditary monarchy by leading a young prince into self-destructive rebellion against his father and king. The centrality of the father-son relationship in this canto of the *Commedia*, which more than any other is steeped in the dynamics of war and enmity, returns us to the starting point of this chapter, the *Monarchia*, and helps us to understand the political role that Dante endeavored to play through his writing. As I have already suggested in my examination of the *Epistola* 7, Dante conceived of his politico-literary responsibility in terms directly opposed to the actions and motivations of the sinners encountered in *Inferno* 28.

After arguing throughout book 3 of the *Monarchia* that both the Papacy and the Empire receive their authority directly from God, in the final chapter of his treatise Dante employs a paternal metaphor to describe the reverence that the Emperor owes to the Pope: "Let Caesar use that reverence towards Peter, therefore, that a first-born son ought to use towards his father; so that being illuminated by the light of paternal grace, he may more powerfully shed his rays on earth's orb, over which he has been placed only by him who is the governor of all things spiritual and temporal" ["Illa igitur reverentia Caesar utatur ad Petrum qua primogenitus filius debet uti ad patrem: ut luce paterne gratie illustratus virtuosius orbem terre irradiet, cui ab Illo solo prefectus est, qui est omnium spiritualium et temporalium gubernator"] (*Mn.* 3.16.17). Much ink has been spilled on the relationship between Church and Empire in Dante's thought, including on this highly controversial passage.[77] The scholarly debate on this issue peaked decades ago in the 1950–60s, but we might still reflect on its implications for Dante's representation of enmity, particularly in *Inferno* 28. Bruno Nardi contended that Dante added this passage when revising the final paragraphs of the *Monarchia* years after its completion in an attempt to counterbalance any potentially unorthodox idea that might have surfaced earlier in the treatise.[78] However, Marjorie Reeves claimed that Dante actually took a hierocratic position at the end of *Monarchia*, acknowledging the supremacy of the Pope over the Emperor and thus fundamentally departing from book 3's central argument for the mutual independence of Church and Empire.[79] Neither interpretation was wholly convincing, and scholars have subsequently accepted—and, in Anthony Cassell's case, further developed—a view first offered by Michele Barbi that Dante simply advocated cooperation between the two authorities.[80]

Following Barbi and Cassell, I would again caution against interpreting Dante's closing words as a reversal of positions that he had staked out earlier in his treatise. I would further add, however, that we should view his remarks on the relationship between Pope and Emperor as paradigmatic of the crucial position that the father-son relationship occupies in his vision of war and peace. By proposing that Pope and Emperor cooperate for the well-being of humankind, in the last paragraphs of the *Monarchia* Dante claims the role of peacemaker that was so central to his authorial stance. This passage, then, far from being a careless throwaway or reversal of an earlier position on the relationship between church and state, might best be viewed as one of the instances in Dante's *oeuvre* when he claims a prophetic mission "in pro del mondo che mal vive" ["for the good of the world that lives ill"] (*Purgatorio* 32.103).[81] As shown in numerous passages of the *Commedia*, Dante considered the hostility between secular and spiritual authorities the most harmful source of the world's conflicts. The final chapter of *Monarchia* allows him to present himself as the poet and prophet of peace, who can harmonize the relationship between these two authorities—between the father, the Pope, and his firstborn son, the Emperor. The contrast could not be greater between Dante's self-conceived poetic role and the actions and motives he ascribes to the sowers of discord, dividers of fathers and sons. The characters depicted in *Inferno* 28 are punished because they have enjoyed the exhilaration of battle, thrived in the midst of conflicts, and nurtured enmity within and among religions, kingdoms, cities, families, and individuals; this enmity is eternally reflected on these sinners' bodies.

CHAPTER 2

The Enemy within the Walls
Treachery, Pride, and Civil Strife in Pulci's *Morgante*

IN THE *DE OFFICIIS*, Cicero argues that justice is the keystone of any political structure aimed at ensuring social order. He celebrated justice as "the crowning glory of the virtues [...] on the basis of which men are called 'good men,'" and noted its close alliance with "charity [*beneficentia*], which may also be called kindness or generosity" ["(iustitia) virtutis splendor est maximus, ex qua viri boni nominantur (...) coniuncta beneficentia, quam eandem vel benignitatem vel liberalitatem appellari licet"] (I, vii, 20). Yet, if justice is the keystone, Cicero seems to have considered it an insufficient guarantee of a virtuous community. A few lines later he tersely adds that "the foundation of justice is good faith [*fides*]—that is, truth and fidelity to promises and agreements" ["Fundamentum autem est iustitiae fides, id est dictorum conventorumque constantia et veritas"] (I, vii, 23). Justice, then, is necessary for the well-being of a *res publica*, but good faith (or trust) is the *conditio sine qua non* for the existence of justice. Thus, treachery—a violation of trust—can be described as a corrosive force capable of undermining justice and with it the integrity of human relationships: treachery is, then, an existential threat to any community. While Dante's sowers of discord, whom I discussed in chapter 1 of this book, openly fostered conflicts among individuals or groups that should have been tied to one another by political and/or familial bonds, traitors nourished their own hostility behind a deceitful facade of friendship and trust. Precisely because these two virtues are crucially important to the life of what Dante in the *Monarchia* termed "the political community of the human race" ["universalis civilitatis humani generis"] (*Mn.* 1.2.8), he assigned traitors to the ninth and lowest circle in his *Inferno*.

It is from this perspective, the understanding of trust and justice as inextricably linked, that we can best analyze the issues of betrayal and internecine enmity that are central to Luigi Pulci's *Morgante*. I should add as a caveat that this is a biased perspective, insofar as it is aligned with Pulci's own pro-Medicean party. Those whom the Medici (and allies like Pulci) considered traitors could be seen from a different viewpoint as defenders of liberty. In this opposing perspective, some of Florence's *ottimati* families viewed with horror the city's turn toward princely power in the fifteenth century and identified as heroes Brutus and Cassius, the men who slayed Julius Caesar in defense of the Republic.[1] In this chapter, then, I address contention within a *polis*, be it the empire centered on Charlemagne's court, which is the ostensible stage of many adventures portrayed in the *Morgante*, or Medici Florence, whose intrigues hover in the background of Pulci's work.

Trust and disloyalty are woven deeply into the fabric of the *Morgante*. Even in strictly quantitative terms, issues of trust and betrayal are pervasive. Variations of *traditore* (traitor) and *tradimento* (treachery) recur in the *Morgante* more frequently even than *cavallo* (horse) and *cavaliere* (knight) or *spada/brando* (sword), all of which readers would expect to find liberally scattered through a chivalric epic. The *Morgante* contains 340 traitors and betrayals, but only 304 horses/knights and 278 swords. By comparison, in Matteo Maria Boiardo's *Orlando Innamorato* and Ludovico Ariosto's *Orlando Furioso*, chivalric poems of comparable length, terms for traitor(s)/treason appear only 105 and 63 times, respectively, far less frequently than references to swords, horses, and knights.

A speech by the half-giant Margutte, one of Pulci's brilliantly grotesque characters and Morgante's companion through some of the poem's most entertaining sections, offers a clue to the centrality of treachery in the *Morgante* and its deep political and theological implications. In cantare 18, Margutte describes his system of beliefs in a blasphemous parody of the Nicene Creed, the Christian profession of faith, and confesses his many sins to Morgante. Margutte, however, explicitly declares that the only sin he has never committed is betrayal:

Io t'ho lasciato indrieto un gran capitolo
di mille altri peccati in guazzabuglio;
che s'i' volessi leggerti ogni titolo,
e' ti parrebbe troppo gran mescuglio;

> e cominciando a sciorre ora il gomitolo,
> ci sarebbe faccenda insino a luglio;
> salvo che questo alla fine udirai,
> che tradimento ignun non feci mai. (18.142)[2]

[I have omitted an important chapter of other thousands of my random sins, for if I only cared to read each title, ah, what a mighty mess at once you'd see! Besides, if I start now, I will stop winding this thread at the beginning of July. But let me tell you at the very end: never, never have I betrayed a friend.]

Though we should take Margutte's exception with a grain of salt, his garrulous display of brazen immorality on all other counts suggests that his disavowal of treachery might actually be genuine. At any rate, Margutte's claim shows that, in Pulci's view, the sin of treachery occupies a unique position: even the self-professed vessel of all vices spurns the title of traitor (or, as one might expect from a traitor, pretends to do so).

Over the last three decades, scholars such as Stefano Carrai and Alessio Decaria have pointed to the importance of treachery in the *Morgante* and noticed the impact of the 1478 Pazzi conspiracy, in which Giuliano de' Medici (brother of Lorenzo il Magnifico) was killed, on both the content and the style of the poem's last five cantari.[3] I would like to develop these observations further with the aim of articulating a threefold argument. I will first unpack some of Pulci's premises about the meaning of treachery, as he exposes them in the crab's killing of Morgante in cantare 20. Here I use a medico-political perspective to argue that Pulci views treachery as a cancerous pathology. I will next revisit the parallel between Morgante's death and Hercules's—foregrounding what I consider the parodic and even ominous undertones of this parallel—to suggest that Pulci challenges the politically symbolic function that the Greek hero had acquired as Florence's avatar in the late Middle Ages and the Renaissance. Finally, I will turn to Pulci's account of Astolfo's near-execution (cantare 11), as well as the agreement between Ganelon and Marsilio (cantare 25) and their ensuing punishment after the Rout of Roncesvalles (cantari 27 and 28), considering these in relation to the simmering tensions within Medici Florence and in relation to Pulci's sources, particularly Dante's views on pride and treachery in the *Commedia*. This chapter's central contention is that, in the *Morgante*, Pulci exposes the primary vulnerability that lies within every community: the internal rivalries that may eventually consume its political body. Even if this political body or the power of its leaders can be envisioned as gigantic, as Pulci may imply via his choice of Morgante as the poem's most iconic character, the giant's Achilles heel is still susceptible to the deadly toxin of betrayal.

Morgante's Death and the Cancer of Treachery

Pulci's brief snapshot of Morgante's death in cantare 20 vividly illustrates the giant's vulnerability to betrayal. Just after Morgante has performed one of his most hyperbolic deeds, the slaying of a whale, a small crab bites the giant's foot, causing an infection that rapidly kills him:

> Ma non potea fuggir suo reo distino:
> e' si scalzò, quando uccise il gran pesce;
> era presso alla riva un granchiolino,
> e morsegli il tallon; costui fuori esce:
> vede che stato era un granchio marino;
> non se ne cura; e questo duol pur cresce;
> e cominciava con Orlando a ridere,
> dicendo:—Un granchio m'ha voluto uccidere:
> forse volea vendicar la balena,
> tanto ch'io ebbi una vecchia paura.—
> Guarda dove Fortuna costui mena!
> Rimmollasi più volte, e non si cura;
> ed ogni giorno cresceva la pena,
> perché la corda del nervo s'indura;
> e tanta doglia e spasimo v'accolse,
> che questo granchio la vita gli tolse. (20.50–51)

[But he cannot escape his evil fate. To kill the whale, he had removed his boots, and now, so near the shore, a little crab bites him right on the heel. Out of the water he comes, and sees that, yes, 't has been a crab: he gives no thought to it, but his pain grows. He starts to laugh about it with Orlando, saying, "I bet a crab has killed Morgante, maybe determined to avenge the whale, according to some ancient fear I had." Ah, look where Fortune leads this man at last! It worsens but he takes no care of it; the pain grows, therefore, sharper every day, because the tendon of the nerve grows stiff: such is, indeed, the lancinating pain, alas, by a tiny crab Morgante's slain.]

Morgante's sudden death takes him well before what scholars presume was the end of the poem's first edition. There is no extant copy of this 1478 edition, but, as noted above, it likely included only cantari 1–23.[4] This unceremonious ending to Morgante's presence in the poem might lead a reader to dismiss the death as one further comic twist in Pulci's comically convoluted work, a quick dispatch for a giant whose narrative function has been exhausted. Even though such a reading would not be entirely inconsistent with Pulci's uproarious account of Margutte's death in the previous cantare (19.147–50), it would be shortsighted here. Given Morgante's obvious prominence in the poem, we should instead look more closely at his passing as a chance to dig more deeply into the thematic and political substrate of Pulci's work.

Pulci's original readers would likely have recognized Morgante's crab as a wily and toxic animal. Pulci had foreshadowed Morgante's death encounter with the crab in a previous passage dedicated to an extensive catalog of animals:

> vedeasi il cancro l'ostrica ingannare,
> e come il fuscelletto in bocca avia,
> e poi che quella vedeva allargare,
> e' lo metteva nel fesso del guscio,
> e poi v'entrava a mangiarla per l'uscio. (*Morgante* 14.65)

[Ready to trap the oyster was the crab: a little straw in his mouth he showed, and when he saw her open up, at once he laid it in the slightly opened shell, sneaked right inside, and swallowed her as well.]

This vignette draws on the crab's reputation as established by numerous ancient and medieval sources. Pulci here appears to paraphrase several lines from Cecco d'Ascoli's *L'Acerba* (1320s),[5] though Cecco had in turn inherited this fable—which exemplifies the crab's cunning and warns against human slyness—from a longstanding and influential encyclopedic tradition: Pliny, *Natural History* IX, 51 (translated into the vernacular and commented on by Cristoforo Landino in 1476); Saint Basil the Great, *Hexaemeron* VII, 3; Saint Ambrose, *Hexaemeron* V, 8; Isidore of Seville, *Etymologies* XII, 7; Vincent of Beauvais, *Speculum Naturale* XVII, 36–38; Albert the Great, *De animalibus* XXIV, 23; and Uguccione da Pisa, *Derivationes* C 112, 12. Moreover, in or around the 1370s, a few decades after Cecco's death, the *topos* of the sly crab resurfaced in the poetic experiments of two Florentine authors: Coluccio

Salutati in his *Fabula de Vulpe et Cancro,* and Domenico Silvestri in his response to Salutati that he titled *Cancer.*[6]

Since many of these texts circulated widely in the fourteenth and fifteenth centuries, it is safe to claim, as Carrai has done,[7] that for Pulci the crab symbolized treachery; and we can assume the same for the *Morgante*'s early readers. While significant in and of itself as a representation of treachery, the presence of crab symbolism in cantari 14 and 20 may also reshape in two key ways our understanding of the *Morgante*'s relationship to contemporary political events. First, assuming that in the 1478 version the *Morgante*'s eponymous hero died in the same fashion and that Margutte had made the same speech I quoted above, then we can understand treachery to have been a key theme in Pulci's poem even before the Pazzi conspiracy and even before Pulci composed the last five cantari. If, moreover, these components were part of the 1478 poem, then it would seem logical to suggest that Pulci had been cognizant of the internal vulnerability of the Medici *de facto* rule well before the plot that killed Giuliano made that weakness apparent and that he understood that this vulnerability derived from the same network of friendships and patronage on which the Medicis' power was founded.[8]

The poem's final cantari are widely viewed as more grave: while Pulci retains a comic nucleus, brutally vital in the battle scenes, the last section of the *Morgante* develops some of the work's most "serious" aspects.[9] For instance, in those final cantari, the theological patterns that intermittently arise through cantari 1–23 acquire a steadier tone. The serious turn is undeniable, though the theological references continue to oscillate between doctrinal orthodoxy and sacrilegious parody throughout the poem, as is made abundantly clear by the dialogue between Rinaldo and the demon Astarotte in cantari 25 and 26. My goal here, however, is not to rehash the arguments about the relationship between the first and the final editions of the *Morgante*, but to stress that treachery is one of the leitmotifs (and probably the most poignant) joining the two otherwise unevenly matched parts of the poem. This element of continuity suggests that scholarly insights regarding the last part of the *Morgante* and concerning Florence's internecine hostilities might be extended to enhance our interpretation of the first twenty-three cantari. Evidence of treachery as a continuing theme linking the two parts of the poem might also help us to reconsider this poem as one comparatively coherent entity, rather than as the haphazard crucible of disparate exploits that critics have perhaps too often made it out to be.

The etymology of the medical terms "cancer" and "gangrene" further underscores the import of the zoological allegory in Morgante's death scene. These words derive from the Greek *karkinos* and the Latin *cancer,* both of which mean crab. In book 2 of the *Method of Medicine to Glaucon,* when describing the progression of breast cancer, the second-century Greco-Roman physician Galen of Pergamon explains why cancer takes its name from this apparently innocuous animal: "we have often seen in the breasts a tumor exactly like a crab. Just as that animal has feet on either side of its body, so too in this affection the veins of the unnatural swelling are stretched out on either side, creating a form similar to a crab."[10] Galen's numerous works were widely available in Latin in the late Middle Ages and became the basis of much medical learning in Western Europe, so his image of the cancerous crab would have been well known.[11] Isidore of Seville likewise noted in his *Etymologies* that "Cancer (*cancer,* lit. 'crab') is named from its resemblance to the sea animal. As physicians say, its lesion can be cured by no medication, and therefore the part of the body where it has arisen is customarily amputated, so that the body may live longer. However, death, even if it has been delayed, will come" ["Cancer a similitudine maritimi animalis vocatum. Vulnus sicut medici dicunt nullis medicamentis sanabile. At ergo praecidi solet a corpore membrum, ubi nascitur, ut aliquantum diutius vivat: tamen inde mortem, quamlibet tardius, adfuturam"] (IV, 8, 14).[12] By the fourteenth century, as illustrated by many texts, the correlation between animal and malady had deepened, encompassing the crab's natural disposition to crawl slowly, backwards, and deceptively while eating away its prey's flesh.[13]

Etymology aside, the symptomatology of Morgante's disease further signals the medico-political valence of his death. We see a suggestive analogy between treachery and *cancer* in Pulci's poem, drawing attention to the risk run by those in power when they underestimate seemingly negligible enemies. Several details in the progress of Morgante's fateful infection seem to substantiate a nosological reading of this crucial episode. First, we should note Pulci's indication that Morgante treats his injury carelessly and worsens his condition by repeatedly immersing the affected part in water ("costui fuori esce: / vede che stato era un granchio marino; / non se ne cura [...] Rimmollasi più volte, e non si cura") ["Out of the water he comes, and sees that, yes, 't has been a crab: he gives no thought to it ... It worsens but he takes no care of it"]. Second, we should closely examine the lines in which Pulci describes the stiffening of Morgante's injured tendon ("corda del nervo") as indicative of physical deterioration and, more precisely, causing intensification of his pain ("ogni giorno cresceva la pena, / perché la corda del nervo s'indura; / e tanta doglia e spasimo v'accolse / che questo granchio la vita gli tolse") ["the pain grows, therefore, sharper every day, because the tendon of the nerve grows stiff: such is, indeed, the lancinating pain, alas, by a tiny crab Morgante's slain]. I will shortly mention a set of texts that might have contributed to Pulci's understanding of how a neglected wound can turn into a lethal cancer, but let me first address Pulci's latter observation about the giant's sinew—in particular the clause "la corda del nervo s'indura" and the word "spasimo," which together reveal a knowledge of medical terminology hitherto unnoticed in criticism of the poet's repertoire. This is a striking omission given Pulci's well-documented interest in bestiaries and scientific curiosities, and, more pertinently, the fairly competent familiarity with current medical language that he displays in several satirical sonnets aimed at doctors.[14] In one of these sonnets, "E' c'è venuto un medico Rosato," probably composed early in his poetic career, Pulci notably uses the word "granchi" (crabs) with the technical meaning of *cancer* to define the deadly disease that the wretched Rosato brought upon many Florentine citizens: "e [medico Rosato] ttanti granchi à fatti per gli avelli" ["has sent many crabs [patients with cancer] to the sepulchers"] (line 3; my translation).[15]

Ancient physiology had developed two prevalent (and largely antithetical) views of the human nervous system—one Aristotelian, the other Galenic. While Aristotle thought that all nerves are hard and originate from the heart, Galen distinguished between sensory (soft) nerves originating from the encephalon (the front part of the brain) and motor (hard) nerves coming from the spinal medulla or *nucha* (the back part of the brain).[16] Most medieval and early modern physicians agreed with Galen. The extremely influential tenth-century Persian polymath Avicenna, for instance, succinctly stated that the nerves arise from the brain and are soft (*Canon of Medicine* §129).[17] Pulci's description of Morgante's hardening "corda del nervo" presumably implies that he had in mind some variation of the Galenic theory.

Indeed, Pulci's use of the phrase "corda del nervo," which is almost certainly technical, finds a direct correspondence in Albert the Great's *On Animals*. In it, Albert referred to the "chorda nervi" (*On Animals* II, 1, 17) as part of a broader explanation on the nature of muscles and nerves partly aimed at comparing, and perhaps integrating, the Aristotelian and Galenic theories. Albert defines a cord as "that which passes through the muscle and is bound to the member it moves" ["hoc enim quod sic transitus per musculum, et membro quod movetur alligatur, vocatur chorda"] (II, 1, 14),[18] and elsewhere in the same chapter adds that the cord functioned essentially as the axis of a muscle. He uses the phrase "chorda nervi" only for the cord connecting the calf to the heel (what we now call the "Achilles tendon"), i.e., only for the exact point where the crab bites Morgante: "It [this large cord] is the cord of a nerve which is connected with the heel bone" ["et ipsa est chorda nervi qui cum osse calcanei in posteriori pedis continuatur"] (II, 1, 17).[19] It seems most unlikely that Pulci's use of such accurate anatomical language was coincidental, especially as "corda" in this sense is a *hapax* in the *Morgante*, appearing only once, while "nervo/i" appears only six times. That the giant's infection results in the hardening of bodily tissue further suggests that he suffers from what Pulci would have regarded as a cancer-like disease. As medical historian Luke Demaitre has highlighted, most scientific sources of the time agreed that "no diagnostic sign was considered more crucial for the recognition of carcinoma than hardness."[20]

The word "spasimo/a," which appears only three times in the *Morgante* (3.47, 20.51, and 25.124), is likewise rare and technical. It can be more accurately translated as such English equivalents as "spasm" or "convulsion," rather than merely as "pain." Only a relatively short list of early modern authors use "spasimo" or its cognates in their writings: Giovanni Villani, in book XII of his *Cronica* (1348) relates how one messer, Pietro Rosso—much like Morgante—had a spasm attack ("spasimò") and died after water got into a wound.[21] Niccolò Machiavelli mentions "spasma" in the prologue to the *Mandragola* (1518),[22] while Matteo Bandello, in novella IV.6 of his 1554 short story collection, uses "spasimo" with a pseudo-specific medical connotation, to describe a side effect of excessive consumption of wine, ironically evoking none other than Galen as authority.[23] But the association of spasms with nerves, the association Pulci evokes in his narrative of Morgante's death, is longstanding. Among the first authors to discuss spasm (*spasmos* in Greek; *spasmus* in Latin) as a clinical condition affecting the nerves were Hippocrates of Cos in the *Aphorisms* and Cornelius Celsus in the *De medicina*. Galen examines spasm in a number of his works, including a short treatise titled *On Tremor, Palpitation, Spasm, and Rigor*, which was translated from an Arabic version into Latin by Arnald of Villanova in the thirteenth century. Here, Galen explains that spasms result from overextension of the nerves, either through excessive moisture (consistent with Morgante's error in exposing his "corda" to water) or excessive dryness.[24] Isidore of Seville, too, pithily registers the connection between nerves and spasms that ancient physicians had recognized: "Spasm is the sudden contraction of body parts or sinews, accompanied by severe pain." ["Spasmus Latine contractio subita partium aut nervorum cum dolore vehementi."] (*Etymologies* IV, 6, 11).[25] By the thirteenth and fourteenth centuries, numerous medical manuals, including those by Teodorico of Lucca and Lanfranc of Milan, conveyed similar notions about spasms, especially that such symptoms may also be caused by a wound to a nerve.[26]

Also prominent in the developing medical literature was the theory that a wound treated carelessly might develop into a "cancerous" lesion. Here again the prognoses and remedies proposed by ancient authors were by and large assimilated in the late Middle Ages into a broader consensus reflected in an extensive body of medical literature. An important though complex example of this documentary paradigm is Celsus's *De medicina*, a work that was "rediscovered" and gained wide recognition quite rapidly in Florence during the fifteenth century.[27] The Florentine humanist and bibliophile Niccolò Niccoli copied a manuscript of Celsus's work in the 1430s, and Bartolomeo Fonzio, another Florentine humanist, published a printed edition in 1478, the year by which Pulci completed the first version of the *Morgante*.[28] Pulci may, then, have had access to a manuscript of the *De medicina* before he wrote his description of Morgante's death. Celsus's own description of a developing cancerous injury in book V may help us better understand how Morgante's small lesion could turn deadly:

> Sometimes the wound becomes the seat of chronic ulceration, and it becomes hardened, and the thickened margins are a livid colour; after which whatever medicament is applied is of little service; and this commonly occurs when the wound has been carelessly treated. At times, whether owing to excessive inflammation, or to unusually hot water, or to excessively cold water, canker (*cancer*) sets in. [...] Canker, whatever its species, corrupts not only the part it attacks, but it also spreads. (*De Medicina* V, 26, 31)[29]

Like most premodern medical theorists, Celsus uses the word "cancer" broadly to describe various forms of physical corruption, including those we would now define as "gangrene." Two aspects of his discussion seem particularly relevant to Pulci's account of Morgante's death: the careless treatment of his wound and the potentially harmful effects of water. Celsus's pattern of cancer-inducing mistreatment corresponds closely to what Morgante did (and should have avoided): "costui fuori esce: / vede che stato era un granchio marino; / non se ne cura [...] Rimmollasi più volte, e non si cura" ["Out of the water he comes, and sees that, yes, 't has been a crab: he gives no thought to it ... It worsens but he takes no care of it"]. Even if Pulci did not directly consult the *De medicina*, Celsus's diagnosis of the progression from a wound to a cancer was, as suggested above, far from unique. Over the centuries it had become a commonplace belief that a neglected wound might provoke cancer, as medieval authors including Teodorico of Lucca and Lanfranc of Milan explained in their treatises on surgery.[30]

Diseases like cancer and gangrene, moreover, were very common in the fifteenth century. The esteemed Florentine physician Antonio Benivieni makes this point in his *De abditis nonnullis ac mirandis morborum et sanationum causis* (published posthumously in 1507),[31] a work deeply influenced by Celsus's *De medicina*. Benivieni began his career around the year 1470 and was close to the circle of intellectuals supported by Lorenzo de' Medici, including Marsilio Ficino, whose interest in medicine was well known, and Angelo Poliziano, who in 1472 dedicated an elegy to Benivieni.[32] In a chapter of the *De abditis* inauspiciously titled "Gangrene is fatal if it begins in the toe," Benivieni states: "I knew Cambino, Carolo and Thoma, all Florentines, and many others too, who being thus affected died within a few days" ["Novimus nos Cambinum, Carolum et Thomam cives florentinos, nec non et alios quam plurimos huiuscemodi affectos vitio paucis diebus vitam finisse"].[33] Cancer was so common that even so-called empirics (*empirici*)—practitioners who, unlike physicians (*fisici*), had not obtained a university medical degree—would treat ailments that were categorized as such.[34] Beyond the information that Pulci could have found in the numerous medical compendia circulating at the time, from his daily life experience he could hardly have ignored the most basic symptoms and conventional treatments of these pathologies.

Because we know little about Pulci's education and the texts to which he might have had access, especially before he began his service with the Florentine patrician Francesco Castellani in the late 1450s, we must proceed with caution when making claims about possible sources for the *Morgante*.[35] The foregoing analysis of Morgante's disease does, however, prove that Pulci was familiar, at least to a rudimentary degree, with the medical literature available at the time. The works of such authors as Galen, Avicenna, Albertus Magnus, and Arnald of Villanova—to name only a few—were relatively easy to access in fifteenth-century Florence and interest in these works extended beyond the community of medical specialists, as some of Angelo Poliziano's poems and his personal collection of medical texts make clear.[36] More to the point, this more detailed attention to the medical specifics of Morgante's death, as contemporaries would have understood them, suggests that Pulci viewed treachery as a disease that can be deceitfully trivial in its beginning, but, if left to metastasize despite signs of its emergence, can utterly corrode a political body. What remains to be seen is how this medico-political view of *cancer* as a treacherous condition contributed to Pulci's understanding of contemporary political tensions in Florence. Taking stock of the similarities and differences between Morgante and Hercules, the classical hero the city had adopted on its insignia, is a necessary step toward this understanding.

Morgante and Hercules

Pulci scholars have long noted the clear and wide-ranging correlation between Morgante and Hercules, usually framing this relationship in positive terms, whereby Morgante inherits only the heroic traits that Hercules exemplified.[37] However, as I will also propose in my discussion of the Greek hero vis-à-vis Orlando's madness in chapter 3, we may do well to problematize the terms of the Morgante-Hercules parallel by examining a shared feature particularly relevant to my consideration of Pulci's poem: that both Morgante and Hercules are killed through treacherous acts of vengeance. What does this narrative similarity reveal about the *Morgante* and how does Pulci's treatment of the Hercules myth compare with the ways in which Florence incorporated the Greek hero into its civic identity? Let us begin to address these questions by quickly surveying the tradition that underlies Florence's use of Hercules.

Classical authors widely praised Hercules as the epitome of human virtue. In one of the most influential examples of this commonplace, an anecdote invented by the fifth-century Sophist philosopher Prodicus and reported by Xenophon in his *Memorabilia* (II, 1, 21), Hercules, upon entering manhood, must choose between the hard road to virtue and the easy road to vice (or pleasure). This *topos* is often known as "Hercules at the crossroads" or "the choice of Hercules."[38] Cicero refers to it in the *De officiis* (I, xxxii, 118), and also repeatedly describes the hero as a benefactor of humankind (*De officiis* III, v, 25; *De finibus* II, 118; *De natura deorum* II, xxiv, 62).[39] Seneca similarly defines Hercules as a selfless defender of the good in *De beneficiis* I, xiii, 3. Notwithstanding opposition from Christian theologians, including Lactantius and Saint Augustine, who treated the alleged deification of pagan mythological figures with a mixture of ironic skepticism and outright contempt, the notion of Hercules as benefactor of humankind originally articulated by Cicero and Seneca would eventually consolidate into a medieval understanding of Hercules as a Christ figure.[40]

The hero's virtue, proverbial by the late thirteenth century, had led the Florentine authorities to choose him as the emblem for their city.[41] Florence's use of the Hercules myth was as extensive as Ferrara's, which I shall treat in the following chapter. The symbolic link between Hercules and Florence was developed through copious cultural production in the fourteenth and fifteenth centuries. In the *Genealogia deorum gentilium* (XIII, 1), Giovanni Boccaccio hailed Hercules—or, rather, the mosaic of avatars Boccaccio believed were recorded under the name of Hercules—as the protagonist of not just twelve, but rather thirty-one labors. A few decades later, the poet Franco Sacchetti matched Hercules's labors with the city's successes as examples of the Florentine Republic's resistance against tyranny.[42] And Coluccio Salutati, the city's chancellor in the last quarter of the fourteenth century, celebrated the exploits of Jove's son in a hefty, albeit incomplete, allegorical treatise titled *De laboribus Herculis* (1406).[43] Under the Medici regime, possibly even more insistently than in the previous century, poets and artists used Hercules to personify the city's strength as well as the wisdom and self-mastery of its leading citizens. We can see the association as it developed in numerous genres and artistic media, including: the pedagogical dialogue *De vita civile* (ca. 1435) by Matteo Palmieri (whom Pulci mentions in *Morgante* 24.109); a series of paintings by Antonio Pollaiuolo commissioned in the waning years of Cosimo de Medici's rule (probably in 1460); and some of Cristoforo Landino's writings, including the *Disputationes Camaldulenses* (1474) and the introduction to his *Comento sopra la comedia* (1481), in which he states that Florence "scelse tra' fiori el giglio; tra gl'animali el lione per suo segno; tra gl'huomini excellenti Hercole imagine di suo sigillo" ["among flowers [Florence] chose the lily; among animals the lion as its sign; among excellent men the image of Hercules for its seal"].[44]

Hercules mythology was so pervasive within the intellectual milieu of the city that there is little doubt that Pulci was aware of its political ramifications. Attention to the parallel between the Greek hero and Morgante thus carries implications that go well beyond a simple review of the possible sources for Pulci's poem. In the *Morgante*, Pulci arguably engages with the Hercules myth—or, more accurately, with the ways that Florence had adapted this myth to the city's political discourse—to illustrate the vulnerability inherent in this adaptation, rather than to passively accept its encomiastic aims. To corroborate this claim, we need only compare Hercules's death with Morgante's.

Two episodes of the Hercules saga shape the way Pulci depicts Morgante's demise. First, during the fight against the Hydra, one of his twelve labors, Hercules is bitten by a crab much as was Morgante. The Greek hero, however, incurs no serious harm as a result of this attack. He instead kills the crustacean, which is then elevated to the sky by Juno and becomes the constellation of Cancer (Hyginus, *Astronomicus* II, 23). Although Pulci does not cite this tale in the *Morgante*, it nevertheless seems clearly relevant to his portrayal of the giant's death. On the other hand, Pulci refers overtly to a second Hercules episode connected to Morgante's passing in the very first cantare, immediately after Orlando converts the giant:

Guarda che non facessi la vendetta,
come fece già Nesso, così morto

(non so se la sua storia hai intesa o letta):
e' ti farà scoppiar, datti conforto. (*Morgante* 1.72)

[See that he does not take his quick revenge, as Nessus did, although so dead and cold. You must have heard his story, so I hope. He'll make you—I am certain of it—burst.]

That Pulci presents the Hercules-Morgante parallel so early in the poem is indicative of the importance he sees in this association of the two heroes. However, the poet's choice of the Nessus story to establish this initial link is surprising, if not altogether ill-omened, and hence invites further inquiry. To be sure, the literal meaning of the cited lines is straightforward: Orlando here advises Morgante not to underestimate the horse that he (Morgante) has just crushed with his weight, because Morgante might end up like Hercules, slain by the posthumous revenge of the centaur Nessus. Yet what does Orlando's early warning entail in the moral and political economy of the poem if, as Carrai has persuasively suggested, the early reference to Hercules's death also portends Morgante's death?[45] How does this reference to Nessus's vengeance eventually converge with the crab's lethal bite in cantare 20?

In the well-known myth that Orlando evokes, Nessus is mortally wounded by Hercules's poisoned arrow. The centaur tells Deianira, the hero's wife, that if her husband should stop loving her and she wanted to regain his love, she should give Hercules the tunic Nessus wore at his death, a tunic imbued with the centaur's blood, as well as the poison from Hercules's arrow. When she later learns that Hercules has fallen in love with Iole, a younger woman from a recently conquered town, Deianira—unaware that the poisonous blood will be deadly to the wearer—asks one of her servants to deliver the tunic to her husband. Hercules puts on Nessus's tunic and dies slowly in excruciating pain, as the venom consumes his flesh. Pulci could have read versions of this story in a large number of classical texts, including Cicero's *Tusculan Disputations* (II, vii-ix, 19–22) and Ovid's *Metamorphoses* (9.101–261), and he was certainly familiar with Dante's encounter with Nessus in the seventh circle of Hell, where the centaurs serve as instruments of justice against tyrants and other violent sinners: "Quelli è Nesso, / che morì per la bella Deianira, / e fé di sé la vendetta elli stesso" ["That is Nessus, who died for the beautiful Dejanira and himself wrought vengeance for himself"] (*Inf.* 12.67–69).[46]

The most extensive account of Nessus's posthumous vengeance is, however, in the *Hercules on Oeta*, a tragedy with disputed attribution to Seneca.[47] This play, which painstakingly details Hercules's agony, is one of the key sources for Salutati's *De laboribus Herculis*. Among the numerous echoes of the *Hercules on Oeta*, three verses the Florentine humanist quotes in passing while discussing the hero's fight against the Hydra and the crab should capture our attention: "Ah, what scorpion inside me, what crab torn from the torrid zone and embedded in me scorches my vitals?" ["Heu qualis intus scorpios, quis fervida / plaga revulsus cancer infixus meas / urit medullas?"] (*Hercules on Oeta*, 1218–20).[48] While the descriptions of Hercules's injury and his ensuing pain are undoubtedly inspired by Sophocles's tragedy *Women of Trachis*, the references to scorpion and crab as equivalents of the hero's affliction ("pestis," ll. 1225 and 1230) are instead Pseudo-Seneca's interpolations reflecting the medical undertones of Hercules's monologue.[49] Lines 1220–32 gruesomely portray the poison's effects on his massive body through a tour de force of anatomical language: "iecur" (liver), "pulmonis" (lung), "ossa" (bones), "cutem" (skin) and "medullas" (marrow).[50]

Although Salutati does not dwell on this scene, we should notice for two reasons his comparatively brief commentary on these lines in the *De laboribus Herculis*. On the one hand, consistent with the *topos* of the sly crab outlined earlier in this chapter, Salutati labels the animal as most insidious ("insidiosissimus"). On the other hand, however, he entirely overlooks the tragic context of the Senecan passage he cites, perhaps to avoid tarnishing the hero's iconic stature. Salutati elects instead to interpret allegorically Hercules's feat against the Hydra and its crustacean ally as a struggle against sophistry and intellectual sloth, explaining that the crab represents a lack of progress, for it moves slowly and backwards ("tardus ac retrogradum").[51] In fact, adds Salutati, the crab is such a small animal, a puny beast indeed ("imbellis fera") if compared to the other monsters Hercules defeated, that he wonders why the story of its slaying is extolled among the hero's exploits: "such an unwarlike beast seems unworthy of consideration among the monsters whose death is attributed to Hercules" ["tam imbellis fera visa non sit dignum monstrum cuius expugnatio Herculi tribuatur"].[52]

It is likely that the lines from Hercules's monologue cited above influenced the way that Pulci imagined Morgante's death, whether Pulci knew them directly from Pseudo-Seneca's tragedy, through the mediation of Salutati's treatise, or from both sources. Beyond the evident lexical correspondence between the "cancer" in the play and the "granchio" in Pulci's poem, the sequence of events leading to the downfall of Hercules appears to also presage the demise of Morgante. In both cases, a treacherous agent—Nessus through his poisoned tunic in the *Hercules on Oeta*, the crab in the *Morgante*—triggers a corrosive infection (a *cancer*) that undoes a heretofore invincible protagonist.

By tying together Nessus's revenge and the crab's bite, this interpretation helps us explain how Morgante's death ultimately fulfills Orlando's warning in cantare 1. Furthermore, I would argue that Salutati's disdain for enemies like the crab—apparently harmless, therefore neglected, and yet ominously associated with betrayal—is symptomatic of what Pulci considered a dangerous flaw in Florence's adoption of the Hercules myth in its civic identity. Pulci lays bare this flaw, which consists in a form of pride, in his account of Morgante's death by engaging with these two key episodes involving the Greek hero. From this viewpoint, then, the Hercules-Morgante parallel reveals the fundamental vulnerability in the ambitious power politics pursued by Lorenzo and his predecessors: Pulci imagines a world contrary to the impervious strength previous reworkings of the Hercules narrative might have indicated, in which the ancient hero and his modern epigones, fictional and otherwise, are vulnerable to even the unlikeliest of foes.

Treason in Paris and Florence, Part 1: The Passion of Astolfo

The reading proposed thus far suggests that Pulci understood treachery as a disease that metaphorically corrodes the body politic from within. As I seek to show in the remainder of this chapter, the allusion to perfidy implicit in the crab's killing of Morgante and underlying the parallel between the giant and Hercules anticipates the tragic outcome of the Battle of Roncesvalles. While there is little doubt, as I have argued above, that treachery was always meant to be a key issue in the *Morgante*, the attempted assassination of Lorenzo de' Medici and the murder of his brother Giuliano in 1478 inevitably reinforced (but did not originate) the centrality of this theme. It is well-documented that Pulci often drew creative inspiration from his experiences, including those he garnered as a diplomat involved in the affairs of various Italian principalities. The mention in *Morgante* 28.22 of Andrea Lampognano, one of the conspirators who in 1476 killed the duke of Milan, Galeazzo Maria Sforza, is one of the most remarkable examples of this poetic praxis. The example holds particular significance because here Pulci weaves the story of a seditious plot that occurred in a powerful city—a city that was, at the time, politically close to Medici Florence—into the fabric of the *Morgante*. And he does so at a momentous point in the poem, when he is explaining why Ganelon decided to betray Orlando and Charlemagne.[53] This is why any discussion of the treasonous pact between Ganelon and Marsilio, and of the rivalries among Charlemagne's paladins leading up to it, should take into account the internecine enmity that rived Florence during the fifteenth century.

An episode from cantare 11 is a useful starting point for this discussion, since it brings to the fore at a fairly early stage in the poem some of the key intertextual, political, and theological questions concerning treachery that would resurface later in the *Morgante*: what texts inspired Pulci's thinking about betrayal and how should we interpret the influence exerted by these texts, particularly Dante's *Commedia*? How did the turmoil in Florence, especially the Pazzi conspiracy and its aftermath, affect Pulci's depiction of the Rout of Roncesvalles? I will address these questions in turn, beginning with an investigation of Pulci's possible sources.

In cantare 11, Pulci depicts Charlemagne as apparently unable to discern Ganelon's scheming against one of the paladins. This kind of doubled vision, with treachery visible to the reader but not to a key character, recurs often in the *Morgante*. In this case, acting on the belief that conflicts among the paladins can bolster his leadership, the Emperor actually foments divisions, thus playing easily into Ganelon's hands. Pulci often allows the reader to glimpse Charlemagne dissimulating what he truly thinks, as he attempts to exploit the very instability that might ultimately upend his reign.[54]

In cantare 11, the English knight Astolfo, designated victim of Ganelon's cunning and Charlemagne's naïve cynicism, is about to be hanged as a thief. His suffering prior to the execution (*manqué*) ambiguously reproduces the Passion of Christ: "I Maganzesi gli sputano nel viso / come facieno a Cristo i Farisei" ["the Maganzans, spitting in his face, did to him as the Pharisees to Christ"] (*Morgante* 11.85), and in the following stanza, "Ch'aspetti tu? Il signor di Montalbano? / E' verrà a te quando a' Giudei Messia; / ed anco Cristo chiamò in croce Elia" ["Whom do you want—the Lord of Montauban? He'll come as the Messiah to a Jew; right from the cross Christ called Elijah, too"] (11.86).[55] While the evocation of the Passion of Christ could hardly be more explicit, it may well be ironic, since Astolfo had in fact been guilty of raiding the French countryside, together with his cousin Rinaldo, to retaliate against Charlemagne's baffling willingness to heed Ganelon's counsel. In their rousing promises to wreak havoc across the large swath of land between Montauban and Paris, Rinaldo and Astolfo boast that they would even assault Saint Peter or the Angel Gabriel if they should happen to encounter them: "e se san Pier trovassimo a camino, / che sia spogliato e messo a fil di spada" ["Whoever's in our way—Saint Peter, too—we'll mug and rob and execute by sword"] (11.20); and

> Se vi passassi con sua compagnia
> sant'Orsola con l'agnol Gabrïello

che annunzïò la Virgine Maria,
che sia spogliato e toltogli il mantello! (11.21)

[And if we run into Saint Ursula, escorted by the Angel Gabriel, who announced Christ's coming to the Virgin Mary, we'll take their cloaks and rob them just as well.]

Later, after he is taken prisoner, Astolfo apologizes to Charlemagne and asks forgiveness for his crimes by implicitly comparing himself to Longinus, the centurion who pierced Christ's side with his lance. According to a widespread legend derived from the apocryphal gospels and reported in the *Legenda Aurea* by Jacobus de Voragine, Longinus subsequently converted to Christianity: "Carlo, or mi perdona, / per quel Gesù che perdonò a Lungino" ["(Charles,) forgive me in the name of Jesus, Who one day forgave Longinus from the Cross"] (11.63).[56]

The unlikely choice of Astolfo as a sacrificial lamb raises legitimate doubts about the significance of Pulci's use of biblical imagery in his poem. But more relevant to our purposes is the poet's (seemingly) impassioned tirade that Pulci inserts just before the Passion of Astolfo. The poet addresses Charlemagne directly to denounce ingratitude as a most heinous sin that, mixed with pride, caused Lucifer's fall:

O Carlo imperador, quanto se' ingrato!
Non sai tu quanto è in odio a Dio tal pecca?
Non hai tu [Carlo] letto che per tal peccato
la fonte di pietà sù in Ciel si secca?
E con superbia insieme mescolato,
caduto è d'Aquilon nella Giudecca
con tutti i suoi seguaci già Lucifero?
Tanto è questo peccato in sé pestifero.
[...]
Questo peccato par che 'l mondo adugge,
e finalmente ogni regno distrugge;
questo peccato scaccia la giustizia,
sanza la qual non può durare il mondo;
questo peccato è pien d'ogni malizia,
questo peccato a gnun è secondo;
Gerusalem per questo precipizia;

questo peccato ha messo Giuda al fondo;
questo peccato tanto grida in Cielo,
che ci perturba ogni sua grazia e zelo. (*Morgante* 11.74–76)

[Emperor Charles, how thankless you can be! Don't you know God abhors ingratitude? Have you not read this is the very sin that dries God's mercy in His heaven above? That, mixed with pride, it was this sin from the high north wind into Judecca plunged Lucifer with his many followers? Than this pestiferous sin no sin is worse [...] This very sin afflicts each continent, and ruins every kingdom in the end. This is the sin that chases justice out (and with no justice can the world endure?). This is the sin that nurtures every fraud, this is the sin that has no equal yet. Because of it Jerusalem collapsed. This sin sent Judas to the deepest hell; this sin before our Lord so loudly cries, because of it His mercy He denies.]

As the first two lines of stanza 74 make plain, Charlemagne's own ingratitude is clearly the primary target of this passage,[57] but further investigation of the intricate web of intertextual references and the possible inconsistencies in Pulci's use of these references reveals more fully the scope of his attack. Let us begin our reconstruction of this intertextual network by highlighting the phrase "fonte di pietà," which appears to echo the mid-thirteenth-century hymn *Dies Irae*: "Rex tremendae maiestatis, / Qui salvandos salvas gratis, Salva me, fons pietatis" ["King of majesty tremendous, By Thy saving grace defend us, Fount of pity, safety send us"].[58] The oldest extant exemplar of the hymn, probably written by the Franciscan friar Thomas of Celano, one of the early biographers of the order's founder, survives as part of a fourteenth-century Dominican missal used in Pisa.[59] Its text is informed by a profound meditation on the Last Judgment and on the quest for God's forgiveness, a meditation whose resonance Pulci amplifies in cantare 11 through a litany of anaphoras (the phrase "questo peccato" is repeated seven times). Moreover, as Franca Ageno pointed out in her commentary on these lines, they contain several biblical allusions as well: specifically, to Isaiah 14:12–13 on the fall of Lucifer, and to Matthew 24:37–25:2, Mark 13:2, and to Luke 21:6 on Jesus's prophecy of the destruction of Jerusalem. The apocalyptic motif and the generally religious overtones of these stanzas are fully developed in the last five cantari of the *Morgante*.

The possible allusion to the *Dies Irae* might provide a fitting explanation for Pulci's use of the phrase "fonte di pietà" and, more broadly, it adequately suits the heavily eschatological tenor of these stanzas. But a connection to the *Dies Irae* would address neither the issue of Charlemagne's ingratitude, which triggered the invective in the first place, nor the relationship between treachery and ingratitude. We can perhaps fill in this lacuna by briefly examining the *incipit* of the *Corbaccio*, the enigmatically misogynistic pamphlet presumably composed by Boccaccio in the mid-1350s: "Qualunque persona, tacendo, i benefici ricevuti nasconde senza di ciò aver cagione convenevole, secondo il mio giudizio assai manifestamente dimostra sé essere ingrato e mal cognoscente di quegli. O cosa iniqua e a Dio dispiacevole e gravissima a' discreti uomini, il cui malvagio fuoco il fonte secca della pietà!" ["Whoever without good reason hides benefits he has received by being silent, in my opinion, most clearly shows himself thankless and ungrateful for them. Oh, what wickedness, displeasing to God, distressing to men of judgment, whose evil fire dries up the fount of pity!"].[60] The last clause of this passage, rather than the hymn by Thomas of Celano, seems more likely to be the actual source of Pulci's rhetorical question in cantare 11: "Non hai tu [Carlo] letto che per tal peccato / la fonte di pietà sù in Ciel si secca?".[61] We do not know if Pulci had knowledge of the *Dies Irae*, but we do have evidence that Francesco Castellani, the patron for whom the poet worked during the late 1450s and the early 1460s, owned a manuscript of the *Corbaccio*. In fact, Castellani noted in his journal that, probably during the year 1458, Pulci had personally delivered this manuscript to Piero di Boccaccino (a relative of Castellani's), who had asked to borrow it.[62]

Leaving aside the significant philological nexus, the most salient element in the proem of the *Corbaccio* is the language of benefits, which underpins Boccaccio's critique of ingratitude and is reminiscent of Seneca's *De beneficiis*, especially I, x, 4 and IV, xviii, 1—two passages in which the Stoic philosopher deems ingratitude the worst of human vices.[63] Much like other Senecan works, including the *Epistles* and the *De clementia*, the *De beneficiis* circulated widely in the late Middle Ages.[64] The authors whom it influenced probably include Dante, who in a chapter of the *Convivio* (1.8) dedicated to "pronta liberalitate" ["complete generosity"] appears to rely extensively not only on Aquinas's commentary on Aristotle's *Ethics*, but also on Seneca's treatise (*De beneficiis* IV, iv, 1—IV, viii, 3).[65] Particularly significant in Dante's discussion of generosity is his definition of God as "universalissimo benefattore" ["the most universal benefactor"] (*Conv.* 1.8.3), for this is essential to our understanding of treachery. Starting with Guido da Pisa in the 1320s, scholars have characterized Dante's sinners in *Inferno* 34—Lucifer, Judas, Cassius, and Brutus— as traitors of benefactors, even though never in the *Commedia* does Dante actually use the word "benefattore."⁶⁶ This conceptual framework connecting treachery and ingratitude by way of the *Inferno* helps explain the otherwise incomplete link between Pulci's outburst against ingratitude in cantare 11 and his mention of Judas and Lucifer, denizens of the same Giudecca that in Dante's *Inferno* is the nethermost area of Hell and that Pulci mentions in the passage cited above.⁶⁷

The reference to Giudecca is but one of many reflecting the debt of Pulci's ethical views to the *Commedia*. It is a relationship that Pulci never seeks to conceal, as we can see from the outset of the *Morgante*.⁶⁸ Although a thorough examination of this relationship goes beyond the limits of the present study, it is nonetheless worth underscoring a few key points of connection to Dante's work that may help us understand why ingratitude and pride—the two faults that comprise Lucifer's treachery—occupy such a prominent space in the moral economy of Pulci's poem, beginning with stanzas 7 and 8 of the first cantare. In introducing the subject of his poem in cantare 1, Pulci traces the greatness of Florence back to the nobility of France:

E tu, Fiorenza, della sua grandezza
possiedi e sempre potrai possedere:
ogni costume ed ogni gentilezza,
che si potessi acquistare o avere
col senno, col tesoro e colla lancia,
dal nobil sangue è venuto di Francia.
Dodici paladini aveva in corte
Carlo, e 'l più savio e famoso era Orlando;
Gan traditor lo condusse alla morte
in Roncisvalle, un trattato ordinando,
là dove il corno e' sonò tanto forte
("dopo la dolorosa rotta quando"
nella sua *Comedìa* Dante qui dice,
e mettelo con Carlo in Ciel felice). (*Morgante* 1.7–8)

[And yet some of his greatness you still own. O Florence, and can yours forever be: every good custom, all the courtesy a man on earth could ever gain and keep through wisdom or through treasure or through lance has come out of the noble blood of France. Within his court Charles lodged twelve paladins: the wisest and most famous was Orlando, whom treacherous Ganelon brought ultimately to death, by ordering a treaty, in Roncesvalles, there where he blew the horn so loud and strong "after the dolorous defeat," as Dante says in his *Comedy*, in which he placed him up in heav'n with Charles, forever blest.]

The context of these Dantean echoes is illuminating for at least three reasons. First, in these *ottave*, Pulci juxtaposes the names of Ganelon and Orlando, invoking their respective places in the afterlife of Dante's poem. As Pulci reminds us, the *Commedia* locates Ganelon in the Antenora, the section of Hell occupied by political traitors: "Gianni de' Soldanier credo che sia / più là con Ganellone e Tebaldello, / ch'aprì Faenza quando si dormia" ["Gianni de' Soldanier I believe is over there with Ganelon and Tebaldello, who opened Faenza when it slept"] (*Inf*. 32.121–23). Orlando is instead in the heaven of Mars: "Così per Carlo Magno e per Orlando / due ne seguì lo mio attento sguardo, / com'occhio segue suo falcon volando" ["Thus for Charlemagne and Roland my attentive gaze followed two of them, as one's eye follows its falcon in its flight"] (*Par*. 18.43–45).[69] From the poem's outset, Pulci thus invites us to consider through a Dantean lens the opposition between the *Morgante*'s two chief antagonists.

Second, because they rebelled against the gods, the giants in *Inferno* 31 represent pride and hence foreshadow the appearance of the first traitorous creature, Lucifer, in canto 34.[70] The presence of the giants at this juncture of the *Commedia*, at a transition point from the *malebolge* of simple fraud to the circle of treachery, suggests that, for Dante, the path to the lowest form of human abasement goes through the disproportionate political ambition embodied by the giants. Third, and perhaps most importantly, in anticipating Orlando's death Pulci cites a line from *Inferno* 31 in which Dante compares the extremely loud sound the pilgrim hears at the hazy appearance of the giants to that of Orlando's horn during the Battle of Roncesvalles: "Dopo la dolorosa rotta, quando / Carlo Magno perdé le sante gesta, / non sonò terribilmente Orlando" ["After the dolorous rout, when Charlemagne lost the holy company, Roland did not sound his horn so terribly"] (*Inf*. 31.16–18). In its evocative quality, this citation is akin to Pulci's mention of Nessus in the other passage from cantare 1 that I have already discussed in relation to Hercules. In *Morgante* 1.72, Orlando warns Morgante not to underestimate the dead horse the giant attempts to carry on his shoulders—as noted above, Orlando's warning foreshadows Morgante's death. In 1.8, on the other hand, Pulci anticipates Orlando's death through Dante's reference to the paladin's defeat at Roncesvalles. According to the Carolingian tradition that Dante echoes in *Inferno* 31,

Orlando decided too late to blow his horn, after initially (and presumptuously) refusing to seek aid from the rest of Charlemagne's army.

Pulci harks back to the same tradition in cantare 26, immediately after Ulivieri and Orlando have sighted the advancing troops of King Marsilio. Here, Orlando's companions repeatedly urge him to blow the horn and call for reinforcements (*Morgante* 26.12–15, 26.33), but he responds to their exhortations by equating himself to Caesar and Scipio, and stating that "per viltà mai non volli sonarlo" ["I never blew the horn for cowardice"] (26.15). This act of pride reveals a rare moral flaw in Orlando's character that contributes to his death: a self-assurance that arguably mirrors Morgante's carelessness when bitten by a crab in cantare 20. It is also noteworthy that in *Inferno* 31 Dante compares the sound of Orlando's horn to Nimrod's horn (31.70–72). Nimrod was traditionally seen as an emblem of pride because he attempted to ascend to heaven by building the Tower of Babel (Genesis 11:1–9). That Pulci conjures up Florence's debt to France while, at the same time, ominously foregrounding Ganelon's betrayal of Orlando and framing it in relation to the giants of Dante's Hell might also help us gauge how to interpret the parallel between Charlemagne's court and the Medici *signoria*.

Treason in Paris and Florence, Part 2: Plots and Vengeance

According to a legend that appears in various Florentine chronicles as indicative of Florence's longstanding ties with France, the city had been destroyed by Totila, King of the Goths, during the fifth century and was then rebuilt by Charlemagne.[71] In 1461, the humanist Donato Acciaiuoli was asked to write the *De vita Caroli*, a biography of Charlemagne, as part of a diplomatic offensive to further strengthen Florence's relations with France. Acciaiuoli himself presented the *De vita Caroli* to the newly crowned King Louis XI in Paris.[72] Roughly in the same year, Lucrezia Tornabuoni, Lorenzo de Medici's mother, commissioned the *Morgante* from Luigi Pulci, partly as a literary counter-narrative to the fall of Constantinople to the Turkish Empire in 1453, an event perceived as a catastrophe across Europe, partly in continuation of the same foreign policy strategy toward France.[73] Yet, if Florence has inherited the nobility of Charlemagne's empire, as the first cantare of the *Morgante* suggests, can we infer that by the same token Florence also suffered from that empire's weaknesses? Pulci's answer to this question, I would argue, is "yes." Envies, rivalries, and conflicts certainly punctuated the life of Quattrocento Florence. Cosimo's (year-long) exile in 1433 (at the behest of the anti-

Medicean faction led by Palla Strozzi and Rinaldo degli Albizzi), the Pitti conspiracy against Piero in 1466, and by the Pazzi attempt to kill Lorenzo and Giuliano in 1478 amply demonstrate the presence of factional strife in Florence.[74] In the closing section of this chapter, I would like to consider how the so-called Pazzi conspiracy—the best known of Florence's fifteenth-century plots—might have affected Pulci's depiction of the Rout of Roncesvalles. To do so, I examine two scenes from the last cantari of the *Morgante*, Ganelon's agreement with Marsilio to ambush Orlando and his troops, and the punishment exacted on the two schemers in the aftermath of the rout, in relation to Poliziano's firsthand account of the tragic events of 1478, the *Pactianae Historia Coniurationis*.

Modern scholars have shown that the Pazzi conspiracy was masterminded by Federico da Montefeltro, Duke of Urbino and former Medici ally, with the involvement of Pope Sixtus IV and Ferdinand of Aragon, King of Naples. That Federico had once been a trusted ally of the Medici regime and was celebrated as the ideal modern ruler in Landino's *Disputationes Camaldulenes* illustrates the fluid nature of alliances among Italian potentates during the Renaissance.[75] Landino had even dedicated his dialogue to Federico, comparing him to none other than Hercules. Moreover, after Federico's victory in Volterra on behalf of Florence in 1472, the *Signoria* had honored him with the gift of a silver helmet surmounted by a figure of the Greek hero.[76] Along with outsiders who could have benefited from ousting Lorenzo, Florentines from circles intimately close to him joined in challenging his position of power. The Pazzi were well known as a long-established Florentine banking family with strong ties to the Medici. Guglielmo de' Pazzi, possibly an accomplice to the core group of plotters formed by the Archbishop of Pisa Francesco Salviati, and Jacopo and Francesco de' Pazzi, was married to Bianca de' Medici, Lorenzo's sister. The remaining co-conspirators also included intellectuals from the coterie led by Pulci's bitter rival at the Medici court, Marsilio Ficino (in the *Morgante*, the poet appears to tie his local nemesis to the disloyal King Marsilio of Spain by means of an onomastic pun).[77]

Among the Ficino associates involved in the plot, Jacopo Bracciolini in particular deserves further attention, for his personal trajectory epitomizes the kind of relationships that existed among the leading families of Florence. The son of Poggio, the famous humanist and former chancellor, Jacopo too had a fairly prolific record of cultural production comprising the translations of his father's *History of Florence* (dedicated to Federico da Montefeltro) and of Xenophon's *Cyropaedia*, as well as a commentary on Petrarch's *Triumph of Fame* (dedicated to Lorenzo de' Medici himself).[78] As part of Florence's elite, Jacopo had participated in the joust held in honor of Lorenzo in 1469, which Pulci celebrated in the *Giostra:* "Iacopo intanto giunse in sulla piazza / di messer Poggio con gran gentilezza."[79] Pulci's depiction of Jacopo blends seamlessly into the gallery of noble Florentine youths described in the 1475 *Giostra*. But just a few years later, in the *Pactianae Historia Coniurationis,* Poliziano would caustically portray the same man as a turncoat and a fickle squanderer of his family fortune: "He [Jacopo] was, on account of his family's straightened circumstances, his debts (of which he had made a great many), and his natural vanity, eager for change of government" ["Hic et ob angustiam rei familiaris aesque alienum, quod grande conflaverat, et ob ingenitam quondam sibi vanitatem, rerum novarum cupidus erat"].[80]

From a philo-Medicean viewpoint, all who participated in the conspiracy were guilty of treason. The well-being of the entire city, not just that of the Medici regime, rested on the network of friendship and patronage that the Pazzi conspirators had betrayed. It is not a coincidence then that, in his *Historia,* Poliziano stresses the benefits that the Medici, especially Lorenzo, had bestowed on Florence. Casting the Medici as benefactors helped Poliziano characterize the Pazzi and in turn their collaborators as committing not only a violent crime against the scions of a powerful family, but also (and more importantly) an assault against the public good. Thus the conspirators appear explicitly as traitors of benefactors: "they had even sought to kill Lorenzo, in whom all the well-being of the whole Florentine republic lay, that very Lorenzo in whom the hope and power of the people were placed" ["ipsum autem Laurentium, in quem unum Florentina omnis res publica recumberet, ipsum illum Laurentium, in quo spes omnes opesque populi sitae forent"].[81] That the plot took place on Easter Sunday inside the Cathedral of Santa Maria del Fiore and that, according to Poliziano, the signal to stab Lorenzo and Giuliano was the raising of the Host—the body of Christ, symbol of communion, and reminder of Judas's betrayal—only reinforces this characterization of the crime as the betrayal of a benefactor.[82] Lorenzo sent the same message with the medal he commissioned from the sculptor Bertoldo di Giovanni only a few months after the execution of the plot: centered on each side of the medal, immediately below towering profiles of Giuliano's and Lorenzo's heads, are the words "luctus publicus" ["public grief"] and "salus publica" ["public welfare"], thus highlighting that the ostensibly personal enmity between the Medici and the Pazzi had unmistakable public ramifications.[83]

Like the Pazzi conspiracy, the Rout of Roncesvalles originated from the efforts of internal and apparently external agents whom Charlemagne considered trustworthy: Ganelon and Marsilio. The latter was only nominally "external," since he had served as a tutor to young Charlemagne (*Morgante* 24.163). Moreover, in an (evidently failed) attempt to establish good political relationships between the Kingdom of Spain and the Frankish Empire, Marsilio's sister Gallerana had been given in marriage to the Christian Emperor (25.21–22). Besides Ganelon and Marsilio, the betrayal's main architects, the plot against the paladins involves two other characters, Bianciardino and Falserone, both of whom serve as advisers to Marsilio. Falserone's name unsubtly broadcasts the quality that best defines him, his deceptiveness. Because of his cunning and eloquence, Marsilio sends Falserone to Paris ostensibly to negotiate a peace agreement with Charlemagne. In his speech to the Emperor and the paladins, Falserone says:

> Tanto è ch'io vengo a dir: '*Quod scripsi,* scrissi,'
> però che 'l mio signor m'impose questo,
> per confirmar con la tua maestate
> pace che sia di buona voluntate. (24.153)
>
> [So here I am, to say, *Quod scripsi, scripsi,* just as my Lord commanded me to say, and to renew with Your Great Majesty our peaceful effort with sincerity.]

These four lines are cast in a Christological light, as the words "*Quod scripsi, scrissi*" echo Pilate's answer to the Jews who complained about the words "Rex Judaeorum" on the Cross (John 19:19–22). Additionally, the last two lines of the stanza ("per confirmar con la tua maestate / pace che sia di buona voluntate") sacrilegiously subvert the Nativity episode in which a choir of angels announce "peace to men of good will" to the shepherds in Luke 2:14 (in the *Vulgate*: "gloria in altissimis Deo et in terra pax in hominibus bonae voluntatis").[84]

Pulci hints at Falserone's deception when the Spanish emissary, in tears, embraces Orlando as a sign of forgiveness for the death of his son Ferraù, whom the Frankish count had killed in battle "lacrimando / [Falserone] si levòe in piè, tanto il dolor l'assale, / ed abbracciò più volte e strinse Orlando" ["in tears he rose and, although overcome with sudden grief, he hugged and hugged Orlando tenderly"] (*Morgante* 24.159). In the very next line, the narrator warns his readers that he does not know how to interpret this emotional outburst: "non so se queste lacrime son false" ["were his tears false? I really don't know"] (ibid.). Pulci develops this initial allusion to Falserone's deceitfulness a few stanzas later, by addressing Charlemagne directly with Jesus's words to Judas at Gethsemane (Matthew 26:50): "O Carlo, a questa volta, o Carlo, io temo, / che: 'Amice,' non sia detto 'ad quid venisti?'" ["O Carlo! Carlo! I'm afraid that someone will say this time, 'Amice, ad quid venisti?'"] (*Morgante* 24.166).

At the start of the next cantare, as Charlemagne directs Ganelon to accompany Falserone back to Spain and seal the peace treaty with Marsilio, Pulci sketches the caricature of a grotesquely vile Ganelon. Feigning affection as he pants and sweats, Ganelon repeatedly embraces Orlando and then betrays Ulivieri with the kiss of Judas:

Abbraccia Orlando poi quel fraudolente,
e, innanzi che la pace si conchiuda,
lo domandò, se gli avea a dir nïente,
che gli scrivessi; e trafelava e suda,
tante abbracciate fa viziatamente;
poi [Gano] baciòe Ulivier, come fe' Giuda. (*Morgante* 25.4)

[And so that traitor even hugged Orlando, and begged him, if he had more things to add concerning that peace treaty, that he write to him; and he was panting and perspiring, repeating all his huggings wickedly; he even kissed, like Judas, Oliver.]

Perceiving Ganelon's insincerity and anticipating the dreadful consequences of Charlemagne's decision, Ulivieri whispers to himself the words that Christ's traitor utters at Gethsemane: "Sorrise e disse fra sé il borgognone: /'O rabi, ave.' Io so che tu ne menti" (25.4–5).[85] As in the Astolfo episode in cantare 11, albeit without parodic tinge, Pulci uses these stanzas to make plain that the betrayal impending in Roncesvalles is bound to reenact Christ's death. The Judas motif therefore remains central throughout the description of the conspiracy's planning and execution, alternately attached to any one of the traitors. This Christological subtext casts the poem's villains as avatars of Judas and Lucifer—that is, as traitors of benefactors, like the sinners in the lowest section of Dante's Hell and Poliziano's plotters.

Despite the paladins' dissent, Charlemagne proceeds with his plan. Ganelon rides with Falserone to Marsilio's court, where he publicly declares that the Emperor wishes to reach a peace agreement with Marsilio. Ganelon is then led into a fabulous garden that evokes a typical *locus amoenus*, but that is also a place of secrecy and temptation like Eden (Genesis 2:8–14). Here he can freely unveil his plan, which Pulci narrates as a renewal of the original sin:

> Posti a sedere e ragguardato un poco,
> laudò la fonte Gan, ch'assai gli piacque,
> però che tutto è circondato il loco
> di pomi, e fresche e cristalline l'acque
> (ma non poterno spegnere il gran foco
> onde principio al gran peccato nacque). (*Morgante* 25.54)
>
> [They sat and looked around a bit; then Ganelon much praised that fountain which he liked so well, the whole place being utterly surrounded with fruit trees, and the water cool and clear (ah, but it could not quench the savage fire that kindled so much in his heart!).]

In this theatrical scene, Ganelon explicitly assigns Marsilio the role of Satan: "O savio, astuto tentatore / che mi costringi a scoprire le mie colpe" ["O you tempter wise and sly, who force me to reveal my faults!"] (25.61; my translation).

When he begins to describe his plan to Marsilio, Ganelon reveals an unexpected, even contradictory, psychological dimension suggesting his desire to deny the full extent of his guilt:

> Ma s'io tel conducessi in Roncisvalle?
> Io non ti chieggo, come Giuda, argento;
> ma vuolsi queste cose ben pensalle
> e misurar, non ch'una volta, cento:
> ché questo è grave peso alle mie spalle.
> Né vo' che sia chiamato tradimento,
> ch'io porto d'Ulivier nel viso il segno,
> e licito ogni cosa è per isdegno. (*Morgante* 25.65)
>
> [But what if I should bring the count to Roncesvalles? For silver coins, like Judas, I ask not, but these are things that need much pondering, and not once—countless times—have to be weighed: this is too heavy a load on this my back. Mine is no treason—it is only vengeance: Oliver's sign is still upon my cheek. Hate legalizes everything we seek.]

Ganelon seems to hesitate, expressing some scruples even as he is about to commit his sin. He wants the Spanish king to realize how heavy a burden it is to deceive Charlemagne and his paladins. He does not want his action to be characterized as treacherous, but rather as legitimate revenge for the offense given by Ulivieri, a public slapping at the presence of all of the paladins

(24.47). This line of defense was already present in the *Chanson de Roland* and reflects a sphere of medieval law based on the principle of honor, according to which any revenge was considered licit if enacted to avenge a public humiliation.[86]

Pulci takes a different religious and ethical stance, condemning Ganelon's action unequivocally. Ganelon, too, is entirely conscious of his actions' gravity; he shows no hope of receiving God's forgiveness, even as he seeks to draw a moral-economic distinction between himself and Judas. Twice he refers to his fears concerning the afterlife: once before (*Morgante* 25.48) and once after (25.67–68) he discloses his "true" intentions to Marsilio. In the latter passage, Ganelon concedes that his soul is already lost: "L'anima mia, dove ella debbe gire, / credo che sia l'alloggiamento or preso" ["I think the place where this my soul will go has been decreed already"] (25.68).[87] Despite the legalistic argument he offers in his own defense, Ganelon ironically follows Judas as a model, at least insofar as both experience the same unyielding despair. Marsilio adopts a similar defensive posture when, later in the cantare, he evokes Judith's beheading of Holofernes (Judith 13) and a passage from Cicero's *De officiis* in support of his claim that any means, including treachery, is justified either to protect one's kingdom or to pursue revenge:

> Cesare disse che, se *iusiurando*,
> cioè la fede che è data ed accetta,
> romper si debba, lecito era quando
> si fa per tener regno, o per vendetta. (25.189)

> [To one who asked him whether, iusiurando, it is illegitimate to break an oath—a solemn promise—made: Caesar replied: "Only to hold a throne or for revenge."]

It is hardly coincidental that Pulci has Marsilio quote a line from a scathing critique of Caesar, a line that anticipates his own undoing, especially since, in the following sentence, Cicero cuttingly asserts that "our tyrant [Caesar] deserved his death for having made an exception of the one thing that was the blackest crime of all" ["(Capitalis Eteocles vel potius Euripides,) qui id unum quod omnium sceleratissimum fuerit, exceperit"] (*De officiis* III, xxi, 82).[88]

The conspirators' agreement to pursue the plot is met by several numinous signs, "gran prodigi e segni" ["many a portent"] (*Morgante* 25.73–79), warning of the harrowing events to come. Some of these signs, an earthquake and the withering of the carob tree upon which Judas supposedly hanged himself, clearly evoke the aftermath of Christ's death.[89] Among the omens depicted in this cantare, one in particular, a thunderbolt that strikes a laurel tree (25.74), might be interpreted as a warning to Lorenzo, even though its actual meaning remains ambiguous. Marsilio interprets the lightning strike as a bad sign for his own rule, and the sorcerers called to decipher the omens consider it, with typical opacity, to be the harbinger of a great kingdom's demise (in light of the poem's ending, the kingdom can only be Marsilio's).[90] The diviners read the carob tree's withering as a portent of Ganelon's destiny, although, as we shall see momentarily, it is Marsilio who will eventually be hanged on it like Judas.

Dismembering the Enemy

Everything is set up for the Battle of Roncesvalles, in which Orlando will prove his prowess by slaying countless enemies. Exhausted by the long fight, however, the Frankish count prepares to die. Consistent with the characterization of Marsilio and Ganelon as traitors of benefactors, as well as the Christological omens that accompanied their pact, Orlando expires while lying as if crucified on his own sword: "questa [Durlindana] sia in luogo di quel santo legno / dove patì la giusta carne umana" ["this is in place of that most holy cross on which Your sinless human body bled"] (*Morgante* 27.152) and "ma prima il corpo compose alla spada, / le braccia in croce e 'l petto al pome fitto" ["But first he placed his sword upon his chest and gently on its pommel crossed his arms"] (27.154). The entire death scene becomes a reenactment of the Crucifixion, including references to the last words of Christ, "Eli, Eli, lamma sabachtani" (Matthew 27:46), and to the beginning of Psalm 113, "*In exitu Israel de Egypto*."[91] The latter foreshadows the immediate ascent of Orlando's soul among the blessed, with a possible nod to the spirits who chant the psalm as they reach the shores of Mount Purgatory in canto 2 of Dante's *Purgatorio* (*Purg.* 2.46–48).

Pulci thus invites his readers to believe that the resurrection of the righteous will follow—and, furthermore, that despite Orlando's death and the menacing events depicted in these cantari, Charlemagne will continue his reign and Christianity will be saved. Yet even this anticipation of future prosperity is fraught with chilling violence. Following the Emperor's order, the Christian army brutally puts to the sword men, women, and children, and sets ablaze Zaragoza, which is reduced to ashes like Sodom (*Morgante* 27.234–54). The traitors are commensurately punished: Marsilio is hanged in the same garden where he orchestrated the plot (27.267–85), while Ganelon is quartered, torn apart by four horses (28.6–15). Their ruthless punishments may evoke the grim spectacle of death in the aftermath of the Pazzi conspiracy. Lorenzo retaliated against its perpetrators with utmost severity: Archbishop Salviati and Francesco de' Pazzi were hanged side by side (like Marsilio and his adviser Bianciardino in Pulci's poem) from the Palazzo della Signoria. Some Pazzi co-conspirators had their bodies dismembered by Medici supporters in a Dionysian outburst of frenzied violence: "Most of those who followed him [Cardinal Riario] were killed by the crowd, all torn apart, their bodies mangled cruelly; in front of Lorenzo's doors someone brought, now a head fixed on a spear, now a shoulder" ["Qui cum assectari consueverant, plerique a plebe occisi. Omnia direpta, cadavera ipsa foede lacerata: iam ante Laurentii fores caput humanum lanceae praefixum, iam humeri partem attulerant"].[92] Worse yet was the case of Jacopo de' Pazzi, who could find no rest even after his execution: his body was exhumed twice and dragged through the streets of Florence by a mob of youths: "Then they [the young boys] seized the dead man by the noose with which he had been strangled, and with much abuse and ridicule they dragged him all over the streets of the city" ["Tum, quo fuerat suffocatus, laqueo apprehendunt multisque conviciis ac ludibriis per omnes urbis vicos passim raptant"].[93] His corpse was then tossed into the Arno.

If, as seems likely, these are the events haunting the last five cantari of the *Morgante*, then Pulci in those concluding cantari also seems to turn the political motifs he treats metaphorically in the poem's first part—particularly in the crab's killing of Morgante and the Morgante-Hercules parallel—into a more literal and far more grisly engagement with murderous Florentine politics. More to the point, both Morgante's demise in cantare 20 and the "triumph of death" enacted in the Battle of Roncesvalles in cantare 27 admonish the reader that even when the political body of a city or the power of its ruler is represented as gigantic, that body nonetheless has an Achilles' heel vulnerable to the bite of its smallest enemy and to the lethal poison of treachery.

In light of Florence's history, the drastic measures adopted by the Medici in the aftermath of the Pazzi conspiracy were only a palliative. Like the amputation of a cancerous limb described by Isidore of Seville as a temporary remedy in his definition of *cancer*, the Medici revenge could not cure Florence from the pervasive internal enmity that would unravel its republican institutions. Just two years after Lorenzo's death in 1492, the Medici regime was overthrown by a new coalition of domestic and foreign forces, including the followers of the fiery Dominican monk Girolamo Savonarola and a new Charlemagne, King Charles VIII of France. This was only the first in a series of regime changes that led to the rise in 1530 of a Medici Duchy installed by the newly crowned Holy Roman Emperor Charles V.[94] As I will discuss in the next chapter in connection with Ariosto's *Orlando Furioso*, Charles had just asserted his power in the fragmented Italian Peninsula over a much weakened Church headed by Pope Clement VII, who was born Giulio de' Medici and was the son of the same Giuliano assassinated in the Pazzi conspiracy.

CHAPTER 3

The Enemy as the Self
Madness and Tyranny in Ariosto's *Orlando Furioso*

IN THE FIRST CHAPTER, I examined the different forms of enmity Dante presents in *Inferno* 28 and contrasted them with the ideal peace he outlines in the *Monarchia*. As noted in the Introduction, the correspondence between micro- and macro-political entities (*polis*, self, world) that inspired Stoic cosmopolitanism and informed Dante's analysis of enmity has also partly shaped the structure of this book. Chapter 2, then, treated hostility within the circle of the *polis* by considering the issue of treachery in Luigi Pulci's *Morgante*. In chapter 3, I move forward chronologically from the *Morgante* to Ludovico Ariosto's *Orlando Furioso*, using this work to explore further the relationship of political communities large and small. Here, this means stepping back with Ariosto from the wider circle of the *polis* to the most narrowly defined of corresponding political entities, as the poet depicts the dire consequences of discord within the individual.

As we shall see below, Plato suggested that harmony within the self—or, more specifically, within an individual's soul—exists when the faculties making up the soul exercise their proper functions, and reason correctly presides over the appetites. When these proper conditions are not in place, the soul is unbalanced and mired in conflict or *stasis*, the Greek word for civil war (*Republic* 444b). Christian theologians including Prudentius, Augustine, and Aquinas generally adopted a viewpoint similar to Plato's.[1] Variations of this motif—namely the idea of *psychomachia*, or battle within the soul—can also be found in various medieval and Renaissance works, including Dante's *Vita*

Nova[2] and Pico della Mirandola's *Oration on the Dignity of Man*. Indeed, in the *Oration*, Pico claims that internal discord can drive individuals to folly (the word he uses to characterize these individuals is *"furenti"*), and he describes the soul as a battleground where grievous wars are fought.[3] No literary figure of the Italian Renaissance embodies this internal struggle more powerfully than Ariosto's Orlando. The strife within the self, a strife that in the *Furioso* culminates in Orlando's metaphorical transformation into a mad beast that exercises unrestrained violence, can be considered the core of my investigation into enmity through the prism of Italian Renaissance epic.

Many scholars have analyzed Ariosto's portrayal of Orlando's madness in the *Furioso*. They have explored the roots of his frenzy, its medical connotations, and its relationship with other great Renaissance portraits of folly, and identified numerous classical and vernacular sources that Ariosto might have considered when he created the central episode of his romance epic.[4] As a consequence, the portrait of Orlando as a melancholic and somewhat caricatured Petrarchan lover, humiliated by his beloved Angelica's passion for the poor Muslim infantryman Medoro, has rightly become canonical. Yet, with few notable exceptions, scholars have paid less attention to the political significance of Orlando's furor. The comparative neglect of political meaning is surprising given that Ariosto fashioned his poem as the foundational myth for the city of Ferrara, explicitly representing the character of Ruggiero as a new Aeneas and an updated avatar of Orlando's heroism. In his excellent *Ariosto's Bitter Harmony*, Albert Ascoli proposes that the parallel between Orlando and Hercules (as portrayed in Seneca's *Hercules Furens*) might veil a polemic against the Este family, Ariosto's patrons, and even against the humanistic conception of education and human dignity.[5] Moreover, Giuseppe Mazzotta has offered a thought-provoking reading of Orlando's madness as a reflection on Stoic (particularly Senecan) views of the passions and as a critique of Niccolò Machiavelli's theories of power.[6] In a later contribution on politics and history in the *Orlando Furioso*, Ascoli also puts forward a theoretical framework that cogently integrates a text-based (intertextual and intratextual) approach to the *Furioso* with a keen attention to the historical crisis during which the poem was written and evolved between its first edition in 1516 and its last in 1532.[7]

In this chapter, I adopt a similar bifocal perspective to foreground the historico-political implications of the *Furioso* by weaving together the following intertextual threads. I will first examine Orlando's loss of his *senno* (wits) in relation to Plato's discussion of the tripartite soul, especially with reference to the city-soul analogy in the *Republic*. Second, I will probe the correlation between the symptoms of Orlando's malady, which has persuasively been described as an extreme form of melancholy akin to lycanthropy, and the depiction of the tyrant as a wolf in several texts Ariosto likely knew, including Plato's *Republic* and Cristoforo Landino's commentary on Dante's *Commedia*. I will then discuss the parallel between Orlando and Hercules, not only in relation to Seneca's tragedy *Hercules Furens*, which the title of Ariosto's own poem plainly references as a key source, but also in relation to Virgil's *Aeneid*. Lastly, I will explore Ruggiero's role as Orlando's alter ego and as forebear of the Este family by juxtaposing Aeneas's slaying of Turnus in the final lines of the *Aeneid* against Ruggiero's killing of Rodomonte at the end of the *Furioso*. I hope to demonstrate via this comparative analysis that Ariosto presents Orlando's madness—a psychological imbalance we will see caused by the lower appetites overcoming reason—as an allusion to tyranny and thus as representing the deepest threat of (and to) political power.[8] I have used the word allusion rather than allegory, for I do not intend to suggest that my political reading is *the* key to interpreting Orlando's furor.[9] I view this political dimension as instead complementary to numerous other explanatory factors offered in the earlier interpretations I will engage in this chapter. Further, I hope to draw attention to Ariosto's reflection on unrestrained power in the *Furioso* as a means to highlight what I consider to be his critique of the foundational myths of Rome and the empire of Charles V, the ruler to whom Ariosto offered a copy of his poem in 1532.

Orlando and Nebuchadnezzar

There is, of course, an obvious possible challenge to the premise of my reading, i.e., to interpreting Orlando's madness as a psychological disorder akin to a tyrant's (or Plato's tyrannical man's) boundless lust for power: why would Ariosto use Orlando, merely a knight and a count, and not Charlemagne, the Holy Roman Emperor, as the image of the tyrant?[10] My answer to this question has two dimensions, one more broadly historical and one specific to Ariosto's own treatment of the subject. First, it is well known that the ranks of tyrants who plagued the Italian Peninsula during the Middle Ages and the Renaissance included petty lords such as counts and dukes, as well as kings and emperors. For instance, Dante's remarks on the rulers of the Romagna region in *Inferno* 27 reveal his own understanding that a ruler need not lord over a large territory to be tyrannical: "Romagna tua non è, e non fu mai, / sanza guerra ne' cuor de' suoi tiranni" ["your Romagna is not, and never was, without war in the hearts of its tyrants"] (27.37–38). Similarly, in a passage from canto 17 of the *Furioso* to which I shall return below, Ariosto mentions such disparate figures as Sulla (a Roman general and dictator), Nero (an emperor), and the notorious thirteenth-century warlord Ezzelino III da Romano (by family lineage a count, and by conquest lord over much of the Veneto) in his list of "tiranni atrocissimi" ["most atrocious tyrants"] and "monstri" ["monsters"] (*Orlando Furioso* 17.1) whom God sent to punish humankind for its sins.

Second, and perhaps more importantly, Ariosto himself compares Orlando to a famous ruler: the biblical king Nebuchadnezzar, who, throughout the medieval and early modern periods, was widely considered an archetype of the tyrant.[11] In canto 34 of the *Furioso*, during one of the poem's most entertaining episodes, Saint John explains to the English knight Astolfo why God had decided to punish Orlando by temporarily depriving him of his reason (34.62–67). In that explanation, John draws a parallel between the Frankish count and Nebuchadnezzar, the king of Babylon, whom God punished by afflicting with madness for seven years (Daniel 4:12–34). The word used in the *Vulgate* to define Nebuchadnezzar's outbursts of violent anger during the seven years he lived like a beast is "furor" (Daniel 2:12 and 3:19). Moreover, as Saint John states in the *Furioso*, the biblical account ascribes Nebuchadnezzar's punishment to his disregard of the Lord's authority over the enormous power that he had acquired as an earthly sovereign. Analogously, although less severely, God punished Orlando when, blinded by his love of a pagan woman, he turned away from the right path and failed to use his God-given superhuman strength to defend "sua santa fede" ["His holy Faith"] (*Orlando Furioso* 34.63)[12]:

> E Dio per questo fa ch'egli va folle,
> e mostra nudo il ventre, il petto e il fianco;
> e l'intelletto sì gli offusca e tolle,
> che non può altrui conoscere, e sé manco.
> A questa guisa si legge che volle
> Nabuccodonosor Dio punir anco,
> che sette anni il mandò di furore pieno,
> sì che, qual bue, pasceva l'erba e il fieno. (34.65)[13]

[Therefore God has sent him mad, to go about with bared chest and belly, and has so clouded his reason that he cannot recognize anyone, still less himself. We read that in this fashion God also punished Nebuchadnezzar, driving him to folly for seven years, when he cropped grass and hay like an ox.]

As the comparison with Nebuchadnezzar indicates, Ariosto believed that the central risk for those who exercise political power lies in the temptation to expand their power so that it might become absolute. We shall see below that this temptation results from a psychological condition that transcends an individual's rank or social status. I begin my analysis of Orlando's madness by briefly pointing out the emergence of his most unsettling traits in the two major fifteenth-century Italian poems of the Carolingian tradition, Pulci's *Morgante* (discussed in the previous chapter) and Matteo Maria Boiardo's *Orlando Innamorato* (1483–95).[14]

Orlando's Madness

In both the *Morgante* and the *Innamorato* Orlando shows a sinister inclination toward rage. He begins to act erratically in the first canto of Pulci's poem: angered by Ganelon's attempts to undermine his position in Charlemagne's court, he leaves Paris, "e dipartissi di Parigi solo, / e scoppia e 'mpazza di sdegno e duolo" ["Bursting with rage and maddened with disdain, alone, embittered, he left Paris then"] (*Morgante* 1.16); he tries to kill his wife Ada, "come colui che la furia consiglia, / e' gli parea a Gan dar veramente" ["Heeding his own unbounded anger still, Gano alone he seemed to find and fight"] (1.18); and, driven by his fury, he decides to travel to Muslim lands, "poi si partì, portato dal furore, / e terminò di passare in Pagania" ["Then, driven by a new fury, home he left, determined not to cross all Pagandom"] (1.19).

Likewise, in the first book of the *Orlando Innamorato*, Boiardo shows Orlando gnashing his teeth during the siege of Albraca, and threatening the perfidious king Truffaldino to overrun the citadel with fury: "stringeva i denti e dicea:– Traditore! [...] pigliarò la rocca a gran furore" ["He gritted his teeth. He shouted, 'Traitor!' ... I will swiftly seize this citadel (with great furor)]" *OI* 1.15.46).[15] The signs of Orlando's madness are further manifest later in the poem, when the Frankish count prepares to resume the fight against his cousin Ranaldo:

> E su ritorna nella rocca ancora
> Guardando se il giorno esce a l'oriente,
> e non può comportar nulla dimora,
> ma rodendo si va l'ongie col dente. (1.25.61)

> Di qua di là va sempre fulminando,
> e batte e denti quella anima fiera;

trasse con ira Durindana il brando,
come davanti a lui fosse la ciera
del re Agolante e del figliol Troiano,
sì furïoso mena ad ambe mano. (1.26.2)

[He went back to the citadel, looked east to see if light appeared, unable to endure delay, and gnawed his fingernails"; and "That fierce soul, like a thunderbolt, went back and forth, and ground his teeth. He drew Durlindana in rage as if, before him, were the face of Agolante and his son Troiano; on all sides he swung.]

Here, Boiardo significantly labels Orlando's soul as "fiera" (a Latinism from the word *fera*, wild beast) and his fighting impetus against Agolante and Agramante as "furïoso." By depicting Orlando anxiously biting his fingernails, Boiardo might also be alluding to a rather perplexing passage of the *Nicomachean Ethics* on brutish and morbid behaviors, in which Aristotle refers to "gnawing the nails"—along with the likes of cannibalism, pederasty, and the plucking of hairs—as a habit resulting from madness (*Nicomachean Ethics* 1148b 25–30). The gnashing of teeth, moreover, was typically considered a sign of frenzy in ancient philosophy and in classical literature. For instance, in book 8 of the *Aeneid*, a text to which I shall return later in this chapter, Virgil portrays Hercules furiously searching for Cacus: "there was the Tirynthian in a frenzy of wrath; scanning every approach, he turned his face this way and that, gnashing his teeth" ["ecce furens animis aderat Tirynthius omnemque / accessum lustrans huc ora ferebat et illuc, / dentibus infrendens"] (*Aeneid* 8.228–30).

Indications of psychological disorder similarly abound in Ariosto's poem. At the outset of the *Furioso*, Ariosto announces that he will narrate the account of "l'ire e i giovenil furori / d'Agramante" ["the anger, the fiery rage of young Agramant their king"] (*OF* 1.1) against Charlemagne's empire and the story of Orlando's madness: "per amor venne in furore e matto, / d'uom che sì saggio era stimato prima" ["driven raving mad by love—and he a man who had been always esteemed for his great prudence"] (1.2). In the following stanzas, the focus decisively shifts to the context of chivalric adventures originating from the emergence of Angelica as a collective focus of desire.[16] The appearance of Orlando's insanity seems to reflect the centrifugal movement of the narrative away from Paris. His mind becomes increasingly unhinged as the poem strays from what should be its geographical center.

In canto 8, Ariosto displays the first symptoms of Orlando's madness. Unable to fall asleep, Orlando imagines Angelica as a lost lamb, chased by wolves and no longer under his loyal protection: "riman tra' boschi la smarrita agnella, / che dal pastor sperando esser udita, / si va lagnando in questa parte e in quella" ["the ewe lamb lost in the wood as the daylight wanes—hither and yon she wanders, bleating, and hopes the shepherd will hear her"] (*OF* 8.76) and, in the following stanza, "o pur t'hanno trovata i lupi rei / senza la guardia del tuo fido Orlando?" ["Or have the wicked wolves found you unprotected by your faithful Orlando?"] (8.77). Given Orlando's own rapacious desire for Angelica—a desire that, as we shall see, will eventually turn him into a wolf-man—it is highly ironic that in these lines he fancies himself a shepherd and a trusty sheepdog. After he finally falls asleep, an ominous dream obliquely prefigures the loss of Angelica and the consequent unraveling of his mind (8.80–83). When he awakens in tears, he dons black armor; this color, as Ariosto notes, represents Orlando's grief and his increasingly melancholic mood, "portar volse un ornamento nero; / e forse acciò ch'al suo dolor simigli" ["[he] chose a black (emblem)—perhaps it was consonant with his sense of mourning"] (8.85).[17] Insomnia and nightmares are typical manifestations of melancholy, a mental disorder that classical and early modern physiology attributed to an excess of black bile (*melancholia*) to the brain. According to the theory of the four humors, the brain's combustion of black bile results in furor.[18] This theory also implies that Orlando's reversal from wisdom to madness should not be surprising: philosophical wisdom and melancholy were understood to be closely linked. In the *Problems*, for example, Pseudo-Aristotle ponders why melancholy so often affected philosophers like Plato and Socrates, as well as heroes like Ajax, who went mad after Ulysses was granted Achilles's weapons, and most significantly Hercules, who killed his wife and children (*Problems* 953a 10–29).[19]

Orlando's dream motivates him to pursue Angelica. He decides to leave Paris even though the city is under siege (*OF* 8.84–86) and embarks on the path to insanity that will eventually culminate at the mathematical center of the *Furioso*. The events narrated in the last stanzas of canto 23 mark Orlando's descent into bestiality. After a duel-turned-brawl against the Saracen warrior Mandricardo—and here Ariosto compares Orlando to Hercules fighting the giant Antaeus (23.83–85)—the Frankish count inadvertently rides to a most delightful (and, for him, insidious) *locus amoenus* (23.101). Here he notices Angelica's calligraphy carved onto the bark of numerous trees, reading her declaration of love for Medoro, a young foot soldier in the Muslim army who had been wounded in a previous episode of the poem (19.13–22). While obsessively reading the story of Medoro and Angelica's passion (23.102–10), Orlando is temporarily turned into a stone: "Rimase al fin con gli occhi e con la mente / fissi nel sasso, al sasso indifferente" ["Finally he fell to gazing fixedly at the stone— stone-like himself"] (23.111). In alluding to the myth of Medusa here in his near-literalized astonishment of Orlando, Ariosto anticipates the loss of identity that his madness will cause. On the verge of losing his "sentimento," and like Seneca's Hercules after slaughtering his family in the *Hercules Furens*,[20] Orlando's head droops on his chest, with his gaze now turned downward: "caduto gli era sopra il petto il mento, / la fronte priva di baldanza e bassa" ["His chin had dropped onto his chest, his head was bowed, his brow had lost its boldness"] (23.112). The shift in visual focus is yet another indication that Orlando is about to shed his human nature, as according to a vast philosophical tradition, humans alone (unlike any other animal) could direct their gaze upward.[21]

The narrative twists that finally lead to Orlando's breakdown represent, in a microcosm, the *Furioso*'s interlacing plots. Orlando arrives at the shepherd's house where Angelica had healed Medoro's wound and the two young lovers had consummated their marriage (*OF* 19.23–36). As a token of gratitude for the hospitality they received, Angelica had given the shepherd a golden bracelet, an earlier gift from Orlando (19.37–40). When he sees the bracelet, the Christian hero's descent into madness reaches its nadir:

> All'ultimo l'istoria si ridusse
> che 'l pastor fé portar la gemma inante,
> ch'alla sua dipartenza, per mercede
> del buon albergo, Angelica gli diede.
> Questa conclusion fu la scure
> che'l capo a un colpo gli levò dal collo. (23.120–21)

> [The herdsman ended his story by having the bracelet brought in—the one Angelica had given him on her departure as a token of thanks for his hospitality. This evidence shown in conclusion proved to be the axe which took his head off his shoulders at one stroke.]

The signs of what Orlando perceives as Angelica's infidelity, from the poems that she and Medoro wrote for each other to her dismissal of the bracelet, cause him to lose his mind. Ariosto's description of the hero's metaphorical beheading effectively captures the fracture within Orlando's soul. Deprived of his reason—properly located in the head—the Frankish count is now driven exclusively by his appetites.

Ariosto's choice to figuratively decapitate Orlando resonates deeply with the Platonic psychology that shaped the thinking of many writers of the

Renaissance and that Ariosto very likely knew from Marsilio Ficino's translations of and commentaries on Plato's works.[22] Through various images in the *Timaeus*, in the *Phaedrus*, and in the *Republic*, Plato explains that the human soul is composed of different parts. A crucial primary distinction exists between a rational component, which uniquely characterizes humans, and an irrational component that is further subdivided into the irascible and the appetitive. Whereas the rational soul is located in the head ("the most divine part of us and the lord of all that is in us," *Timaeus* 44d), the irascible and appetitive parts are located in the heart and in the liver, respectively (*Timaeus* 69d-71c). Plato articulates a similar view in the *Phaedrus* through a myth that would become enormously popular through the ancient and early modern periods: he describes the soul as the "union of powers in a team of winged steeds and their winged charioteer" (*Phaedrus* 246a-b). In humans, the charioteer (reason) controls two horses: one white and noble, the other dark and with the opposite character. The former coincides with the irascible soul and is a "lover of glory, but with temperance and modesty," and responds positively to the charioteer's command; the latter is "hot-blooded, consorting with wantonness and vainglory" and defies any control (*Phaedrus* 253 d-e).[23] In book IX of the *Republic*, Plato further depicts the soul as a chimerical form made of three elements: a) appetitive, fashioned like a multi-headed beast; b) irascible, in the shape of a lion; and c) rational, shaped like the figure of a human being. Through the words of Socrates, Plato states: "Then mold about them outside the likeness of one, that of the man, so that anyone who is unable to look within but who can see only the external sheath it appears to be only one creature, the man" (*Republic* 588e).[24]

Viewed from the Platonic perspective just outlined, Orlando's metaphorical beheading concretizes the loss of his *senno* (the highest faculty of the soul) and his consequent transformation into a beast. As Ariosto tersely notes, Orlando is now alienated, divided within himself: "Io son lo spirto suo da lui diviso" ["I am his spirit sundered from him"] (*OF* 23.128).[25] The only passions left in his soul are "odio, rabbia, ira, e furore" ["hate, fury, wrath, and violence"] (23.129). After leaving the shepherd's abode, Orlando begins to wander in a nearby wood and, after three days without eating or speaking,[26] tears off his body armor and garments (23.132–33). He then drops his weapons (emblems of his knighthood) and forsakes his human identity, naked in his bestial folly.[27] In Ariosto's solemn words:

> e cominciò la gran follia, sì orrenda,
> che la più non sarà mai ch'intenda.

> In tanta rabbia, in tanto furor venne,
> che rimase offuscato in ogni senso. (23.133–34)
>
> [Now began the great madness, so horrifying that none will ever know a worse instance. He fell into a frenzy so violent that his every sense was darkened.]

The accumulation of terms like folly, wrath, and fury suggests the complete collapse of Orlando's intellect. Thus, armed only with his strength beyond measure ("vigore immenso"), the count begins his dishonorable exploits: "Quivi fé ben de le sue prove eccelse" ["He now performed some truly astonishing feats"] (23.134).

In a narrative reversal of his interior monologue from canto 8, the first victims of Orlando's uncontrolled violence are two herdsmen and their sheep (OF 24.4–6). The shepherd with his sheepdog who earlier dreamed himself as Angelica's protector has now morphed into a wolf-man. Orlando roams through the fields and slays horses, oxen, and scores of peasants who try to stop him from decimating their cattle: "Fece morire diece persone e diece, / che senza ordine alcun gli andaro in mano" ["Out of that disorderly throng ten he killed who came within his reach, and then another ten"] (24.10).[28] He eventually enters a village abandoned by its inhabitants, who had fled in terror from Orlando's blind rage: "Dentro non vi trovò piccolo né grande; / che 'l borgo ognun per tema avea lasciato" ["Here he found not a soul, man or child, for everyone had abandoned the place in terror"] (24.12). Ariosto here stages not only the undoing of a political animal (fashioned after the model of the Greek hero Bellerophon in Homer's *Iliad* 6.155–220 and Aristotle's *Politics* 1253a 2–5), but also the potential for unlimited power, when no longer curbed by reason, to dissolve the community around itself. Ravenous after several days of fasting, Orlando indiscriminately devours foods of all sorts, regardless of whether they are cooked or raw (24.12).[29] He then leaves the forsaken village and begins wandering through France, hunting humans and beasts alike, as befits his brutish state: "E quindi errando per tutto il paese, / dava la caccia e agli uomini e alle fere" ["After this he roamed about the countryside, preying upon men and wild beasts"] (24.13). The trail of destruction he leaves behind him amounts to a wasteland, the carcass of a *polis* consumed by a tyrant.

Focusing on the symptoms and causes of Orlando's madness as they would have been viewed through premodern physiology and Platonic psychology, we understand Ariosto's portrait of Orlando as a bestial, wolf-like, creature operating from powerful passions unchecked by reason. But by further probing the political element embedded in Plato's theory of the soul—including Plato's embedding of wolfish symbolism in his illustration of the tyrant's *psyche*—we can now recognize that the physio-psychological symptoms of Orlando's breakdown are situated within a larger reflection on political power.

The Tyrant's Lycanthropy

During his exposition on justice in book II of the *Republic* (368e–69a), Plato introduces an analogy between the city and the individual soul that he develops throughout the dialogue.[30] Particularly in book IV, he states that identical features "are to be found in the state and in the soul of each one of us" (441c) and that justice resides in the appropriate division of tasks among the three faculties of the soul and the three classes (philosopher kings, soldiers, and the people) of the *polis*. In both microcosm and macrocosm, the rational part shall preside over the others (441d–e). The city-soul analogy is so crucial to the *Republic*'s structure and concepts that in book VIII, Plato lists the parallels between each form of government and its corresponding individual soul. The correspondence Plato here elaborates between tyranny and the soul of a tyrannical person is most consequential for my discussion of Orlando's insanity and its political import. In books VIII and IX, Plato suggests that a man's drive to power, nourished by unlimited desire, leads to tyranny (565d–580d). He first notes that the tyrant's *psyche* is dominated by the lowest appetites (571a–573b), and then goes on to assert that this "madman, the deranged man, attempts and expects to rule over not only men but gods," and that "a man becomes tyrannical in the full sense of the word when either by nature or by habits or by both he has become even as the drunken, the erotic, the melancholic" (573c).[31] The last two attributes that he cites here—the erotic and the melancholic—coincide with the form of mad love that afflicts Orlando and renders his traditionally superhuman strength entirely unrestrained during the three months of his bestial fury. Moreover, Plato defines the tyrant, dominated and driven to madness by erotic passion, as the unhappiest of men. His life is controlled by the paranoid fear that anyone might potentially be his enemy (578a–b and 580a). This failure to distinguish friend from foe is again a symptom of Orlando's madness, as we see in canto 39 of the *Furioso*, when he attacks his fellow paladins, who have approached him seeking to restore his wits (*OF* 39.44–57).

The *topos* of the desire-driven tyrant, ruling only to satisfy his own pleasure with no regard for the public good or the laws of the commonwealth, lasted through antiquity and the Middle Ages and well into the Renaissance.

Aristotle discussed tyranny at length in *Politics* 1310a 39–1315b 10 and defined the tyrant as he who "has no regard to any public interest" and whose "aim is pleasure" (1311a 2–3).[32] According to Seneca, whose *De Clementia* exerted a profound influence in medieval and Renaissance political thought, the tyrant is a ruler who takes pleasure in cruelty.[33] Fifteenth-century humanists including Coluccio Salutati and Leon Battista Alberti described the tyrant as a leader who disregards the law and as a ferocious beast.[34] Yet it is Cristoforo Landino's commentary on Dante's *Commedia* (1482) that might best illustrate the relevance of Plato's political psychology to Ariosto's *Furioso*. In *Inferno* 12, a canto to which Ariosto refers in his poem (*OF* 13.36), Dante and Virgil encounter the centaurs, who serve as instruments of divine justice against sinners who have committed violence against others. This group of sinners includes the Macedonian emperor Alexander the Great and the above-mentioned Ezzelino da Romano, whom Dante presents as tyrants: "E' son tiranni / che dier nel sangue e ne l'aer di piglio" ["These are tyrants who took to blood and plunder"] (*Inferno* 12.104–5). In his commentary to *Inferno* 12.55–57, Landino allegorizes the centaurs as "effrenati et crudeli desiderii" ["unchecked and cruel desires"], since they are "figliuoli d'Ixione, cioè del tyranno" ["Ixion's children — that is, a tyrant's children"]. In mythological accounts of the centaurs' birth, their father, Ixion, is described as the first man who sought to become a tyrant. As Landino notes in the same section of his commentary, Ixion tried to rape Juno, Jove's wife and goddess of kingdoms. Jove mockingly turned Juno into a cloud, and the centaurs were generated from the ethereal union between Ixion and the cloud. The Florentine humanist then explains that Ixion's thwarted assault on Juno was doomed to fail, for "nessuno è che possa congiungersi con Giunone come desidera, cioè acquistare tanta signoria quanta si propone nell'animo, el quale nella vita tyrannica è insatiabile" ["no one can possess Juno to the full extent of his desire — that is, no one can aquire as much power as he wishes — for that desire is insatiable in the life of a tyrant"] (Commentary to *Commedia*, *Inferno* 12.55–57).

Landino continues his commentary with an etymological excursus on the definitions of kings among the Greeks, among the Romans, and lastly among the Christians. He uses the word "shepherds" ("pastores") to identify Christian rulers, underscoring the religious inspiration and selflessness of such ideal sovereigns: "Chiamongli e christiani 'pastores,' perchè chome e buoni pastori non cerchono e proprii commodi, ma quegli della gregge a lloro commessa, chosì e buoni principi cerchono la salute di quegli che sono commessi al lor governo; et ricordonsi delle parole della verità che'l buon pastore mette la vita per le sue pecore. Questo è adunque l'officio et el debito di chi governa et regge. Et chi fa el contrario di questo non è re nè governatore, ma tyranno. Non è pastore ma lupo."[35] The Christological precept of self-sacrifice and the image of the good shepherd ("le parole della verità che 'l buon pastore mette la vita per le sue pecore") provide the theological groundwork for Landino's definition of power's legitimate boundaries.[36] Landino's allegorization likely also adapts the profile of the tyrant's soul identified in the *Republic*, most strikingly in the use of a zoomorphic parallel with the wolf in book VIII: "is it not the inevitable consequence and a decree of fate that such a one [a bloody and murderous ruler] be either slain by his enemies or become a tyrant and be transformed from a man into a wolf?" (*Republic* 565d–566a).[37]

Traditionally presented as an archetype of ferociousness and voracity (not least of all in the first canto of Dante's *Commedia*),[38] the wolf seems a well-suited analogue for Plato's mad tyrant. This analogy of wolf and tyrant is by no means limited to the *Republic*. We can find examples of it that Ariosto would surely have known in both the classical and biblical traditions. In the text immediately preceding the above-cited passage from the *Republic*, Plato evokes the example of Lycaon (*Republic* 565d–e), the tyrant who tried to serve Jove human flesh and who was then turned into a wolf as a punishment. Lycaon's transformation, the first of Ovid's *Metamorphoses* to involve a human (*Met.* 1.163–243), literalizes the tyrant's cruelty and appetite for power. Given that the first victims of Orlando's madness in canto 24 of the *Furioso* are shepherds and their flocks, it is particularly relevant for the *Furioso* that when Lycaon is transformed into a wolf his first victims are a flock of sheep: "His mouth of itself gathers foam; and with his accustomed greed for blood he turns against the sheep" ["ab ipso / colligit os rabiem solitaeque cupidine caedis / vertitur in pecudes"] (*Met.* 1.233–35).[39] Equally significant, at the beginning of canto 17, is Ariosto's description of the tyrants whom God sends to earth to punish sinful humanity as ravenous wolves: "spesso dà regno / a tiranni atrocissimi" ["(God) Has monstrous and destructive tyrants crowned"] (*OF* 17.1); and "lupi arrabbiati" ["mad wolves"] (17.3–4).[40]

The notion of wolf-like unjust rulers as instruments of God's vengeance against a corrupt community might derive from Ezekiel 22:27: "Her princes in the midst of her, are like wolves ravening the prey to shed blood, and to destroy souls, and to run after gains through covetousness."[41] Ariosto adds a further wolf-tyrant comparison to the last edition of the *Furioso* in the episode of the tyrant Marganorre:

Marganor il felon (così si chiama
il signore, il tiran di quel castello),

> del qual Nerone, o s'altri è ch'abbia fama
> di crudeltà, non fu più iniquo e fello,
> il sangue uman, ma 'l feminil più brama,
> che 'l lupo non lo brama de l'agnello. (*OF* 37.43)

[Marganor is the name of the tyrant of this place. Neither Nero nor any other who had a reputation for savagery was more evil or sinister; he thirsts after human blood, especially female, more than the wolf after the lamb's.]

Massimo Ciavolella and Marina Beer have convincingly argued that Orlando suffers from a form of melancholy akin to lycanthropy.[42] And from the long-standing association of lycanthropy and erotic melancholy with tyrants that I have sketched above, we can plausibly extend these scholars' strictly psychological reading to submit that Orlando's madness also functions as an allusion to tyranny.

Before asking how Orlando's frenzy influences our understanding of the *Furioso*'s historical entanglements, I should like to make two additional points on the question of tyranny within the economy of Ariosto's poem. First, it is only in the third edition of the *Furioso* that the tipping point of Orlando's insanity occupies the poem's structural center; this shift presumably indicates greater attention to this theme on Ariosto's part. It is also noteworthy and, I would suggest, not unrelated to the new centrality of madness that at least two of the major additions included in the 1532 edition—the Cimosco and Marganorre episodes in cantos 9–10 and 37, respectively—hinge on the issue of tyranny and occupy almost exactly symmetrical positions.[43] The first of these two episodes is especially suggestive and raises a number of questions. We should note to begin with that Cimosco uses an arquebus, the ancestor of the modern rifle, which toward the conclusion of this episode Orlando famously throws into the sea (*OF* 9.90–91). Why, in this added episode, does Ariosto appear to condemn the use of firearms, given that his patrons were among the most advanced producers of those weapons in Europe?[44] Moreover, Cimosco is from Frisia, a northern region of the Netherlands (9.25). Is it significant (and, if so, how) that Cimosco rules over the same region in which the future Emperor Charles V of Habsburg began to consolidate his reign?

We can answer these questions by better addressing Ariosto's engagement with history in the *Furioso*. My discussion has so far concentrated on the political psychology that lies at the heart of the poem's reflection on power: that psychology presents an unvarnished, and often disturbing, insight into apparently universal human desires, ambitions, and vulnerabilities. What makes the universal insight even more compelling here is Ariosto's fashioning of his romance epic by incorporating Trojan and Roman etiological narratives into the foundational myth of Ferrara. In the second half of this chapter I will therefore consider a twofold interplay that I hope will further our understanding of Orlando's madness and its political significance in an early sixteenth-century context. By examining the parallel between Orlando and Hercules on the one hand, and between Ruggiero and Aeneas on the other, we can gain considerable insight into Ariosto's view of his Este patrons, and his concern regarding the growing power of Charles V's Holy Roman (and global) Empire.

Hercules Renewed

As the previous chapter discussed in detail, the myth of Hercules figured prominently in the civic identity of Florence and in the writings of Florentine humanists. Two points are worth further emphasis here: first, that in the writings of many authors, Hercules epitomized reason, the highest faculty of the soul;[45] second, that Hercules was as symbolically dominant in Ferrara as he was in Florence. The *Furioso* itself is dedicated to Ippolito d'Este, whom Ariosto describes as "Erculea prole" ["Seed of Ercole"] (*OF* 1.3) and "figliuol d'Ercole invitto" ["invincible son of Ercole"] (40.1), for Ippolito was a son of Duke Ercole I (1431–1505), who ruled the city for more than three decades and whose name unequivocally attests to Hercules's emblematic value.[46] When he inherited the dukedom at his half-brother's death in 1471, Ercole undertook to fundamentally reshape the profile of Ferrara. In accordance with the association of Hercules and reason, this majestic urban project, the so-called *Addizione erculea*, aimed to reflect a renewed spirit of rationality. With its straight avenues and right corners, this addition was conceived in contrast to the winding intricacy of Ferrara's medieval section.[47]

Since as early as the sixteenth century, commentators of the *Furioso* have argued that Ariosto clearly intended for Orlando to evoke Hercules. In 1554, Giovan Battista Pigna noted in his *I Romanzi* that Ariosto's title echoes that of Seneca's tragedy[48] the *Hercules Furens*, a play in which the Greek hero slays his wife and children. In various passages of the *Furioso*, Orlando displays—as does, to a lesser extent, Ruggiero—characteristics usually attributed to Jove's son.[49] Since numerous studies have addressed the Orlando-Hercules analogy, I will only draw attention here to two key references in the Cimosco episode mentioned above. When Olimpia, Countess of Holland and victim of Cimosco's intrigues, begs Orlando to free her beloved Bireno, she does so with reference to his "erculeo aspetto" ["Herculean aspect"] (*OF* 9.56). Later in the same episode, though, when describing the fight between Cimosco and Orlando, Ariosto compares the latter to Antaeus, Hercules's giant opponent who regained strength whenever he touched the earth:

> Quale il libico Anteo sempre più fiero
> surger solea da la percossa arena,
> tal surger parve, e che la forza, quando
> toccò il terren, si radoppiasse a Orlando. (9.77)

> [Like the Libyan Anteus who, after hitting the ground, used always to arise with renewed ferocity, so did Orlando appear on getting up, as though when he touched the earth his strength was redoubled.]

These apparently contradictory similes (Orlando is at once Hercules and the giant he defeats) point to the ambivalence inherent in classical depictions of Hercules and, by the same token, to the ambivalence in any parallel involving the Greek hero. At any rate, Orlando does free Bireno and eventually kills Cimosco (9.80), thus performing a typical Herculean exploit as tyrant-slayer.[50]

As suggested above, however, Ariosto knew well that, in the classical tradition, Hercules was also associated with madness.[51] Euripides's *Heracles* and, more notably, Seneca's *Hercules Furens* are the most recognizable materials Ariosto could have utilized in the *Furioso*.[52] These tragedies are of particular interest because they crucially join a political element with the psychological dimension vividly expressed by the hero's frenzy. Both Euripides and Seneca expose the limits of Hercules's power by dramatizing his madness as an internal strife wherein he is his own enemy. Indeed, at the outset of the *Hercules Furens*, Juno proclaims that, since none of the monstrous antagonists she has forced Hercules to fight has prevailed over him, his defeat can best be achieved by having the hero fight against himself: "Do you need a match for Alcides? There is none but himself. Now with himself let him war" ["quaeris Alcidae parem? / nemo est nisi ipse / bella iam secum gerat"] (*H. F.* 85).[53] In view of the terminological history of *hostis* and *inimicus* outlined in the Introduction, it is noteworthy that Seneca's Juno foreshadows the war Hercules will wage on himself with the phrase "bella [...] gerat," the same formula Cicero uses in the *De officiis* ("bellum geras," I, xii, 37) to illustrate the function of the word *hostis*.

In the first part of the *Hercules Furens*, we also learn that Lycus, usurper of Thebes's throne and the embodiment of tyranny as Seneca articulates it in the *De Clementia*, took advantage of Hercules's absence (on a mission to

Hades for Juno) to kill the father and two brothers of the hero's wife Megara.[54] Lycus (whose name means "wolf" in Greek) then offers to marry Megara to consolidate his power, but she refuses his offer. Lycus's course of action possibly prefigures the first part of the Cimosco episode in the *Furioso*, in which Cimosco usurps Olimpia's dominion by murdering her father and two brothers (*OF* 9.28–31). The main difference between the two narratives is that Olimpia's father initially arranges for her to marry Cimosco's son Arbante, an arrangement she rejects with disastrous consequences (9.25–27).[55] On returning from Hades, however, Hercules slays Lycus and re-establishes the rightful political order. The Chorus cheers Hercules's victory, celebrating the wolf-slaying hero as a peacemaker: "Peace reigns by the hands of Hercules" ["pax est Herculea manu"] (*H. F.* 882). In the following lines, which immediately precede the eruption of his frenzy, Hercules proudly states that "no greater, richer victim can be sacrificed to Jove than an unrighteous king" ["victima haud ulla amplior / potest magisque opima mactari Iovi, / quam rex iniquus"] (922–24) and vows,

> non saevi ac truces
> regnent tyranni, si quod etiamnum est scelus
> latura tellus, properet, et si quod parat
> monstrum, meum sit. (936–39)

[savage and cruel tyrants rule no longer. If earth is still to produce any wickedness, let her make haste, and if she is preparing any monster, let it be mine.]

Hercules's ominous pledge will be fulfilled paradoxically and in a way that destabilizes the stark contrast between good and evil on which his words rely; he will not have to search afar to find his new enemy.

Falling victim to his own madness, Hercules then mistakes his children for the children of his enemy: "But look! here lurk the children of the king, my enemy, the abominable spawn of Lycus; to your detested father this hand forthwith shall send you" ["sed ecce proles regis inimici latet, / Lyci nefandum semem. Inviso patri / haec dextra iam vos reddet"] (*H. F.* 987–89). When he awakens from his blind fury, still unaware of the atrocious misdeed he has just perpetrated, Hercules sees the dead bodies of his kin and wonders against whom he should retaliate: "my foeman is he who points not out the foe. Vanquisher of Alcides, hidest thou?" ["hostis est quisquis mihi / non monstrat hostem. Victor Alcidae, lates?"] (1167–68), and, later on, "To whom have I fallen prey?" ["cui praeda iacui?"] (1186). Hercules's murderous act and subsequent reaction trigger a sequence of mirror images that infinitely reflect the figure of the tyrant and that of his slayer as one and the same.⁵⁶ Indeed, by killing his own family, Hercules finally executes the plan that Lycus had devised before the hero's arrival at Thebes (350–51, 506–8, 629–30).

Although in the *Furioso* neither Orlando nor Ruggiero commits crimes as heinous as Hercules's slaughter of his own family, the underlying association of the *Furioso*'s heroes with Jove's son jeopardizes the encomiastic quality of the poem. Ariosto's allusive adaptation of material from Seneca's political satire *Apocolocyntosis* (a mock-apotheosis of the Emperor Claudius, probably written in 54 CE at Nero's accession to the throne) further complicates the connections the *Furioso* draws between its characters and Hercules, who has turned against himself. As David Quint has demonstrated, Seneca's praise of Nero in the *Apocolocyntosis* is a key source of Ariosto's encomium of Ippolito d'Este in canto 35 of the *Furioso* (OF 35.3).⁵⁷ Upon Claudius's death, moreover, Seneca returned to Rome, where he served as tutor, speechwriter, and advisor to the young Nero, who had just become emperor and who would eventually force his former teacher to commit suicide. Nero himself, as Ariosto probably learned from Suetonius's highly popular *Lives of the Caesars*, enjoyed playing the role of the mad Hercules in the theater.⁵⁸ Had Ariosto not opted for a title so candidly reminiscent of Seneca's tragedy, one might overlook the ominous ambiguity rooted in the phrase "Erculea prole," with which the poet dedicates the *Furioso* to Ippolito d'Este:

> Piacciavi, generosa Erculea prole,
> ornamento e splendor del secol nostro,
> Ippolito, aggradir questo che vuole
> e darvi sol può l'umil servo vostro. (1.3)

> [Seed of Ercole, adornment and splendour of our age, Hippolytus, great of heart, may it please you to accept this which your lowly servant would, and alone is able to, give you.]

Yet in light of the overt reference to the *Hercules Furens* and the foregrounding of Orlando's fury in the preceding stanza, introducing a patron as one of the Greek hero's children can hardly be considered unambiguous flattery. That Seneca wrote a tragedy of destructive power like the *Hercules Furens* and a treatise of political pedagogy like the *De Clementia* (which he envisioned as a mirror that would help reveal Nero to himself)⁵⁹ during the years in which he was the young emperor's mentor makes Ariosto's decision to coopt the title of the Roman tragedy all the more ironic.

While Seneca's tragedy provides the most obvious reference point for the *Furioso*, I would also suggest that, in his depiction of Orlando, Ariosto evokes the Virgilian Hercules. More broadly, the constant presence of *furor* in the *Aeneid* hovers over Ariosto's engagement with madness in his own poem.[60] The strife within Aeneas's soul — the challenge to overcome both his own *furor* and the temptation to make a new home before he has reached his intended destination — complements his mission to establish the new city. In the *Furioso*, Ruggiero, whom Ariosto envisions as a descendant of Hector (OF 36.70), the ill-fated prince of Troy, takes on the role that Aeneas plays in the *Aeneid*. Within this framework, the relationship between Orlando and Ruggiero mirrors that between Hercules and Aeneas: Ariosto thus follows a relationship that is unequivocally established in book 8 of the *Aeneid*, where Aeneas's status as proto-founder of Rome is projected onto the imposing shadow of the Greek hero. Virgil's portrait of Hercules in the heat of battle against the half-human monster Cacus (*Aeneid* 8.203–61) reveals the same ambivalence embodied by Jove's son in the *Hercules Furens*.[61]

When Aeneas arrives in Arcadia, aiming to forge an alliance with its king Evander, he is welcomed into the Arcadians' rites in homage to Hercules, a former visitor and benefactor. The noble host invites Aeneas to sit on a throne covered by a cushion made of a lion's skin (*Aeneid* 8.176–78), which evokes Hercules's garment and his Nemean labor. Evander explains that the rocky site where this ceremony takes place was formerly a cave of immeasurable depth, where Cacus dwelled, spreading terror in the surrounding land and feasting on its inhabitants (8.193–98). Like the cannibal Cyclops, Cacus, whose name in Greek means "bad" or "evil" (*kakos*),[62] is Vulcan's child and represents the chthonic forces of primordial lawlessness that persistently threaten the development of societal life. After describing Hercules's arrival, Evander narrates the furious fight between the bestial Cacus and the great hero, slayer of monsters and tyrants, who is destined to ascend among the Olympian gods. Virgil's depictions of these two antithetical figures blend into each other, as both display the inexorable power of *furor*:

> For to us, too, in our need, the mightiest of avengers, glorying in the slaughter and spoils of triple Geryon, Hercules came, and this way drove his huge bulls in triumph, and his oxen filled vale and riverside. But Cacus, his wits wild with frenzy (*furiis*), that no crime or craft might prove to be left undared or untried, drove from the stalls four

bulls of surpassing form, and as many heifers of peerless beauty [...]
One heifer returned the cry, lowed from the high cave's depths,
and from her prison baffled the hopes of Cacus. At this the wrath
of Alcides furiously (*furiis*) blazed forth with black gall. (8.203–8,
8.217–20).[63]

The equivalent passions expressed by the repeated word "furiis" incite the actions of the two foes; much as we saw in the *Hercules Furens*, the hero and the villain become mirror images of each other. For Virgil's Hercules in particular, a wrathful grief (*dolor*) ignites his black bile or gall (*atro felle*). I have noted earlier in this chapter that in ancient and early modern medical theories, the inflammation of this humor causes madness in melancholic individuals.[64] This diagnosis of melancholy conventionally applies to Hercules, but also to Ariosto's Orlando (*OF* 8.72, 8.85, and 23.126–27). Enraged by the theft of his cattle, Hercules seeks revenge against Cacus, who finds refuge in his cave and blocks its entrance with a massive rock, thus making his pursuer even more furious ["furens animis"] (*Aeneid* 8.228). As he looks for an opening into the den, the hero gnashes his teeth (8.228–32).[65] Hercules then manages to rip a boulder off the mountain and, dashing through the flames coming out of Cacus's mouth, finally kills the monster (8.251–61).

After completing his commemoration of Hercules, Evander leads Aeneas into his home and invites him not to disdain the humble abode where Hercules was previously a guest. The king's words manifestly join the two heroes:

> Haec limina victor
> Alcides subiit, haec illum regia cepit.
> aude, hospes, contemnere opes et tequoque dignum
> finge deo rebusque veni non asper egenis. (*Aeneid* 8.362–65)

> [These portals victorious Alcides stooped to enter; this mansion had room for him. Have the courage, my guest, to scorn riches; make yourself, too, worthy of deity, and come not disdainful of our poverty.]

As he crosses the threshold into Evander's house, Aeneas is quite literally framed as a new Hercules. His noble but humble host advises Venus's son that he should dare to scorn ("aude, hospes, contemnere") wealth and embrace humility to achieve a divine stature like that of his magnanimous predecessor. More precisely, Evander exhorts Aeneas to make, fashion, forge, or even feign ("finge") himself worthy like a god, like Hercules. The verb *fingere*, laden with ambiguity, might convey any of these meanings.

The figure of Hercules was of course paramount in Rome's mythology. As Livy narrated in his *Ab urbe condita* (I, 15), rites in honor of the Greek hero were the only vestiges of foreign cults that Romulus retained in the newly founded city. In Livy's history, Romulus, too, was directly compared to Hercules as a man destined to join the gods after his death. Virgil further extended the mythological genealogy to Augustus whom, like Hercules and Romulus, he hailed as a peacemaker bound to ascend among the Olympians (such comparisons grew increasingly common after the rise of the Empire). Significantly, Virgil's *ekphrasis* of Aeneas's shield, which concisely represents this genealogy, occupies the last part of book 8, visualizing the Roman trajectory toward the establishment of the Empire heralded by Hercules's victory over Cacus.[66] A necessary step toward the fulfillment of this prophecy is the Trojans' victory over the Latins led by the Rutulian warrior Turnus: this is a victory that is achieved only in the last lines of the poem in ways that undoubtedly, albeit ambiguously, foreshadow the conclusion of the *Furioso*.

Ruggiero and Aeneas

In the final battle of the *Aeneid*, the proverbially pious portrait of Aeneas shows the same passions that previously sullied all of the characters who tried to oppose his fateful journey and his effort to found the new city. The actions of Juno, Dido, and Turnus have all exposed the power of madness.[67] In book 1, a wrathful Juno asks Aeolus to raise a storm and shipwreck Aeneas's ships (*Aeneid* 1.34–80) and in book 7, she summons the Fury Allecto to sow discord among the Latins and the Trojans (7.308–30), while in book 12, Jove urges her to abandon her mad anger (12.830–40). In book 4, after learning that Aeneas is about to depart from Carthage, Dido describes herself as possessed by frenzy (4.376) and kills herself with her lover's sword (4.660–65). Through the second half of Virgil's epic, Turnus, perhaps more than any other character, personifies the *furor* that Juno unleashed against Aeneas. In book 12, however, we see Turnus stand silently, torn by mixed emotions, not far from the battlefield and only a few hundred lines from his death: "within that single heart surges mighty shame, and madness mingled with grief, and love stung by fury, and the consciousness of worth" ["Turnus et obtutu tacito stetit; aestuat ingens / uno in corde pudor mixtoque insania luctu / et furiis agitatus amor et conscia virtus"] (12.666–68). Virgil induces the reader to commiserate with Turnus for the grievous fate that his demise is about to fulfill. The ruthless fighter who earlier in the poem wreaked havoc among the Trojans and who, in a reenactment of the grisly scene in Cacus's cave, went to battle displaying his slain enemies' heads (9.465–67 and 12.511–12) is turned into a defenseless youth waiting to face a formidable opponent supported by the gods (12.676–80).

In the poem's final lines, after an unheroic pursuit and Turnus's plea for mercy (*Aeneid* 12.930–38), Virgil depicts Aeneas as being overcome by furor as he slays the embodiment of the very madness he has battled since his departure from Troy: "Aeneas, as soon as his eyes drank in the trophy, that memorial of cruel grief, ablaze with fury and terrible in his wrath: 'Clad in the spoils of one of mine, are you to be snatched from my hands? Pallas it is, Pallas who sacrifices you with this stroke, and takes retribution from your guilty blood!' So saying, in burning rage he buries his sword full in Turnus's breast. His limbs grew slack and chill and with a moan his life fled resentfully to the Shades below" (12.945–52).[68] The fight between the two men thus literalizes the strife within Aeneas himself, and culminates as Aeneas violates his father's warning to spare the vanquished.[69] The picture of Turnus's body collapsing under Aeneas's blow mirrors the first snapshot of the Trojan hero at the beginning of the poem: when the storm demanded by Juno begins to rise, "Aeneas's limbs weaken with chilling dread" ["Aeneae solvuntur frigore membra"] (1.92). Again, as in Virgil's description of Cacus's death at the hand of Hercules, furor and wrath blur the boundaries between Aeneas and Turnus. Hence, by killing his enemy Aeneas also kills a part of himself. As several scholars have noted, moreover, Aeneas's slaying of Turnus prefigures Romulus's foundational fratricide and Rome's future civil wars.[70] The hotly debated question of whether Aeneas's rage and his desire to avenge Pallas are justified arises from the fundamental tension that Virgil highlights when describing the killing of Cacus and Turnus: can those who, like Hercules and Aeneas, exercise violence to fight the forces of chaos and furor remain untarnished by the forces they combat?[71] Even when we assume that their opponents do in fact embody the forces of chaos and furor—and therefore that there is a more or less overt ethical distinction between Hercules or Aeneas, on the one hand, and their antagonists, on the other—the uncanny specularity between heroes and villains in Virgil's and Seneca's works points to the ambiguity intrinsic to the exercise of political power. The same ambiguity is also exemplified in the *Aeneid* by the double meaning of the verb *condere*, which means both "to found," for instance when Virgil presents Aeneas's goal to found a new city at the beginning of the poem ("conderet urbem," 1.5), and "to bury," when Virgil describes Aeneas plunging his sword into Turnus's breast ("ferrum adverso sub pectore condit," 12.950).

The tragic quality of the *Aeneid*'s closure did not elude its medieval and Renaissance readers. Dante himself captured the greatness and, from his viewpoint, the limits of Virgil's poem with implacable conciseness, calling it an "alta tragedìa" ["lofty tragedy"] (*Inferno* 20.113). In the fifteenth century, questions about Aeneas's susceptibility to furor raised concerns for humanists such as Francesco Filelfo and Maffeo Vegio. In the *Aeneidos liber XIII*, Vegio resumes Virgil's narrative from the last line of the *Aeneid*. In Vegio's version, Turnus's sacrifice engenders peace, and Aeneas seals this peace by allowing the Rutulians to bury their former lord. As King Latinus beholds Turnus's body, he pithily encapsulates the relationship between furor and lust for power as follows: "How precarious is the scepter's transient power! O wildness [*furor*], o native lust for overweening power, whither in your blindness do you drag us mortals?" ["O fragilis ruitura superbia sceptri! / O furor, o nimium dominandi innata cupido, / mortales quo caeca vehis?"] (*Aeneidos liber XIII*, lines 145–47).[72] By describing Aeneas's wedding with Lavinia and the hero's deification, Vegio's sequel to the *Aeneid* tacitly reveals a sense of discomfort with the ending of Virgil's poem and the need to impart a more wholesome moral character to its Trojan hero. Ariosto's own rewriting of the *Aeneid*'s ending suggests that we should count him beside Vegio and Filelfo as a troubled reader of Virgil's original.[73]

After the long episode involving Ruggiero and the Greek Emperor's son Leone, which Ariosto added to the 1532 edition of the *Furioso*, Ruggiero and Bradamante are finally allowed to marry. Their wedding seals the foundation of the House of Este, whose future successes the newlyweds have seen prefigured in the tapestry that the Trojan prophetess Cassandra originally wove for her brother Hector (*OF* 46.80–99). The nuptials between Ruggiero and Bradamante thus enact a new beginning while harking back to an ancient Trojan-Roman mythology and supplementing a part of the story that Virgil omitted from his epic, Aeneas's wedding with Lavinia. On the last day of the festivities, an armed knight, completely clad in black like Orlando in canto 8, arrives in Paris to disrupt the celebrations: "venne / contra le mense un cavalliero armato, / tutto coperto egli e 'l destrier di nero" ["a knight in armour appeared (...), riding full tilt towards the banqueters. Like his steed, the knight was all in black"] (46.101). We soon learn that he is Rodomonte, the irredeemable archenemy of the Christian camp who set Paris ablaze earlier in the *Furioso*. During his account of the battle in Paris, Ariosto labels Rodomonte as a "demonio" ["devil"] (16.86), a "Satanasso" ["Satan"] (16.87), and a "can che gli uomini divora" ["man-eating dog"] (17.15). Departing from Virgil's ambivalent presentation of Turnus in the *Aeneid*, Ariosto never provides his readers with any reasons to sympathize with Rodomonte, even in the *Furioso*'s final stanzas.[74]

In the poem's last canto, Rodomonte challenges Ruggiero to a duel on a charge of treachery (OF 46.106–7). The ensuing battle offers an evident contrast between Ruggiero's skills and Rodomonte's mounting furor: "a maggior rabbia, a più furor si mosse" ["the pagan (...) was goaded to a greater fury"] (46.121). The Saracen eventually succeeds in turning their chivalric duel into a brawl. As they wrestle on the ground, Rodomonte bleeds copiously from the many wounds Ruggiero has inflicted upon him. The Christian hero at this point offers to spare his enemy's life: "e che si renda, minacciando, tenta, / e di lasciarlo vivo gli fa patto" ["he tried with menaces to make him surrender, offering to spare his life in exchange"] (46.137). This apparently small detail pointedly sets Ruggiero apart from Aeneas: as noted above, the Virgilian hero disregards Turnus's plea for mercy. Ariosto thus suggests that Ruggiero is a more reliable interpreter than Aeneas of Anchises's warning to spare the vanquished. Even so, when Rodomonte refuses to yield and instead seeks to stab his opponent, the grim closure of the *Aeneid* is ultimately reenacted:

> E due e tre volte ne l'orribil fronte,
> alzando, più ch'alzar si possa, il braccio,
> il ferro del pugnale a Rodomonte
> tutto nascose, e si levò d'impaccio.
> Alle squallide ripe d'Acheronte,
> sciolta dal corpo più freddo che giaccio,
> bestemmiando fuggì l'alma sdegnosa,
> che fu sì altiera al mondo e sì orgogliosa. (46.140)

[So two or three times he raised his arm to its full height and plunged the dagger to the hilt in Rodomont's forehead, thus assuring his own safety. Released from its body, now ice-cold, the angry spirit which, among the living, had been so proud and insolent, fled cursing down to the dismal shores of Acheron.]

The parallel between Aeneas and Ruggiero is all too obvious, and the violence of this scene undeniably evokes the bloody conclusion of the *Aeneid*. Yet, beyond Rodomonte's refusal of Ruggiero's mercy, we can detect meaningful, if subtle, shifts that reveal Ariosto's effort to create distance between his text and its Virgilian model, and therefore between Ruggiero and Aeneas. For instance, even though Rodomonte still poses a threat (unlike the suppliant Turnus), Ruggiero plunges his knife into his adversary's forehead without showing any sign of the furor that seizes Aeneas in Virgil's poem. Ariosto also qualifies Rodomonte's "fronte" with "orribil," while Virgil simply registers that Aeneas stabs Turnus in the chest ("pectore"). It perhaps bears repeating here that in platonic psychology, the chest, which Aeneas strikes "furiis accensus et ira terribilis" ["in burning rage"] (*Aeneid* 12.946–47), is the site of wrath and the head is the site of reason. Lastly, the verb "bestemmiare" connotes Rodomonte more negatively than does the adjective "indignata" in reference to Turnus in the last line of the *Aeneid*.

The contrast that Ariosto draws in this passage should not be surprising. It is consistent with his critique of Aeneas in canto 35: "Non sì pietoso Enea, né forte Achille / fu, come è fama, né sí fiero Ettorre" ["Aeneas was not as devoted, nor Achilles as strong, nor Hector as ferocious as their reputations suggest"] (*OF* 35.25). I shall return to this canto momentarily, for Ariosto's polemic there expands well beyond the meaning of these two lines. Let us first, however, briefly trace the dynastic lineage that the *Furioso* allegedly extols by outlining the parallel foundational narratives of Ferrara and Rome with the following scheme:

Rome:	Hercules	Aeneas	Augustus
Ferrara:	Orlando	Ruggiero	Ippolito/Alfonso d'Este

In the *Orlando Furioso*, Ruggiero is to Aeneas what Ippolito (who died in 1520) and Alfonso d'Este are to Augustus. In light of the historical context and the power jockeying that characterized Europe between the invasion of the Italian Peninsula by the French King Charles VIII in 1494 and the Sack of Rome by the Imperial troops of Charles V in 1527, the comparison between Augustan Rome and Este Ferrara is quite puzzling. Indeed, I would suggest that, even taking into account the rhetoric of praise typical of the epic genre, such a parallel should be taken as ironic. Ariosto surely recognized the political and military imbalance between the small Italian city-states and growing nation-states like France and England, and the Empire of Charles V. The poet's lamentation of the Italian wars in canto 33, another section added to the 1532 edition of the *Furioso*, bears clear witness to his awareness of this woeful reality. A closer look at cantos 35 and 15 can also help us to evaluate Ariosto's engagement with questions of politics and history, including the parallel between madness and tyrannical power that underlies this chapter.

Ariosto and the Empire of Charles V

After escorting Astolfo to the moon in search of Orlando's wits, Saint John explains to the paladin that poets can grant fame to princes and emperors even when they do not deserve it (*OF* 35.20–30). As noted above, the names of Aeneas and Hector figure prominently in the Evangelist's list of undeserving heroes and rulers. In this section of the poem, another name stands out in addition to those of the two Trojans, specifically that of Augustus: "Non fu sì tanto santo né benigno Augusto / come la tuba di Virgilio suona" ["Augustus was not as august and beneficent as Virgil makes him out in clarion tones"] (35.26). The parallel sketched above between Ferrara and Rome would suggest that Ariosto aims the biting irony of this passage at Ippolito and Alfonso d'Este. I would argue, however, that if Ariosto's patrons and other Italian rulers such as the Medici Pope Leo X appear to bear the brunt of his attack, and in fact they probably do in the 1516 and 1521 editions of the poem,[75] then it would seem fitting for an author as cognizant of contemporary historical reality as Ariosto was to choose a more ambitious target, one whose power could actually match or even exceed that of a Caesar. A passage from canto 15 that, once again, was added in the last edition of the *Furioso* gives us a hint of who could be the object of Ariosto's critique.

After celebrating the new Argonauts who journeyed beyond Hercules's pillars, crossed the Atlantic in pursuit of India, and discovered a previously unknown continent (*OF* 15.21–22), Ariosto goes to great lengths to praise Emperor Charles V, with whom the Este had forged an alliance in the late 1520s:

> Veggio la Santa Croce: e veggio i segni
> imperial: nel verde lito eretti:
> veggio altri a guardia de i battuti legni
> altri all'acquisto del paese: eletti,
> veggio da dieci cacciar mille: e i regni
> di là da l'India ad Aragon suggetti:
> *e veggio i Capitan di Carlo quinto*
> *dovunque vanno haver per tutto vinto.*
> Dio vuol ch'ascosa antiquamente questa
> strada sia stata: e anchor gran tempo stia,
> ne che prima si sappia che la sesta
> e la settima età passata sia,
> *e serba a farla al tempo manifesta*

che vorra porre il mondo a Monarchia,
sotto il più saggio Imperatore e giusto
che sia stato o sara mai: dopo Augusto.
Del sangue d'Austria e d'Aragon io veggio
nascer su'l Reno alla sinistra riva
un Principe: al valor del qual Pareggio
nessun valor: di cui si parli o scriva.
Astrea veggio per lui riposta in seggio
anzi di morta ritornata viva:
e le virtù che cacciò il mondo: quando
lei cacciò anchora, uscir per lui di bando.
Per questi merti la bontà suprema
non solamente di quel grande impero
ha disegnato c'habbia Diadema
c'hebbe Augusto Traian Marco e Severo
ma d'ogni terra e quinci e quindi estrema
che mai né al sol né all'anno apre il sentiero
e vuol che sotto a questo imperatore
solo un'ovile sia, solo un pastore. (15.23–26, emphasis mine)

[I see the Holy Cross and the imperial standards set up on the verdant shore; some guard the storm-tossed ships, others are taking possession of the territory; they are picked men—I see ten of them routing a thousand, and kingdoms beyond the Indies being subjected to Aragon; and I see Charles V's captains sweeping all before them. / God willed that this route should in the past have remained concealed, and should so continue for still many a year: not before the sixth and seventh ages have elapsed shall it become known, for He has reserved its discovery until the day when He places the world under the monarchy of the wisest and most just emperor who ever lived or shall live, after Augustus.

I see the birth of a prince on the left bank of the Rhine; in his veins flows the blood of Austria and Aragon, and no valour ever mentioned in speech or writing can compare with his. I see Astrea restored from death to life; and the virtues, too, which the world banished when it banished her, shall return from exile by his power. / Because of such merits the Supreme Good has awarded him the crown of the great empire once ruled over by Augustus, Trajan, Marcus Aurelius, and Septimus Severus; not only this, but also that he should rule over every land East and West. However far flung, that sees the sun and the passage of the year. He wills that under this emperor there should be but one fold, one shepherd.]

This long quotation condenses the ideological drive underpinning the resurgent idea of world empire at the time of Charles V's reign, particularly after the consolidation of the Spanish settlements in the West Indies. Ariosto notes that the new Habsburg sovereign, who had received the title of Holy Roman Emperor, extended his rule on both sides of the Atlantic and beyond. Although outnumbered by indigenous populations, his captains, including Hernán Cortés (whose name is mentioned in stanza 27), managed to conquer large swaths of the newly discovered continent. In the eyes of his contemporaries, these missions legitimately qualified Charles V to be considered an epigone of Augustus destined to establish a Christian world monarchy ("vorrà porre il mondo a monarchia, / sotto il più saggio imperatore e giusto / che sia stato o sarà mai dopo Augusto"). This is the only time in which Ariosto mentions Augustus as a proper name in the sections added to the 1532 edition.[76] Charles, as the new Augustus, will also restore to life Astrea, symbol of justice in Virgil's fourth *Eclogue* ("Astrea veggio per lui riposta in seggio, / anzi di morta ritornata viva").[77] The above-cited passage ends with a reference ("vuol che sotto a questo imperatore / solo un ovile sia, solo un pastore") to a verse from the Gospel of John—indeed the same John who in canto 35 describes himself as one of the many writers who lie to serve their powerful patrons (*OF* 35.28–29)—in which Jesus prophesies the unification of humankind under one faith: "And other sheep I have, that are not of this fold: them also I must bring, and they shall hear my voice, and there shall be one fold and one shepherd" (John 10:16).

The myth of a transnational, cosmopolitan (and Catholic) government that could revive Rome's vestiges and ensure peace remained a significant *topos* in Renaissance political discourse from the fifteenth century until well into the seventeenth century, as pope Pius II's *De ortu et auctoritate imperii romani*, Ficino's translation of Dante's *Monarchia* into the vernacular, and Tommaso Campanella's appeals to world unity make plain.[78] In the years during which Ariosto was revising the *Furioso*, a few statesmen at the court of Charles V were crafting the narrative of this imperial ideology around that very *topos*. Most active among these figures was the Piedmontese jurist Mercurino di Gattinara, one of Charles's most trusted and influential advisors, who loyally served the young sovereign as Grand Chancellor from 1518 until his death in 1530, four months after Charles was crowned Emperor.[79] One of Gattinara's most noteworthy steps in advancing his agenda was his invitation to Desiderius Erasmus to prepare the critical edition of Dante's *Monarchia*.[80] The Dutch humanist, who in 1516 edited Seneca's works and authored a tract on political education (*The Education of a Christian Prince*) dedicated to the young Prince Charles, declined the offer from his friend and fellow alumnus of the University of Turin. Despite Erasmus's refusal, Gattinara's efforts reveal a keen interest in forging a cultural framework to support Charles V's imperial policies in Europe and in the West Indies. The royal emblem chosen to epitomize such a vision features a motto, *"Plus Ultra"* ("further beyond"), and an image representing Hercules's pillars, the sign that marked the limit of the known world in antiquity.[81] The overt comparison with Hercules aimed to represent the Emperor's power as greater than that of the Greek hero. Moreover, at the time of Charles's election in 1519, Chancellor Gattinara issued a memorandum celebrating Charles's rising universal empire in which he quoted the verse from the Gospel of John that Ariosto echoes in canto 15 of the *Furioso*.[82]

It is unclear whether Ariosto genuinely believed that Charles was the shepherd under whose rule humankind could be unified as one, or if instead he saw Charles as the wolf that in the same parable comes to scatter the sheep (John 10:12). Since Ariosto's Saint John challenges Virgil's praise of Augustus in canto 35 of the *Furioso*, it seems plausible in turn to interpret as ironic Ariosto's own praise of Charles. This view is, I would argue, corroborated by the snapshot of the Sack of Rome that Ariosto provides in *OF* 33.55–56 and by his invective against firearms that follows Orlando's killing of Cimosco in *OF* 9.90–91. In a possible allusion to Charles V, the tyrant Cimosco is a ruler of Frisia who relies on the deadly new weapons. It is true that Ariosto notes that Charles, a native of the city of Ghent in what is now Belgium, was born on the left bank of the Rhine ["su'l Reno alla sinistra riva"] (*OF* 15.25), while Frisia occupies the right side of that river. Yet it was Charles who established the Lordship of Frisia in 1524 after purchasing its territory from Duke Georg of Saxony and after quelling a violent rebellion with the help of the landsknechts, the same German mercenaries who eventually marauded through the Italian Peninsula and sacked Rome in 1527 (in the process making ample use of the arquebus, Cimosco's weapon of choice).[83] Ariosto was therefore more likely to see Charles as an agent of violence and chaos than as a peacemaking "pastore." Assuming that my reading is correct, one might ask why Ariosto was so cautious in his criticism. I would echo here Albert Ascoli's observation, in discussing Ariosto's veiled slight against Ippolito d'Este, that the price for offending a patron was extremely high: poverty or death.[84]

In February 1530, less than three years after the Sack of Rome, Pope

Clement VII crowned Charles as Emperor in Bologna. Ariosto, shortly after completing the third edition of his masterpiece in 1532, accompanied Alfonso d'Este to meet Charles in Mantua and presented a copy of the *Orlando Furioso* to the Emperor. Implicit in this gift was the poet's rebuke of those who wield political power imprudently. It is unlikely, of course, that Charles ever read the *Furioso*, but if he had, he would have probably realized that Ariosto—in the footsteps of Seneca and Virgil, among others—saw behind every hero's feats the struggle the hero waged against the tyrannical forces within himself. Charles would have also found that these heroes' struggles against monsters and tyrants symbolized the perpetual conflict within their own souls, a conflict that often represents a sovereign's most formidable challenge. At stake in this internal war is whether the hero exemplifies a just ruler or a mad tyrant. Thus, if Augustus, Nero, Ippolito and Alfonso d'Este, and Charles V had followed Seneca's advice in the *De Clementia* to look at themselves in a mirror, they would have seen the image of their enemy.

CHAPTER 4

The Geography of the Enemy
Christian and Islamic Empires from the Fall of Constantinople to Tasso's *Gerusalemme Liberata*

And other sheep I have that are not of this fold
them also I must bring. And they shall hear my voice:
And there shall be one fold and one shepherd.
— John 10:16, quoted by Christopher Columbus
in his *Libro de las Prophecías*

THE PREVIOUS CHAPTERS on Luigi Pulci and Ludovico Ariosto have explored enmity within the *polis* and within the individual. I have considered Pulci's exposure of treachery and civic discord in the *Morgante* and examined Orlando's madness as an allusion to political tyranny in the *Furioso*. In Pulci's poem, we have seen treachery characterized as a disease—a *cancer*, in Morgante's case—that corrodes the political body from within, breaking the bonds of friendship and trust that hold a community together. My investigation of Ariosto's poem has also revealed that tyranny, like Orlando's insanity, can be understood as a manifestation of imbalance or, in Platonic terms, as a dangerous domination of the lowest appetites over reason. In chapter 4, I will focus on the *Gerusalemme Liberata*, in which Torquato Tasso portrays the Muslim enemy as a rebel force in a cosmic struggle between good and evil. Tasso's development of Islam as a manifestation of rebellion against universalizing Christendom is in part consistent with the representation of Muhammad as a schismatic in *Inferno* 28, which I discussed in chapter 1. The expanding scale of conflict introduced in my analysis of Dante's treatment of war in *Inferno* 28 and the *Monarchia*'s vision of universal peace thus culminates in this chapter, where I move outward from individual and *polis* to the global-scale conflicts described in the late-sixteenth-century *Liberata*. As noted in the Introduction, this change of perspective from the political dynamics of the Italian city-states to those of a world arena in which multinational empires compete for hegemony across different continents reflects a concurrent shift in the history of Western Europe and beyond.

Many scholars have observed the apparent suppression of multiplicity for the sake of unity in Tasso's poem and have characterized that suppression as follows: on the one hand, it mirrors the Crusaders' victory over a diverse assortment of Muslim armies; on the other hand, it affirms the dominant authority embodied by the Crusaders' commander Goffredo over the humanistic-chivalric lures epitomized by Rinaldo, the poem's indispensable hero and future founder of the Este House, and by his ill-fated doubles, the seditious Italian knight Argillano and the young Danish prince Sveno. The domestication of romance and individualism within the epic structure of the *Liberata* in turn mirrors the purported conversions to Christianity of the female characters in the enemy camp: the Ethiopian fighter Clorinda, who is mortally wounded and baptized by her unrequited lover Tancredi; the princess of Antioch Erminia, who pledges loyalty to her beloved Tancredi as she heals the wounds he suffered in his fight with the Circassian warrior Argante; and, above all, the Damascene sorceress Armida, who in the poem's final canto echoes the Virgin Mary's reply to the angel Gabriel at the Annunciation, possibly suggesting a sudden metamorphosis from seducer of men to handmaid of God. In each of these conversion moments, Tasso uses the words *ancella* or *ancilla* (handmaid)—as opposed to *rubella* (rebel), the default keyword applied to the Crusaders' foes—to label the submission, religious or otherwise, of the poem's three main female characters.

For scholars who understand the *Liberata* primarily in relation to this dynamic of suppression, the poem's process of controlling or containing unorthodox forces enacts an unapologetically Eurocentric vision of power relations, a vision rooted in the tenets of the Catholic Reformation. In the influential reading of Sergio Zatti, Tasso's sympathetic depiction of some vanquished enemies of the Crusaders has been diagnosed as a symptom of the poet's repressed "emotive identification with the defeated pagans"; this emotive identification is, however, "rejected at the ideological level," in a poem that Zatti and others have characterized as unequivocally imperialistic.[1] This perspective productively accounts for Tasso's well-known personal restlessness and his response to the revival of Aristotle's *Poetics* in the sixteenth century. Zatti's critical approach also sheds light on important aspects of Tasso's representation of the "Other" in the *Liberata*. His reading acknowledges the centrifugal pressures that could potentially undermine the longing for unity that pervades the poem, but at the same time protects what is generally considered its ideological integrity. In relation to this last count, the poem's purported ideological integrity, re-situating the *Liberata*'s representation of the enemy in its cultural-historical context can help us view Tasso's political theology in a different light. Although the *Liberata* ostensibly reflects the attraction of a unified world under the "holy standards" ["santi segni"] (*GL* 1.1) of a Christian Empire,² its ideology is not at all monolithic. I would argue, in fact, that Tasso deliberately exposes the instability of such an imperial project by keeping the poem's romantic-chivalric thread running in the poem's last cantos and by expressing his dismay at the friend-enemy dichotomy violently enacted in the battle for Jerusalem.³

Without turning Tasso into a harbinger of multicultural relativism, it is possible to acknowledge that the ideological thrust of his poem reflects underlying tensions inherent in the emerging political, religious, and economic hegemony of the early modern European nation-states. In the *Liberata*, Tasso captures a lucid snapshot of a developing new world order, centered in Europe, but ultimately irreducible to a single political or religious authority. Echoing the title of a recent book by Ayesha Ramachandran, we might consider Tasso one of the "worldmakers" who, during the Renaissance, helped inform how modernity would conceive of the world.⁴ The *Liberata* participates in this worldmaking process in part by asking its Crusaders to confront an array of enemies hailing from every corner of the Earth, from Egypt to India and from Ethiopia to Turkey, with even a diversion beyond the Strait of Gibraltar to the Canary Islands (or the Fortunate Isles, as they were called during the Renaissance). My reading aims to challenge the assumption that the battle for Jerusalem depicted in the *Liberata* operates as a microcosm for a worldwide clash of civilizations,⁵ wherein Catholic European nations kill or convert all of humankind at sword-point. It is true that Tasso introduces the First Crusade in stark ethico-theological terms as the strife between God and Satan, good and evil, Christianity and Islam, and as an ideal pilgrimage toward the salvation offered by the Holy Sepulchre in Jerusalem, the city whose etymology means "vision of peace."⁶ Yet he also acknowledges that such peace cannot be achieved through the exercise of political power, including holy war.

As I will show in this chapter, Tasso's representation of his Muslim characters is grounded in the debates that animated primarily, but by no means exclusively, the intellectual life of the Italian Peninsula during the fifteenth and sixteenth centuries. The controversies that I will outline below accompanied seismic historical events that reverberated throughout the world, with profound implications for the whole of Christendom: first, multi-layered religious conflicts, including the Protestant Reformation initiated by Martin Luther in 1517 and military challenges from the Islamic East as experienced most dramatically in the Fall of Constantinople to the Turks in 1453, the Siege of Vienna in 1529, and the Battle of Lepanto between the fleets of the Holy League and the Ottoman Empire in 1571; and second, Columbus's voyage to the West Indies, and the subsequent colonization of the new continent by the Spanish and Portuguese in the early decades of the sixteenth century. These events fostered both the renewal and the problematization of two concepts that, as we have seen in chapter 1 of this book, lay at the heart of medieval political theology: the legacy of Rome as a world empire and the perception of Islam as a renegade limb torn from the universal body of the Catholic Church, rather than an autonomous religion. The Roman legacy and the notion of a "rebel" Islam are key issues in my reading of the *Liberata*, and both deserve to be addressed at some length.

Before turning more closely to Tasso's poem, then, it will be helpful to consider how Islam, and particularly its manifestation in the Ottoman Empire, was depicted in Western Europe, especially in the aftermath of the Fall of Constantinople. Remarkably, the idea of world monarchy was used both by various Ottoman sultans and by those who, like Cardinal Nicholas of Cusa and Pope Pius II, opposed the Turkish advance into Eastern Europe. As Mehmed II (1432–1481) and Suleiman the Magnificent (1494–1566), two of the most prominent Ottoman rulers in the fifteenth and sixteenth centuries, adapted to their own purposes the traditional motif of Rome's universal empire as bulwark of global unity and peace, Mercurino di Gattinara and other advocates did the same on behalf of Charles V's Holy Roman Empire. In the second part of the chapter, I will focus on what I would term Tasso's geography of the enemy, first by taking stock of Satan's speech to the other fallen angels in canto 4 of the *Liberata* and then by mapping the Crusaders' adversaries throughout Africa and Asia. I will also probe Erminia's and Armida's alleged conversions to suggest that neither character actually embraces Christianity. Lastly, I will argue that Goffredo's choice to spare the Persian king Altamoro in the poem's final canto confirms my view that the *Liberata* does not unequivocally sustain a universalist ideology of Catholic imperialism.

The Roman Empire Between the Habsburgs and the Ottomans

I concluded my chapter on Ariosto with a discussion of the imperial propaganda developed by the advisers of Charles V. We have seen that Charles's rule over enormous swaths of Western Europe and the Americas renewed hopes for a world empire, and that the Emperor's supporters fashioned his public image after the model of classical conquerors, as exemplified by the emblem featuring the Pillars of Hercules accompanied by the phrase *"Plus Ultra"* ("further beyond"). Tasso, too, referred to Charles's columnar insignia in one of his dialogues, *Il conte overo de l'imprese:* "Poiché mi concedete ch'io trapassi l'ordine, comincerò dal fine, cioè da le colonne di Carlo Quinto, imperadore oltre tutti gli altri gloriosissimo, il quale trapassò tutti i termini della gloria mondana: però a le colonne di Ercole aggiunse questo *plus ultra*" ["since I am allowed to follow a different order, I will begin from the end, namely from the columns of Charles V, the emperor, more glorious than any other, who surpassed all limits of worldly glory: that is why he added 'plus ultra' to the Pillars of Hercules"].[7] As a new Hercules, Charles was to recover the cities of Constantinople and Jerusalem from what Christianity considered the infidels' usurpation in the East, spread the Lord's message to the American Indians in the West, and restore unity, justice, and peace within a divided Christian Commonwealth.

Achieving this threefold objective remained, unsurprisingly, elusive for both Charles and his son and successor Philip (1527–1598). The strife among the European nation-states continued throughout the sixteenth century and extended into the colonized territories in the Americas, as well as to Africa and East Asia, where Portugal had established numerous colonies.[8] At the same time, the Ottoman Empire strengthened its positions in the Balkans and in the Near East. The threats to Charles's dominions in Europe came not only from the Turks, led by the sultan Suleiman the Magnificent, whose troops laid siege to Vienna in 1529, but also from the divisions within Christianity that burst into the open with the Protestant Reformation. Sharp divisions existed even within the Habsburg Empire: Spain was a bastion of Catholicism, while the epicenter of Lutheranism was located within the German states. Indeed, Philip, who inherited a religiously divided Europe when his father abdicated between 1554 and 1556, was never elected Emperor because of these intra-European enmities.[9] Western Europe's interactions with the Ottomans were still deeply affected by the 1453 conquest of Constantinople, the former capital of the Eastern Roman Empire, by Mehmed II.[10] The naval battle of Lepanto in 1571, won by a heterogeneous fleet of Christian powers led by Philip's half-brother John of Austria, marked another milestone—at least in the eyes of Western Europeans—in the history of encounters between the Islamic Empires and Christianity.[11]

The fall of Constantinople, the last bastion of the Eastern Roman Empire and one of the capitals of Christendom, sent shockwaves across Europe. Even a cursory survey of texts written in the immediate aftermath of this traumatic defeat testifies to the widespread fear and contempt that engulfed most courts in Italy and elsewhere.¹² The tone of these laments ranges from apocalyptic and bellicose in support of a crusade to rueful and irate because of the discord among Christian nations. Conflicting interests among European states hampered all efforts to muster the resources needed to recover the lands that the Muslims had subjugated. Moreover, as Aeneas Silvius Piccolomini (the future Pope Pius II) made clear in a well-known letter to Nicholas of Cusa in July 1453, contemporaries understood the fall of Constantinople as, among other things, a fatal blow to the classical legacy of Ancient Greece.¹³

Over the past two decades, several scholars have documented the historiographical, ethnic, and political facets that define humanist portraits of the Turks, effectively suggesting a shift toward a more secular characterization of Muslims between the fourteenth and sixteenth centuries.¹⁴ Theological components were, however, still central to humanist critiques of Islam in the Renaissance; these theological aspects, moreover, were in large part still anchored to principles and legends formulated during the Middle Ages. These religiously inflected portrayals of Islam significantly influenced both renewed calls for a crusade in the fifteenth century and a number of surprising appeals for conversion addressed to the sultan Mehmed II. Indeed, in the same epistle to Cusa, after Piccolomini's invective against the destruction of Greek letters with the fall of Constantinople, he turns to bewail what he describes as the even greater loss consisting of the forced retrenchment of Christianity within the narrow boundaries of Europe: "This is a great loss; but it is even worse that we see the Christian faith undermined and driven into a corner" ["Magnum est hoc detrimentum, sed multo maius illud, quod fidem Christianam comminui et in angulum coartari videmus"].¹⁵

As I have noted in the first chapter of this book, a vast anti-Islamic tradition that gained currency in Europe during the Middle Ages branded the Prophet Muhammad as a cunning pseudo-prophet, who, after receiving instruction from a renegade monk named Sergius, founded a powerful sect that spread rapidly thanks to its military might. Among the most influential medieval critics of Islam were John of Damascus, Peter the Venerable, and Riccoldo da Montecroce. Nicholas of Cusa's 1460 critique of the Qur'an in the *Cribatio Alkorani* retains many of these earlier critics' polemical arguments, particularly those put forward by Riccoldo in his *Contra legem Sarracenorum*.¹⁶ However, Cusa reveals a remarkable interest in furthering his understanding of Islam, as his efforts were partly aimed at finding a reasonable common ground between Christianity and Islam. In an earlier dialogue, *De pace fidei* (1453), the conversation among Cusa's various speakers even culminates with the following appeal for concord and peace: "nations are entitled to their own devotions and ceremonies, provided faith and peace be maintained" ["permittantur nationes—salva fide et pace—in suis devotionibus et cerimonialibus"].[17] Yet both the *De pace fidei* and the *Cribatio* show that the theological disagreement between Christians and Muslims still pivoted around a crucial issue: that Islam rejected the doctrine of the Trinity. Cusa discusses this primary point of contention in books 1 and 2 of the *Cribatio*, illustrating in painstaking detail the relationships among the three persons of the Trinity and the hypostatic union of Christ's two natures, divine and human.

After completing his scrutiny of the Qur'an, in the final chapters of the *Cribatio*, Cusa addresses Mehmed II (whom Cusa erroneously calls Caliph of Baghdad and Sultan of Babylon), exhorting him to embrace the Christian faith. He urges Mehmed to command all his subjects "to believe the Gospel in such manner as the Egyptians, the Africans, the Romans, and the Asians believed and glorified the Virgin Mary at the time of Muhammad [...] Then your command will be just and will be pleasing to God, to Christ, and to the chaste Virgin" ["Si itaque praeceperis in omni imperio tuo omnes credere evangelio modo tali, quo Aegyptii, Afri, Romani Asianique crediderunt et glorificaverunt virginem Mariam tempore Mahumeti (...) iustum erit mandatum tuum deo, Cristo et virgini intemeratae acceptum"] (*Cribatio* 3.17).[18] Here—in terms similar to those that we will also see Pius II use in his *Epistle to Mohammed II*—Cusa argues that Mehmed's rule would become legitimate if he should decide to become a Christian, thus drawing to the Gospel all the peoples under his authority. Mehmed's embrace of Christianity would, further, mirror the Prophet Muhammad's own alleged conversion from idolatry: "Muhammad was converted from idolatry through Sergius [...] But because he [Muhammad] was a Christian, even though a Nestorian, assuredly he was baptized" ["Mahometus de idolatria conversus (fuit) per Sergium Christianum et Nestorianum (...) Sed quia Christianus licet Nestorianus utique baptizatus fuit"] (3.18).[19]

Cusa's approach to the conflict with Islam paid particular attention to doctrinal issues. Pius II, in his *Epistle to Mohammed II*, articulated a more vehement discourse, though it too was apparently aimed at converting Mehmed II.[20] Pius's pamphlet begins with a *captatio benevolentiae* in which the Pope notes that his letter does not originate from hatred, even though Mehmed is an enemy of the Christian faith. To the contrary, following the teaching of the Gospel (Matthew 5:43–48), Pius contends that Christians should love their enemies and seek to correct their actions through reason, rather than attack them with weapons. Pius's rhetorical flourish scarcely masks his frustration and disillusionment with the fractiousness among European nations, which had mired his efforts to launch a crusade. Although he begins by addressing the Ottoman sultan as "an enemy of our religion" ("nostrae religionis hostis"),²¹ in chapter 2 of the *Epistle*, Pius offers Mehmed a somewhat shocking proposal:

> If you want to extend your power over Christians and render your name as glorious as possible, you do not need gold, weapons, armies, or fleet. A little thing can make you the greatest, most powerful and illustrious man of all who live today [...] it is a little bit of water by which you may be baptized and brought to Christian rites and to the belief in the Gospel. If you receive this, there will not be any leader in the world who can surpass you in glory or equal you in power. We will call you ruler over the Greeks and the East; what you now hold by force and injustice, you will rightfully possess.²²

According to Pius, the only flaw that keeps Mehmed from exercising his authority legitimately is his faith. Neither his often disparaged ethnic identity, nor the form of his government makes the Turkish sovereign unfit to rule over the Christian Commonwealth, or at least its eastern half. The rejection of Mehmed's conquests here rests solely on theological grounds and, therefore, a "little bit of water" would turn this ruthless enemy into "the greatest, most powerful and illustrious man of all who live today."

Should this passage have left some readers indifferent, Pius II drives his point home later in the *Epistle* by drawing a parallel between Mehmed and none other than Augustus and by echoing the same texts that, as discussed in chapter 3 of the present study, Ariosto evokes in canto 15 of the *Furioso*, namely Virgil's fourth *Eclogue* and the Book of Isaiah: "O how great would the abundance of peace be, how great the exultation of Christian folk, how great the joy in the whole world! The Augustan era and the Golden Age of the poets would be renewed! The leopard would lie down with the kid and the calf with the lion; swords would be beaten into pruning hooks, plowshares, and hoes [...] O how great would be your glory for being the one who restored peace to the world!"²³ Although it is unclear what Pius hoped to achieve with such a provocative suggestion,²⁴ it is certain that his letter circulated widely in Western Europe. In light of the enduring debates on the legitimacy of the Holy Roman Empire, Pius's reference to the *pax augusta* acquires further significance, especially if we take into account Mehmed's interest in ancient history and particularly in the depictions of Julius Caesar and Alexander the Great as global rulers. As the Venetian diplomat Nicola Sagundino, a witness to the fall of Constantinople, noted in an oration to King Alfonso V of Aragon and later repeated in an extended report to Pius II, Mehmed aspired to "world domination" ["imperium orbis"] and hoped to take over the city of Rome as the legitimate seat of his empire: "he [Mehmed] said that the seat of Constantine is bestowed from heaven, and that this seat seems to be Rome, not Constantinople" ["ait sibi concedi coelitus Constantini sedem, hanc vero Romam esse, non Constantinopolim videri"].[25]

Like Sagundino, Pius also refers to the Emperor Constantine, the first Christian Roman emperor. In another important passage of his *Epistle*, after extolling Constantine's feats, Pius promises that the same triumphs await "you [Mehmed] if you worship Christ in your wisdom and imitate Constantine the Great. Just as the Romans became Christians with their emperor, so the Turks will be baptized together with you" ["si nobiscum sapiens Christum colas et magnum Constantinum imiteris: quemadmodum Romani cum suo imperatore Christiani sunt effecti, ita et Turcae una tecum"].[26] The narrative of Constantine's conversion and the subsequent impact of that conversion on the Roman Empire were at the center of late medieval arguments regarding the proper relationship between the Catholic Church and European states; during the fourteenth century, Constantine's purported decision to place the Roman Empire under papal control drew criticism from such figures as Dante and Marsilius of Padua.[27] As is well known, the attacks against the Church's meddling in political affairs reached a tipping point in the first half of the fifteenth century, when Nicholas of Cusa in book 3 of *The Catholic Concordance* and, more forcefully, Lorenzo Valla in the *Oration on the Donation of Constantine* (1440) demonstrated the inauthenticity of the document used to attest Constantine's alleged donation of the Empire to Pope Sylvester and thus further undermined the papacy's claim to secular power.[28]

Pius II was less interested in the donation controversy than in divisions within Christendom, especially as he saw his efforts to launch a crusade defeated by the personal interests of his coreligionists. For him, the *exemplum* of Constantine was particularly poignant in the aftermath of the fall of Constantinople. Formerly a general in the service of Diocletian during some of the most violent persecutions against the Christians, Constantine subsequently converted to Christianity.[29] Few, if any, historical figures provided a similarly compelling archetype to use in framing Mehmed's victories and the Christians' suffering within a providential historical narrative. Given that, before he became Pope, Aeneas Silvius Piccolomini had written a tract arguing in favor of the Roman Empire's universal authority, his references to Constantine and Augustus might well be considered insincere, but his deployment of these key historical actors here certainly reflect a keen awareness of the implications of their examples.[30] As I pointed out earlier in my discussion of *Monarchia*, many authors, including Augustine and Dante, argued that the Roman Empire rose to power under providential auspices to allow for the expansion of Christianity.[31] Yet Pius radically subverts the conventional European perspective on universal monarchy (which, of course, assumed outward expansion of European power) by positing that the Turkish Emperor could bring peace to a unified world if only he were baptized.[32]

It must be added that Mehmed II was well respected in some European centers of power. The case of Florence is particularly relevant, given the fruitful relationship between the Medici and the Ottoman ruler and his successor Beyazid II. Two overt signs of this relationship followed Mehmed's handing over of Bernardo Bandini, one of the perpetrators of the 1478 Pazzi conspiracy, who had fled to Constantinople after the assassination of Giuliano de' Medici. To express his gratitude, Lorenzo the Magnificent asked Bertoldo di Giovanni—the same artist who, as noted in chapter 2, made the medal to memorialize the Pazzi conspiracy as a public crime—to craft a medallion for Mehmed II. Then, in 1482, barely a year after the brief Turkish occupation of the town of Otranto in the Southern Italian region of Apulia, the humanist Francesco Berlinghieri dedicated a copy of his translation of Ptolemy's *Geographia* to the sultan. (Since, however, Mehmed II died while the volume was being completed, the book was eventually addressed to his son Beyazid II.)[33] It would seem singularly appropriate that Berlinghieri offered a book that seeks to represent the world to a ruler who cultivated a narrative of global imperialism.

Mehmed's ambitions were consistent with a central tenet of Islam, a religion that had since its inception seen itself as a universal faith, therefore analogous to Christianity.[34] It is not entirely surprising, then, that the Ottoman Empire, particularly after the conquest of Constantinople and during the long reign of Suleiman the Magnificent (r. 1520–1566), would appropriate the claim of world domination that in Western Europe was commonly ascribed to the Holy Roman Empire.[35] Those committed to the millenarian narrative of Muslim world conquest destined to occur under the aegis of the Ottoman Empire drew attention to the coincidence of the Christian era's sixteenth century with the tenth century of the Islamic calendar, which dated from Muhammad's journey (*hijrah*) from Mecca to Medina in 622. Indeed, Ibrahim Pasha, Suleiman's extremely powerful grand vizier, only addressed his master with the title of "universal ruler of the inhabited world."[36] We might reasonably infer, then, an ideological kinship between Latin Christianity and

Ottoman Islam, if only in their respective commitments to universality.³⁷ Indeed, the respective Habsburg and Ottoman claims to world empire produced a geopolitical scenario with Christian and Islamic enemies functioning as mirror images of each other. The two sides created competing myths to assert the legitimacy of their claims. The political universalists in each camp also faced opposition within their respective religions: the Habsburgs saw diverging interests forming among the nascent European states and political-religious divisions emerging with the rise of Protestantism; meanwhile, on their Eastern border, the Ottomans confronted the Shiite Safavid Empire, which through the sixteenth and seventeenth centuries stretched over a vast territory that included Persia as well as parts of modern-day Iraq, Afghanistan, and Uzbekistan.³⁸

The politico-religious tensions that simmered within the Habsburg dominions played out in the intellectual arena as well. Desiderius Erasmus, one of the most influential humanists of the sixteenth century, rejected the idea of the crusade in the *Education of a Christian Prince* (addressed to Charles V in 1516) and in the *Complaint of Peace* (1517). His irenic skepticism rested on the belief that war breeds war and that, rather than confronting the Turkish menace with violence, Europeans ought to be mindful that "war against the Turks should [not] be hastily undertaken, remembering first of all that the kingdom of Christ was created, spread, and secured by very different means [...] First make sure that we are truly Christians ourselves and then, if it seems appropriate, let us attack the Turks" ["in Turcas bellum temere suspiciendum esse censeo primum illud mecum reputans Christi ditionem longe diversa via natam propagatam et constabilitam (...) Primus hoc agamus, ut ipsi simus germane Christiani, deinde si visum erit, Turcas adoriamur"].³⁹ As Turkish forces advanced inexorably through the Balkans, culminating in the Ottoman siege of Vienna in 1529, the intellectuals of Charles V's court grew increasingly bellicose. One of the strongest advocates for an anti-Turkish crusade was Spanish theologian and humanist Juan Gines de Sepulveda. After studying in Bologna under the philosopher Pietro Pomponazzi, Sepulveda had entered the service of the papal curia where he stayed until 1536, when he became the official chronicler of Charles V. As we can see in the *Cohortatio ad Carolum V* (a pamphlet he published in Bologna in 1529, only a few months before Charles's coronation as Holy Roman Emperor),⁴⁰ Sepulveda regarded the Turks as an imminent threat to the entire *respublica christiana*. His portrayal retrieved and revived some of the most conventional ingredients of medieval anti-Muslim invectives, caricaturing Charles's Islamic enemies as ferocious barbarians who despised the liberal arts.⁴¹

While the primary targets of Sepulveda's attacks were the Turks, he also attacked those Christians who did not favor the campaign against the Ottoman Empire. His words reveal the discord still present in Europe even as Islamic expansion threatened the Catholic Church's center. Among this cohort of "internal" enemies, Sepulveda included those who argued that "it is not consistent with Christian tolerance to fight the Turks with weapons" ["non esse Christianae tolerantiae Turcarum violentiae (...) ferro et armis repugnare"].[42] These arguments he described as heretical opinions and their authors as "capital enemies of the Christian religion" ["capitalior hostis Christianae religionis"].[43] In condemning the proponents of these sacrilegious views, Sepulveda was likely alluding to Erasmus for his reluctance to support a military response to the Ottoman Empire, and to Martin Luther for his (initial) justification of the Turkish invasion as divine punishment for the corruption of the Church.[44] Given the circumstances, even Erasmus eventually softened his pacifism and warily endorsed the defensive war against the Turkish invasion in the *Utilissima consultatio de bello Turcis inferendo* (1530),[45] just a few months after the publication of Sepulveda's pamphlet. In the final pages of the *Cohortatio*, Sepulveda urges Charles V to rescue the territories occupied by the Muslims, including Constantinople, "the court of the Roman emperors until not too long ago" ["regia non pridem Romanorum imperatorum"], and the city of Jerusalem, "the holiest shrine of the Christian religion" ["praecipuo Christianae religionis sacrario"].[46] Charles's ultimate goal should be to exercise his power "as emperor and annex the rest of the world to the dominion of the holy Christian religion" ["te imperatore (...) reliquus terrarum orbis dicioni Christianorum et sanctissime religioni adiciatur"].[47] Sepulveda's argument fits into the myth of the "last world emperor" that both the Habsburgs and the Ottomans adopted. The notion of just war that he developed in his *Cohortatio* is consistent with his writings in support of the Spanish occupation of the West Indies and the forceful conversion of the American Indians. Even Sepulveda's arch-rival, the Dominican friar Bartolomé de Las Casas, who fiercely rejected the view that the Spaniards had a right to subjugate the inhabitants of the West Indies, used the Turks as the example of a people against whom Christians might legitimately take up arms, for this was an enemy who had attacked Christian territories.[48]

Military confrontations, as well as trade and cultural exchanges, continued to characterize the relationships between Islamic and Christian states throughout the sixteenth century. The best-known episode in this conflict-ridden engagement was the 1571 naval battle of Lepanto, which pitted the Ottoman fleet against the armada of the Holy League, an alliance formed by Spain, Venice, and various Italian city-states and led by John of Austria, an illegitimate son of Charles V. Seen as long overdue revenge for the numerous Christian setbacks since the fall of Constantinople, the Holy League's victory was hailed in Europe with a flurry of poems, many of which were first published in a 1572 anthology and were recently collected in a volume for the I Tatti Library.[49] Many of these poems cast the Battle of Lepanto in the mold of Octavian's defeat of Mark Antony and Cleopatra at Actium in 31 BCE, and emphasize John of Austria's lineage as son of the Holy Roman Emperor. As the editors of the I Tatti anthology have noted, "high-profile converts to Islam led the contingents at Lepanto."[50] These cross-religious ties were consistent with the legend of Muhammad as a renegade Christian, which had been perpetuated in Europe during the Middle Ages and the early Renaissance. The longest, and perhaps most complex, of the poems included in the collection is Juan Latino's *Song on the Victory of the Christian Fleet*. Formerly a slave, the Black-African Latino became a humanist and teacher in the Spanish city of Granada.[51] In several passages of his *Song*, he brands Muslim enemies as heretics and Islam as a sect (book 1, lines 64–65; book 2, line 1396; book 2, lines 1758–59).

Among numerous examples of the interplay between classical leitmotivs and religious themes in post-Lepanto literary production, Ottaviano Manini's short poem "The Long-Desired Day" is also worth noting. Steeped in classicizing references, much of Manini's work rehashes commonplaces of long-lost Roman greatness, as illustarated by such mythological figures as Mars and Tisiphone and famed conquerors as the Scipios and the Camilli. After extolling the virtues of Ancient Rome, Manini's call to arms in "The Long-Desired Day" exhorts European readers to make the territories under infidel occupation embrace the Christian faith again:

> Let us rise up as a united people, and whatever remains of the Roman race, whoever rejoices to follow the gleaming white standards of the world's Savior, let us hasten to this one purpose: we must prevail at last. It is not right to abandon the path begun before these lands are free from eternal terror. Let them accept again our laws and better governance.[52]

That Ottoman rule is described as tyrannical throughout this text explains why Manini would characterize a Roman—and Christian—conquest as a transition to "better governance." The key point here, however, is that this transition would amount to a reassimilation of the occupied lands into their legitimate Roman-Christian dominion.

What emerges from the foregoing historical excursus of Christian-Islamic encounters between the fifteenth and sixteenth centuries can be summarized with the following three main themes: a consistent pattern of internal discord within both the Christian and Muslim worlds; the lingering notion that Islam usurped territories that had rightfully belonged to Christendom; and the enduring myth of a universal Roman Empire. By the time news of the Holy League's triumph was spreading across Europe, Tasso had already begun to craft the poetic materials that would eventually comprise the *Gerusalemme Liberata* (the *Rinaldo* and the *Goffredo* were completed in 1562 and 1575, respectively). As I will show in the following pages, there is little doubt that the multifaceted conflicts involving the European states and the Turkish Empire in the roughly 120 years between the fall of Constantinople and the Battle of Lepanto helped shape the development of Tasso's thought on politics and religion and thus his conception of the *Liberata*.

Satan's Geopolitics

To assess the impact of the events and ideas outlined above on Tasso's view of empire in the *Liberata*, I will begin by playing, quite literally, devil's advocate. In canto 4, Satan offers a defiantly antagonistic take on world history, challenging the hegemonic ideology that many have argued sustains Tasso's work. The enemy of humankind ["'l gran nemico de l'umane genti"] (GL 4.1), as Tasso brands Satan, following the etymology of his name, suggests that the fallen angels are considered "alme rubelle" ["rebel souls"] (4.9) only because God's army won the "war in heaven." Might has made right, says Satan, and has written history to boot. In the same stanza, he defines his fellow devils' attempt to overthrow the divine Sovereign as an "alta impresa" ["lofty enterprise"] (ibid.). These are the same words Tasso uses to describe the crusade, and the same words God employs when urging the angel Gabriel to encourage Goffredo to undertake the liberation of Jerusalem: "Già 'l sesto anno volgea, ch'in oriente / passò il campo Cristiano a l'alta impresa" ["Now the sixth year was come since the Christian host passed into the Orient on the lofty enterprise"] (1.6); and "Chiami i duci a consiglio, e i tardi mova / a l'alta impresa" ["Let him call the chiefs to council and stir up the sluggish to the lofty enterprise"] (1.12). The phrase "alta impresa" appears only occasionally in the *Liberata*, and always at crucial moments, to connote a variety of missions, irrespective of who undertakes them. In canto 12, for example, an "alta impresa" is Clorinda and Argante's night raid to destroy the siege tower the Crusaders have built to breach the walls of Jerusalem (12.15). In cantos 14 and

15, another "alta impresa" is Carlo and Ubaldo's journey beyond the Pillars of Hercules to rescue Rinaldo from his erotic captivity on Armida's island (14.71 and 15.38). In one of the poem's most memorable passages, Tasso uses the phrase "alte imprese" to describe the battle raging on the plain outside the city that the Turkish warrior Solimano watches in awe from the keep of Jerusalem: "e desiò trovarsi anch'egli in atto / nel periglioso campo a l'alte imprese" ["(he) wanted to find himself in action too, in lofty enterprises on the perilous field"] (20.74). "Alta/e" therefore exclusively denotes the gallantry of an action, and both Christians and Muslims are said to undertake such worthy deeds.

During the demonic council in Hell, Satan further describes the God-willed war against the Muslims as an imperialistic undertaking whose goal is to superimpose Christian rule over the entire world:

> Deh! Non vedete omai com'egli tenti
> tutte al suo culto richiamar le genti?
> Noi trarrem neghittosi i giorni e l'ore,
> né degna cura fia che 'l cor n'accenda?
> e soffrirem che forza ognor maggiore
> il suo popolo fedele in Asia prenda?
> e che Giudea soggioghi? e che 'l suo onore,
> che 'l nome suo si dilati e stenda?
> che suoni in altre lingue, e in altri carmi
> si scriva, e incida in novi bronzi e marmi?
> Che sian gl'idoli nostri a terra sparsi?
> ch'i nostri altari il mondo a lui converta?
> ch'a lui sospesi i voti, a lui sol arsi
> siano gl'incensi, ed auro e mirra offerta?
> ch'ove a noi tempio non solea serrarsi,
> or via non resti a l'arti nostre aperta?
> che di tant'alme il solito tributo
> ne manchi, e in voto regno alberghi Pluto? (GL 4.12–14)

[Ah, do you not see even now how He is trying to call back all the peoples to His religion? Shall we draw out in idleness our days and hours, and shall there be no worthy task to kindle your hearts? And shall we suffer it that His faithful gather in Asia and daily a great power? And that they bring Judaea under the yoke? And that His honor, His name be the more extended and spread abroad? That it resound in other tongues, and be written in other oracles, and cut in new bronzes and marbles? That our idols be scattered on the ground? That the world convert our altars to Him? That for Him trophies be hung up, for Him alone incense burned, and gold and myrrh offered? That where no temple was wont to be closed against us, now there should be no avenue open to our arts? That the customary tribute of so many souls be withdrawn, and Pluto have his dwelling in an empty kingdom?]

Satan's address is overtly political. He exhorts his infernal troops to prevent efforts to draw all peoples to God's faith and to make His "name" and "honor" worshipped throughout the world.[53] That people across the globe have been Christianizing altars previously vowed to Satan not only testifies to God's aggressive expansionism, but also implies some degree of affinity between the adoration of non-Christian deities or idols and the practice of Christianity. In stanza 14, the juxtaposition between "voti" (holy vows) and "voto" (void/empty) suggests that vows fulfilled in the name of the Lord will ultimately empty Hell ["che di tant'alme il solito tributo / ne manchi, e in voto regno alberghi Pluto?"].[54] The anti-imperialist quality of Satan's complaints becomes clearer if they are read in relation to a passage of the *Giudicio sopra la Conquistata*, in which Tasso describes a poem as a microcosm, pointing out that "il poeta, a guisa di geografo, gli figura quasi la forma dell'imperio e i confini delle provincie soggiogate da gl'infedeli" ["the poet, like a geographer, depicts the shape of the empire and the boundaries of the provinces subjugated by the infidels"].[55] Both Satan in the *Liberata* and Tasso in the *Giudicio* appear to establish a correlation between poetry and geopolitics: by drawing boundaries among Christian and Islamic regions, Tasso suggests, poets can draw what we might describe as a "geography of the enemy."

The interplay of the political and religious dimensions articulated in this passage of Satan's speech mirrors the twofold goal of Goffredo's military campaign: he is both religious pilgrim and field marshal of the crusading army, simultaneously pursuing the discharge of his vows and the liberation of the Holy Sepulcher from the Saracen occupation. Yet here Tasso highlights the eschatological contrast between Pluto's realm (a kingdom of inevitable and eternal loss) and Christ's tomb (which is at once a place of death, and a place of rebirth and salvation). These dyads—emptiness vs. fulfillment, the diabolical vs. the divine, authority vs. rebellion, unity vs. multiplicity—seem to configure the conflict between the Christians and the Muslims as two radically foreign entities.[56] As Sergio Zatti has demonstrated,[57] however, even if Tasso's narrative apparently proposes clear dichotomies between two different religions, the strife dramatized in the *Liberata* takes place within one politico-theological system. The body of the Church is divided into many different sects that need to be brought back together. In this regard, David Quint has shown that, through Rinaldo's self-imposed exile and Argillano's revolt, both of which undermine the unity of the Christian camp from within, Tasso alluded to the Protestant Reformation.[58]

The Crusaders' disunity is a critical challenge for the liberation of Jerusalem, just as, from the outset of the *Liberata*, Goffredo's first objective is the submission to his authority of "i suoi compagni erranti" ["his wandering companions"] (*GL* 1.1). Furthermore, the Islam of Tasso's poem is presented as something akin to a renegade offshoot of Christianity, although less explicitly so than in Dante's and Cusa's works. The parallel between the "compagni erranti" and the Saracens is confirmed in Goffredo's address to his troops in canto 1, where he describes the territories under Muslim control as "ribellanti provincie" ["rebelling provinces"] (1.21), a phrase implying that they originally (and rightfully) belonged to Christendom. Thus, even an "external enemy" must share a process of assimilation similar to that imposed on the wandering crusaders.

Tasso spelled out the divisions corresponding to the fault lines between Catholicism and Lutheranism, on the one hand, and between Christianity and Islam, on the other, in a text often mentioned alongside the *Liberata*: the dedicatory letter to Scipione Gonzaga with which Tasso introduces his dialogue *De la dignità*.[59] Tasso began this dialogue in 1580, the year before the publication of the *Liberata*, then resumed and completed it in 1585. In it, Tasso indicates that the forces hampering the unity of the Church correspond to the "eretica pravità" of the Lutheran heresy and to the "ottomana tirannide." The dialogue's passage on unity ends with reference to a line from the Gospel of John that we have already seen quoted by Ariosto, Gattinara, and Columbus:

> E benché molti siano i rivi de l'operazioni e molti i rami pieni de' suoi [of the Church] fatti e molti i raggi ch'ella semina de la sua dottrina, uno è nondimeno il fonte, uno il tronco fondato sovra tenerissima radice, uno il sole che sparge la chiarissima luce: e l'unità si conserva ne l'origine, e un capo solamente regge molte membra, parte de le quali sono divise da questo corpo per l'eretica pravità, altre per l'ottomana tirannide, la quale usurpa le più belle parti de l'Oriente e del Mezzogiorno. Ma vostra signoria con gli altri può considerare i mezzi co' quali si possono ricongiungere, accioché uno sia l'ovile e uno il pastore, sì come una è la fede e uno il battesimo. (Tasso, *Dialoghi*, I, 448)

[Although the Church operates through many rivers, and although there are many branches full with its deeds, and although it shines through many rays, there is nonetheless one fountain, one tree founded on a most tender root, and one sun that spreads its light. Unity is preserved beginning with its source, one head alone rules over many limbs, some of which are severed from the body of the Church because of wicked heresies, some others because of the Ottoman tyranny, which usurps the most beautiful regions of the East and of the South. But you can consider what are the best ways with which to rejoin these limbs to their body, so that there will be one fold and one shepherd, and one faith and one baptism. (my translation)]

Beyond its explicit aspiration to established religious unity, I find two aspects of this passage particularly striking: first, Tasso refers solely to the concord of the Church, not to the foundation of a universal empire; second, he tasks Scipione Gonzaga, then Patriarch of Jerusalem, and unspecified others with considering ("considerare") what means would best suit such a glorious objective. It is important to stress here that Tasso makes no mention of war as an instrument to achieve the Church's unification.

If we accept the point of view adopted in the preface of *De la dignità*—i.e., the view of a unified mystical body—then Tasso's depiction of the Crusade in the *Liberata* transcends the limits of its historical objective, at least insofar as this war against Muslim powers is supposedly part of a broader mission to unite the world under Christ's standard. That the whole world participates in the struggle to redeem the errant knights and fight the rebellious Muslims is confirmed in the opening stanza of the poem, where Tasso asserts that Asia and Africa are joined with Satan's infernal forces in opposition to Goffredo's task: "in van l'Inferno vi s'oppose, e in vano / s'armò d'Asia e di Libia il popol misto" ["vainly Hell opposed herself to it, and vainly the combined peoples of Asia and of Lybia took up arms"] (GL 1.1). "Asia" and "Libia" (i.e., Africa) are the two additional continents that appeared with Europe in medieval world maps. On the surface, the goal of a Christian global empire would be achieved by killing or converting the enemies who hail from these two continents; or, in the exceptional case of the non-Muslim and non-Christian female warrior Clorinda, by doing both. In Tasso's narrative, conversions ostensibly apply to women, whereas men generally die in battle.[60] We shall see in the rest of the chapter, however, that these patterns of submission, on which most scholarly assumptions about the ideology of the *Liberata* are based, are flawed. Three important cases—those of Erminia, Armida, and Altamoro—arguably work against the poem's larger movement toward imperialistic unity. To highlight this tension between centrifugal and centripetal forces, I will now sketch out the geography of the enemy charted in the *Liberata*, starting with three prominent slain foes: Argante, Solimano, and Clorinda.

Dead Enemies

In the drama that unfolds in the *Liberata*, Argante and Solimano are the two leading male characters in the Muslim camp. Tasso portrays them as the perfect enemies, for they seem to represent the evil that the Crusaders are determined to extirpate. Both have a Luciferian quality that Tasso repeatedly invokes through reptilian similes (GL 9.25 and 19.25).[61] At the same time, though, the tragic stature of these characters, particularly in the moment of suspension that precedes their engagement in final duels with Tancredi and Rinaldo (19.10 and 20.73, respectively), both fascinates the reader and engages his or her sympathy. There are also clear differences between these two Muslim fighters. Argante hails from the mountainous region of Caucasus, where the realms of fantasy and romance meet; he is a character with no historical background. Solimano is a fictional representation of Kilij Arslan in Sulaiman, the eleventh-century ruler of Nicaea; he is, consequently, imbued with a sense of history. In the *Liberata*, Solimano's past defeats seem to haunt him as much as his present concern for the defense of Jerusalem does.[62] Argante, conversely, is a sheer force of nature. He belongs to no socio-political structure and relies exclusively on his strength and his sword (2.59).[63] As a Turk, Solimano also evokes an enemy, the above-mentioned Suleiman the Magnificent, who was undoubtedly present in Tasso's imagination and in the minds of his sixteenth-century readers as the man who led the Ottoman conquests of Belgrade (1521) and Rhodes (1522), and later laid siege to Vienna (1529).

Together with Clorinda, both Argante and Solimano are compared to towering giants on the walls of Jerusalem:

e quinci in forma d'orrido gigante
da la cintola in su sorge il Soldano,
quindi tra' merli il minaccioso Argante
torreggia, e discoperto è di lontano,
e in su la torre altisima Angolare
sovra tutti Clorinda eccelsa appare. (GL 11.27)[64]

> [And from one side looms the Sultan, from his waist up, in the shape of a fearsome giant; from another the menacing Argante towers between the battlements and is discovered from afar; and, upon the tallest tower Angolar, above them all Clorinda appears on high.]

The architectonic similes involving the three warriors evoke canto 31 of Dante's *Inferno*, where the pilgrim mistakenly identifies the giants Anteus, Briareus, and Nimrod as towers (*Inf.* 31.19–57).[65] As noted in chapter 2, in the *Commedia*, the giants embody disproportionate political ambition and the downfall this ambition inevitably precipitates. All of the giants, like Lucifer, whom they foreshadow in the *Commedia*, rebelled against divine authority and were then cast to the lowest sections of Hell. Yet Tasso diverges from Dante's model by allowing Clorinda to repent and convert to Christianity immediately before dying. Her two male companions, on the other hand, await an even less comforting fate. Tasso cannot allow them to be redeemed, not even in the bloody style of Clorinda's Christianization. The only way he can "assimilate" Argante and Solimano within the literary conventions of his poem is by killing them unconverted. Tasso thus adapts the legacy of some twenty-five centuries of defeated antagonists, including Turnus and Rodomonte; their literary function evokes a long heroic tradition, even though their deaths do not occur at the end of the *Liberata*, the end being where heroes dispatched comparable antagonists in the *Aeneid* and in the *Furioso*. Argante is killed—not as a public foe, but as a private enemy, as his rival Tancredi brands him shortly before their fatal duel ["proprio mio più che commune nemico"] (*GL* 19.5)—in a "solitary struggle" ["solinga guerra"] (19.29), distant from the battleground where Christians and Muslims fight for Jerusalem. Solimano is slain just outside of the city in Rinaldo's last heroic feat before he turns his attention to Armida (20.107–8).

Clorinda, the third warrior the cited passage places on the walls of Jerusalem, is a multi-layered character with multiple, and often clashing, identities. She was born a princess in Ethiopia. Her parents were Black, but she is white, for her mother stared intently at a picture of Saint George during her pregnancy. Fearful that her husband, the king, might consider the baby's skin color the result of an extramarital affair, Clorinda's mother gave the infant to the Muslim eunuch Arsete and ordered him to leave the country (*GL* 12.20–40). As David Quint has effectively pointed out,[66] Clorinda's story maps onto the geography of a religiously divided Ethiopia. At the time, Ethiopia was divided into Muslim and Christian areas. Clorinda's father ruled the latter region, which was itself schismatic as a branch of Coptic, not Catholic, Christianity. When Clorinda's mother left her to the eunuch Arsete, he raised the child according to his own faith, Islam. Clorinda discovers her origins only shortly before what proves to be her last mission, when Arsete finally tells her the real story of her life. She is, moreover, a woman and a warrior whom Tasso introduces with a masculine noun:

> ecco un guerriero
> (ché tal parea) d'alta sembianza e degna;
> e mostra, d'arme e d'abito straniero,
> che di lontan peregrinando vegna (2.38)

[behold a warrior (for so he seemed) of noble and commanding appearance; and he shows, by his weapons and his foreign clothes, that he is coming from traveling afar]

Tasso's use of the word "peregrinando" suggests that Clorinda's journey entails a spiritual dimension that is about to be fulfilled in the battle for Jerusalem, the city of pilgrimage *par excellence*. Her pilgrimage's conclusion in baptism immediately before her death at the hand of Tancredi in canto 12 can be regarded as the punishment of a rebel and as the metonymic reintegration of an unorthodox sect of Christianity:

> Ella, mentre cadea, la voce afflitta
> movendo, disse le parole estreme:
> parole ch'a lei un novo spirto ditta,
> spirto di fé, di carità, di speme:
> virtù, ch'or Dio le infonde, e se rubella
> in vita fu, la vuole in morte ancella.
> "Amico, hai vinto: io ti perdon ... Perdona
> tu ancora, al corpo no, che nulla pave,
> a l'alma sì; deh! per lei prega, e dona
> battesmo a me ch'ogni colpa lave." (12.65–66)

[She, while she was falling, with weakened voice was uttering her last words: words that a new spirit is teaching her, a spirit of faith, of charity, of hope: a grace that God now sheds upon her, and she has been a rebel in her life, He wants her now in death as His handmaiden. "Friend, you have won; I grant you pardon. Now you grant pardon too—not to my body, which nothing fears, but to my soul. Ah, pray for it, and give me baptism that it may cleanse my every sin."]

The word "rubella" ("rebel"), the same used to define the devils ("rebel souls") and the provinces under Muslim control ("rebelling provinces") earlier in the *Liberata*, is juxtaposed—and tied—in rhyming position to "ancella" ("handmaid"), pithily capturing the sudden reversal of Clorinda's condition in the last two lines of stanza 65. She is integrated into the body of the Catholic Church through the baptism her Coptic lineage prevented her from receiving at birth. Her demise—the consequence of her rebelliousness—literalizes the metaphoric death of her old self that, in Pauline and Augustinian terms, is required for a genuine conversion.[67] In her last moments, God inspires her with the three theological virtues: faith, hope, and charity. These three gifts transform her into an "ancella" of God, causing her to forgive Tancredi, who has just mortally wounded her, and to beseech forgiveness for the salvation of her own soul.

Erminia's Conversion Manqué

While there is no doubt that Clorinda experiences a conversion, the cases of Erminia and, as we shall see in the following section, of Armida are more equivocal. Erminia is related to Clorinda through a succession of reflections and disguises, skillfully interweaving the two women's stories with Tancredi's: while the Christian hero loves Clorinda, Erminia secretly loves him.[68] Daughter of the former king of Antioch, Erminia was Tancredi's prisoner for some time after the fall of Antioch, but she was eventually freed to return with her mother to an allied city. However, as Tasso writes, "se 'l corpo libertà riebbe, / fu l'alma sempre in servitude astretta" ["if her body regained its liberty, her soul was forever bound into slavery"] (*GL* 6.58). We first see her enclosed within the walls of Jerusalem looking at the Crusader army and indicating each warrior to Aladino (3.12–20, 3.37–40, and 3.58–63), the ruler of the holy city, in a scene that clearly echoes the passage in the *Iliad* where Helen points at the Greeks approaching Troy (*Iliad* 3.191–319). Erminia's love for Tancredi has placed her geographically at Jerusalem's wall, on the literal and figurative boundary between the Muslim and Christian systems. When she tries to bridge the distance that separates her from Tancredi, to heal his wounds after his first duel with Argante, she must disguise herself as Clorinda, the Frankish hero's beloved enemy (6.92–105).

As her attempt fails, Erminia eventually experiences the "errors" of the pastoral literary genre (*GL* 7.1–15), becoming a "donzella errante" ["wandering maid"] (19.91) and "cittadina de' boschi e pastorella" ["a shepherdess and citizen of the woods"] (19.98). After this evasion from the confines of her prison, Erminia can at last find Tancredi and restore him to health (19.103–14). Immediately before finding the beloved crusader almost mortally wounded and lying next to Argante's dead body, Erminia expresses a wish to return to her romantic servitude: "pietoso [Tancredi] gradisca il mio ritorno / e ne l'antica mia prigion m'accoglia!" ["But in his mercy may he take kindly my return and receive me back, into my old prison!"] (19.101). Although we can suppose that she will follow Tancredi as an "ancella errante" ["handmaiden"] (ibid.), Erminia exits the stage without a clear geographical destination and, given her allusive command to her ailing patient, with no evident trace of having converted: "'Salute avrai, prepara il guiderdone.' / Ed al suo capo, il grembo indi suppone" ["You shall have your health: make ready the fee. And then she makes of her lap a support for his head"] (19.114). Aside from its obvious physicality, the word "grembo" (literally, "womb") is particularly suggestive in that it evokes the garden hidden in the innermost part of Armida's palace (16.1) and, even more closely, the sensual scene in which Rinaldo's head rests on Armida's lap: "vede pur certo il vago e la diletta, / ch'egli è in grembo a la donna, essa a l'erbetta" ["it sees for certain the lover and his beloved, how he is in his lady's lap, she on the lawn"] (16.17); and "Sovra lui pende [Armida]; ed ei nel grembo molle / le posa il capo" ["she bends above him and he lays his head in her soft lap"] (16.18).[69] The erotic allusions underlying the two scenes involving Armida and Erminia significantly undermine an argument that the latter experiences a conversion akin to Clorinda's. I would, to the contrary, read Erminia's eroticized re-encounter with Tancredi as a sign that the kill-and/or-convert paradigm the Christians of the *Liberata* follow in subduing their opponents is not as implacable as is often assumed.

Let us recapitulate the exploration of the *Liberata*'s geography of the enemy conducted thus far. One character from Africa, Clorinda, is both converted and killed.[70] We have also seen Tasso's treatment of three characters from various regions of Asia: the Circassian Argante and the Turk Solimano, both of whom are killed without converting, and the Antiochian princess Erminia, who is not killed and does not convert. In view of the Christian universalism that allegedly underpins the *Liberata*'s ideology, readers would expect to see the kill-and/or-convert paradigm extended to all Muslim enemies. Erminia's case might then be considered the exception that proves the rule or a minor concession to the romance genre that Tasso apparently repudiates in his epic. Yet, as we shall see in the remainder of this chapter, Tasso's representation of Armida's reconciliation with Rinaldo and of Goffredo's treatment of Altamoro—two crucial points in the *Liberata*'s political geography—cautions the reader against one-sided assumptions concerning the ideology of the poem.

Armida Between East and West

Of the *Liberata*'s three female protagonists, Armida has drawn the greatest attention, from literary scholars as well as from artists including Guido Reni and Nicolas Poussin. Before I, too, turn to her reunion with Rinaldo, I would like to make one key point about her narrative and its implications for a geopolitical reading of the *Liberata*: the Armida episode extends significantly westward Tasso's geography of the enemy, as Carlo and Ubaldo travel beyond the Strait of Gibraltar to rescue Rinaldo from Armida's island in the Atlantic Ocean, and dramatically eastward, when Rinaldo kills the Indian King Adrasto. Armida, a sorceress from Damascus, first appears in canto 4, where she succeeds in sowing discord among the Crusaders and in diverting numerous Christian knights from their mission to conquer Jerusalem. The knights follow her to a castle by the Dead Sea, where they become her prisoners (*GL* 14.47–71). Rinaldo eventually sets the knights free, but finds himself entangled when Armida falls in love with him and decides to move with him to one of the Fortunate Isles (the Canary Islands) in the Atlantic Ocean.[71] For the crusade to succeed, Rinaldo must be freed from his enchanted captivity. Under guidance from Fortuna and the Magus of Ascalon, Ubaldo and Carlo rapidly sail across the Mediterranean Sea, witnessing the ruins of history, from Alexandria to Carthage, and the frailty of empires:

> Muoiono le città, muoiono i regni,
> copre i fasti e le pompe arena ed erba,
> e l'uom d'esser mortal par che si sdegni:
> oh nostra mente cupida e superba! (15.20)

> [Cities perish, kingdoms perish; sand and grass cover their monuments and displays; and it seems that man would be restive at being mortal; oh our greedy and aspiring minds!]

The two Crusaders eventually travel beyond the Pillars of Hercules, following the tracks of Dante's Ulysses: "ma quei segni sprezzò ch'egli [Ercole] prescrisse, / di veder vago e di saper, Ulisse" ["but Ulysses, eager to see and to learn, scorned those boundaries that he (Hercules) prescribed"] (15.25).[72]

In revising the *Liberata*, Tasso removed several stanzas initially intended for canto 15, stanzas that, as Ted Cachey has shown, were fashioned after Antonio Pigafetta's account of Magellan's circumnavigation of the world.[73] This excision deprives the poem of a deeper excursion into the territories recently colonized by Europeans, but does not entirely erase the traces of Tasso's interest in the century's new geographic discoveries. During the journey to Armida's island, Ubaldo asks Fortuna whether God had decided to neglect such a great part of the Earth. In response, she prophesies that the Christian faith will prevail over the "barbaric" laws and cults of the diverse peoples inhabiting the "mondo occulto" ["hidden world"] (GL 15.27):

> Gli soggiunse colei: "Diverse bande
> diversi riti ed abiti e favelle:
> altri adora le belve, altri la grande
> comune madre, il sole altri e le stelle;
> v'è chi d'abominevol vivande
> le mense ingombra scelerate e felle.
> E 'n somma ognun che 'n qua da Calpe siede
> barbaro è di costume ed empio di fede."
> "Dunque" a lei [Fortuna] replicava il cavaliero
> "quel Dio che scese ad illuminar le carte
> vuol ogni raggio ricoprir del vero
> a questa che del mondo è sì gran parte?"
> "No," rispose ella "anzi la fé di Piero
> fiavi introdotta ed ogni civil arte;
> né già sempre sarà che la via lunga
> questi da' vostri popoli disgiunga."
> [...]
> Un uom de la Liguria avrà ardimento
> a l'incognito corso esporsi in prima;
> né 'l minaccievol mar, né il dubbio clima,
> né s'altro di periglio o di spavento
> più grave e formidabile or si stima,
> faran che 'l generoso entro a i divieti
> d'Abila angusti l'alta mente accheti.
> Tu spiegherai, Colombo, a un nuovo polo
> lontane sì le fortunate antenne,
> ch'a pena seguirà con gli occhi il volo
> la fama ch'a mille occhi e mille penne.

Canti ella Alcide e Bacco, e di te solo
basti a i posteri tuoi ch'alquanto accenne,
ché quel poco darà lunga memoria
di poema dignissima e d'istoria. (15.28–29, 31–32)

[She continued to him: "Divers groups have divers customs and dress and speech: some worship beasts, some the great universal Mother; others the sun and the stars; there is one that loads its wicked and cruel tables with abominable repast: and in sum, every place that sits between here and Calpe is barbarous in customs, impious in faith." "Is it then the will (replied the knight to her—Fortune) of that God who descended to illuminate the pages that every ray of the truth be concealed for this that is so large part of the world?" "No (she answered); on the contrary, the faith of Peter will be introduced there, and every civilizing art: nor will it always be that the long voyage disjoins these people from our own. [...] A man of Liguria will have the daring first to set himself on the unknown course: and not the menacing howling of the wind, nor inhospitable seas, nor doubtful clime, nor anything else that now may be esteemed more formidable and filled with fear or danger will make the proud spirit content his lofty mind within the narrow prescriptions of Abyla. You, Columbus, will spread your fortunate sails so far toward an unknown pole that Fame (that has a thousand eyes and a thousand wings) will scarcely follow with her eyes your flight. Let her sing of Alcides and Bacchus, and of you let it be enough that she only give some hint for your posterity: for that little will give you a lasting memorial most worthy of Poetry and History."]

Fortuna's *ex post facto* prediction evokes the blend of religious zeal and intellectual curiosity that led Columbus to embark on his voyage. Tasso's poem celebrates the Genoese admiral's audacity and proclaims that his journey, which would lead to a drastic reshaping of the balance of power between nation-states and eventually usher in a new world order, is destined to expand Christianity into the Americas and to be engraved in the parchments of poetry and history. By the time Tasso began drafting the poem that would eventually become the *Gerusalemme Liberata*, Columbus's endeavors had been publicized through the reports of various Italian ambassadors in Spain and the works of historians like Pietro Martire d'Anghiera, author of the *De Orbe Novo Decades* and friend of both Columbus and Mercurino di Gattinara, and Giovan Battista Ramusio, who collected a variety of different travel books in three hefty volumes published in Venice in 1556. These works' success attests to the enormous popular interest in accounts of Columbus's journeys, and stories of other travelers, including Amerigo Vespucci, Vasco de Gama, and Ferdinand Magellan, also circulated widely.[74] Particularly relevant to understanding the relationship between Tasso and Columbus is the latter's argument, presented in his *Journal*, that the new world would provide the resources the Spanish monarchs needed to recover Jerusalem.[75] In the *Liberata*, Carlo and Ubaldo's journey across the Atlantic is similarly instrumental to the conquest of Jerusalem.

In the passage cited above, Tasso also echoes widespread accounts about some of the American Indians' practices, including cannibalism ("v'è chi d'abominevol vivande / le mense ingombra scelerate e felle," GL 15.28). Beginning with the dispatches of Columbus himself, travelers in the West Indies made anthropophagy a recurrent motif, contributing to a hegemonic narrative casting the European conquerors as a civilizing force against the indigenous populations' alleged barbarity.[76] Indeed, the dehumanization of natives through the overstatement of what Europeans considered their most atrocious practices became pivotal in formulating the rationale for the colonization that followed Columbus's first encounters. The debate over cannibalism eventually culminated in a famous essay by Michel de Montaigne, *Des Cannibales* (1578–80, nearly contemporary to the *Liberata*), in which the French thinker questioned the assumption that even a custom so horrific to Europeans as anthropophagy could qualify as a sign of barbarism.[77] By contrast, Tasso's Fortuna is far more ready to label the people beyond the Pillars of Hercules as barbaric ("E 'n somma ognun che 'n qua da calpe siede / barbaro è di costume ed empio di fede," ibid.).

At this juncture, it would be tempting to accept that the violation of Armida's garden, together with her possible conversion later in the poem, represents the subjugation of the New World by force. This interpretation would be wholly consistent with an argument that the *Liberata* reiterates in hendecasyllables the most ardent claims put forward by thinkers like the abovementioned Juan Ginés de Sepulveda, who perhaps more vehemently than any other sixteenth-century author devoted his energies to legitimizing the Spanish conquests overseas (a legitimizing project he continued in the face of significant opposition, especially from Bartolomé del Las Casas).[78] In his *Apología en favor del libro sobre las justas causas de la guerra* (published in Rome in 1550), Sepulveda contends that, because of their alleged barbaric customs and defects of reason, America's indigenous populations should be treated as natural slaves and must therefore obey—by coercion, if necessary—more rational and advanced peoples. According to Sepulveda, the Spaniards' role in fostering the cause of virtue over vice in the Americas would correspond to that of the Romans in antiquity: "Romani propter gloriam multa vitia comprimebant, id est, virtutes colebant. Ergo eadem potioreque ratione Hispani possunt Indos in suam ditionem redigere" ["The Romans gained glory repressing many vices; which is to say that they cultivated the virtues. The Spaniards, too, can therefore place the Indians under their (the Spaniards') authority"].[79]

To the contrary, in his *In Defense of the Indians* (ca. 1551), Las Casas noted that Sepulveda should not use "the tyranny of the Romans as a justification of our tyranny toward the Indians" ["Romanorum tyrannidem nobis obiiciat, ut nostram in Indos"].[80] He also highlighted an essential flaw that should have been obvious to any student of ancient history and any proponents of a legitimate universal monarchy: that, even at the time of its widest expansion, "the Roman Empire is and has always been marked by certain boundaries" ["Imperium enim Romanum certis limitibus distinctum est semperque fuit"], and "the Roman Emperors were not the lords of the whole world" ["Non ergo Romani caesares domini fuerunt totius orbis"].[81] Therefore, Las Casas argues that even if "it is true that the Roman Emperor is the universal lord of Christians, [...] to say that the Roman Emperor is the lawful master of the whole world is an utterly vain bit of nonsense and a way of deceiving the Emperors by flattery and an occasion for involving the world in strife" ["Verum tamen est Romanum Caesarem esse dominum universalem Christianorum (...) Asserere autem Romanum Imperatorem legitimum esse totius orbis dominum, vanissimum nugamentum est et adulatione depiere imperatores ansaque miscendi orbem dissidiis"].[82] Beyond dismissing the Roman Empire from its position as traditional model for the Habsburgs (and for their Ottoman rivals, as we have seen earlier in this chapter), Las Casas here also crucially posits that any claim to a universal government would lead to a world war rather than to peace, thus rejecting out of hand a pillar of medieval and early modern political theology. Much like Erasmus, who suggested that Muslims should be peacefully brought into the Christian faith, Las Casas believed that the American Indians should be redeemed by preaching to them, even if such efforts exposed the missionaries to the same risks that Christ's Apostles faced when the Church began its growth. To convert the indigenous peoples of the newly discovered lands, the Spanish kingdom should therefore organize peaceful task forces of pious messengers.

A middle ground between Sepulveda's and Las Casas's positions was articulated by another prominent Spanish jurist and theologian, Francisco de Vitoria, in his works *On the Evangelization of the Unbelievers* (1535) and

On the American Indians (1539). Vitoria's legal framework would become the mainstream imperial doctrine with respect to American policies. He asserted that Charles V's soldiers had the right to wage war only in self-defense or to defend innocents against tyranny.[83] Furthermore, although Vitoria stated that the Spaniards had the right to preach the Christian faith, they could not convert the local populations by force: "if the barbarians permit the Spaniards to preach the Gospel freely and without hindrance, then whether or not they accept the faith, it will not be lawful to attempt to impose anything on them by war" ["Si barbaru permittant Hispanos libere et sine impedimento praedicare Evangelium, sive illi recipient fidem sive non, non licet hac ratione intentare illis bellum"].[84]

Whether or not Tasso was directly familiar with the arguments of Sepulveda, Las Casas, or Vitoria,[85] his references to Columbus and the eventual conversion of the Amerindians inevitably involved the *Liberata* in the contemporary debate over the colonization of the West Indies. We should ask then, especially in light of the *Liberata*'s larger engagement with the politics of universal politico-religious monarchy, whether Tasso believed that the indigenous populations of the Americas should be converted through violence, and further, whether such a view can be logically supported by a reading of the Armida episode's conclusion. Two signs in the *Liberata* suggest that the answer to these questions is negative, contradicting the view that Tasso adopted a hard-nosed position à la Sepulveda.[86] We will first briefly look at how Carlo and Ubaldo face the threats they encounter on Armida's island, and then we will reconsider whether Armida actually converts to Christianity in one of the poem's last scenes.

In canto 14, the Magus of Ascalon tells Carlo and Ubaldo how they must proceed once they have landed on Armida's island (GL 14.71–79).[87] The Magus describes at some length the threats, including wild beasts and seductive sirens, that the two Crusaders will encounter on reaching their destination. He makes no mention of offensive weapons to deploy against these threats, warning Carlo and Ubaldo that the only tools they may use for their protection are a diamond shield to awaken Rinaldo from his languor and a wand ("verga") to fend off snakes and lions (14.73). In fact, when the travelers arrive on Armida's island, and Carlo prepares to attack a snake with his sword, Ubaldo immediately reproaches his companion for not heeding the Magus's instructions:

Già Carlo il ferro stringe e 'l serpe assale,
ma l'altro grida a lui: "Che fai? Che tente?

per isforzo di man, con arme tale
vincer avisi il difensor serpente?" (15.49)

[Already Charles is drawing his steel and is attacking the serpent; but the other shouts to him: "What are you doing? What are you trying to do? By manual strength, with weapons such as that, do you think to overcome the guardian snake?"][88]

Ubaldo then waves the wand that the Magus had given him and successfully chases the snake away. The magic wand has the same effect on the many other diverse, ferocious creatures that seek to halt the Crusaders' mission (15.50–52). With the Magus's decree that the adversaries that Carlo and Ubaldo face may not be defeated with deadly weapons, Tasso arguably implies that warfare is not the proper response to the challenges symbolized by Armida's island, be they the peoples of recently discovered lands, the pleasures of the senses that Rinaldo experienced with Armida, or other forms of intellectual temptations. Tasso's position thus seems to be closer to those of Vitoria and Las Casas than to the bellicose view espoused by Sepulveda.

As we reassess Armida's alleged conversion, we might well turn next to the role played by the Indian fighter Adrasto. He is one of Armida's paladins, and thus one of the last living emblems of the romance code that Rinaldo apparently abandoned when he deserted Armida on her island. In canto 19, we see Adrasto overwhelmed by Armida's beauty. Tasso's portrait captures Adrasto's ecstatic gaze and his resulting obliviousness to the collective goal of the war he is supposed to be fighting:

Vedele incontra il fero Adrasto assiso
che par ch'occhio non batta e che non spiri,
tanto da lei pendea, tanto in lei fiso
pasceva i suoi famelici desire. (GL 19.68)

[He sees seated opposite to her the fierce Adrastus, who seems not to bat an eye and not to breathe, so much he hung upon her, so fixed on her he fed his ravenous desire.]

This image strikingly resembles that of Rinaldo reveling in Armida's servitude during their stay on her island. Much like Adrasto, Rinaldo is transfixed and engaged in a narcissistic game, staring into Armida's eyes while she enjoys her own image in a mirror: "L'uno di servitù, l'altra d'impero / si gloria, ella in se stessa ed egli in lei" ["The one of them glories in his servitude, the other in her power, she in herself and he in her"] (16.21). Like Argillano and Sveno, both killed while pursuing Rinaldo's model (8.36 and 9.87), Adrasto can be considered an ill-starred avatar of the Christian hero.

The Indian warrior's final lines in the *Liberata* form a challenge to Rinaldo. Adrasto proclaims his devotion to Armida in religious terms; in accordance with the chivalric ethos he champions, the beloved lady becomes a deity ("nume") to whom the knight must pledge his vows:

Or solverò de la vendetta i voti
co 'l tuo capo al mio nume. Omai facciamo
di valor, di furor qui paragone,
tu nemico d'Armida ed io campione. (*GL* 20.102)

[Now with your head to my deity I shall discharge my vows of vengeance. Now let us make right here our proof of valor, of fury— Armida's enemy you, and I her champion.]

As expected, Adrasto will not live to discharge his vows. His sudden death and the futility of his oath elicit a sarcastic smile in the reader and a chilling sense of horror in Solimano, who witnessed Rinaldo's dreadful blow (20.103–4). The slaying of Adrasto appears to suggest the suppression of the chivalric values that he embodied and perhaps signals the spread of Christian arms to India, the kingdom lying at the easternmost boundary of the Earth, "i confin de l'aurora" ["borders of the dawn"] (19.125). His death, however, also serves as a prelude to the reconciliation between Rinaldo and Armida, which apparently insinuates the sorceress's conversion, but in fact leaves the door open to the chivalric individualism that Goffredo has tried to subdue since the poem's outset.

After quickly dispatching Solimano and Tisaferno (*GL* 20.113–16), Rinaldo can at last turn to Armida. He remembers that he had promised to be her knight once the battle for Jerusalem was won: "gli sovien che si promise in fede / suo cavalier quando da lei partia" ["he recalls that he faithfully pledged himself her knight when he parted from her"] (20.122). The "fede" Tasso mentions here is not the Christian faith, but the devotion that the chivalric code demanded a knight show toward his lady. Consistent with this promise of knightly service is Rinaldo's offer to help Armida regain a kingdom (possibly her uncle's): "non a gli scherni, al regno io ti riservo, / nemico no, ma tuo campione e servo" ["I keep you for a kingdom, not for spite—no enemy I, but your faithful champion knight"] (20.134).[89] It is surprising—and hardly congruent with the Christian imperialism that Tasso allegedly espoused—that Rinaldo would fight for Armida, especially before receiving any commitment on her part to become a Christian. When, in the following stanza, Rinaldo adds a sentence suggesting (obliquely) that he might marry her if only God helped her find the right path, the reservation does not amount to a *conditio sine qua non* for his chivalric service:

ed oh piacesse al Cielo
cha la tua mente alcun de' raggi suoi
del paganesimo dissolvesse il velo,
com'io farei che 'n Oriente alcuna
non t'agguagliasse di regal fortuna. (20.135)

[And oh if it should please Heaven that some of its rays should dissolve the veil of paganism from your mind, how would I see to it that nobody in the Orient should equal you for royal fortune.]

It is also worth noting that the rhyme words "riservo" and "servo" appear together only one other time in the poem, in canto 5, when Goffredo reserves for himself the authority to establish the number of knights (only ten) allowed to follow Armida after she successfully infiltrated the crusaders' camp: "non già di diece il numero trascenda, / ch'in questo il sommo imperio mi riservo: / non fia l'arbitrio suo per altro servo" ["The number, however, is not to exceed ten, for in this I reserve to myself the final word. In other matters his judgment will not be controlled"] (5.5). Ironically, dozens of Goffredo's soldiers disregard his "sommo imperio" and instead flock to Armida. Given Tasso's repetition of the same rhyming words in *GL* 20.134, it is conceivable that Rinaldo's reservation is just as likely to be disregarded. Thus his service on Armida's behalf would result in another diversion from the unifying politico-theological *telos* that purportedly underpinned Tasso's representation of the Crusade and, more broadly, of the clash between Islam and Christianity.

Furthermore, in describing himself as Armida's "campione," Rinaldo repeats the word that Adrasto used to describe himself when he challenged Rinaldo ("tu nemico d'Armida e io campione," *GL* 20.102). In canto 16, Ubaldo had mockingly used the same term to shame Rinaldo into returning to the world war being fought outside Jerusalem's walls:

Te solo, o figlio di Bertoldo, fuora
del mondo, in ozio, un breve angolo serra:
te sol de l'universo il moto nulla move,
egregio campion d'una fanciulla. (16.32)

[You alone, O son of Bertoldo, away from the world, in idleness, a
little corner of the earth shuts in; you alone are nothing moved by the
universal movement, the gallant champion of a girl.]

In short, as the Armida plotline draws close to its end, Rinaldo replaces his enemy Adrasto, who had previously replaced Rinaldo.

The Rinaldo-Adrasto mirroring relationship shows the ambiguity between the tropes of the chivalric ethos and the *Liberata*'s Christian epic motif of subjugation. If Rinaldo reclaims his chivalric role as Armida's "campione" by killing Adrasto, then how should we interpret Armida's promise to become Rinaldo's handmaid later in canto 20? We should first notice that here, in a remarkably short answer for a speaker who is ordinarily eloquent and loquacious, Armida famously echoes the words of the Virgin Mary to the angel Gabriel at the time of the Annunciation: "'Ecco l'ancilla tua: d'essa a tuo senno / dispon,' gli disse 'e le fia legge il cenno'" ["'Behold your handmaid; dispose of her at your discretion (she said), and your command shall be her law'"] (GL 20.136). Walter Stephens has explored in an elegant essay the presence of Saint Paul's letters, especially 1 Corinthians, and of Petrarch's *Canzoniere*, in Tasso's characterization of Armida in order to argue that her "subordination [...] embraces both Christianity and a specifically Pauline wifely virtue."[90] Armida's conversion would thus be consistent with an affirmation of the epic, patriarchal, and Christian teleology of the *Liberata*. Jo Ann Cavallo, on the other hand, has examined the Armida story in relation to similar episodes in other chivalric epics to contend that Armida's conversion for love does not suggest a deep acceptance of Christianity and that "Tasso does not have any intention of renouncing the elements of romance from his poem."[91] Cavallo's reading also implies that Tasso does not offer the all-encompassing epic closure around which the imperialist ideology of the poem purportedly gravitates.

Given the systematic ambiguity of the stanzas leading to Armida's reconciliation with Rinaldo and the slight but significant shift from the phrase "ancilla Domini" in Luke 1:38 to "ancilla tua" in the *Liberata*, I find Cavallo's interpretation of this scene quite persuasive. In my view, Armida's Marian imitation mirrors Rinaldo's decision to return to Armida's service as a champion dedicated to regaining her kingdom. It denotes, at best, a half-hearted conversion for love, not a genuine metamorphosis into an "ancilla Domini." That Armida intends to become Rinaldo's handmaid does not necessarily entail her conversion to Christianity, for she expressed the same desire earlier in the poem, after she had realized that he was about to return to fight in Palestine:

> Vattene, passa il mar, pugna, travaglia,
> struggi la fede nostra: anch'io t'affretto
> Che dico nostra? Ah non più mia! Fedele
> sono a te solo, idolo mio crudele. (GL 16.47).

> [Go your way; pass over the sea, fight, struggle, destroy our faith; I even urge you to it. Why do I say *our* faith? ah no more mine! I am faithful only to you, my idol cruel.][92]

If we are to take Armida's words at face value, it is clear that she had abandoned her previous faith to idolize Rinaldo well before her supposed conversion in the last canto. Even if we assume that she experienced a religious conversion, Rinaldo's promise to make Armida the greatest queen of the East nonetheless puts him at odds with Goffredo's imperial (and unified) authority.

Further, that the reconciliation between Rinaldo and Armida occurs far from the battlefield confirms the geopolitical distance between the strife for Jerusalem and the *hortus conclusus* (enclosed garden) where chance has led Armida's (and Rinaldo's) "wandering tracks":

> Giunge ella intanto in chiusa opaca chiostra,
> ch' a solitaria morte atta si mostra.
> Piacquele assai che 'n quelle valli ombrose
> l'orme sue erranti il caso abbia condutte. (GL 20.122–23).

> [Meanwhile she is arrived at a dark and sheltered spot that appears a place suitable for a solitary death. It pleased her well that chance had led her wandering tracks into those shadowy vales.]

Tasso's use of the word "erranti" in these lines echoes (and reverses) the "erranti" of the *Liberata*'s first stanza, when the poet suggested that Goffredo's primary task consisted in bringing his "compagni erranti" ("wandering companions") under his command. It would thus appear that Rinaldo and Armida's reunion could best be characterized as a reconciliation between an individual Christian and an individual non-Christian. Taking place as it does in geographical isolation from the overarching Christian-Islamic conflict, this reconciliation cannot be interpreted as a step toward global peace under Christian rule.

The foregoing analysis suggests that among the three main female characters of Tasso's poem, the Coptic princess Clorinda alone is (re-)assimilated within the body of the Church, when she receives the baptism she had been denied at birth. Both Erminia and Armida follow independent trajectories that take them into a more ambiguous relationship with the Catholic Church. These two female characters are not, however, the only "infidels" to survive the Crusade without embracing Christianity. A few *ottave* after the Armida episode's open-ended conclusion, Goffredo spares the Persian king Altamoro, allowing him to return to his kingdom. This last twist, to which I will dedicate the final pages of this chapter, further upsets the movement toward political and theological unity in Tasso's poem.

Sparing Altamoro and the Limits of Warfare

After Rinaldo and Armida leave the stage for an undisclosed location, Tasso returns to the battle for Jerusalem by describing Goffredo's slaying of Emireno, the commander of the Egyptian Army (*GL* 20.137–39). The last recognizable Muslim chief still on the battlefield is thus Altamoro, whom Tasso presents to the reader covered in blood, with his weapons irremediably damaged, and surrounded by scores of Crusaders (20.140). It is at this point that Goffredo orders his soldiers to spare Altamoro: "Grida egli a' suoi: 'Cessate; e tu, barone, / renditi, io son Goffredo, a me prigione'" ["He shouts to his troops: 'Give over; and you, baron, yield yourself my prisoner; I am Godfrey'"] (ibid).[93] Walter Stephens has shown the multilayered intertextual significance of Tasso's decision—here, in allowing Goffredo to spare Altamoro—to break from the ending of Classical epics such as the *Iliad* and the *Aeneid*: unlike its predecessors, the *Liberata* emphasizes conjugal love over filial piety. I would add to Stephens's discussion that Altamoro's survival, much like Tasso's ambiguous conclusion to the Erminia and Armida episodes, further undermines the argument that Tasso's epic flatly affirms the ideology of a Catholic, universal, empire. More plausibly, Tasso allows Altamoro to return to Persia because (as noted earlier in this chapter) the Persian-centered Safavid Empire had throughout the sixteenth century been a thorn in the eastern flank of the Ottoman Empire, the most imminent and formidable Islamic threat to Christendom.[94] It is true, then, that Tasso depicted a conflict between two enemies with universalist ambitions. But he did not write that conflict advancing a totalitarian Eurocentric world order. Such an outcome would have also been historically incongruous, since Saladin, the Sultan of Egypt, reconquered Jerusalem in 1187, less than a century after the First Crusade. Thus, rather than resolving its geopolitical enmities in a unified global monarchy, the *Liberata* hints at the tense coexistence of different religions, and multiple political actors, in the world arena.

Even before Altamoro replies to Goffredo's exhortation to surrender, Tasso inserts lines that suggest a geographical limit to the Christian commander's fame and, perhaps, undercut his authority: "ora ch'ode [Altamoro] quel nome, onde si spande / sì chiaro il suon da gli Etiòpi a l'Orse" ["now that he hears that name, the sound of which spreads itself so clear from the Ethiopes to the Bears"] (*GL* 20.141). First, the geographical and astronomical coordinates Tasso uses here draw a north-south line from Ethiopia to the North Pole ("l'Orse" are the constellations Ursa Major and Ursa Minor, which point to the polar star). This is undoubtedly a vast territory, encompassing Europe, Ethiopia, Anatolia, and the Mediterranean Sea. But it is also a territory that largely coincides with the historical boundaries of Christendom during the Byzantine Empire, before the rise of Islam. Here, then, Tasso appears to be implementing the above-cited theoretical point he made in the *Giudicio sopra la Conquistata,* where he wrote that "il poeta, a guisa di geografo, gli figura quasi la forma dell'imperio e i confini delle provincie soggiogate da gl'infedeli."[95]

Furthermore, the phrase "quel nome, onde si spande" clearly echoes canto 26 of *Inferno,* where Dante also rhymes the word "spande" with "grande": "Godi, Fiorenza, poi che se' sì grande / che per mare e per terra batti l'ali / e per lo 'nferno tuo nome si spande!" ["Rejoice, Florence, since you are so great that on sea and land you beat your wings, and your name spreads through Hell!"] (*Inf.* 26.1–3). This is not a flattering way to frame Goffredo's virtue, for in the opening of *Inferno* 26, these lines sarcastically refer to the reputation Florence has gained in Hell thanks to the numerous Florentine thieves whom Dante and Virgil encounter in the seventh *bolgia* (ditch) (*Inf.* 24–25). Tasso was of course quite familiar with canto 26 of *Inferno,* as he clearly evokes it in narrating Carlo and Ubaldo's journey to the Fortunate Isles. His choice to reference Dante's scathing critique of Florence in his praise of Goffredo can hardly be coincidental. Indeed, the reference to Florence's thieves might cast an intensely ironic light on Goffredo's refusal to accept Altamoro's offer of gold and jewels in return for his life: "'Me l'oro del mio regno e me le gemme / ricomperan de la pietosa moglie.' / Replica a lui Goffredo: 'Il Ciel non diemme / animo tal che di tesor s'invoglie'" ["'The gold of my kingdom will ransom me, and the jewels of my loving wife.' Godfrey replies to him: 'Heaven did not give me such a mind that it should be covetous of treasure'"] (GL 20.142).[96]

The echo of *Inferno* 26 could perhaps be described as one more "chink in [the] ideological armor" of the *Liberata*, to paraphrase David Quint's remark on Tancredi's inability to slay Clorinda's ghost in canto 13 (GL 13.40–46).[97] My conclusion, however, is that the damage Tasso inflicted to this ideological armor was far too extensive for it to sustain a vision of unified empire. Tasso's departures from a hegemonic narrative of universal conversion and political conquest are too numerous, and too extensive, to dismiss them as the byproduct of the poet's emotive identification with the enemy. It is instead more likely that, through the episodes discussed above, Tasso aimed to present a more nuanced politico-theological vision, a vision that acknowledged the attractions of a universal peace that would at last unite the *corpus mysticum* of the Church, while recognizing that such an outcome was unlikely to be achieved by military means.

Erminia's and Armida's conversions manqués, the Magus's warning that Carlo and Ubaldo must not use their swords to fight the threats of Armida's island, the uncertainty surrounding Rinaldo's relationship with Armida, Altamoro's survival—these exceptions to the ostensible guiding principle of forced conversion collectively indicate that political and military victories cannot entirely fulfill the objective of religious unity described in the dedicatory letter to the *De la dignità*. For all their ambiguity, these episodes express, I would argue, a fundamental longing for coexistence and the possibility of life beyond the horrors of war. Tasso was far too aware of the pervasiveness of conflicts in human history to embrace a naïve utopianism, but he also appears to suggest in his work that the cycle of enmity that underlies human conflicts can, however temporarily, be broken.

Goffredo's dream in canto 14 further limits the sense of what can be achieved through warfare. Here, following a long tradition of visionary literature that includes the likes of Scipio and Dante, the head of the Crusader army ascends to the heavens to learn that he will only achieve true peace when he becomes a "cittadin de la città celeste" ["citizen of the Heavenly city"] (GL 14.7). From the privileged standpoint of his dream, Goffredo also sees the Earth as a "picciolo cerchio" ["tiny circle"] and the ocean as a "bassa palude e breve stagno" ["low swamp and a narrow pond"] (14.10).[98] Thus, as Tasso narrates what, according to the prevailing ideology of his time, was a holy war against another faith (or sect) with equally universal ambitions, he also is the Renaissance poet who recalls most lucidly Dante's voice in the heaven of Saturn: even in the greatest epics, heroes come into sight as shadowy miniatures fighting in a bloody pantomime over what Dante defined as "l'aiuola che ci fa tanto feroci" ["The little threshing-floor which makes us so fierce"] (*Paradiso* 22.151).

Epilogue
The Mirror of the Friend?

I WILL CLOSE THIS BOOK by returning briefly to a text mentioned only in passing in the Introduction: *The Iliad*. Even a fragmentary summary of the *Iliad*'s chain of events shows that this foundational text is a microcosm containing all of the elements of the story that *The Enemy in Italian Renaissance Epic* tries to tell. From Paris's initial seduction of Helen, the *Iliad* is a tale of discord and betrayals—of father-son divisions, treachery and civil discord, madness and tyranny, and war. As in the family feuds of *Inferno* 28 and Pulci's *Morgante*, the *Iliad*'s initial personal slight turns a *hospes* into a *hostis* (to paraphrase Cicero's etymological excursus in book 1 of the *De officiis*) and triggers a military confrontation across two continents. This confrontation would serve as the archetype for many epic East-West conflicts to come, not least of which the Crusade as depicted by Tasso in the *Gerusalemme Liberata*. Tasso's fractious Crusader army recalls the Achaean force mustered by the tyrannical chieftain Agamemnon to reclaim Helen. This force is a heterogeneous coalition of militias riven by fierce internecine quarrels that temporarily drives its best warrior, Achilles, from the battlefield. The death of his closest friend Patroklos, however, finally sends Achilles back into battle and into a violent rage (*lyssa*, in Greek, from the word *lykos*, "wolf")[1] analogous to the wolfish madness experienced by Hercules in the ancient tragedies and by Orlando in Ariosto's *Furioso*.

But thematic links are only a small part of the story. There are two key reasons why I now turn to Homer's work. First, by engaging, however briefly, with this archetypal poem, I would like to suggest that my approach to the epic genre via the pervasive theme of enmity might also yield fruitful insights outside the confines of the Italian Renaissance. By extending this perspective to other literary traditions or epochs, we might gain a longer historical view of how enemies and enmity have been represented across national and chronological boundaries. Second, I should like to offer a counterpoint to the violent narratives that underlie my examination of the texts discussed thus far by revisiting Homer's account of the peaceful reconciliation, however tentative, between Achilles and Priam in book 24 of the *Iliad*. The scene's climactic resolution, I propose, is consistent with the argument this book advances, namely that enmity is an endogenous political pathology that violates the bonds of humanity.

In one of the twentieth century's most poignant readings of Homer's work, written shortly after Nazi troops invaded France in 1940, philosopher Simone Weil famously argued that the *Iliad* was the poem of force. More specifically, she asserted that for those "who perceive force, today as yesterday, as the very center of human history, the *Iliad* is the purest and the loveliest of mirrors."[2] Weil went on to define force pithily as "that x that turns anybody who is subjected to it into a thing. Exercised to the limit, it turns man into a thing in the most literal sense: it makes a corpse out of him."[3] In this latter sense, of course, Weil was right in recognizing the *Iliad* as a mirror of force: Homer's epic tells the stories of countless men who, struck by their enemies, bite the earth with blood gushing out of their wounds, quickly turning into corpses. Yet the *Iliad* is also, in the most dramatic fashion, a mirror of pity and human kindness. Indeed, the climax of the poem, in book 24, is a moment of intense pity built around a corpse, the "thing" into which Achilles had turned Hector, the prince of Troy. In this scene, Priam ransoms his son's body, which Achilles had repeatedly (and in vain) sought to defile in his efforts to sate his gnawing rage over the death of his beloved Patroklos.

In this well-known episode from the *Iliad*'s last book, Achilles has just performed the funeral rites in honor of Patroklos, but still keeps Hector's body in his hut, close to the Achaean ships (24.1–24). Grieving in Troy, but now encouraged by the divine messenger Iris, Priam decides to travel alone (accompanied only by a herald) to Achilles's camp and retrieve Hector's body (24.159–331), which had been kept intact by Apollo's intervention (24.18–21). Together with the funeral games for Patroklos in book 23, the gods' protection of Hector's corpse from Achilles's fury demonstrates the critical significance of proper burial in Homer's understanding of human civilization and thus underscores the prominence of Priam's mission in the *Iliad*'s moral structure. Escorted by the god Hermes, disguised as one of Achilles's soldiers, Priam enters the shelter of the man who until then had been his mortal foe, responsible for the death of many of his sons (24.339–475). Scholars have characterized Priam's journey as a *catabasis*—a descent into Hades, the pagan underworld, whose lord in this case is Achilles himself.[4] From this realm of death, however, arises an astonishing, if temporary, reconciliation. Priam kneels before

Achilles, kisses his hand, and begs him to release Hector's body, so that the Trojans may honor their dead prince with proper funeral rites (24.476–506).[5] In a poem that offers such an unvarnished representation of death, allowing an enemy to rest in peace—to return home, so to speak, and gain through a different path the *nostos* (triumphant, heroic return) that war has denied him—signifies an enduring glimmer of humanity amidst the horror of war.

Priam begins and ends his supplication by appealing to Achilles's memory of his own father, Peleus; struck by Priam's words, Achilles recognizes his old father's suffering in Priam's pain for his dead son: "Achilleus like the gods, remember your father, one who is of years like mine, and on the door-sill of sorrowful old age [. . .] Honour then the gods, Achilleus, and take pity upon me remembering your father, yet I am still more pitiful; I have gone through what no other mortal on earth has gone through; I put my lips to the hands of the man who has killed my children." So he spoke, and stirred in the other a passion of grieving for his own father (24.486–87 and 24.503–8).[6] The effect of Priam's words is intensified by Achilles's keen awareness that, because of his own imminent death, he will never see his father again. To Peleus, in other words, Achilles is as dead as Hector is to Priam. In the previous lines, Homer had obliquely alluded to the parallel between Priam and Peleus through a counterintuitive simile in which the poet had apparently compared the king of Troy to a fugitive murderer (24.480–84). This comparison becomes clearer and further emphasizes the Priam-Peleus correspondence if we remember that Peleus had been a fugitive for murdering his half-brother.[7] The simile also blurs the distinction between Priam, who is in fact traveling in his own land, and Achilles, who is the actual murderer in a foreign country. Homer's use of the phrase "heart of iron" later on further highlights the symmetry between Achilles and Priam. While in book 22 dying Hector had described Achilles as having a "heart of iron" after the Achaean warrior promised to let dogs and birds feast on Hector's body (22.357), in book 24 it is Achilles who uses the same phrase to address Priam for his willingness to meet the man (Achilles) who slayed so many of his sons (24.521).[8]

Thus, as they grieve, the two former enemies look at each other, as if through a mirror, admiring each other's appearance and acknowledging their shared fate: "Priam, son of Dardanos, gazed upon Achilles wondering at his size and beauty, for he seemed like an outright vision of gods. Achilleus in turn gazed on the Dardanian Priam and wondered, as he saw his brave looks and listened to him talking" (24.629–32). In this recognition scene, which Homer depicts almost as a religious epiphany, each sees in the other the reflected image of his own humanity; and Achilles and Priam glimpse the possibility of peace beyond the sorrows that force—to use Weil's key word—has brought upon their lives. Even the Stoics, who typically criticized Homer's Achilles for his proclivity toward intense passions, and particularly toward anger, praised his conduct here: Chrysippus of Soli, for instance, described Achilles's actions in *Iliad* 24 as therapeutic, in that they helped heal Priam's grief.[9] Achilles's therapeutic function in this episode amounts to a stunning reversal of the very meaning of his name, whose etymology is intimately associated with pain (*ákhos*).[10] From a Stoic (and cosmopolitan) standpoint, moreover, Achilles's kindness toward Priam highlights the bond that joins all humans, even those divided by fierce hostility. This scene, then, splendidly captures the contrast I outlined in the Introduction between Carl Schmitt's concept of the enemy as an essentially alien being and the cosmopolitan view of humankind as a universal community. Indeed, toward the end of their encounter, Achilles calls Priam *phile* ["friend" or "dear one"] (24.650), fulfilling the old man's earlier call for *philon* ["friendship" or "love"] (24.309).[11] In this chiastic relationship emerging from the abyss of war, Priam sees in Achilles a recipient for his paternal love and Achilles in Priam a recipient for his filial love. *Pace* Schmitt, some eight centuries before Christ would urge his followers to love their enemies (Matthew 5:44 and Luke 6:27), Homer had already told the story of two enemies who found the strength to love each other.

Notes

Introduction

1. All citations and translations are from Lucan, *Civil War*, trans. J. D. Duff (Cambridge: Harvard University Press, 1997):

Bella per Emathios plus quam civilia campos
iusque datum sceleri canimus, populumque potentem
in sua victrici conversum viscera dextra
cognatasque acies, et rupto foedere regni
certatum totis concussi viribus orbis
in commune nefas, infestisque obvia signis
signa, pares aquilas et pila minantia pilis.

For a detailed discussion of the poem's *exordium*, see Roche's commentary to Lucan, *De bello ciuili*, ed. Paul Roche (Oxford: Oxford University Press, 2009), 91–107. On Lucan's extensive use of corporeal imagery, see: Martin Dinter, *Anatomizing "Civil War": Studies in Lucan's Epic Technique* (Ann Arbor: The University of Michigan Press, 2012), especially 19–21 on Lucan's use of the word "*caput*"; Shadi Bartsch, *Ideology in Cold Blood: A Reading of Lucan's Civil War* (Cambridge: Harvard University Press, 1997), especially 10–47; Michael Lapidge, "Lucan's Imagery of Cosmic Dissolution," *Hermes* 107.3 (1979): 344–70; David Quint, *Epic and Empire: Politics and Generic Form from Virgil to Milton* (Princeton, NJ: Princeton University Press, 1993), 140–47; and Elaine Fantham, "Discordia Fratrum: Aspects of Lucan's Conception of Civil War," in *Citizens of Discord: Rome and Its Civil Wars*, ed. Brian W. Breed, et al. (Oxford: Oxford University Press, 2010), 207–20. More broadly on the use of violent body imagery in first-century Roman literature, see Glenn Most, "*Disiecti membra poetae*: The Rhetoric of Dismemberment in Neronian Poetry," in *Innovations of Antiquity*, eds. Ralph Exeter and Daniel Selden (New York: Routledge, 1992), 391–419.

2. All citations and translations are from Virgil, *Aeneid*, trans. H. Rushton Fairclough (Cambridge: Harvard University Press, 1999). On the contrast between this passage of the *Aeneid* and the beginning of *Civil War*, see Joseph Reed, "The *Bellum Civile* as a Roman Epic," in *Brill's Companion to Lucan*, ed. Paolo Asso (Leiden: Brill, 2011), 21–31, especially 24.

3. Seneca, *De clementia*, in *Moral Essays*, trans. John Basore (Cambridge: Harvard University Press, 1998).

4. Cf. Shadi Bartsch, *The Mirror of the Self: Sexuality, Self-Knowledge, and the Gaze in the Early Roman Empire* (Chicago: The University of Chicago Press, 2006), especially 183–88 on the *De Clementia*, and 24–26 and 203–4 on the Apollonian injunction to "know thyself." For a history of the injunction "know thyself," see Pierre Courcelle, *Connais-toi toi-même; de Socrate à saint Bernard* (Paris: Études augustiniennes, 1974–75).

5. Carl Schmitt, *The Concept of the Political*, trans. George Schwab (Chicago: The University of Chicago Press, 2007), 27.

6. Ibid., 28.

7. Ibid., 28–29. Schmitt would then return to the question of the enemy in the 1963 *Theory of the Partisan*, where he grapples with what he described as "the problem of the partisan," which he viewed as a distinctly modern phenomenon whose emergence he traced to the anti-Napoleonic guerrilla war waged by the Spanish people between 1808 and 1813. See Carl Schmitt, *Theory of the Partisan: Intermediate Commentary on the Concept of the Political*, trans. G. L. Ulmen (New York: Telos Press, 2007), 3–4. For a wide-ranging overview of Schmitt's life and works, see Gopal Balakrishnan, *Enemy: An Intellectual Portrait of Carl Schmitt* (London: Verso, 2000), especially 101–15. For a lucid critique of Schmitt's clear-cut distinction between private and public enemy, see David Lloyd Dusebury, "Carl Schmitt on *Hostis* and *Inimicus*: A Veneer for Bloody-Mindedness," *Ratio Juris* 28.3 (September 2015): 431–39. See also Jacques Derrida, *Politics of Friendship*, trans. George Collins (London: Verso, 1997), 83–93.

8. On the definition of civil war in relation to interstate conflicts, see Cécile Fabre, *Cosmopolitan War* (Oxford: Oxford University Press, 2012), 130–65, especially 132.

9. Schmitt, *The Concept of the Political*, 28.

10. Moreno Morani, et al., *Amicus (Inimicus) Hostis. Le radici concettuali della conflittualità "privata" e della conflittualità "politica"* (Milan: Giuffrè Editore, 1992), especially 33–40.

11. Cf. Nicole Loraux, "*Oikeios polemos*: La guerra nella famiglia," *Studi Storici* 28.1 (Jan.–Mar. 1987): 5–35; Giorgio Agamben, *Stasis: Civil War as a Political Paradigm* (Homo Sacer II, 2), trans. Nicholas Heron (Stanford, CA: Stanford University Press, 2015), 1–24. For an insightful discussion of the relationship between family loyalty and enmity (and on the tension between private and civic duty), particularly in Sophocles's *Antigone*, see Martha Nussbaum, *The Fragility of Goodness: Luck and Tragedy in Greek Tragedy and Philosophy* (Chicago: The University of Chicago Press, 1986), 54–67.

12. Cf. Morani, *Amicus (Inimicus) Hostis*, 38–40, who refers to Aeschylus's *Prometheus* (line 120) and Sophocles's *Philoctetes* (lines 1302–3), among other texts.

13. All citations and translations are from Cicero, *De officiis*, trans. Walter Miller (Cambridge, MA: Harvard University Press, 2005). On Cicero's definition and its influence, see: Morani, *Amicus (Inimicus) Hostis*, 43–55; Ian Baucom, "Cicero's Ghost: The Atlantic, the Enemy, and the Laws of War," in *States of Emergency: The Object of American Studies*, ed. Russ Castronovo and Susan Gillman (Chapel Hill: University

of North Carolina Press, 2009), 124–42; and Dusebury, "Carl Schmitt on *Hostis* and *Inimicus*," 433–38.

14. On the influence of Cicero's *De officiis* in the early modern age, see Baucom, "Cicero's Ghost."

15. Cicero, *Philippics*, ed. and trans. D. R Shackleton Bailey (Cambridge, MA: Harvard University Press, 2009).

16. All citations and translations of the *Hercules Furens* are from Seneca, *Tragedies*, trans. John Fitch (Cambridge, MA: Harvard University Press, 2002–4), vol. 1.

17. All citations and translations of the *De beneficiis* are from Seneca, *De beneficiis*, trans. John Basore, in *Moral Essays* (Cambridge, MA: Harvard University Press, 1989), vol. 3.

18. Giovanni Boccaccio, *Famous Women*, ed. and trans. Virginia Brown (Cambridge, MA: Harvard University Press, 2001), 94, and 126 and 132.

19. Coluccio Salutati, *De laboribus Herculis*, ed. B. L. Ullmann (Zurich: Thesauri Mundi, 1951), 134.

20. Leon Battista Alberti, *Momus*, eds. Virginia Brown and Sarah Knight, and trans. Sarah Knight (Cambridge, MA: Harvard University Press, 2003), 80 and 82.

21. Schmitt, *The Concept of the Political*, 29.

22. See Juan Ginés de Sepulveda, *Cohortatio ad Carolum V*, ed. J. M. Rodríguez Peregrina, in *Obras Completas* (Pozoblanco, Esp.: Exmco. Ayuntamento de Pozoblanco, 2003), vol. 7, 335 (chapter 9). See also Carl Schmitt, *Glossario*, translated into Italian by Petra Dal Santo (Milan: Giuffrè Editore, 2001), 35 (October 3, 1947).

23. For Peter the Venerable, see an anthology of his writings in James Kritzeck, ed., *Peter the Venerable and Islam* (Princeton, NJ: Princeton University Press, 1964), especially 215–16. I will further discuss Peter's role in anti-Islamic polemics in chapter 1. For Piccolomini, see his July 1453 letter to Nicholas of Cusa in Rudolf Wolkan, ed., *Der Briefwechsel des Eneas Silvius Piccolomini*, in *Fontes Rerum Austriacarum* (Vienna: A. Hölder, 1909–18), ser. 2, vol. 68, 201. I will return to Piccolomini's epistles in chapter 4.

24. On the etymology of the words "church" and "catholic," see Isidore of Seville, *Etymologies*: "'Church' (*ecclesia*) is a Greek word that is translated into Latin as 'convocation' (*convocatio*), because it calls (*vocare*) everyone to itself. 'Catholic' (*catholicus*) is translated as universal (*universalis*), after the term καξ ὅλου, that is, 'with respect to the whole,' for it is not restricted to some part of a territory, like a small association of heretics, but it is spread widely throughout the entire world" ["Ecclesia Graecum est, quod in Latinum vertitur convocatio, propter quod omnes ad se vocet. Catholica, universalis, APO TOU KATH OLON, id est secundum totum. Non enim sicut conventicula haereticorum in aliquibus regionum partibus coartatur, sed per totum terrarum orbem dilatata diffunditur"] (Book VIII, i, 1). All Latin citations from the *Etymologies* are from The Latin Library, http://www.thelatinlibrary.com/isidore.html. All translations of the *Etymologies* are from *The Etymologies of Isidore of Seville*, trans. Stephen A. Barney, et al. (Cambridge: Cambridge University Press, 2006).

25. Unless otherwise noted, all biblical passages are cited from the Douay-Rheims 1899 American Edition (DRA) at http://www.biblegateway.com/. Cf. Michelle V. Lee, *Paul, the Stoics, and the Body of Christ* (Cambridge: Cambridge University Press, 2006), 27–102; Dale Martin, "The Promise of Teleology, the Constraints of Epistemology, and Universal Vision in Paul," in *St. Paul among the Philosophers*, eds. John Caputo and Linda Martin Alcoff (Bloomington: Indiana University Press, 2009), 91–108; Karin B. Neutel, *A Cosmopolitan Ideal: Paul's Declaration 'Neither Jew Nor Greek, Neither Slave Nor Free, Nor Male and Female' in the Context of First-Century Thought* (London: Bloomsbury, 2015).

26. Martha Nussbaum, "Patriotism and Cosmopolitanism," in *For Love of Country: Debating the Limits of Patriotism*, ed. Joshua Cohen (Boston: Beacon Press, 1996), 3–17; eadem, "Kant and Stoic Cosmopolitanism," in *Perpetual Peace: Essays on Kant's Cosmopolitan Ideal*, eds. James Bohman and Matthias Lutz-Bachmann (Cambridge, MA: The MIT Press, 1997), 25–57. Among the most valuable works on the foundations of cosmopolitanism, see also Anthony Pagden, "Stoicism, Cosmopolitanism, and the Legacy of European Imperialism," in *Constellations* 7.1 (2000): 3–22; Denis Cosgrove, "Globalism and Tolerance in Early Modern Geography," *Annals of the Association of American Geographers* 93.4 (2003): 852–70; Eric Brown, "The Stoic Invention of Cosmopolitan Politics," delivered as a lecture at "Cosmopolitan Politics: On the History and Future of a Controversial Idea," Frankfurt am Main, 2006 (accessed online at https://pages.wustl.edu/files/pages/imce/ericbrown/invention.pdf on December 22, 2016); Daniel S. Richter, *Cosmopolis: Imagining Community in Late Classical and the Early Roman Empire* (Oxford: Oxford University Press, 2011); Katja Maria Vogt, *Law, Reason, and the Cosmic City: Political Philosophy in the Early Stoa* (Oxford: Oxford University Press. 2008); Tamara T. Chin, "What is Imperial Cosmopolitanism? Revisiting *Kosmpopolitēs* and *Mundanus*," in *Cosmopolitanism and Empire: Universal Rulers, Local Elites, and Cultural Integration in the Ancient Near East and Mediterranean*, ed. Myles Lavan, et al. (Oxford: Oxford University Press, 2016), 129–51; and David Armitage, "Cosmopolitanism and Civil War," in *Cosmopolitanism and the Enlightenment*, eds. Joan-Pau Rubiés and Neil Safier (Cambridge: Cambridge University Press, forthcoming). Primarily on the modern implications of cosmopolitanism, see Jürgen Habermas, *The Postnational Constellation: Political Essays*, ed. and trans. Max Pensky (Cambridge: Polity, 2001); Kwame Appiah, *Cosmopolitanism: Ethics in a World of Strangers* (New York: W.W. Norton, 2006); Fabre, *Cosmopolitan War*; and eadem, *Cosmopolitan Peace* (Oxford: Oxford University Press, 2016); David D. Kim, *Cosmopolitan Parables: Trauma and Responsibility in Contemporary Germany* (Evanston, IL: Northwestern University Press, 2017), especially 29–56.

27. Diogenes Laertius, *Lives of Eminent Philosophers*, ed. R. D. Hicks (Cambridge, MA: Harvard University Press, 1925), book 6, chapter 2.

28. Vogt, *Law, Reason, and the Cosmic City*, 65–110.

29. Marcus Aurelius, *The Meditations of Marcus Aurelius*, trans. A. S. L. Farquharson (Oxford: Oxford University Press, 1989), 24 (4.4). See also Cicero, *De officiis* III, vi, 26–32; and Seneca, *De beneficiis* I, xv, 2; IV, xviii, 2–3.

30. Ilaria Ramelli, ed., *Hierocles the Stoic: Elements of Ethics, Fragments, and Excerpts*,

trans. David Konstan (Atlanta: Society of Biblical Literature, 2009), 91. Cf. Cicero, *De officiis* I, xvii, 54; and *De amicitia* V, 19–20.

31. Nussbaum, "Kant and Stoic Cosmopolitanism," 32–33.

32. Armitage, "Cosmopolitanism and Civil War," especially 6–10.

33. Dante, *De Vulgari Eloquentia*, trans. Steven Botterill (Cambridge: Cambridge University Press, 1996), 1.6.3. The Latin text is taken from Dante, *De Vulgari Eloquentia*, ed. Pier Vincenzo Mengaldo, in *Opere minori* (Milan: Ricciardi, 1979), 5:2:50–52. On Dante's cosmopolitanism, see Ernst H. Kantorowicz, *The King's Two Bodies: A Study in Medieval Political Theology* (Princeton, NJ: Princeton University Press, 1957), 451–95; and Gregory Stone, "Sodomy, Diversity, and Cosmopolitanism: Dante and the Limits of the Polis," *Dante Studies* 123 (2005): 89–132, especially 116–29.

34. For an overview of the political history in late medieval and early modern Italy, see Quentin Skinner, *The Foundations of Modern Political Thought* (Cambridge: Cambridge University Press, 1978), 1:3–189; Philip Jones, *The Italian City-State: From Commune to Signoria* (Oxford: Clarendon Press, 1997), 333–650; Christine Shaw, *Popular Government and Oligarchy in Renaissance Italy* (Leiden: Brill, 2006); and Dale Kent, *Friendship, Love, and Trust in Renaissance Florence* (Cambridge, MA: Harvard University Press, 2009).

35. Michael Murrin, *History and Warfare in Renaissance Epic* (Chicago: Chicago University Press, 1994); Murrin, *Allegorical Epic: Essays in its Rise and Decline* (Chicago: The University of Chicago Press, 1980); Quint, *Epic and Empire*; Jo Ann Cavallo, *The Romance Epics of Boiardo, Ariosto, and Tasso: From Public Duty to Private Pleasure* (Toronto: Toronto University Press, 2004); Cavallo, *The World Beyond Europe in the Romance Epics of Boiardo and Ariosto* (Toronto: Toronto University Press, 2013); Dennis Looney, *Compromising the Classics: Romance Epic Narrative in the Italian Renaissance* (Detroit: Wayne State University Press, 1996); and Tobias Gregory, *From Many Gods to One: Divine Action in Renaissance Epic* (Chicago: The University of Chicago Press, 2006).

36. Schmitt, *The Concept of the Political*, 26: "the specific political distinction to which political actions and motives can be reduced is that between friend and enemy."

37. See, for instance, the volume of collected essays *Political Theology and Early Modernity*, eds. Graham Hamill and Julia Reinhard Lupton (Chicago: The University of Chicago Press, 2012), and the Autumn 2006 issue of the journal *Religion and Literature*, also eds. Hamill and Lupton. A few other studies have considered analogies and differences between Schmitt's and Machiavelli's political writings: see John McCormick, "Addressing the Political Exception: Machiavelli's 'Accidents' and the Mixed Regime," *American Political Science Review* 87.4 (1993): 888–900; Gabriele Pedullà, "Una 'tirannide elettiva.' Ovvero: ciò che gli umanisti e Machiavelli possono insegnarci sulla dittatura e lo 'stato d'eccezione,'" in *Il governo dell'emergenza. Poteri straordinari e di guerra in Europa tra XVI e XX secolo*, ed. Francesco Benigno (Rome: Viella, 2007), 35–73; and Andrea Moudarres, "On the Threshold of Law: Dictatorship and Exception in Machiavelli and Schmitt," *I Tatti Studies* 18.2 (Fall 2015): 349–70.

38. Julia Reinhard Lupton, *Citizen-Saints: Shakespeare and Political Theology*

(Chicago: The University of Chicago Press, 2005); Jacques Lezra, *Wild Materialism: The Ethic of Terror and the Modern Republic* (New York: Fordham University Press, 2010); Victoria Kahn, *The Future of Illusion: Political Theology and Early Modern Texts* (Chicago: The University of Chicago Press, 2014); and Nichole E. Miller, *Violence and Grace: Exceptional Life between Shakespeare and Modernity* (Evanston, IL: Northwestern University Press, 2014).

39. In view of this book's scope, I have found Victoria Kahn's discussion of Ernst Kantorowicz's reading of Dante's *Commedia* particularly thought-provoking: see Kahn, *The Future of Illusion*, 75–80. It is also worth noting that Julia Reinhard Lupton and Nichole Miller dedicate prominent sections of their works to Saint Paul's epistles. See Lupton, *Citizen-Saints*, 21–48, and Miller, *Violence and Grace*, 161–86.

40. Partial exceptions are the above-mentioned section dedicated to Kantorowicz's reading of Dante in Kahn's *The Future of Illusion* and Justin Steinberg's *Dante and the Limits of Law* (Chicago: The University of Chicago Press, 2013), especially 5–8.

1. Between Fathers and Sons

1. All cited translations of the *Monarchia* (*Mn.*) are from Dante Alighieri, *Monarchia*, trans. Richard Kay (Toronto: Pontifical Institute of Medieval Studies, 1998). The Latin text is from Dante Alighieri, *Monarchia*, ed. Prue Shaw (Florence: Le Lettere, 2009): "Et ad evidentiam eius quod queritur advertendum quod, quemadmodum est finis aliquis ad quem natura producit pollicem, et alius ab hoc ad quem manum totam, et rursus alius ab utroque ad quem brachium, aliusque ab omnibus ad quem totum hominem; sic alius est finis ad quem singularem hominem, alius ad quem ordinat domesticam comunitatem, alius ad quem viciniam, et alius ad quem civitatem, et alius ad quem regnum, et denique optimus ad quem uniersaliter genus humanum Deus ecternus arte sua, que natura est, in esse producit."

2. All translations of Aristotle's works are from *The Complete Works of Aristotle*, ed. John C. Barnes (Princeton, NJ: Princeton University Press, 1984).

3. See Livy, *Ab urbe condita* 2.3.8–12; John of Salisbury, *Policraticus* 4.1 and 5.2. On the concept of the body politic, see Otto Gierke, *Political Theories of the Middle Ages*, trans. Frederic Maitland (Cambridge: Cambridge University Press, 1927), especially 7–8 on the macrocosm-microcosm analogy; and Ernst H. Kantorowicz, *The King's Two Bodies* (Princeton, NJ: Princeton University Press, 1957). See also Leonard Barkan, *Nature's Work of Art: The Human Body as Image of the World* (New Haven, CT: Yale University Press, 1975), 8–115.

4. See Bernardus Silvestris, *Cosmographia*, in *Poetic Works*, ed. and trans. Winthrop Wetherbee (Cambridge: Harvard University Press, 2015), especially 152–53, describing man as a "second universe" ("alter mundus"); and Alan of Lille, *The Plaint of Nature*, in *Literary Works*, ed. and trans. Winthrop Wetherbee (Cambridge: Harvard University Press, 2013), especially 70–71: "Ego illa sum quae ad exemplarem mundanae machinae similitudinem hominis exemplavi naturam" ["I am she who modeled the nature of man in imitation of the model of the cosmic order"]. On the influence of Alan de Lille and Bernardus Silvestris on Dante, see Giuseppe Mazzotta, *Dante, Poet of the Desert: History*

and Allegory in the Divine Comedy (Princeton, NJ: Princeton University Press, 1979), 14–65, especially 24–25.

5. All cited translations of the *Summa Theologiae* are from Thomas Aquinas, *Summa Theologica*, trans. the Fathers of the English Dominican Province (New York: Benziger, 1948). The Latin text is from Corpus Thomisticum, Fundación Tomás de Aquino and Universidad de Navarra, http://www.corpusthomisticum.org/iopera.html (accessed August 17, 2016).

6. All citations from the *De officiis* are taken from Cicero, *De officiis*, trans. Walter Miller (Cambridge: Harvard University Press, 1913). As mentioned in the Introduction, Dante himself described the entire world as his "patria" ("fatherland") in the *De Vulgari Eloquentia* (1.6.3). On Dante and Cicero, see: Mazzotta, *Dante, Poet of the Desert*, 76–83; Guy Raffa, "Enigmatic 56's: Cicero's Scipio and Dante's Cacciaguida," *Dante Studies* 110 (1992): 121–34; and Claudia Di Fonzo, *Dante e la tradizione giuridica* (Rome: Carocci, 2016), 97–156.

7. See also *Convivio*, in *Opere minori*, ed. Cesare Vasoli and Domenico De Robertis (Milan: Ricciardi, 1995), 4.4.1–7, where Dante articulates the same concept. On Dante's vision of a universal empire and the emperor's authority in *Monarchia*, see: Francesco Ercole, *Il pensiero politico di Dante* (Milan: Edizioni Alpes, 1928), 2:9–164; Bruno Nardi, *Saggi di filosofia dantesca* (1930; Florence: La Nuova Italia, 1967), 215–75; Etienne Gilson, *Dante the Philosopher*, trans. David Moore (London: Sheed & Ward, 1948), 162–224; Alessandro Passerin d'Entrèves, *Dante as a Political Thinker* (Oxford: Oxford University Press, 1952), 26–51; Donna Mancusi-Ungaro, *Dante and the Empire* (New York: Peter Lang, 1987); and Albert Ascoli, *Dante and the Making of the Modern Author* (Cambridge: Cambridge University Press, 2008), especially 248–63. On the polemics surrounding the *Monarchia*, see Anthony Cassell, *The "Monarchia" Controversy* (Washington: The Catholic University of America Press, 2004).

8. On the relationship between *charitas* and justice, see *Paradiso* 18.91–93. Cf. Vittorio Montemaggi, "'E 'n sua volontade è nostra pace': Peace, Justice and the Trinity in the *Commedia*," in *War and Peace in Dante*, ed. John C. Barnes and Daragh O'Connell (Dublin: Four Court Press, 2015), 195–225. On Dante's understanding of peace in *Monarchia*, see in the same volume Matthew Kempshall, "The Utility of Peace in 'Monarchia,'" 141–72. See also: Gian Roberto Sarolli, *Prolegomena alla "Divina Commedia"* (Florence: Olschki, 1971), 291–98; Giuseppe Mazzotta, *Dante's Vision and the Circle of Knowledge* (Princeton, NJ: Princeton University Press, 1993), 86–87; Ugo Dotti, *La Divina Commedia e la città dell'uomo* (Rome: Donzelli Editore, 1996), especially 110–15; and Gregory Stone, *Dante's Pluralism and the Islamic Philosophy of Religion* (New York: Palgrave Macmillan, 2006), 25–41.

9. Cf. Mark 12:29: "Hear, O Israel: the Lord thy God is one God" ["audi Israhel Dominus Deus noster Deus unus est"]; and Deut. 6:4: "Hear, O Israel, the Lord our God is one Lord" ["audi Israhel Dominus Deus noster Dominus unus est"].

10. See Jane Chance, "Monstra-naturalità distorte: Betram dal Bornio, Ecuba," in *I monstra nell'Inferno dantesco: tradizione e simbologie* (Spoleto: Centro italiano di studi sull'alto Medioevo, 1997), 235–75, especially 252–53.

11. Cf. John C. Barnes, "'Guerre conviene surgere': Dante and War," in *War and Peace in Dante*, 11–32; and in the same volume his "Storming the Barbican: A Military Reading of *Inferno* VIII-IX," 73–94; Zygmunt G. Barański, "'E cominciare stormo': Notes on Dante's Sieges," in *"Legato con amore in un volume"*: *Essays in Honour of John A. Scott*, eds. John Kinder and Diana Glenn (Florence: Olschki, 2013), 175–203; and Robert Hollander, "Dante and the Martial Epic," *Mediaevalia* 12 (1986): 67–91.

12. Mazzotta, *Dante's Vision and the Circle of Knowledge*, 215; and Montemaggi, "'E 'n sua volontade è nostra pace,'" 197–98.

13. See *Convivio*, 2:11:80–81. All translations are from Dante, *Il Convivio*, ed. and trans. Richard Lansing (New York: Garland, 1990).

14. On the father figures in Dante's works, see: John Freccero, "The Eternal Image of the Father," in *The Poetry of Allusion: Virgil and Ovid in Dante's "Commedia,"* ed. Rachel Jacoff and Jeffrey Schnapp (Stanford, CA: Stanford University Press, 1991), 62–76; Warren Ginsberg, *Dante's Aesthetics of Being* (Ann Arbor: University of Michigan Press, 1999), 96–114; and Ricardo Quinones, *Foundation Sacrifice in Dante's "Commedia"* (University Park: Pennsylvania State University Press, 1994), 102–22.

15. *Inferno* 28.37–42:

> Un diavolo è qua dietro che n'accisma
> sì crudelmente, al taglio de la spada
> rimettendo ciascun di questa risma,
> quand'avem volta la dolente strada;
> però che le ferite son richiuse
> prima ch'altri dinanzi li rivada

> [There is a devil back there who carves us so cruelly, putting the edge of his sword to each of this ream once we have circled through the suffering road, for the wounds have closed before any confronts him again.]

All quotations from the *Commedia* are taken from Dante Alighieri, *La Commedia secondo l'antica vulgata*, ed. Giorgio Petrocchi, 4 vols. (Florence: Le Lettere, 1994); the translations are from Dante Alighieri, *The Divine Comedy of Dante Alighieri*, ed. and trans. Robert Durling, notes by Ronald Martinez and Robert Durling, 3 vols. (Oxford: Oxford University Press, 1996–2011). All further parenthetical in-text citations indicate book, canto, and verse.

16. On Dante's sources for the first section of the canto, see Mario Fubini, "Canto XXVIII," in *Lectura Dantis Scaligera. Inferno* (Florence: Le Monnier, 1967), 997–1021; Mazzotta, *Dante's Vision and the Circle of Knowledge*, especially 89–90; Paola Allegretti, "Canto XXVIII," in *Inferno. Lectura Dantis Turicensis*, eds. Georges Güntert and Michelangelo Picone (Florence: Franco Cesati Editore, 2000), 393–406; and Piero Beltrami, "L'epica di Malebolge," *Studi Danteschi*, LXV (2000): 119–52.

17. See Maria Esposito Frank, "Dante's Muhammad: Parallels between Islam and Arianism," *Dante Studies* 125 (2007): 185–206, on the significance of the Arian heresy in medieval European polemics against Islam; and, in the same issue, Karla Mallette, "Mu-

hammad in Hell," 207–24, on Dante's possible use of a passage from the Qur'an itself in his depiction of Muhammad. On Dante and Islam, and on the portrait of Muhammad in *Inferno* 28, see also Miguel Asín Palacios, *Islam and the Divine Comedy*, trans. Harold Sutherland (New York: Dutton, 1926); Bruno Nardi, *Saggi di filosofia dantesca* (Florence: La Nuova Italia, 1967); Enrico Cerulli, *Nuove ricerche sul Libro della Scala e la conoscenza dell'Islam in Occidente* (Vatican City: Biblioteca Apostolica Vaticana, 1972); Rasha Al-Sabah, "*Inferno* XXVIII: The Figure of Muhammad," *Yale Italian Studies* 1 (Winter 1977): 147–61; Maria Corti, "'La *Commedia* di Dante e l'oltretomba islamico," *Belfagor* 50 (1995): 301–14; Brenda Schildgen, *Dante and the Orient* (Urbana: University of Illinois Press, 2002), 45–91; Daniela Boccassini, *Il volo della mente. Falconeria e Sofia nel mondo mediterraneo: Islam, Federico II, Dante* (Ravenna: Longo, 2003); Stone, *Dante's Pluralism and the Islamic Philosophy of Religion*, especially 53–56 on Muhammad's presence in *Inferno* 28; Andrea Celli, *Dante e l'Oriente. Le fonti islamiche nella storiografia novecentesca* (Rome: Carocci, 2013); idem, "'Cor per medium fidit'. Il canto XXVIII dell'*Inferno* alla luce di alcune fonti arabo-spagnole," *Lettere italiane* 65.2 (2013): 171–92; and the other articles in the 2007 issue of *Dante Studies*. See also Elizabeth Coggeshall, "Dante, Islam, and Edward Said," *Telos* 139 (Summer 2007): 133–51, and Karla Mallette, "Dante e l'Islam: sul canto III del *Purgatorio*," *Rivista di Storia e Letteratura Religiosa* 41 (2005): 39–62, both of whom persuasively reject Edward Said's claim about the radical otherness of Islam in Dante's *Commedia*. Cf. Edward Said, *Orientalism* (London: Penguin Books, 1978), 69–70.

18. Andrea Moudarres, "Crusade and Conversion: Islam as Schism in Pius II and Nicholas of Cusa," *Modern Language Notes* 128.1 (2013): 40–52.

19. In discussing apostasy, Aquinas quotes a passage from the Book of Proverbs that includes the following verse: "[the apostate] who plots evil with deceit in his heart—he always stirs up [*seminat*] dissension (6:12–21, especially 6:14)." For an analysis of this biblical passage and its medieval commentaries with reference to *Inferno* 28, see Al-Sabah, "*Inferno* XXVIII: The Figure of Muhammad," especially 151–57.

20. On this section of the *Summa Theologiae* and its relevance to *Inferno* 28, see also Mazzotta, *Dante's Vision and the Circle of Knowledge*, 90–91.

21. Aquinas also employs a maternal metaphor to describe charity's relation to other virtues: "And since a mother is one who conceives within herself and by another, charity is called mother of other virtues, because, by commanding them, it conceives the acts of the other virtues, by the desire of the last end" (*S. T.* II-II, q. 23, a. 8). See also Isidore's definition of charity as "love (*dilectio*), because it binds (*ligare*) two (*duo*) in itself. Indeed, love begins from two things because it is the love of God and the neighbor" (*Etymologies* 8.2). On the distinction between sins against faith and sins against charity in relation to Dante's decision to place Muhammad among the schismatics, see Jacopo della Lana's introductory note to *Inferno* 28 and Francesco da Buti's commentary to *Inferno* 28.22–27. I consulted all medieval and Renaissance commentaries of the *Commedia* on dante.dartmouth.edu. Unless otherwise noted, all translations of these commentaries are my own.

22. In an early fourteenth-century Italian translation of Brunetto Latini's *Tresor*, Muhammad is a cardinal; see Alessandro d'Ancona, *Il Tesoro di Brunetto Latini* (Rome:

Accademia della Crusca, 1888), especially 211. We can assume that this version of the legend had gained some popularity since the author of the *Ottimo Commento* to the *Commedia* feels that he needs to dismiss it, in favor of a tale of Muhammad receiving instructions from a monk named Sergio. Among the many studies on Islam in Western Europe during the Middle Ages, see Alessandro D'Ancona, *Studi di critica e storia letteraria* (Bologna: Nicola Zanichelli, 1912); Norman Daniel, *Islam and the West: The Making of an Image* (1960; Oxford: One World, 1993); R. W. Southern, *Western Views of Islam in the Middle Ages* (Cambridge, MA: Harvard University Press, 1962); Jaroslav Pelikan, *The Growth of Medieval Theology* (Chicago: Chicago University Press, 1978), 229–55; Maria Rosa Menocal, *The Arabic Role in Medieval Literary History: A Forgotten Heritage* (Philadelphia: University of Pennsylvania Press, 1987); Stefano Mula, "Muhammad and the Saints: The History of the Prophet in the *Golden Legend*," *Modern Philology* 101.2 (2003): 175–88; Thomas Burman, *Reading the Qur'an in Latin Christendom* (Philadelphia: University of Pennsylvania Press, 2007); John Tolan, *Saracens: Islam in the Medieval European Imagination* (New York: Columbia University Press, 2002); idem, *Sons of Ishmael: Muslims through European Eyes in the Middle Ages* (Gainesville: University Press of Florida, 2008); David Nirenberg, *Neighboring Faiths: Christianity, Islam, and Judaism in the Middle Ages and Today* (Chicago: The University of Chicago Press, 2014), especially 15–33.

23. In Peter the Venerable, *Peter the Venerable and Islam*, ed. James Kritzeck (Princeton, NJ: Princeton University Press, 1964), 215. All translations of the passages from Peter the Venerable's works are mine. In addition to Kritzeck's extensive introduction, on the crucial role of Peter the Venerable in the development of Western European views of Islam, see Tim Rayborn, *The Violent Pilgrimage: Christians, Muslims and Holy Conflicts, 850–1150* (Jefferson, NC: McFarland & Company, 2012), 97–111; Tolan, *Sons of Ishamel*, 46–63; and Esposito Frank, "Dante's Muhammad," 189–90.

24. In Kritzeck, ed., *Peter the Venerable and Islam*, 212.

25. Ibid., 213.

26. Ibid., 207.

27. The Latin text is taken from Riccoldo da Montecroce, *Contra legem Sarracenorum*, ed. J.-M. Mérigoux, in "Fede e controversia nel '300 e '500," *Memorie domenicane* 17 (1986): 60–144, especially 63 (all English translations of the *Contra legem Sarracenorum* are mine). An Italian translation is available in Riccoldo da Montecroce, *I Saraceni. Contra legem Sarracenorum*, ed. and trans. Giuseppe Rizzardi (Florence: Nardini Editore, 1992). The Latin texts of Riccoldo da Montecroce's works can also be consulted at emiliopanellaweb, at http://www.e-theca.net/emiliopanella/riccoldo/index.htm.

28. Riccoldo narrates his journey to the Near East and his stay in Baghdad in the *Liber peregrinationis*, available in Latin, in French translation in *Riccold de Monte Croce: Pérégrination en Terre Sainte et au Proche-Orient et Lettres sur la chute de Saint-Jean d'Acre*, ed. and trans. René Kappler (Paris: Champion, 1997), 36–205, and in English translation in Rita George-Tvrtković, *A Christian Pilgrim in Medieval Iraq: Riccoldo da Montecroce's Encounter with Islam* (Turnhout, Belgium: Brepols, 2012), 175–227. George-Tvrtković's book includes her English translation of Riccoldo's *Epistole ad Eccle-*

siam triumphantem, as well. On Riccoldo da Montecroce, see Ugo Monneret de Villard, *Il libro della peregrinazione nelle parti d'Oriente di Frate Ricoldo da Montecroce* (Rome: Institutum historicum fratrum predicatorum, 1948); Thomas Burman, "How an Italian Friar Read His Arabic Qur'an," *Dante Studies* 125 (2007): 93–109; Mallette, "Muhammad in Hell," 214–19; and George-Tvrtković, *A Christian Pilgrim in Medieval Iraq*.

29. On Dante's use of scatological language and, more broadly, on the issues of style and genre in his works, see Zygmunt G. Barański, "Scatology and Obscenity in Dante," in *Dante for the New Millennium*, eds. Teodolinda Barolini and H. Wayne Storey (New York: Fordham University Press, 2003), 259–73; idem, "'Tres enim sunt manerie dicendi . . .': Some Observations on Medieval Literature, Dante, and 'Genre,'" in Zygmunt G. Barański, ed., *"Libri poetarum in quattuor species dividuntur." Essays on Dante and 'Genre,'* Supplement 2 of *The Italianist* 15 (1995): 9–60. On the linguistic register of *Inferno* 28, see Tiziano Zanato, "Inferno XXVIII," in *Lectura Dantis Bononiensis*, eds. Emilio Pasquini and Carlo Galli (Bologna: Bononia University Press, 2014), 4:157–81, especially 161–65; and Ettore Paratore, "Il Canto XXVIII," in *Inferno*, ed. Silvio Zennaro (Rome: Bonacci, 1977), 683–704, especially 691–94.

30. Two exceptions to this rather widespread reading of this passage can be found in Benvenuto da Imola's and Cristoforo Landino's commentaries, both of which interpret the phrase "quel che si trangugia" as the doctrines that Muhammad corrupted by founding Islam. On Dante's depiction of Muhammad's wound, see also Mallette, who, in "Muhammad in Hell," 210–13, suggests that a passage of the Qur'an itself, translated by the team put together by Peter the Venerable in the twelfth century and Mark of Toledo in the early thirteenth century, might be a source that Dante used in his description of Muhammad's punishment; Al-Sabah, "*Inferno* XXVIII: The Figure of Muhammad," especially 147–51; and Elizabeth Mozzillo-Howell, "*Divina Anatomia*: Laying Bare Body and Soul in the '*Commedia*,'" in *Dante and the Human Body*, eds. John C. Barnes and Jennifer Petrie (Dublin: Four Court Press, 2007), 139–57, especially 144–48.

31. Cf. Saint Thomas Aquinas, *Reasons for the Faith against Muslim Objections (and one Objection of the Greeks and Armenians) to the Cantor of Antioch*, trans. Joseph Kenny, in *Islamochristiana* 22 (1996): 31–52, especially 32: "They also hold against Christians their claim to eat God on the altar" ["Improperant etiam Christianis, quod cotidie in altari comedunt Deum suum"]; hereafter cited as *Reasons for the Faith against Muslim Objections*. The Latin text of the *De rationibus fidei* is available from the Corpus Thomisticum, University de Navarro and Foundation Tomas Aquino, at http://www.corpusthomisticum.org/ocg.html. See also Aquinas, *Summa contra Gentiles*, book 1, chapter 6; and Riccoldo da Montecroce, *Contra legem Sarracenorum*, 96–99.

32. It is worth noting that Riccoldo mentions the schism that Alì caused within Islam both in the *Liber peregrinationis* (in George-Tvrtković, *A Christian Pilgrim in Medieval Iraq*, 204–5) and in the *Contra legem Sarracenorum* (121).

33. In addition to the passage cited below from John of Damascus's *De Haeresibus*, see chapter VII of Peter John of Olivi's *Lectura super Apocalipsim*, in *Scritti scelti*, ed. Paolo Vian (Rome: Città Nuova Editrice, 1989), 122, where the Franciscan theologian defines Islam as a sect of the Antichrist, while advocating for a missionary, peaceful

effort to convert the Muslims. See also the third epistle of Riccoldo di Montecroce, in George-Tvrtković, *A Christian Pilgrim in Medieval Iraq*, 156, where Muhammad is labeled a precursor of the Antichrist.

34. On the *corpus mysticum*, see Henri de Lubac, *Corpus Mysticum: The Eucharist and the Church in the Middle Ages*, trans. Gemma Simmonds, et al. (1944; London: SCM Press, 2006). I will further discuss the parallel between Christianity and Islam as universal religions in Chapter 4.

35. *Ottimo Commento* to the *Commedia*, *Inferno* 28.22–31.

36. John of Damascus, *De Haeresibus* 100–1, in *John of Damascus on Islam: The "Heresy of the Ishmaelites,"* ed. and trans. Daniel Sahas (Leiden: Brill, 1972), 133. The works of John of Damascus, whom Dante mentions in his *Epistle* 11 to the Italian cardinals as an example of authors to be studied, were translated from Greek into Latin by Robert Grosseteste during the thirteenth century.

37. John of Damascus, *De Haeresibus* 100–1, in *John of Damascus on Islam*, 137 (emphasis mine).

38. In Kritzeck, ed., *Peter the Venerable and Islam*, 206 and 208–9, with a specific analogy between Arius and Muhammad. Cf. Riccoldo da Montecroce, *Contra legem Sarracenorum*, 65.

39. Aquinas mentions the Muslims ("Mahumetistae") and Muhammad in passing in the *Summa contra gentiles*, book 1, chapters 2 and 6. Cf. Aquinas, *Reasons for the Faith against Muslim Objections*, especially 32, where he writes: "The Christian faith principally consists in acknowledging the Holy Trinity, and it specially glories in the cross of our Lord Jesus Christ" ["Fides autem Christiana principaliter consistit in sanctae Trinitatis confessione, et specialiter gloriatur in cruce domini nostri Iesu Christi"].

40. Riccoldo da Montecroce, *Contra legem Sarracenorum*, 63–66.

41. In George-Tvrtković, *A Christian Pilgrim in Medieval Iraq*, 141 and 149.

42. Riccoldo da Montecroce, *Contra legem Sarracenorum*, 106. See also George-Tvrtković, *A Christian Pilgrim in Medieval Iraq*, 164.

43. We see confirmation of this passage's historical significance when Boniface VIII quotes it in the first paragraph of his famous 1302 bull *Unam Sanctam* to explain the corporeal unity of the Church in relation to the sacredness of the Trinity.

44. On the geography of *Inferno* 28, see Theodore J. Cachey, "Cartographic Dante: A Note on Dante and the Greek Mediterranean," in *Dante and the Greeks*, ed. Jan Ziolkowski (Washington, D.C.: Dumbarton Oaks Research Library and Collections, 2014), 197–226.

45. On Pier da Medicina, see Ignazio Baldelli, "'Lo dolce piano che da Vercelli a Marcabò dichina': *Inferno* XXVIII, 74–75," *Lettere Italiane* 47 (1995): 193–202.

46. See the *Chronica de Origine Civitatis* and the *Libro Fiesolano* in *Quellen und Forschungen zur ältesten Geschichte der Stadt Florenz*, ed. Otto Hartwig (Marburg, Germany: Elwert, 1875), 1–69. See also the *Sanzanomis Gesta Florentinorum*, which can be consulted in *Cronache dei secoli XIII e XIV* (Florence: Tipi di M. Cellini, 1876), 125–54. On Dante's use of Florentine chronicles in his works, see John C. Barnes, "Dante's Knowledge of Florentine History," in *Dante and his Literary Precursors*, eds. John C. Barnes

and Jennifer Petrie (Dublin: Four Court Press, 2007), 93–116; Nicolai Rubinstein, "The Beginnings of Political Thought in Florence: A Study in Medieval Historiography," *Journal of the Warburg and Courtauld Institutes* 5 (1942): 198–227; Passerin d'Entrèves, *Dante as a Political Thinker*, 1–25; and Charles Till Davis, *Dante and the Idea of Rome* (Oxford: Oxford University Press, 1957), 86–100. See also *Convivio* 1.3.4, where Dante refers to Florence as "la bellissima e famosa figlia di Roma" ["the most beautiful and famous daughter of Rome"]; and Dante's letter to the Emperor Henry VII, where he refers to it as the city that Rome "created in its own image and likeness" ["ad imaginem suam atque similitudinem fecit"] (*Epistles* 7.25) in Dante Alighieri, *Four Political Letters*, trans. Claire Honess (London: Modern Humanities Research Association, 2007), 79.

47. See Brunetto Latini, *Tresor*, ed. Pietro Beltrami (Turin: Einaudi, 2007), I, 37 (my translation). See also Brunetto's "own" words in *Inferno* 15.61–64 and 73–78. On Florentine factionalism, see Edward Peters, "Pars, Parte: Dante and an Urban Contribution to Political Thought," in *The Medieval City*, ed. Harry Miskimin, et al. (New Haven, CT: Yale University Press, 1977), 113–40; John Najemi, "Dante and Florence," in *The Cambridge Companion to Dante*, ed. Rachel Jacoff (Cambridge: Cambridge University Press, 1993), 80–99; Francesco Bruni, *La città divisa. Le parti e il bene comune da Dante a Guicciardini* (Bologna: Il Mulino, 2003); Claire Honess, *From Florence to the Heavenly City: The Poetry of Citizenship in Dante* (London: Legenda, 2006); and on the kinship between Rome and Florence, see Jeffrey Schnapp, *The Transfiguration of History at the Center of Dante's Paradise* (Princeton, NJ: Princeton University Press, 1986), 14–69.

48. On the providential expansion of the Roman Empire, see Augustine, *De Civitate Dei* 5.1 and 5.21; and Orosius, *Adversus Paganos* 6.20, 6.22, and 7.1. On Dante and Rome, see Davis, *Dante and the Idea of Rome*; and Mazzotta, *Dante, Poet of the Desert*, 147–91. On the notion of just war, see Frederick Russell, *The Just War in the Middle Ages* (Cambridge: Cambridge University Press, 1975).

49. See, for instance, Nicola Fosca's commentary on *Inf.* 28.94–99 in *Commentary on the "Commedia,"* which can be accessed via the *Dartmouth Dante Project* at https://dante.dartmouth.edu.

50. On the context of this letter, see Honess's Introduction to *Dante Alighieri, Four Political Letters*, 5–41. On Henry VII, see William Bowsky, *Henry VII in Italy: The Conflict of Empire and City-State, 1310–1313* (Lincoln: University of Nebraska Press, 1960).

51. Curio's sentence in the *Civil War* is also quoted in Latini, *Tresor* 2.57. On the allegorical value of the tongue as a potential instrument of discord, see Bernardus Silvestris, *Cosmographia*, 174–75:

> Quae tamen exprompsit et nudas prodidit artes,
> cognita multiplici lingua nocere malo.
> Nam male discreta quotiens insibilat aure
> livida mordaces vipereosque sonos,
> separatat unanimos fratres, inimicat amicos
> abrumpitque fidem, dissociatque thoros,
> turbat agros praedis, fora litibus, oppida bellis.

[Yet the tongue which gave voice to the needy arts and transmitted them, is known for doing harm in many evil ways. For whenever it carelessly whispers in the jealous ear backbiting and poisonous words, it separates loving brothers, unfriends friends, breaks bonds of trust, divides marriages, makes the land teem with robbery, the forum with quarrels, the city with war.]

52. See, for example, Anna Maria Chiavacci Leonardi's commentary to *Inf.* 28.97–99. Cf. Lino Pertile, "Dante Looks Forward and Back: Political Allegory in the Epistles," *Dante Studies* 115 (1997): 1–17, especially 11–12.

53. Cf. Jacques Goudet, "La 'parte per se stesso' e l'impegno politico di Dante," in *Nuove Letture Dantesche* 7 (1974): 289–316, especially 313–16. On the emphatically messianic tone of Dante's political letters, see Pertile, "Dante Looks Forward and Back," 1–17; Paola Nasti, *Favole d'amore e "saver profondo": la tradizione salomonica in Dante* (Ravenna, Longo: 2007) 131–57; and Elisa Brilli, "Reminiscenze scritturali (e non) nelle epistole politiche dantesche," *La Cultura* 45.3 (2007): 439–55. Compare with Francesco Mazzoni, "Le epistole di Dante," in *Conferenze aretine 1965* (Bibbiena, Italy: Società Dantesca Casentinese, 1966), 47–100, especially 77. Among the numerous studies on Dante as a prophet, see Bruno Nardi, *Dante e la cultura medievale* (Bari: Laterza, 1983), 265–326; Nicolò Mineo, *Profetismo e apocalittica in Dante. Strutture e temi profetico-apocalittici in Dante: dalla "Vita nuova" alla "Divina commedia"* (Catania, Italy: Università di Catania, Facoltà di lettere e filosofia, 1968), especially 143–60 on the political letters; Zygmunt G. Barański, *Dante e i segni: saggi per una storia intellettuale di Dante Alighieri* (Naples: Liguori, 2000), 147–72; Robert Wilson, *Prophecies and Prophecy in Dante's "Commedia"* (Florence: Olshki, 2008); and Elisa Brilli, *Firenze e il profeta: Dante tra teologia e politica* (Rome: Carocci, 2012), especially 271–354.

54. "Haud alium tanta civem tulit indole Roma, / Aut cui plus leges deberent recta sequenti. / Perdita tunc urbi nocuerunt saecula, postquam / Ambitus et luxus et opum metuenda facultas / Transverso mentem dubiam torrente tulerunt; / Momentumque fuit mutates Curio rerum / Gallorum captus spoliis et Caesaris auro / ius licet in iugulos nostros sibi fecerit ensis / Sulla potens Mariusque ferox et Cinna cruentus / Caesareaeque domus series, cui tanta potestas / concessa est? emere omnes, hic uendidit urbem."

55. On Curio in the *Civil War*, see Charles Saylor, "Curio and Antaeus: The African Episode of Lucan *Pharsalia* IV," *Transactions of the American Philological Association* 112 (1982): 169–77; and Frederick Ahl, *Lucan: An Introduction* (Ithaca, NY: Cornell University Press, 1976), 88–115.

56. On Cato's role in the *Civil War*, see Ahl, *Lucan: An Introduction*, 231–79; Shadi Bartsch, *Ideology in Cold Blood: A Reading of Lucan's* Civil War (Cambridge, MA: Harvard University Press, 1997), especially 29–35 and 114–23; Alex Long, "Lucan and Moral Luck," *The Classical Quarterly* 57.1 (May 2007): 183–97, especially 185–90; and Erica Bexley, "Replacing Rome: Geographic and Political Centrality in Lucan's *Pharsalia*," *Classical Philology* 104.4 (October 2009): 459–75. For Dante's admiration for Cato, see also *Conv.* 4.28.15. On Dante's depiction of Cato, see Mazzotta, *Dante, Poet of the Desert*, 14–65. On Lucan and Dante, see William Stull and Robert Hollander, "The Lucanian

Source of Dante's Ulysses," *Studi Danteschi* 63 (1997): 1–52, especially 28–33; and Ettore Paratore, "Lucano e Dante," in *Antico e nuovo* (Caltanissetta, Italy: Salvatore Sciascia Editore, 1965), 165–210.

57. For more information on the structure of the *Civil War*, see Bexley, "Replacing Rome," especially 465. Compare with Charles Martindale, "The Politician Lucan," *Greece & Rome* 31.1 (April 1984): 64–79, especially 65.

58. The English translation is taken from *Dante Alighieri, Four Political Letters*, 75–76. The Latin text of Dante's letters is taken from Dante, *Epistole*, ed. Arsenio Frugoni and Giorgio Brugnoli, in *Opere di Dante*, ed. Arsenio Frugoni, et al. (Milan: Ricciardi, 1996), 3:2:566–68: "Intonet iterum vox illa Curionis in Cesarem: 'Dum trepidant nullo firmate robore partes, tolle moras; semper nocuit differre paratis: par labor atque metus pretio maiore petuntur.' Intonet illa vox increpitantis Anubis iterum in Eneam: 'Si te nulla movet tantarum gloria rerum, nec super ipse tua moliris laude laborem, Ascanium surgentem et spes heredis Iuli respice, cui regnum Ytalie Romanaque tellus debentur.' Iohannes namque, regius primogenitus tuus et rex, quem, post diei orientis occasum, mundi successiva posteritas prestolatur, nobis est alter Ascanius."

59. Mosca's words in the *Cronica fiorentina compilata nel secolo XIII* read as "Cosa fatta cappa à." See *Testi fiorentini del Dugento e dei primi del Trecento*, ed. Alfredo Schiaffini (Florence: Sansoni, 1926), 82–150, especially 119.

60. Durling's translation of this line ("A thing done is done") does not quite convey the sharpness of Dante's pun, which becomes evident only at the appearance of Bertran de Born.

61. On Dante's rejection of vengeance, see Mazzotta, *Dante's Vision and the Circle of Knowledge*, 79–80 and 84–86; and Chance, "Monstra-naturalità distorte," 252–53.

62. Dante, *De Vulgari Eloquentia*, trans. Steven Botterill (Cambridge: Cambridge University Press, 1996). The Latin text is taken from Dante, *De Vulgari Eloquentia*, ed. Pier Vincenzo Mengaldo, in *Opere minori* (Milan: Ricciardi, 1979), 5:2:152–54. See also *Convivio* 4.11.14, where Dante praises Bertran de Born for his liberality.

63. Danuta Hanzer, "The Punishment of Bertram de Born," *Yearbook of Italian Studies* VIII (1989): 95–97; and Chance, "Monstra-naturalità distorte," especially 250–54.

64. Alan of Lille, *Anticlaudianus*, in *Literary Works*, 490–91.

65. See Justinian, *Institutes* with the Accursian Gloss, book 3, chapter 1 ("De hereditatibus"), as cited in Kantorowicz, *The King's Two Bodies*, 391. See also Kantorowicz, *The King's Two Bodies*, 336–83 (on the crown as fiction and Accursius's gloss to Justinian's *Institutes*), 386 (on Bernard Botone's gloss to the *Decretales* of Gregory IX), and 391–92 (on Frederick II's interpretation of sameness or unity of father and son). On the nature of kingship and on Dante's knowledge of medieval law, see Kantorowicz, *The King's Two Bodies*, especially 451–54; Passerin d'Entrèves, *Dante as a Political Thinker*, 27–28; Nardi, *Dante e la cultura medievale*, 176–78; and Richard Kay, *Dante's Swift and Strong* (Lawrence: Regent Press of Kansas, 1978), 29–66; Lorenzo Valterza, "Dante's Justinian, Cino's Corpus," *Medievalia et Humanistica* 37 (2011): 89–110; Justin Steinberg, *Dante and the Limits of the Law* (Chicago: University of Chicago Press, 2013); Sara Menzinger, "Law," in *Dante in Context*, eds. Zygmunt G. Barański and Lino Pertile (Cambridge:

Cambridge University Press, 2015), 47–58; and Claudia Di Fonzo, *Dante e la tradizione giuridica* (Rome: Carocci, 2016).

66. On *lèse-majesté* in relation to Bertran de Born, see Steinberg, *Dante and the Limits of the Law*, 47.

67. On the relationship between poetry and ethics in *Inferno* 28, see also the chapter entitled "The Poetry of Politics: Bertran and Sordello" in Teodolinda Barolini, *Dante's Poets: Textuality and Truth in the "Comedy"* (Princeton, NJ: Princeton University Press, 1984), 153–73; and Mazzotta, *Dante's Vision and the Circle of Knowledge*, 75–95. On the issue of poetry and violence within the larger question of Dante and medieval law, see Steinberg, *Dante and the Limits of the Law*, especially 40–49. On Bertran de Born in *Inferno* 28, see also Marianne Shapiro, "The Fictionalization of Bertran de Born (*Inf.* XXVIII)," *Dante Studies* 92 (1974): 107–16; Michelangelo Picone, "I trovatori di Dante: Bertran de Born," *Studi e problemi di critica testuale* 19 (1979): 71–94, especially 80–84; and Claire Honess, "Dante and the Political Poetry in the Vernacular," in *Dante and his Literary Precursors*, eds. John Barnes and Jennifer Petrie (Dublin: Four Court Press, 2007), 116–51, especially 146–49.

68. Cf. *Inferno* 30.1–12 for Athamas's madness; *Inferno* 32.10–12 for Amphion's foundation of the city walls, and 32.130–32 with Tydeus's gnawing of Melanippus; *Inferno* 33.89, where Dante, after Ugolino's speech about his death and that of his children, defines Pisa as "novella Tebe." On the archetypical value of Thebes as a tragic city, see Mazzotta, *Dante, Poet of the Desert*, 23. On Dante and Statius, see Dotti, *La Divina Commedia e la città dell'uomo*, 78–93; and Teresa Hankey, "Dante and Statius," in *Dante and his Literary Precursors*, 37–50.

69. See Statius, *Thebaid* 12.429–32. Dante explicitly conjures up this image in *Inferno* 26, where the souls of Ulysses and Diomedes are trapped in a two-pronged flame (26.52–54). Offspring of the incestuous relationships between Oedipus the father-slayer and Jocasta, Eteocles and Polynices killed each other in battle in book 11 of the *Thebaid*.

70. On friendship as "foretaste" of the Garden of Eden and as antidote to civil strife, see Mazzotta, *Dante, the Poet of the Desert*, 119–20. Cf. Teodolinda Barolini, "*Amicus eius*: Dante and the Semantics of Friendship," *Dante Studies* 133 (2015): 46–69, especially 65 on Virgil and Statius. See also *Monarchia* 1.4.4, where Dante quotes those same words of peace from Luke 24. On the relationship between the *Monarchia* and the encounter with Statius as messenger of peace, see Stone, *Dante's Pluralism and the Islamic Philosophy of Religion*, 5–10.

71. Cf. Barolini, *Dante's Poets*, 172.

72. *Vida* I, in *L'amour et la guerre. L'œuvre de Bertran de Born*, ed. G. Gourain (Aix en Provence: Université de Provence, 1985), 1:1: "et era seigner totas vez, qan se volia, del rei Henric d'Englaterra e del fill de lui. Mas totz temps vlia qu'ill aguesson gerra ensems lo paire e-l fills, e-ill fraire l'uns ab l'autre [...] E s'il avian patz ni treva, ades se penava e-is percassava ab sos sirventes de desfar la patz, e demonstrava cum chascuns era desonratz en la patz." See also Bertran de Born, *Liriche*, ed. Thomas Bergin (Varese, Ita.: Magenta, 1964), 14–17. On the influence of this *Vida* in Dante's depiction of the Provençal poet, see William Paden, Jr., "Bertran de Born in Italy," in *Roots and Branches: Essays in Honor*

of *Thomas Goddard Bergin*, eds. Giose Rimanelli and Kenneth John Atchity (New Haven, CT: Yale University Press, 1976), 39–66.

73. On Dante's use of military language in *Inferno* 8–9, see Barański, "'E cominciare stormo,'" 175–203.

74. The English translation is taken from Dante Alighieri, *Epistolae*, ed. and trans. Paget Toynbee (Oxford: Oxford University Press, 1966), 202.

75. For Aquinas's definition of *contrapasso*, see *S. T.* II-II, q. 62, a. 4. On Dante's use of the term *contrapasso*, see Anthony Cassell, *Dante's Fearful Art of Justice* (Toronto: University of Toronto Press, 1984), 3–14; Mazzotta, *Dante's Vision and the Circle of Knowledge*, 79–82; Chance, "Monstra-naturalità distorte," 247–49; Peter Armour, "Dante's Contrapasso: Context and Texts," *Italian Studies* 55.1 (2000): 1–20; and Steinberg, *Dante and the Limits of the Law*, 42–47.

76. On Dante's knowledge of anatomy in *Inferno* 28, see Vittorio Bartoli, "Il midollo spinale 'principio' del 'cerebro' (*Inf.* XXVIII 140–1): un errore causato dalle scoperte scientifiche di fine Settecento," *La Cultura* 48.2 (2010): 303–22; and Simon Gilson, "Human Anatomy and Physiology in Dante," in *Dante and the Human Body*, 11–42, especially 32–36. Cf. Armour, "Dante's Contrapasso," 5–6. See chapter 3 of this book for a discussion of Aristotelian and Galenic theories of the nervous system.

77. Among the primary sources on the relationship between State and Church, the two following groups of texts correspond roughly to the two sides of the struggle between supporters of the independent temporal power versus and supporters of papal supremacy over secular rulers: on the temporal side, see Peter John Olivi, *Quaestiones de Romano Pontifice*, especially XVIII "De universalissima potestate Papae" (1282–85); John of Paris, *Tractatus de Potestate regia et Papali* (1302–03); Marsilius of Padua, *Defensor Pacis* (1324); William of Ockham, *Octo quaestiones de potestate papae* (1340–42). In support of papal power, see the letter of Innocent III to the prefect Acerbus and the nobles of Tuscany (1198); Giles of Rome, *De ecclesiastica potestate* (1301); James of Viterbo, *De Regimine christiano* (1301–02); Boniface's papal bulls *Clericis Laicos* (1296) and *Unam Sanctam* (1302); Ptolemy of Lucca, *De Regimine Principum* (1301–03). On the historical-theological context of the controversy, see Gierke, *Political Theories of the Middle Ages*, 9–21; Walter Ullmann, *Growth of Papal Government in the Middle Ages* (London: Metheun, 1955); Brian Tierney, *The Crisis of Church and State* (Englewood Cliffs, NJ: Prentice-Hall, 1964), especially 172–92 on the struggle between Boniface VIII and Philip IV; Quentin Skinner, *The Foundations of Modern Political Thought* (Cambridge: Cambridge University Press, 1978), especially 1:3–22; and Joseph Canning, *Ideas of Power in the Late Middle Ages, 1296–1417* (Cambridge: Cambridge University Press, 2011), 11–59. Among the many works on Dante's view of the relationship between Church and State, see especially Nardi, *Dante e la cultura medievale*, 265–82; idem, "La Donatio Constantini e Dante," in *Nel mondo di Dante* (Rome: Edizioni di Storia e Letteratura, 1944), 107–59; Gilson, *Dante the Philosopher*, 180–224; Passerin d'Entrèves, *Dante as a Political Thinker*, 52–75; Michele Maccarone, "Il terzo Libro della 'Monarchia,'" *Studi Danteschi* XXXIII, 1, (1955): 5–142; Michele Barbi, *Problemi fondamentali per un nuovo commento della Divina Commedia* (Florence: Sansoni, 1956), especially 65–67 and

91–114; Davis, *Dante and the Idea of Rome*, 195–235; and more recently Cassell, *The "Monarchia" Controversy*, especially 5–22; and Matthew Kempshall, "Accidental Perfection: Ecclesiology and Political Thought in *Monarchia*," in *Dante and the Church*, eds. Paolo Acquaviva and Jennifer Petrie (Dublin: Four Court Press, 2007), 127–71.

78. Cf. Bruno Nardi, *Dal "Convivio" alla "Commedia"* (Roma: Nella sede dell'Istituto, 1960), 301 and 309–10. Nardi's argument is fatally undermined by his assumption that the *Monarchia* was written circa 1307. On the vexed question of the *Monarchia*'s date of composition, see the recent Diego Quaglioni, "Un nuovo testimone per l'edizione della 'Monarchia' di Dante: il Ms. Add. 6891 della British Library," in *Laboratoire italien* 11 (2011): 231–79; Quaglioni's "Introduzione" to Dante Alighieri, *Monarchia*, in *Opere*, ed. Gianfranco Fioravanti, et al. (Milan: Mondadori, 2014), especially 2:828–37 and 2:887–92; and Alberto Casadei, *Dante oltre la "Commedia"* (Bologna: Il Mulino, 2013), 107–27.

79. Cf. Marjorie Reeves, "Marsiglio da Padova and Dante Alighieri," in *Trends in Medieval Political Thought*, ed. Beryl Smalley (Oxford: Blackwell, 1965), 86–104, especially 91–92.

80. Barbi, *Problemi fondamentali per un nuovo commento della Divina Commedia*, 102–5; and Maccarone, "Il terzo Libro della 'Monarchia'," 128–36. For a review of this controversy, with additional bibliography, see John Scott, *Understanding Dante* (Notre Dame, IN: University of Notre Dame Press, 2004), 164; Anthony Cassell, "The Exiled Dante's Hope for Reconciliation: 'Monarchia' 3.16.16–18," *Annali d'Italianistica* 20 (2002): 425–49; and Kempshall, "Accidental Perfection," 163–64. The point I am making in this conclusion partly overlaps with Sarolli, *Prolegomena alla "Divina Commedia,"* 321–24.

81. See, for instance, *Inferno* 16, *Purgatorio* 32, and *Paradiso* 17 and 27.

2. The Enemy within the Walls

1. An exemplary case is that of the humanist Alamanno Rinuccini, who was actively involved in the civic life of Florence under the Medici regime and who, in 1479, shortly after the plot carried out by the Pazzi family and their allies, published a short polemical dialogue titled *De libertate* in which he attacked Lorenzo de' Medici, accusing him of being a tyrant, and praised the Pazzi conspirators as the new Brutus and Cassius. See Alamanno Rinuccini, *On Liberty*, in *Humanism and Liberty*, ed. Renée Neu Watkins (Columbia: University of South Carolina Press, 1978), 185–224, especially 196 and 221. On the Florentine debate on Cassius's and Brutus's killing of Caesar in the early fifteenth century, see Christopher Bond, "Lucan the Christian Monarchist: The Anti-Republicanism of the *De tyranno* and the *De bello civili*," *Renaissance Studies* 20.4 (September 2006): 478–93; and Brian Jeffrey Maxson, "Kings and Tyrants: Leonardo Bruni's Translation of Xenophon's *Hiero*," *Renaissance Studies* 24.2 (April 2010): 188–206.

2. All citations from the *Morgante* are from Luigi Pulci, *Morgante*, ed. Franca Ageno (1955; Milan: Mondadori, 1994); all translations are from Luigi Pulci, *Morgante: The Epic Adventures of Orlando and His Giant Friend Morgante*, trans. Joseph Tusiani (Bloomington: Indiana University Press, 1998).

3. Stefano Carrai, "*Morgante* di Luigi Pulci," in *Letteratura italiana. Le Opere*, ed.

Alberto Asor Rosa (Turin: Einaudi, 1992), 1:772–73; Alessio Decaria, "Tra Marsilio e Pallante: una nuova ipotesi sugli ultimi cantari del *Morgante*," in *L'entusiasmo delle opere: studi in memoria di Domenico De Robertis*, ed. Isabella Becherucci, et al. (Lecce: Pensa Multimedia, 2012), 299–339. Cantari 24–28 are dedicated primarily to the battle of Roncesvalles, in which the Frankish paladin Orlando dies because of the treasonous plot hatched by his fellow Christian Ganelon and the Muslim King of Spain Marsilio.

4. On the history of the poem, see Franca Ageno's introduction and commentary to Pulci, *Morgante*; Ernest Wilkins, "On the Dates of Composition of the *Morgante* of Luigi Pulci," *PMLA* Vol. 66, No. 2 (March 1951): 244–50; idem, "On the Earliest Editions of the 'Morgante' of Luigi Pulci," *The Papers of the Bibliographical Society of America* 45.1 (First Quarter, 1951): 1–22; Domenico De Robertis, *Storia del* Morgante (Firenze: Le Monnier, 1958); Salvatore S. Nigro, *Pulci e la cultura medicea* (Bari: Laterza, 1972), especially 23–26; Lorenz Boninger, "Notes on the Last Years of Luigi Pulci (1477–84)," *Rinascimento* 27 (1987): 259–71; and Decaria, "Tra Marsilio e Pallante," 299–316.

5. See Cecco d'Ascoli, *L'Acerba* (Ascoli Piceno, Ita.: Casa Editrice di Giuseppe Cesari, 1977), lines 2587–609, especially 2601–7:

L'ostrica quando v'é Luna piena
Apresi tutta; qual veggendo il cancro,
Immagina d'averla a pranzo o a cena:
Mettele dentro pietra ovver festuca
Per qual lo suo coprire le vien manco:
Così lo cancro l'ostrica manduca.

[The oyster opens when the moon is full; when the crab sees that, he thinks about having her for lunch or dinner: he then puts a pebble or a straw inside her shell and so she remains uncovered: thus the crab eats the oyster. (my translation)]

Pulci mentions "l'ascolano Cecco" in *Morgante* 24.112. On Pulci's zoological interests, see Franca Ageno, "Ancora sui bestiari del 'Morgante,'" *Studi di filologia italiana*, 14 (1956): 485–93; Rossella Bessi, "Santi, Leoni e Draghi nel 'Morgante' di Luigi Pulci," in *Umanesimo volgare. Studi di letteratura tra Tre e Quattrocento* (Florence: Olschki, 2004), 103–36; John Raymond Shulters, *Luigi Pulci and the Animal Kingdom* (Baltimore: J. H. Furst Company, 1920).

6. Cf. Richard C. Jensen and Marie Babr-Volk, "The Fox and the Crab: Coluccio Salutati's Unpublished Fable," *Studies in Philology* 73.2 (Apr. 1976): 162–68 on Salutati's fable and Silvestri's response and 170–75, which includes Salutati's poem. See also Domenico Silvestri, *The Latin Poetry*, ed. Richard C. Jensen (Munich: Wilhelm Fink Verlag, 1973), especially 54–66.

7. Stefano Carrai, *Le muse dei Pulci* (Naples: Guida Editori, 1985), 102.

8. As I will discuss later in the chapter, moreover, two conspiracies had already challenged Medici power in 1433 and 1466. On the relationship between private friendship and politics in Quattrocento Florence, see Dale Kent, *Friendship, Love, and Trust in*

Renaissance Florence (Cambridge, MA: Harvard University Press, 2009); and Annalisa Ceron, *L'amicizia civile e gli amici del principe. Lo spazio politico dell'amicizia nel pensiero del Quattrocento* (Macerata, Ita.: EUM, 2011), especially chapters 1, 3, and 6 on the question of friendship and politics in the works of Leon Battista Alberti, Matteo Palmieri, and Platina, respectively.

9. On the "seriousness" of the *Morgante*, see Ruggero Ruggieri, *L'Umanesimo cavalleresco italiano. Da Dante all'Ariosto* (Naples: Fratelli Conte Editori, 1977), 217–41, particularly 224–25. Cf. Mark Davie, *Half-Serious Rhymes: The Narrative Poetry of Luigi Pulci* (Dublin: Irish Academic Press, 1998). On the battles in the last five cantari, and their possible historical connotations, see Michael Murrin, *History and Warfare in Renaissance Epic* (Chicago: The University of Chicago Press, 1994), 21–39. See also Annalisa Perrotta, "Lo spazio della corte: la rappresentazione del potere politico nel Morgante di Luigi Pulci," *The Italianist* 24 (2004): 141–68, who effectively argues in favor of the poem's unity.

10. Galen, *Method of Medicine to Glaucon*, ed. and trans. Ian Johnston (Cambridge, MA: Harvard University Press, 2016), 553 (M 141). On the study of cancer-like pathologies in antiquity, see Francois Pieter Retief and Louise Cilliers, "Tumours and Cancers in Graeco-Roman Times," *South African Medical Journal* 91.4 (2001): 344–48.

11. Cf. Nancy Siraisi, *Medieval and Early Renaissance Medicine* (Chicago: The University of Chicago Press, 1990), especially 14–15. See also Ian Johnston's introduction to Galen, *Method of Medicine to Glaucon*, ed. and trans. Ian Johnston (Cambridge, MA: Harvard University Press, 2016), 325, noting that this work was first translated into Latin by Niccolò da Reggio in the early fourteenth century.

12. Isidore of Seville, *Etymologies*, ed. and trans. Stephen A. Barney, et al. (Cambridge: Cambridge University Press, 2006), 113. See also Uguccione da Pisa, *Derivationes* C 38, 1.

13. For a highly informative discussion of the cancer-crab analogy in the Middle Ages, see Luke Demaitre, "Medieval Notions of Cancer: Malignancy and Metaphor," *Bulletin of the History of Medicine* 72.4 (1998): 609–37, especially 619–23.

14. See sonnets XLIV ("Un medico, se Nencio di Butone"), XLV ("Il medico mi dice ch'io ho male"), and XLVI ("E' c'è venuto un medico Rosato") in Luigi Pulci, *Sonetti extravaganti*, ed. Alessio Decaria (Florence: Società Editrice Fiorentina, 2013), 88–90 and 95. Two of these sonnets, XLIV and XLVI, had previously been published in Guglielmo Volpi, "Pulci contro i medici," *Rassegna* ser. III, vol. 1 (1916): 181–85. On Pulci's interest in the sciences, see also Rossella Bessi, "Luigi Pulci e Lorenzo Buonincontri," *Rinascimento* 14 (1974): 289–95.

15. For this sonnet's date of composition, see Decaria's commentary to Pulci, *Sonetti extravaganti*, ccxi.

16. On these two views of the nervous system in thirteenth- and fourteenth-century Italy, see Nancy Siraisi, *Taddeo Alderotti and His Pupils: Two Generations of Italian Medical Learning* (Princeton, NJ: Princeton University Press, 1981), 192–95.

17. Avicenna, *The Canon of Medicine*, adapted by Laleh Bakhtiar (Chicago: Great Books of the Islamic World, 1999), 46: "Nerves arise from the brain or the spinal cord."

They are white, soft, pliant, difficult to tear and were created to subserve sensation and movement of the limbs."

18. Albertus Magnus, *On Animals: A Medieval Summa Zoologica*, translated and annotated by Kenneth Kitchell and Irven Resnick (Baltimore: The Johns Hopkins University Press, 1999), 158. For the original text in Latin, see idem., *De animalibus*, in *Alberti Magni Opera Omnia*, ed. August Borgnet (Paris: Ludovicum Vivès, 1891), 11:76.

19. Magnus, *On Animals*, 176. Idem, *De animalibus*, 11:88.

20. Demaitre, "Medieval Notions of Cancer," 625.

21. Giovanni Villani, *Nuova cronica*, ed. Giuseppe Porta (Parma: Ugo Guanda Editore, 1991), 1313.

22. Niccolò Machiavelli, *La mandragola*, in *Opere*, ed. Mario Bonfantini (Milan: Ricciardi, 1954), 987.

23. Matteo Bandello, *Le novelle del Bandello*, in *Tutte le opere di Matteo Bandello*, ed. Francesco Flora (Milan: Mondadori, 1942), 1986.

24. Galen, *Translatio Libri Galieni De rigore et tremore et iectigatione et spasmo*, ed. Michael McVaugh, in *Arnaldi de Villanova Opera Medica Omnia*, vol. 16 (Barcelona: Publicacions i Edicions de la Universitat de Barcelona, 1981), especially 90–92. The English translation of the Greek text is available in David Sider and Michael McVaugh, "Galen *On Tremor, Palpitation, Spasm, and Rigor*," *Transactions and Studies of the College of Physicians of Philadelphia* 1.3 (1979): 183–210.

25. Isidore, *Etymologies*, 110. See also Uguccione da Pisa, *Derivationes* S 281.

26. Teodorico of Lucca, *Chirurgia*, in *La chirurgia italiana nell'Alto Medioevo*, ed. Mario Tabanelli (Florence: Olschki, 1965), 1:256–57; and Lanfranc of Milan, *Chirurgia magna*, in ibidem, 2:853–54 and 887–90.

27. On the circulation of Celsus's *De medicina*, see Leighton Durham Reynolds, ed., *Text and Transmission: A Survey of the Latin Classics* (Oxford: Clarendon Press, 1983), 46–47.

28. Niccoli donated his vast collection of manuscripts to the library of the Dominican Church of San Marco, to which laymen as well as clergymen had access. See Berthold L. Ullman and Philip A. Stadter, *The Public Library of Renaissance Florence: Niccolò Niccoli, Cosimo de' Medici and the Library of San Marco* (Padua: Antenore, 1972), 3–121, and 199. Even though the *De medicina* was less widely known than other works of its genre, Marsilio Ficino mentions Celsus in his *Oratio de laudibus medicinae*, which Paul Oskar Kristeller attributed to Ficino's youth. See Kristeller, ed., *Svpplementvm ficinianum. Marcilii Ficini florentini philosophi platonici opvscvla inedita et dispersa* (Florence: Olschki, 1937), c. Cf. Teodoro Katinis, *Medicina e filosofia in Marsilio Ficino* (Rome: Edizioni di Storia e Letteratura, 2007), 72 and 92.

29. Celsus, *De medicina*, trans. W. G. Spencer (Cambridge, MA: Harvard University Press, 1989): "Sed quaedam tamen periculosa incidere consuerunt: interdum enim vetustas ulcus occupat, induciturque ei callus, et circum orae crassae livent; post quae quicquid medicamentorum ingeritur, parum proficit; quod fere neglegenter curatio ulceri supervenit. Interdum vel ex nimia inflammatione, vel ob aestus inmodicos, vel ob nimia frigora, vel quia nimis vulnus adstrictum est, vel quia corpus aut senile aut mali habitus

est, cancer occupat. [...] Omnis autem cancer non solum id corrumpit, quod occupavit, sed etiam serpit."

30. Teodorico of Lucca, *Chirurgia*, 1:386–88; and Lanfranc of Milan, *Chirurgia magna*, 2:883–85.

31. Giovanni Rosati, a student of Marsilio Ficino, compiled *De abditis* using Benivieni's notes. The work was published posthumously by Antonio's brother, the poet Girolamo, who in a letter to Rosati introducing the first edition of the *De abditis* says the notes reflected Antonio's thirty-two years of medical practice. Cf. Antonio Benivieni, *De abditis nonnullis ac mirandis morborum et sanationum causis*, ed. Giorgio Weber (Florence: Olschki, 1994), 46.

32. On Benivieni, see Nancy Siraisi, *The Clock and the Mirror: Girolamo Cardano and Renaissance Medicine* (Princeton, NJ: Princeton University Press, 1997), 153–58. On Celsus's influence on Benivieni, see Giorgio Weber's Introduction to Benivieni, *De abditis* (1994), 33–39; and Antonio Costa and Giorgio Weber, *L'inizio dell'anatomia patologica nel Quattrocento fiorentino, sui testi di Antonio Benivieni, Bernardo Torni, Leonardo da Vinci* (Florence: Edizioni Riviste Mediche, 1963), especially 764–65. On Benivieni's own list of his books, see Bindo de Vecchi, "I libri di un medico umanista fiorentino del sec. XV dai 'Ricordi' di maestro Antonio Benivieni," *La Bibliofilia* 34 (1932): 293–302; Susanna Sclavi, "La biblioteca di Antonio Benivieni," *Physis* 17 (1975): 255–68; and Angelo Poliziano, "Ad Antonium Benivenium, medicum," in *Prose volgari inedite e poesie latine e greche edite e inedite*, ed. Isidoro del Lungo (Florence: Barbera Editore, 1867), 236–38. On Pulci's own possible connection to the Benivieni family, see Carlo Pellegrini, *Luigi Pulci. L'uomo e l'artista* (Pisa: Nistri, 1912), 16.

33. The English translation is from Antonio Benivieni, *De abditis nonnullis ac mirandis morborum et sanationum causis*, trans. Charles Singer (Springfield, IL: Charles C. Thomas Publisher, 1954), 145. For the original text in Latin, see Benivieni, *De abditis nonnullis ac mirandis morborum et sanationum causis*, 131 (chap. LXXI).

34. Katharine Park, *Doctors and Medicine in Early Renaissance Florence* (Princeton, NJ: Princeton University Press, 1985), 58–59 and 68. For an overview on medical knowledge in the late Middle Ages and Renaissance, see Victor Robinson, *The Story of Medicine* (New York: The New Home Library, 1943), especially 238–80; Eugenio Garin, ed., *La disputa delle arti nel Quattrocento* (Florence: Vallecchi, 1947); and Nancy Siraisi, *Medicine and the Italian Universities, 1250–1600* (Leiden: Brill, 2001), especially 226–52.

35. On the early years of Pulci's life and his work at Francesco Castellani's service, see Decaria's introduction to Luigi Pulci, *Sonetti extravaganti*, xi–xvii; and Alessio Decaria, *Luigi Pulci and Francesco di Matteo Castellani: novità e testi inediti da uno zibaldone magliabechiano* (Florence: Società Editrice Fiorentina, 2009).

36. On Poliziano's interest in medicine, see Juliana Hill Cotton, "Materia medica del Poliziano," in *Il Poliziano e il suo tempo. Atti del IV convegno internazionale di studi sul Rinascimento* (Florence: Sansoni, 1957), 237–45; Alessandro Perosa, "*Febris*: A Poetic Myth Created by Poliziano," *Journal of the Warburg and Courtauld Institutes* 9 (1946): 74–95; idem, "Codici di Galeno postillati dal Poliziano," in *Umanesimo e Rinascimento. Studi offerti a Paul Oskar Kristeller* (Florence: Olschki, 1980), 75–109.

37. On the analogy between Morgante and Hercules, see Carrai, *Le muse dei Pulci*, 95–112; and Alessandro Polcri, *Luigi Pulci e la Chimera. Studi sull'allegoria nel* Morgante (Florence: Società Editrice Fiorentina, 2010), especially 121–27 and 132–48. On Morgante's similarity to other classical heroes such as Achilles and Philoctetes, see Andrea Gareffi, *L'ombra dell'eroe. 'Il Morgante'* (Urbino, Ita.: Quattroventi, 1986), 42–44; Gennaro Savarese, *La cultura a Roma tra Umanesimo ed Ermetismo* (Anzio, Ita.: De Rubeis, 1993), 105–11.

38. Among the numerous studies of this myth, see Erwin Panofsky, *Hercules am Scheidewege und andere anitike Bildstoffe inder neueren Kunst* (Leipzig: B.G. Teubner, 1930), who examines the presence of the "Hercules at the crossroads" motif in Renaissance iconography; and Theodore Mommsen, "Petrarch and the Story of the Choice of Hercules," *Journal of the Warburg and Courtauld Institutes* 16 3/4 (1953): 178–92, who corrects Panofsky's classic study by pointing out that Petrarch in his *De vita solitaria*, not Salutati, was the first to coin the phrase "Hercules *in bivio*" ("Hercules at the crossroads)."

39. In book I of the *De vita solitaria*, Petrarch cites both passages from the *De officiis*. See Francesco Petrarca, *Prose*, ed. Giorgio Martellotti, et al. (Milan: Ricciardi, 1955), 322 and 332.

40. For a useful survey of the Hercules myth as it evolved through the ancient and medieval periods, see Franco Gaeta, "L'avventura di Ercole," *Rinascimento* 5 (December 1954): 227–60. On Hercules as a figure of Christ, see Marcel Simon, *Hercule et le Christianisme* (Paris: Les Belles Lettres, 1955).

41. See Goro Dati, *Istoria di Firenze dall'anno 1380 all'anno 1405* (Florence: Stamperia di Giuseppe Manni, 1735), 127. On the use of the Hercules myth in Florentine propaganda, particularly under the Medici regime, see Leopold Ettlinger, "Hercules Florentinus," *Mitteilungen des Kunsthistorischen Institutes in Florenz* 16.2 (1972): 119–42; Alison Wright, "The Myth of Hercules," in *Lorenzo il Magnifico e il suo mondo*, ed. Gian Carlo Garfagnini (Florence: Olschki, 1994), 323–39; Maria Monica Donato, "Hercules and David in the Early Decoration of the Palazzo Vecchio: Manuscript Evidence," *Journal of the Warburg and Courtauld Institutes* 54 (1991): 83–98; and Alison Brown, "De-Masking Renaissance Republicanism," in *Renaissance Civic Humanism: Reappraisals and Reflections*, ed. James Hankins (Cambridge: Cambridge University Press, 2000), 179–99.

42. Franco Sacchetti, *Il libro delle rime*, ed. Alberto Chiari (Bari: Laterza, 1936), 210 and ff., where Sacchetti defines Florence as "Ercole novo."

43. Coluccio Salutati, *De laboribus Herculis*, ed. B. L. Ullman (Zurich: Thesauri Mundi, 1951). On Salutati's work, see Ronald Witt, *Hercules at the Crossroads: The Life, Works, and Thought of Coluccio Salutati* (Durham, NC: Duke University Press, 1983), especially 212–26.

44. See also Matteo Palmieri, *Della vita civile*, ed. Felice Battaglia (Bologna: Nicola Zanichelli Editore, 1944), 41, with a reference to the above-mentioned *exemplum* narrated in Xenophon's *Memorabilia*; and Cristoforo Landino, *Disputationes Camaldulenses*, ed. Peter Lohe (Florence: Sansoni, 1980), 186, 235, and most significantly 32, where he retrieves the notion of Hercules as benefactor via the character of Lorenzo de' Medici, one

of the participants in Landino's fictional dialogue. By the same author, but written after Pulci's death in 1484, is the *De vera nobilitate*, ed. Maria Teresa Liaci (Florence: Olschki, 1970), 107–9. See also Girolamo Savonarola, *Prediche sopra Ezechiele*, ed. Roberto Ridolfi (Rome: Belardetti, 1955), 208; as late as 1497, one of Savonarola's sermons still decries the popularity of the Hercules myth.

45. Carrai, *Le muse dei Pulci*, 95–96.

46. Antonio Pollaiuolo's *The Rape of Deianira*, one of the paintings dedicated to the hero's deeds, captures the instant in which Hercules is about to strike Nessus with his arrow. Currently held at the Yale Art Gallery in New Haven, CT, this painting was commissioned roughly in the same years during which Pulci began writing the *Morgante*.

47. On the authorship of this tragedy, see Richard J. Tarrant, "Greek and Roman in Seneca's Tragedies," *Harvard Studies in Classical Philology* 97 (1995): 215–30, especially 215–16. On the circulation of Seneca's tragedies in the late Middle Ages, see Claudia Villa, "Le tragedie di Seneca nel Trecento," in *Seneca e il suo tempo*, ed. Piergiorgio Parroni (Rome: Salerno Editrice, 2000), 469–80; and Carla Maria Monti and Francesca Pasut, "Episodi della fortuna di Seneca tragico nel Trecento," *Aevum* 73.2 (Maggio-Agosto 1999): 513–47.

48. In Seneca, *Tragedies*, 2:436–37. These lines are quoted in Salutati, *De laboribus Herculis*, 205–6.

49. On the influence of Sophocles's *Women of Trachis* on this passage of the *Hercules on Oeta*, see Felix Budelmann, "The Reception of Sophocles' Representation of Physical Pain," *American Journal of Philology* 128.4 (Winter 2007): 443–67, especially 446–51. For a thorough analysis of the play and its sources, see Silvia Marcucci, *Analisi e interpretazione dell'Hercules Oetaeus* (Pisa: Istituti Editoriali e Poligrafici Internazionali, 1997).

50. On Seneca's interest in medicine, see Fabio Stok, "Celso in Seneca?," *Orpheus* 6 (1985): 417–21; and Paola Migliorini, *Scienza e terminologia nella letteratura latina di età neroniana. Seneca, Lucano, Persio, Petronio* (Frankfurt: Peter Lang, 1997), 21–94.

51. Salutati, *De laboribus Herculis*, 206.

52. Ibid., 206; my translation.

53. From the early 1470s, Pulci spent much of his time in Milan on diplomatic missions at the service of both Lorenzo and the condottiere Roberto da Sanseverino. See Marcello Simonetta, *Rinascimento segreto. Il mondo del Segretario da Petrarca a Machiavelli* (Milan: Franco Angeli, 2004), 196–210. On Pulci's reference to Andrea Lampognano, see Perrotta, "Lo spazio della corte," 163–66.

54. See, for instance, *Morgante* 10.108, in which Pulci's Charlemagne conceals his gladness at seeing a fight between Orlando and Rinaldo: "Carlo diceva:—Io ne son mal contento—/ dicea di fuor, ma nol diceva drento" ["Charlemagne whispered, 'I don't like all this,' but deep within he was full of bliss"].

55. Cf. Nigro, *Pulci e la cultura medicea*, 33; and Ruggieri, *L'umanesimo cavalleresco italiano*, 239.

56. For the Longinus story, see Iacopo da Varazze, *Legenda Aurea*, ed. Giovanni Paolo Maggioni (Florence: Sismel—Edizioni del Galluzzo, 1998), 307–8 (XLVII).

57. I have discussed this passage previously in my "The Giant's Heel: Pride and Treachery in Pulci's *Morgante*," *Modern Language Notes* 127.1 (2012): 164–72, but did not then adequately consider the issue of ingratitude. On pride and ingratitude in relation to the fallen angels, see also *Morgante* 25.152.

58. From the *Graduale Romano Serafico*, Ordinis Fratrum Minorum (Paris: Typis Societatis S. Joannis Evangelistae, Desclee & Socii, 1932), 97–100, in the sequence for the *Missa pro Defunctis*. The English translation is taken from *Dies Irae*, trans. W. J. Irons, in *Seven Great Hymns of the Medieval Church*, ed. Charles C. Nott (New York: Anson D. F. Randolph, 1870), 61. On Thomas of Celano, see Gilbert Wdzieczny, "The Life and Works of Thomas of Celano," *Franciscan Studies*, New Series 5.1 (March 1945): 55–68; on the possible pagan and Christian sources of the *Dies Irae*, see John Savage, "Virgilian Echoes in the 'Dies Irae,'" *Traditio* 13 (1957): 443–51.

59. Cf. John Julian, ed., *A Dictionary of Hymnology: Setting Forth the Origin and History of Christian Hymns of All Ages and Nations* (New York: Dover Publications, 1907), 1:295–301, especially 295.

60. Giovanni Boccaccio, *Corbaccio*, ed. Tauno Nurmela (Helsinki: Suomalainen Tiedeakatemia, 1968), 39. The translation is from Giovanni Boccaccio, *The Corbaccio*, trans. and ed. Anthony Cassell (Urbana: University of Illinois Press, 1975), 1. On the *Corbaccio* and its possible sources, see Anthony Cassell, "Il *Corbaccio* and the *Secundus* Tradition," *Comparative Literature* 25.4 (Autumn 1973): 352–60; and Dante Nardo, "Sulle fonti classiche del 'Corbaccio,'" in *Medioevo e Rinascimento Veneto* (Padua: Antenore, 1979), 1:245–54.

61. Dante, too, uses the term "Fonte pietatis" in *Monarchia* 2.5.5 and in *Epistles* 5.3, but in a rather different context, as he asserts the legitimacy of the Roman Empire; he also cites a passage from Jacobus de Voragine's *Legenda Aurea*. That the *Corbaccio* possibly served as a bridge between the *Dies Irae* and cantare II of the *Morgante* is further suggested by the presence of a punishing fire in the final sentence, which may echo the feared punishments in the *Dies Irae* (ll. 42, 46–47).

62. See Francesco Castellani, *Ricordanze*, ed. Giovanni Ciappelli (Florence: Olschki, 1992), 2:52.

63. Among the most recent studies on Boccaccio's knowledge and use of Seneca's works, see Igor Candido, *Boccaccio umanista. Studi su Boccaccio e Apuleio* (Ravenna: Longo, 2014), especially 77–83; Jonathan Usher, "Apicius, Seneca, and Surfeit: Boccaccio's Sonnet 95," *Modern Language Notes* 118.1 (January 2003): 46–59; and Elsa Filosa and Luisa Flora, "Ancora su Seneca (e Giovenale) nel *Decameron*," *Giornale storico della letteratura italiana* 115 (1998): 210–19.

64. On the transmission of the *De beneficiis* in the Middle Ages, see Giancarlo Mazzoli, "Ricerche sulla tradizione medievale del *De beneficiis* e del *De clementia* di Seneca," *Bollettino del comitato per la preparazione dell'edizione nazionale dei classici greci e latini*, ser. 2, 26 (1978): 85–109; idem, "Ricerche sulla tradizione medievale del *De beneficiis* e del *De clementia* di Seneca. III Storia della tradizione manoscritta," *Bollettino dei Classici*, ser. 3, 3 (1982): 165–223.

65. On Dante and Seneca, see Santorre Debenedetti, "Dante e Seneca filosofo," *Studi danteschi* 6 (1923): 5–24; Giorgio Brugnoli, "Ut patet per Senecam in suis tragediis," *Rivista di cultura classica e medioevale* 5 (1963): 146–63; and Giuseppina Mezzadroli, *Seneca in Dante. Dalla tradizione medievale all'officina dell'autore* (Florence: Le Lettere, 1990), especially 43–60.

66. Cf. Guido da Pisa, *Expositiones et glose super Comediam Dantis* (commentary to *Inferno* 34.10–12).

67. Given Hercules's common depiction as benefactor of humankind, it would not be inconceivable to argue that his death and, for that matter, Morgante's death should be seen as examples of treason against benefactors.

68. On Dante's influence on Pulci, see Maria Cristina Cabani, *L'occhio di Polifemo: studi su Pulci, Tasso e Marino* (Pisa: ETS, 2005), 17–57.

69. On Dante's traitors, see John Scott, "Treachery in Dante," in *Studies in the Italian Renaissance: Essays in Memory of Arnolfo B. Ferruolo*, ed. Gian Paolo Biasin, et al. (Naples: Società Editrice Napoletana, 1985), 27–42.

70. On Dante's giants, see Peter Dronke, *Dante and Medieval Latin Traditions* (Cambridge: Cambridge University Press, 1986), 32–54.

71. See Giovanni Villani, *Nuova Cronica* IV, 1; Giovanni Boccaccio, *Ninfale fiesolano*, lines 461–63; and the partial criticism of this story in Leonardo Bruni, *History of the Florentine People*, 3 vols., ed. and trans. James Hankins with D.J.W. Bradley (Cambridge, MA: Cambridge University Press, 2001–7), 1:94–95 (I, 76–77).

72. See Donato Acciaiuoli, *La "Vita Caroli" di Donato Acciaiuoli*, ed. Daniela Gatti (Bologna: Paltron Editore, 1981). On Acciaiuoli, and his discussion of Charlemagne and the relationship between trust and justice, see Eugenio Garin, *Medioevo e Rinascimento* (Bari: Laterza, 1984), 199–267, especially 250–54. See also Nigro, *Pulci e la cultura medicea*, 23; and Constance Jordan, *Pulci's "Morgante": Poetry and History in Fifteenth-Century Florence* (Washington, D.C.: The Folger Shakespeare Library, 1986), 20–23.

73. Toward the end of the *Morgante*, in cantare 28, Pulci describes Charlemagne, once crowned Holy Roman Emperor by Pope Leo III, as the (re-)founder of Florence:

> dunque Carlo fu Magno e imperatore
> di tutto l'universo e re di Roma,
> ed aggiunse al suo segno, per più onore,
> il grande uccel che di Giove si noma.
> E licenziato dal santo Pastore,
> poi ch'egli aveva ogni arroganza doma,
> nel suo tornar, per più magnificenzia,
> rifece e rinnovòe l'alma Florenzia. (28.100)

[Thus Charles was Charlemagne and Emperor of the Whole Universe and King of Rome, and added on his flag—for greater fame—the noble eagle that's the bird of Jove. After the pontiff gave him leave to go—every rebellion having been subdued—on his way back, with high munificence, he renovated and rebuilt great Florence.]

The version of the poem we currently read was first published in 1483, a year after Lucrezia Tornabuoni's death. For the references to Lorenzo's mother, see *Morgante* 1.4 and 28.131–36.

74. On Cosimo's exile and struggle for power in the 1430s, see Dale Kent, *The Rise of the Medici: Faction in Florence 1426–1434* (Oxford: Oxford University Press, 1978), especially 211–351. On the 1466 plot, see Margery Ganz, "Perceived Insults and Their Consequences: Acciaiuoli, Neroni, and Medici Relationships in the 1460's," in *Society and Individual in Renaissance Florence*, ed. William Connell (Berkeley: University of California Press, 2002), 155–72. Among the numerous studies on the Pazzi conspiracy, see Tobias Daniels, *La congiura dei Pazzi: i documenti del conflitto fra Lorenzo de' Medici e Sisto IV* (Florence: Edifir-Edizioni, 2013); Marcello Simonetta, *The Montefeltro Conspiracy: A Renaissance Mystery Decoded* (New York: Doubleday, 2008); and Lauro Martines, *April Blood: Florence and the Plot against the Medici* (Oxford: Oxford University Press, 2003). For a detailed history of Florentine politics under the Medici regime, see Nicolai Rubinstein, *The Government of Florence under the Medici (1434–1494)* (Oxford: Clarendon Press, 1997).

75. Landino, *Disputationes Camaldulenses*, 32.

76. Giovanni Santi, *La vita e le gesta di Federico da Montefeltro duca d'Urbino: poema in terza rima (Codice Vat. Ottob. lat. 1305)*, ed. Luigi Michelini Tocci (Vatican City: Biblioteca Apostolica Vaticana, 1985), 406 (book XIII, chapter 54). Cf. Wright, "The Myth of Hercules," 332.

77. Cf. Luigi Pulci, *Morgante e le lettere*, ed. Domenico De Robertis (Florence: Sansoni, 1984), especially 991–92, letter XXXVI to Lorenzo, in which Pulci complains of both Ficino and Franco; and Luigi Pulci, *Opere minori*, ed. Paolo Orvieto (Milan: Mursia, 1986), 151–90 (for his sonnets against Franco) and 197–201 (for his poems of religious parody aimed mainly at Ficino's *Platonic Theology*). On the Ficino associates' involvement in the Pazzi conspiracy, see Garin, *Medioevo e Rinascimento*, 269–70; and Giuseppe Mazzotta, *Cosmopoiesis: The Renaissance Experiment* (Toronto: Toronto University Press, 2001), 7–10. See also Giuseppe Mazzotta, "Modern and Ancient Italy in *Don Quijote*," *Poetica* 38 (2006): 91–106, especially 97–99. On the tensions among Medici courtiers, see Nigro, *Pulci e la cultura medicea*, and Ruggeri, *L'Umanesimo cavalleresco italiano*, particularly 242–68. Regarding the possible Ficino pun and, more generally, Pulci's rivalry with the philosopher, see also Paolo Orvieto, *Pulci medievale* (Rome: Salerno Editrice, 1978), 12 and 213–83.

78. For a comprehensive portrait of Jacopo, see Francesco Bausi, "'Paternae artis haeres.' Ritratto di Jacopo Bracciolini," *Interpres* 8 (1988): 103–98.

79. "Iacopo, son of Poggio, displayed great nobility as he arrived at the square" (translation mine). See Pulci, *Opere minori*, 82–83 (stanzas LIV-LV).

80. The English translation is from Agnolo Poliziano, *The Pazzi Conspiracy*, in *The Earthly Republic*, eds. Benjamin G. Kohl and Ronald G. Witt (Philadelphia: University of Pennsylvania Press, 1978), 305–22, especially 308. The Latin text is from Agnolo Poliziano, *Della congiura dei Pazzi (Coniurationis commentarium)*, ed. Alessandro Perosa (Padova: Antenore, 1958), 17.

81. Poliziano, *The Pazzi Conspiracy*, 317; Poliziano, *Della congiura dei Pazzi*, 47.

82. Other sources differ from Poliziano on this point. See Perosa's commentary to Poliziano, *Della congiura dei Pazzi*, 30.

83. On this commemorative medal, see James Draper, *Bertoldo di Giovanni, Sculptor of the Medici Household: Critical Reappraisal and Catalogue Raisonné* (Columbia: University of Missouri Press, 1992), 86–95.

84. Luke 2:14: "Glory to God in the highest: and on earth peace to men of good will."

85. "Smiling the knight from Burgundy replied, 'O Rabbi, hail! I know that you are lying.'" Cf. Matthew 26:49. On this passage, see Carrai, *Le muse dei Pulci*, 138.

86. For Ganelon's trial and the duel to establish whether he should be condemned for treason, see *La Chanson de Roland*, 3780–959. In his treatise on chivalry, *Libre del orde de cavalleria* (ca. 1275), Ramon Llull unequivocally states that traitors should be executed: see Raimondo Lullo, *Libro dell'ordine della cavalleria*, edited and translated into Italian by Giovanni Allegra (Carmagnola, Ita.: Edizioni Arktos, 1983), 94–98. For a critical assessment of this complex legal issue and its historical background, see Ruggero Ruggieri, *Il processo di Gano nella "Chanson de Roland"* (Firenze: Sansoni, 1936); Silvio Pellegrini, *Studi rolandiani e trobadorici* (Bari: Adriatica Editrice, 1964), particularly 122–35; Simon Cuttler, *The Law of Treason and Treason Trials in Later Medieval France* (Cambridge: Cambridge University Press, 1981); Emanuel Mickel, *Ganelon, Treason and the "Chanson de Roland,"* (University Park: The Pennsylvania State University Press, 1989); and Giuseppe Monorchio, *Lo specchio del cavaliere* (Ottawa: Canadian Society for Italian Studies, 1998), 11–42.

87. Much like Ganelon, right before the moment of his execution Marsilio claims that his soul will be damned: "Del corpo mio, fa tu quel che ti pare; / l'anima so nell'inferno è dannata" ["Do with my body as you wish; my soul, I know, will be forever damned in hell"] (*Morgante* 27.284).

88. Cicero here translates a passage from Euripides's *The Phoenician Women*.

89. For the earthquake, see Matthew 27:51–54; Mark 15:38; and Luke 22:45. The legend of Judas's hanging on a carob tree is not found in the gospels, but probably derives from a folk tradition.

90. Everywhere in his letters and later in the poem (*Morgante* 28.146) Pulci calls Lorenzo "alloro" or "lauro." For an identical image of a laurel tree struck by lightning, see Petrarca, *Rerum Vulgarium Fragmenta*, 323.25–36. On this sign as a warning to Lorenzo, see also Jordan, *Pulci's "Morgante,"* 165. For a reference to similar signs in the *Chanson de Roland*, see Cesare Segre, *La tradizione della "Chanson de Roland"* (Milan: Ricciardi, 1974), 3–8.

91. On the Christological echoes of Orlando's death, see Stefano Carrai, "La morte di Orlando nel *Morgante*," in *Luigi Pulci in Florence and Beyond: New Perspectives on His Poetry and Influence*, eds. James K. Coleman and Andrea Moudarres (Turnhout: Brepols, 2017).

92. Poliziano, *The Pazzi Conspiracy*, 316; Poliziano, *Della congiura dei Pazzi*, 42. Poliziano's description of the dismemberment of the conspirators in the *Historia* resembles his account of the dismemberment of Orpheus by the Maenads in the *Fabula di Orfeo*,

probably written in the late 1470s. Cf. Agnolo Poliziano, *Fabula di Orfeo*, in Antonia Tissoni Benvenuti, *Orfeo del Poliziano* (Padua: Antenore, 1986), 163–65 (lines 293–308).

93. Poliziano, *The Pazzi Conspiracy*, 321; Poliziano, *Della congiura dei Pazzi*, 60. On the desecration of Jacopo de' Pazzi's body, see Gian-Paolo Biasin, "'Messer Iacopo Giù Per Arno Se Ne Va . . . ,'" *Modern Language Notes* 79.1 (January 1964): 1–13.

94. On the establishment of the Duchy of Florence, see John Najemy, *A History of Florence 1200–1575* (Malden, MA: Blackwell Publishing, 2006), 446–68; and Catherine Fletcher, *The Black Prince of Florence: The Spectacular Life and Treacherous World of Alessandro de' Medici* (London: The Bodley Head, 2016).

3. The Enemy as the Self

1. On the strife within the soul, see Augustine, *Confessiones* IV, 10 and VIII, 7–11, especially VIII, 10: "Therefore was I at strife with myself, and distracted by mine own self. Which distracting befell me much against my mind" ["ideo mecum contendebam et dissipabar a me ipso, et ipsa dissipatio me invito quidem fiebat"], in Saint Augustine, *Confessions*, trans. W. Watts (Cambridge, MA: Harvard University Press, 1960); Prudentius, *Psychomachia*, lines 5–11: "say, our King [Christ], with what fighting force of the soul is furnished and enabled to expel the sins from our breast; when there is disorder among our thoughts and rebellion arises within us, when the strife of our evil passions vexes the spirit, say what help there is then to guard our liberty" ["dissere, rex noster, quo milite pellere culpas / mens armata queat nostri de pectoris antro, / exoritur quotiens turbatis sensibus intus / seditio atque animam morborum rixa fatigat, / quod tunc praesidium pro libertate tuenda / uaeve acies furiis inter praecordia mixtis / obsistat meliore manu. nec enim, bone doctor"], in Prudentius, *Works*, trans. H. J. Thompson (Cambridge, MA: Harvard University Press, 1949); and the passage cited in chapter 1 of this book from Aquinas's *Summa theologiae*: "[concord] denotes union of appetites among various persons, while peace denotes, in addition to this union, the union of appetites even in one man," Thomas Aquinas, *Summa Theologica*, trans. the Fathers of the English Dominican Province (New York: Benziger, 1948), II-II, q. 29, a. 1.

2. Dante, *Vita Nova* 38.4: "Onde io, avendo così più volte combattuto in me medesimo, ancora ne volli dire alquante parole; e però che la battaglia de' pensieri vinceano coloro che per lei parlavano, mi parve che si convenisse di parlare a lei" ["Finally, having battled like this within myself many times, I wished to write more poetry about it, and since in the battle of the thoughts those won which spoke in the lady's favor, it seemed right that I address myself to her"]. The original text is from Dante, *Vita Nuova*, in *Le Opere di Dante*, ed. Michele Barbi (Florence: Società Dantesca Italiana, 1960), vol. 1. The English translation is from *Dante's "Vita Nuova,"* trans. Mark Musa (Bloomington: Indiana University Press, 1973).

3. The Latin text and the translation are both from Pico della Mirandola, *Oration on the Dignity of Man*, ed. Francesco Borghesi, et al. (Cambridge: Cambridge University Press, 2013), 150–51: "Manifold indeed, o fathers, is the discord in us; we have grave internal, more than civil, wars" ["Multiplex profecto, patres, in nobis Discordia; gravia et intestina domi habemus, et plus quam civilian bella"].

4. The following list includes only a selection of the numerous studies on Orlando's madness: Pio Rajna, *Le fonti dell'Orlando furioso* (1900; Florence: Sansoni, 1975), 394–408; Robert Durling, *Figure of the Epic Poet in Renaissance Epic* (Cambridge, MA: Harvard University Press, 1965), 112–81, especially 160–68; Paolo Valesio, "The Language of Madness in the Renaissance," *Yearbook of Italian Studies* (1971): 199–234; Andrea Di Tommaso, "'Insania' and 'Furor': A Diagnostic Note on Orlando's Malady," *Romance Notes* 14 (1972/73): 583–88; Giuseppe Della Palma, "Una cifra per la pazzia d'Orlando," *Strumenti Critici* 9 (1975): 367–79; Giulio Ferroni, "L'Ariosto e la concezione umanistica della follia," in *Atti del convegno internazionale "Ludovico Ariosto"* (Rome: Accademia Nazionale dei Lincei, 1975), 73–91; Massimo Ciavolella, "La licantropia d'Orlando," in *Il Rinascimento. Aspetti e problemi attuali*, ed. Vittore Branca, et al. (Florence: Leo Olschki Editore, 1982), 311–23; Elizabeth Chesney, *The Countervoyage of Rabelais and Ariosto: A Comparative Reading of Two Renaissance Mock Epics* (Durham, NC: Duke University Press, 1982), 171–204; Ernesto Grassi and Maristella Lorch, *Folly and Insanity in Renaissance Literature* (Binghamton, NY: Medieval and Renaissance Texts and Studies, 1986), 87–109; Marina Beer, *Romanzi di cavalleria. Il "Furioso" e il romanzo italiano del primo Cinquecento* (Rome: Bulzoni Editore, 1987), 35–111; Cesare Segre, *Fuori del mondo. I modelli nella follia e nelle immagini dell'aldilà* (Turin: Einaudi, 1990), 89–119; Sergio Zatti, *Il Furioso tra epos e romanzo* (Lucca: Maria Pacini Fazzi Editore, 1990), 96–102 and 127–33; Dennis Looney, *Compromising the Classics: Romance Epic Narrative in the Italian Renaissance* (Detroit: Wayne State University Press, 1996), 19–29; Rinaldo Rinaldi, *Le imprese imperfette. Studi sul Rinascimento* (Turin: Tirrenia Stampatori, 1997), 41–88; Franco Masciandaro, "La follia e lo specchio di Narciso nell'*Orlando Furioso*," in *La conoscenza viva. Letture fenomenologiche da Dante a Machiavelli* (Ravenna, Ita.: Longo Editore, 1998), 99–116; Franco Picchio, *Ariosto e Bacco. I codici del sacro nell'Orlando Furioso* (Turin: Paravia, 1999), 27–30 and 78–90; Elissa Weaver, "A Reading of the Interlaced Plot of the *Orlando Furioso*: The Three Cases of Love Madness," in *Ariosto Today: Contemporary Perspectives*, ed. Donald Beecher, et al. (Toronto: University of Toronto Press, 2003), 126–53; and Marion Wells, *The Secret Wound: Love-Melancholy and Early Modern Romance* (Stanford, CA: Stanford University Press, 2007), 96–136.

5. Albert Ascoli, *Ariosto's Bitter Harmony: Crisis and Evasion in the Italian Renaissance* (Princeton, NJ: Princeton University Press, 1987), 46–70, especially 58–59, and 304–31.

6. Giuseppe Mazzotta, *Cosmopoiesis: The Renaissance Experiment* (Toronto: Toronto University Press, 2001), 25–51.

7. Albert Ascoli, "Ariosto and the 'Fier Pastor': Form and History in *Orlando Furioso*," *Renaissance Quarterly* 54.2 (Summer 2001): 487–522.

8. In this chapter, I will use terms such as "psychology" and "psychological" according to their etymological root, namely the Greek word *psyche*, which means "soul."

9. Cf. Ascoli, "Ariosto and the 'Fier Pastor,'" 510, regarding whether and how the term "allegory" can appropriately be used in relation to the *Furioso*.

10. It should be noted that Charlemagne plays a much larger role in the incomplete *Cinque Canti* than in the *Orlando Furioso*. On the *Cinque Canti*, see David Quint's

Introduction to Ludovico Ariosto, *Cinque Canti*, trans. Alexander Sheers and David Quint (Berkeley: University of California Press, 1996), 1–44, especially 25–36 on Charlemagne.

11. On Nebuchadnezzar in the *Furioso*, see Ascoli, *Ariosto's Bitter Harmony*, 279–80. On Nebuchadnezzar as a paradigm of madness in the Middle Ages, see Penelope Doob, *Nebuchadnezzar's Children: Conventions of Madness in Middle English Literature* (New Haven, CT: Yale University Press, 1974), 54–94 and especially 63–79, on Nebuchadnezzar as a tyrant in post-biblical commentaries; and Richard Bernheimer, *Wild Men in the Middle Ages: A Study in Art, Sentiment, and Demonology* (Cambridge, MA: Harvard University Press, 1952), 12–13.

12. In the same stanza, Orlando's role in defense of Christianity is compared to Samson's mission on behalf of the Jews in Judges 13–16. It is also worth noting that Astolfo is compared to the prophet Elijah (34.59 and 34.68). Moreover, while Orlando's seven-fold baptism that cures his madness (39.56) evokes the seven deadly vices, it also—and more pertinently, I believe—evokes the cure of Naaman the Syrian, a gentile captain sick with leprosy who converts after Elijah tells him to bathe seven times in the Jordan River (2 Kings 5). Orlando is thus repeatedly cast as an Old Testament figure, while Ruggiero is associated with New Testament figures, including Saint Paul in 41.53. Since my focus here is primarily on the classical antecedents of the *Furioso*, a discussion of Orlando and Ruggiero in biblical terms exceeds the limits of this chapter; I hope to return to this topic in a future study.

13. All citations are from Ludovico Ariosto, *Orlando furioso*, ed. Lanfranco Caretti (Turin: Einaudi, 1992). All translations are from Ludovico Ariosto, *Orlando Furioso*, trans. Guido Waldman (Oxford: Oxford University Press, 1998). Hereafter cited as *OF*.

14. On the relationship between the *Orlando Innamorato* and the *Furioso*, see: Peter Marinelli, *Ariosto and Boiardo: The Origins of "Orlando Furioso"* (Columbia: University of Missouri Press, 1987), 17–51; Riccardo Bruscagli, *Stagioni della civiltà estense* (Pisa: Nistri-Lischi, 1983), 87–126; Bruscagli, *Studi cavallereschi* (Florence: Società Editrice Fiorentina, 2003), 55–73; Jo Ann Cavallo, *The Romance Epics of Boiardo, Ariosto, and Tasso: From Public Duty to Private Pleasure* (Toronto: Toronto University Press, 2004); and Cavallo, *The World Beyond Europe in the Romance Epics of Boiardo and Ariosto* (Toronto: Toronto University Press, 2013).

15. All citations are from Matteo Maria Boiardo, *Orlando innamorato*, ed. Riccardo Bruscagli (Turin: Einaudi, 1995). All translations are from Matteo Maria Boiardo, *Orlando Innamorato*, trans. C. S. Ross (Berkeley: University of California Press, 1989). Hereafter cited as *OI*.

16. On desire in the *Furioso*, see Eugenio Donato, "'Per selve e boscherecci labirinti': Desire and Narrative Structure in Ariosto's *Orlando Furioso*," in *Literary Theory/Renaissance Texts*, eds. Patricia Parker and David Quint (Baltimore: Johns Hopkins University Press, 1986), 33–62. On Angelica as "embodiment of desire," see Valeria Finucci, *The Lady Vanishes: Subjectivity and Representation in Castiglione and Ariosto* (Stanford, CA: Stanford University Press, 1992), 109–44.

17. See also *OF* 14.33: "lasciato Orlando avea il quartiero; / che come dentro l'animo

era in doglia, / così l'imbrunir di fuor volse la spoglia" ["Orlando had left off his insignia: his heart was in mourning, so he chose black for his outward trappings"].

18. On Orlando's melancholy, see Di Tommaso, "'Insania' and 'Furor,'" 583–88; Ciavolella, "La licantropia d'Orlando," 311–23; Beer, *Romanzi di cavalleria*, 35–111; Wells, *The Secret Wound*, 96–136; and Rinaldi, *Le imprese imperfette*, 41–48. On melancholy in antiquity and in the early modern age, see the classic Raymond Klibansky, Erwin Panofsky, and Fritz Saxl, *Saturn and Melancholy: Studies in the History of Natural Philosophy, Religion, and Art* (1964; Nendeln, Lie.: Klaus Reprint, 1979), especially 3–66 on ancient physiological literature (pages 1–15 on the Pythagorean and Hippocratic notions of *melancholia* and pages 15–41 on the pseudo-Aristotelian *Problems* XXX, 1), and 241–74 on Marsilio Ficino and Florentine Neoplatonism. See Aristotle, *Problems* 954a 32–35: "those who possess a large quantity of hot black bile become frenzied or clever or erotic or easily moved to anger and desire [...] Many too, if this heat approaches the region of the intellect, are affected by diseases of frenzy and possession." Ficino discusses the causes and effects of melancholy and lovesickness in several of his works: see, for instance, Marsilio Ficino, *Platonic Theology*, eds. James Hankins and William Bowen, and trans. Michael J. B. Allen and John Warden (Cambridge, MA: Harvard University Press, 2001–6): "if some vapor of black bile, which the Greeks call melancholy, besieges and then storms the body's citadel, we immediately experience the sensation of our queen, the reason, being dethroned as it were, and of [her] subjects being gripped by manifest insanity" ["si vapor aliquis bilis atrae, quam melancholiam Graeci vocant, arcem corporis obsederit expugnaveritque statim reginam inde nostrum, ipsam videlicet rationem, ut ita dicam, praecipitari, ac manifesta homines insania corripit"] (XIV, vii, 7); Marsilio Ficino, *Three Books on Life*, ed. and trans. C. Kaske and J. Clark (Binghamton, NY: Medieval and Renaissance Texts and Studies, 1989), especially 113–29; and Marsilio Ficino, *Commentary on Plato's* Symposium *on Love*, trans. Sears Jayne (Dallas: Spring Publications, 1985), especially 122 (on the connection between love and melancholy), 185 (on the different kinds of frenzy), and 168 (on the effects of burning black bile). On Ficino's discussion of black bile, see Paul Oskar Kristeller, *The Philosophy of Marsilio Ficino* (New York: Columbia University Press, 1943), 211–14. See also Andreas Capellanus, *The Art of Courtly Love*, trans. John Jay Parry (New York: Columbia University Press, 1990), 199: "The loss of sleep also causes frequent alterations in the brain and in the mind, so that man becomes raging mad" ["Somni quoque amissio cerebri et mentis saepissime alterationes inducit, unde homo efficitur amens et furiosus"]. All Latin citations from Capellanus's work are from The Latin Library, http://www.thelatinlibrary.com/capellanus.html. For the etymology of melancholy, see Isidore of Seville, *Etymologies* IV, 7, 9. On ancient and premodern theories of melancholy, see also Doob, *Nebuchadnezzar's Children*, 1–53; Robert Klinsman, "Folly, Melancholy and Madness: A Study in Shifting Styles of Medical Analysis and Treatment," in *The Darker Vision of the Renaissance: Beyond the Fields of Reason*, ed. Robert Klinsman (Berkeley: University of California Press, 1974), 273–320; Massimo Ciavolella, *La "malattia d'amore dall'Antichità al Medioevo* (Rome: Bulzoni Editore, 1976); and Wells, *The Secret Wound*, 19–59.

19. Regarding Hercules's fury, Aristotle mentions the episode that formed the basis

Euripides's *Heracles* and would eventually become the subject of Seneca's *Hercules Furens*. Cf. Debra Hershowitz, *The Madness of Epic: Reading Insanity from Homer to Statius* (Oxford: Oxford University Press, 1998), 17–22. In the *Tusculan Disputations*, Cicero similarly states that "frenzy can come upon the wise man" ["furor in sapientem cadere possit"] (III, v, 11). See Cicero, *Tusculan Disputations*, trans. J. E. King (Cambridge, MA: Harvard University Press, 2001). See also Klibansky, Panofsky, and Saxl, *Saturn and Melancholy*, 43–44. On black bile's potentially negative influence on learned people, see Ficino, *Three Books on Life*, 113. See also Capellanus, *The Art of Courtly Love*, 199–200: "For yet another reason I urge you not to love: that is because in a wise man wisdom loses its function if he loves [...] Indeed it is said that wise men become more wild with love and indulge more ardently in the pleasures of the flesh than those who have less knowledge to control them" ["Alia quoque ratione te non amare compello, quia sapientia propter amorem suum in sapiente perdit officium. Nam, quantumcunque sit aliquis sapientia plenus, si ad Veneris opera deducatur, nescit habere modum vel sua sapientia motus luxuriae moderari aut actus mortiferos refrenare. Immo magis sapientes insanire dicuntur amore et ardentius carnis voluptates implere quam qui minori scientia gubernantur"].

20. *Hercules Furens* 1044–45: "his tired neck sinks beneath his drooping head" ["vultus in somnum cadit / et fessa cervix capite summisso labat"].

21. See Plato, *Timaeus* 91e; Aristotle, *Parts of Animals* 686a 27; Ovid, *Metamorphoses* 1.84; Boethius, *Consolation of Philosophy* V, 5; Bernardus Silvestris, *Cosmographia* book II, chapter 10; and Leon Battista Alberti, *Momus* II, 111. On this notion in relation to Ariosto, see Ascoli, *Ariosto's Bitter Harmony*, 311; and Mazzotta, *Cosmopoiesis*, 41.

22. In a letter to Aldo Manuzio (January 1498), Ariosto requests a number of books, including Ficino's commentaries on Plato's works; see Ariosto, *Lettere* (Verona: Mondadori, 1965), letter no. 1. See Giulio Bertoni, *La biblioteca estense e la coltura ferrarese* (Turin: Loescher, 1903), especially 142; and Cesare Segre, *Eperienze ariostesche* (Pisa: Nistri—Lischi, 1966), 45–50. See also Ariosto, *Satire* VI, 130–50.

23. See Ficino's *Commentarium in Phaedrum*, in *Marsilio Ficino and the Phaedran Charioteer*, ed. Michael Allen (Berkeley: University of California Press, 1981), especially 74–79 and 140–42, on the Platonic distinction among the different kinds of *furor*. On Plato's influence on Renaissance thought, see James Hankins, *Plato in the Italian Renaissance* (Leiden: Brill, 1990), especially 267–359 on Ficino. See also Michael Allen, *The Platonism of Marsilio Ficino: A Study of His Phaedrus Commentary, Its Sources and Genesis* (Berkeley: University of California Press, 1984), especially 86–112 on "the soul's flight" and 165–84 on "the soul's descent."

24. In a letter to Giovanni Nesi on the preeminence of reason, Ficino summarizes these same passages from the *Republic*, the *Phaedrus*, and the *Timaeus*; see Marsilio Ficino, *The Letters of Marsilio Ficino*, translated by members of the Language Department of the School of Economic Science, London (London: Shepheard-Walwyn, 1975–2003), 3:59–62. On "self-mastery" as the distinctive expression of Plato's moral psychology, see Charles Taylor, *Sources of the Self: The Making of the Modern Identity* (Cambridge: Cambridge University Press, 1989), 115–26, especially 115–16: "To be master of one-

self is to have the higher part of the soul rule over the lower, which means reason over desire [...] When reason rules, a quite different kind of order reigns in the soul. Indeed, we can say that order reigns there for the first time. By contrast, the realm of desire is that of chaos. The good souls enjoy order (*kosmos*), concord (*xumphonia*), and harmony (*harmonia*), where the bad are torn every which way by their desires and are in perpetual conflict. Plato even describes them as suffering from a kind of 'civil war' (*stasis*)." See also Bennett Simon, *Mind and Madness in Ancient Greece: The Classical Roots of Modern Psychiatry* (Ithaca, NY: Cornell University Press, 1978), 157–99; Martha Nussbaum, *The Fragility of Goodness: Luck and Ethics in Greek Tragedy and Philosophy* (Chicago: The University of Chicago, 1986), 200–39; Hendrik Lorenz, *The Brute Within: Appetitive Desire in Plato and Aristotle* (Oxford: Oxford University Press, 2006), 1–52; Kenneth Dorter, "Weakness and Will in Plato's *Republic*," in *Weakness of Will from Plato to the Present*, ed. Tobias Hoffmann (Washington, D.C.: The Catholic University of America Press, 2008), 1–21; and Hershowitz, *The Madness of Epic*, 8–10.

25. See also, at the beginning of the second half of the *Orlando Furioso*, Ariosto's direct comments to the reader: "E quale è di pazzia segno più espresso / che, per altri voler, perder sé stesso?" ["what clearer sign of lunacy than to lose your own self through pining for another?"] (24.1).

26. As we read in the Pseudo-Aristotelian *Problems*, some melancholic individuals "maintain a complete silence, especially those atrabilious subjects who are out of their minds" (953b 13–14). Together with reason, speech is obviously the other peculiar faculty that distinguishes human beings from other animals: see Aristotle, *Rhetoric* 1355b 1–3; Cicero, *De officiis* I, 50. Cf. Ascoli, *Ariosto's Bitter Harmony*, 50 and 80–81.

27. Hercules, too, in Euripides's eponymous tragedy, strips himself of his clothes when he is assailed by madness (*Herakles* 957–59).

28. See Sophocles, *Ajax* 295–308, where the Greek hero, deceived and disoriented by Athena, goddess of reason, slaughters animals, thinking that they are his foes Agamemnon, Menelaus, and Odysseus.

29. On the symptoms of Orlando's furor in relation to the medieval tradition of wild men, including chivalric characters like Yvain and Tristan, see Rajna, *Le fonti dell'Orlando Furioso*, 394–408; and Segre, *Fuori del mondo*, 90–93. On Yvain, see Doob, *Nebuchadnezzar's Children*, 134–58; and on the wild men's nakedness, see also Bernheimer, *Wild Men in the Middle Ages*, 1–20. For a broader overview of the wild man in Western culture, see Hayden White, "The Forms of Wildness: Archaeology of an Idea," in *The Wild Man Within: An Image in Western Thought from the Renaissance to Romanticism*, eds. Edward Dudley and Maximilian Novak (Pittsburgh: University of Pittsburgh Press, 1972), 3–38. On the eating of raw flesh and its connection with Dionysian frenzy, see Lillian Feder, *Madness in Literature* (Princeton, NJ: Princeton University Press, 1980), especially 46–47.

30. For a more comprehensive analysis of the city-soul analogy, see Julia Annas, *An Introduction to Plato's* Republic (Oxford: Oxford University Press, 1981), 109–52; Bernard Williams, "The Analogy of City and Soul in Plato's *Republic*," in *Plato's "Republic": Critical Essays*, ed. Richard Kraut (Lanham, MD: Rowman & Littlefield Publishers,

1997), 49–59; Ioannis Evrigenis, "The Psychology of Politics: The City-Soul Analogy in Plato's Republic," *History of Political Thought* 23.4 (Winter 2002): 590–610; Giovanni Ferrari, *City and Soul in Plato's "Republic"* (Sankt Augustin, Germany: Academia Verlag, 2003); and Norbert Blössner, "The City-Soul Analogy," in *The Cambridge Companion to Plato's "Republic,"* ed. Giovanni Ferrari (Cambridge: Cambridge University Press, 2007), 345–85. For a thought-provoking discussion of the key issues articulated in the *Republic*, see Ernst Cassirer, *The Myth of the State* (New Haven, CT: Yale University Press, 1946), 61–77, particularly 61–62: "What is written in 'small characters' in the individual soul, and is therefore almost illegible, becomes clear and understandable only if we read it in the larger letters of man's political and social life. This principle is the starting point of Plato's *Republic*. From now on the whole problem of man was changed: politics was declared to be the clue to psychology."

31. On the wretchedness of the tyrant, see also *Phaedrus* 248e. On the tyrant's melancholic temperament, see Klibansky, Panofsky, and Saxl, *Saturn and Melancholy*, 17. See also Simon, *Mind and Madness in Ancient Greece*, 166–70. On the tyrant in Plato's *Republic*, see Richard Parry, "The Unhappy Tyrant and the Craft of Inner Rule," in *The Cambridge Companion to Plato's "Republic,"* 386–413. See also Ferrari, *City and Soul in Plato's "Republic,"* especially 94–99. On *eros* and the tyrant in the *Republic*, see Waller Newell, *Tyranny: A New Interpretation* (Cambridge: Cambridge University Press, 2013), especially 85–94.

32. On tyranny as the worst form of government and as a corruption of monarchy, the most effective regime, see Aristotle, *Nicomachean Ethics* 1160b 1–2, and *Politics*, 1289a 39-b 2, 1292a 15–24, 1295a 17–23.

33. Seneca, *De Clementia*, in *Moral Essays*, 390–91 (I, 11, 4): "What difference is there between a tyrant and a king [...] except that tyrants are cruel to serve their pleasure, kings only for a reason and by necessity?" ["Quid interest inter tyrannum ac regem (...) nisi quod tyranny in voluptatem saeviunt, reges non nisi ex causa ac necessitate?"]. On tyranny in the *De Clementia*, see Peter Stacey, *Roman Monarchy and the Renaissance Prince* (Cambridge: Cambridge University Press, 2007), 30–72, especially 58–61; and Miriam Griffin, *Seneca: A Philosopher in Politics* (Oxford: Oxford University Press, 1976), 141–48. On the influence of Seneca's political philosophy, especially of the *De Clementia*, in the Middle Ages and the Renaissance, see Peter Stacey, "Senecan Political Thought from the Middle Ages to Early Modernity," in *The Cambridge Companion to Seneca*, eds. Shadi Bartsch and Alessandro Schiesaro (Cambridge: Cambridge University Press, 2015), 289–302.

34. See Coluccio Salutati, *De Tyranno*, in *Political Writings*, ed. Stefano U. Baldassarri and trans. Rolf Bagemihl (Cambridge, MA: Harvard University Press, 2014), 78–79: "Proprium autem est tyranni non iure principari" ["the particular quality of the tyrant is that he does not rule according to law"]; and Leon Battista Alberti, *Defunctus*, in *De commodis litterarum. Defunctus*, edited and translated into Italian by Giovanni Farris (Milan: Marzorati, 1971), 249, in which he describes the effects of tyrants' "furore": "Primum stadium tyrannis est, non secus atque teterrime, horrendeque bellue, omnia per vim, temeritatem atque immanitatem posse" ["The first concern of a tyrant is to

rule over everything through strength, temerity, and cruelty like ferocious beasts"] (my translation). On Salutati's *De tyranno*, see Hans Baron, *The Crisis of the Italian Renaissance: Civic Humanism and Republican Liberty in an Age of Classicism and Tyranny* (1955; Princeton, NJ: Princeton University Press, 1966), 146–66. Compare with Brian Jeffrey Maxson, "Kings and Tyrants: Leonardo Bruni's Translation of Xenophon's *Hiero*," *Renaissance Studies* 24.2 (April 2010): 188–206; and Claudio Fiocchi, *Mala Potestas. La Tirannia nel Pensiero Politico Medioevale* (Bergamo, Ita.: Lubrina Editore, 2004), 144–51. On Alberti, see Eugenio Garin, *Rinascite e rivoluzioni. Movimenti culturali dal XIV al XVIII secolo* (Bari: Laterza, 1975), 133–92, especially 189–91, where he notes the influence of Plato's *Republic* on Alberti's denunciation of tyrants.

35. "Christians call them [princes] 'pastores,' for—like good shepherds—they do not seek their own benefit, but rather that of the fold under their responsibility. Likewise, good princes seek the well-being of the people placed under their authority and remember that truthful adage: that the good shepherd puts his life on the line for his sheep. This is a ruler's responsibility and duty. He who does the opposite is neither a king nor a statesman, but a tyrant. He is not a shepherd, but a wolf."

36. Cf. John 10:11: "I am the good shepherd. The good shepherd lays down his life for the sheep." For the Davidic prefiguration of the Christian Good Shepherd, see Ezekiel 34:1–31.

37. On the wolf in Greek political discourse before Plato, see Elizabeth Irwin, *Solon and Early Greek Poetry: The Politics of Exhortation* (Cambridge: Cambridge University Press, 2005), 245–61. On the wolf in political theory from Plato to Carl Schmitt, see Jacques Derrida, *The Beast and the Sovereign*, ed. Michel Lisse, et al., and trans. Geoffrey Bennington (Chicago: The University of Chicago Press, 2009), 1–106; and Giorgio Agamben, *Homo Sacer: Sovereign Power and Bare Life*, trans. Daniel Heller-Roazen (Stanford, CA: Stanford University Press, 1998), 104–11. On the relationship between tyranny, melancholy, and lycanthropy, see Klibansky, Panofsky, and Saxl, *Saturn and Melancholy*, especially 15–17.

38. See *Inferno* 1.49–54. On the wolf in the folktale tradition, see Jack Zipes's Introduction to *The Trials and Tribulations of Little Red Riding Hood*, ed. Jack Zipes (New York: Routledge, 1993), 17–88. On lycanthropy in literature, see Caroline Walker Bynum, *Metamorphosis and Identity* (New York: Zone Books, 2001), especially 166–70 on Ovid; and Jan Veenstra, "The Ever-Changing Nature of the Beast: Cultural Change, Lycanthropy and the Question of Substantial Transformation (from Petronius to Del Rio)," in *The Metamorphosis of Magic from Late Antiquity to the Early Modern Period*, eds. Jan Bremmer and Jan Veenstra (Leuven: Peeters, 2002), 133–66. For a medical history of lycanthropy, see Nadine Metzger, "Battling Demons with Medical Authority: Werewolves, Physicians and Rationalization," *History of Psychiatry* 24.3 (2013): 341–55.

39. Ovid, *Metamorphoses*, trans. Frank Justus Miller (Cambridge, MA: Harvard University Press, 1977).

40. On canto 17, see Ascoli, "Ariosto and the 'Fier Pastor': Form and History in *Orlando Furioso*," 494–509.

41. Aquinas cites this passage in *Summa Theologiae* II-II, q. 66, a. 8; and Pietro Alighieri uses it in his commentary on *Inferno* 12.46–48.

42. See Ciavolella, "La licantropia d'Orlando," 311–23; and Beer, *Romanzi di cavalleria*, 83–88.

43. On Ariosto's additions included in the 1532 edition of the *Furioso*, and particularly their political content, see Alberto Casadei, *La strategia delle varianti. Le correzioni storiche del terzo* Furioso (Lucca, Ita.: Maria Pacini Fazzi, 1988); Walter Moretti, *L'ultimo Ariosto* (Bologna: Pàtron Editore, 1977), 11–64; Eduardo Saccone, "Prospettive sull'ultimo Ariosto," *Modern Language Notes* 98.1 (January 1983): 55–69; Stefano Jossa, *Ariosto* (Bologna: Il Mulino, 2009), 104–10; and Mario Santoro, *Ariosto e il Rinascimento* (Napoli: Liguori, 1989), 275–316.

44. See Murrin, *History and Warfare in Renaissance Epic*, 124–27. On Ariosto's invective against firearms as a possible critique of Alfonso d'Este, see Ugo Balzaretti, "L'*Orlando Furioso* in filigrana: Ravenna, le armi da fuoco, la corte, l'ascesa negata di Ruggiero," *Aevum* 70.3 (Sept.-Dec. 1996): 563–96, especially 574–76. On the growing use of firearms in Renaissance warfare, see Michael Mallett and Christine Shaw, *The Italian Wars, 1494–1559: War, State and Society in Early Modern Europe* (Harlow, UK: Pearson, 2012), especially 177–97; and Piero Pieri, *La crisi militare italiana nel Rinascimento nelle sue relazioni con la crisi politica ed economica* (Naples: Ricciardi, 1934), especially 462–516.

45. Michael Allen has discussed the association of reason with Hercules in an essay on the Greek hero as intellectual paragon in Ficino's use of Boethius's *De consolatione philosophiae*. See Michael J. Allen, "Homo ad Zodiacum: Marsilio Ficino and the Boethian Hercules," in *Plato's Third Eye: Studies in Marsilio Ficino's Metaphysics and Its Sources* (Aldershot, UK: Variorum, 1995), (XIII) 205–21.

46. Several other works celebrating Jove's son were written in the fifteenth and sixteenth centuries: Piero Andrea de' Bassi, *Le fatiche de Hercule* (1430–35); Lilio Gregorio Giraldi, *Vita Herculis* (1514); and Giovan Battista Giraldi-Cinzio, *Dell'Ercole Canti 26* (1557). Hercules's labors also became the subject of numerous works of art, including paintings by Andrea Mantegna (*Ercole e Anteo* and *Ercole e il leone Nemeo*) and Cosmè Tura (again, *Ercole e il leone Nemeo*). On the myth of Hercules in Ferrara, see Antonia Tissoni Benvenuti, "Il mito di Ercole. Aspetti della ricezione dell'antico alla corte estense nel primo Quattrocento," in *Omaggio a Gianfranco Folena* (Padua: Programma, 1993), 1:773–92; and Tina Matarrese, "Il mito di Ercole a Ferrara nel Quattrocento tra letteratura e arti figurative," in *L'ideale classico a Ferrara e in Italia nel Rinascimento*, ed. Patrizia Castelli (Florence: Olschki Editore, 1998), 191–203. See also Alberto Casadei, *Il percorso del "Furioso". Ricerche intorno alle redazioni del 1516 e del 1521* (Bologna: Il Mulino, 1993), 25–28.

47. On the Este artistic patronage, see *Corte di ferrara e il suo mecenatismo, 1441–1598*, ed. Marianne Pade, et al. (Modena: Panini, 1990); and Thomas Tuohy, *Herculean Ferrara: Ercole d'Este, 1471–1505, and the Invention of a Ducal Capital* (Cambridge: Cambridge University Press, 1996). On Ferrara as the "first modern European city," see

Jakob Burckhardt, *The Civilization of the Renaissance in Italy*, trans. S. D. C. Middlemore (New York: The Modern Library, 2002), 35–40. See also Bruscagli, *Stagioni della civiltà estense*, 15–32.

48. See Giovan Battista Pigna, *I romanzi di M. Giouan Battista Pigna divisi in tre libri. Ne quali della poesia, & della vita dell'Ariosto con nuouo modo* (Venice: Valgrisi, 1554), 78.

49. On the parallels between Hercules and the two protagonists of Ariosto's poem, see Eduardo Saccone, *Il "soggetto" del* Furioso (Naples: Liguori Editore, 1974), 201–47; Remo Ceserani, "Due modelli culturali e narrativi nell'*Orlando Furioso*," *Giornale storico della letteratura italiana*, Vol. CLXI, Fasc. 516 (1984): 481–506; Ascoli, *Ariosto's Bitter Harmony*, especially 46–70; Marinelli, *Ariosto and Boiardo*, 148–65; Marianne Shapiro, *The Poetics of Ariosto* (Detroit: Wayne State University Press, 1988), 25–34; Mazzotta, *Cosmopoiesis*, 34–39 (with reference to the myth of Hyppolitus as well); and Silvia Longhi, *Forme di mostri. Creature fantastiche e corpi vulnerati da Ariosto a Giudici* (Verona: Edizioni Fiorini, 2005), 10–31.

50. See, for instance, Landino's commentary on *Inferno* 12.64–66, echoing the motif of Hercules as tyrant-slayer, shortly after presenting the tyrant-wolf analogy. In it the Florentine Neoplatonist allegorizes Hercules's killing of the centaur Nessus as the triumph of prudent and strong men over *furiosi tyranni*: "et certo tutte le 'mprese inconsiderate de' furiosi tyranni sono uccise da Hercole, cioè sono vinte da gl'huomini prudenti et forti, chome intendiamo per Hercole" ["and that Hercules soundly defeats all the furious tyrants' senseless endeavors means that prudent and strong men, whom Hercules exemplifies, defeat these endeavors"]. On Hercules as benefactor of humanity in the struggle against tyrants, see also Cristoforo Landino, *Disputationes Camaldulenses* (Florence: Sansoni, 1980), 32. Cf. Karl Galinsky, *The Herakles Theme: The Adaptations of the Hero in Literature from Homer to the Twentieth Century* (Totowa, NJ: Rowman and Littlefield, 1972), 185–230.

51. On the ambivalent quality of Hercules's power, see Galinsky, *The Herakles Theme*, especially 3–7; John Fitch's Introduction to *Seneca's "Hercules Furens,"* a critical text with introduction and commentary by John Fitch (Ithaca, NY: Cornell University Press, 1987), 15–20 and 30–32; and Thalia Papadopoulou, "Herakles and Hercules: The Hero's Ambivalence in Euripides and Seneca," *Mnemosyne* 57.3 (2004): 257–83. Cf. Georges Dumézil, *The Destiny of the Warrior*, trans. Alf Hiltebeitel (Chicago: The University of Chicago Press, 1970), 96–107, with reference to Diodorus Siculus's extensive account of Hercules's life; see Diodorus of Sicily, *The Library of History*, trans. C. H. Oldfather (Cambridge, MA: Harvard University Press, 1935), book IV, chapters 7–58.

52. On Hercules as a tragic figure, see Galinsky, *The Herakles Theme*, 40–80 and 167–84, especially 168–72, on the similarities and differences between Euripides's and Seneca's plays. See also Kathleen Riley, *The Reception and Performance of Euripides' "Herakles": Reasoning Madness* (Oxford: Oxford University Press, 2008), 14–91.

53. On Juno's role in the prologue of the *Hercules Furens*, see Alessandro Schiesaro, *The Passions in Play: Thyestes and the Dynamics of Senecan Drama* (Cambridge: Cambridge University Press, 2003), 183–86.

54. See Amy Rose, "Seneca's HF: A Politico-Didactic Reading," *The Classical Journal* 75.2 (Dec. 1979-Jan. 1980): 135–42, especially 136. On the recurrent theme of tyranny in Seneca's plays, see Paolo Mantovanelli, *Patologia del potere. Studi sulle tragedie di Seneca* (Bologna: Pàtron Editore, 2014), especially 21–46.

55. The (mostly Ovidian) sources for the second part of the Olimpia episode, in which Bireno abandons her for a younger woman (*OF* 10.1–34), are fairly clear and have been widely examined. Little has been written, however, about possible inspirations for the section that revolves around Cimosco (cf. Rajna, *Le fonti dell'Orlando Furioso*, 209–19). See also Barbara Pavlock, *Eros, Imitation, and the Epic Tradition* (Ithaca, NY: Cornell University Press, 1990), 149–70; Irene Zanini-Cordi, "The Seduction of Ariosto's Olimpia: Mythopoetic Rescue of an Abandoned Woman," *Pacific Coast Philology* 42.1 (2007): 37–53; and Ita Mac Carty, "Olimpia: Faithful or Foolhardy?," *Olifant* 22 (2003): 103–18; and Finucci, *The Lady Vanishes*, 145–68.

56. Cf. Papadopoulou, "Herakles and Hercules," especially 271–73; and Rose, "Seneca's HF," 137–38. On the mirrored relationship between the tyrant and the martyr, see Walter Benjamin, *The Origin of German Tragic Drama*, trans. John Osborne (London: NLB, 1977), 69: "In the baroque the tyrant and the martyr are but two faces of the monarch. As far as the tyrant is concerned, this is clear enough. The theory of sovereignty which takes as its example the special case in which dictatorial powers are unfolded, positively demands the completion of the image of the sovereign, as tyrant."

57. Cf. David Quint, *Origin and Originality in Renaissance Literature* (New Haven, CT: Yale University Press, 1983), especially 88–90; and Clare Carroll, *The "Orlando Furioso": A Stoic Comedy* (Tempe, AZ: Medieval and Renaissance Texts and Studies, 1997), 185–88.

58. See Suetonius, *Life of Nero* XXI, 3. Cf. Riley, *The Reception and Performance of Euripides' "Herakles,"* 54–63; Margarethe Billerbeck, "Hercules Bound: A Note on Suetonius, Nero 21.3," *American Journal of Philology* 102.1 (Spring 1981): 54–57, who notes that Suetonius probably refers to Euripides's play; and Rose, "Seneca's HF," 140–42. On the relationship between Seneca and Nero, see Griffin, *Seneca*, 67–128.

59. Seneca, *De Clementia* I, 1, 1: "I have undertaken, Nero Caesar, to write on the subject of mercy, in order to serve in a way the purpose of a mirror, and thus reveal you to yourself" ["Scribere de clementia, Nero Caesar, institui, ut quodam modo speculi vice fungerer et te tibi ostenderem"].

60. On the presence of the *Aeneid* in Ariosto's epic, see Patricia Parker, *Inescapable Romance: Studies in the Poetics of a Mode* (Princeton, NJ: Princeton University Press, 1979), 39–44; Marinelli, *Ariosto and Boiardo*, 125–47; Ascoli, *Ariosto's Bitter Harmony*, 6–7, 151–55; Daniel Javitch, "The Grafting of Virgilian Epic in *Orlando furioso*," in *Renaissance Transactions: Ariosto and Tasso*, ed. Valeria Finucci (Durham, NC: Duke University Press, 1999), 56–76; and Jane Everson, *The Italian Romance Epic in the Age of Humanism: The Matter of Italy and the World of Rome* (Oxford: Oxford University Press, 2001), 244–58, 334–46, with reference to both Boiardo and Ariosto.

61. On the influence of the *Aeneid*, particularly of book 8, on the *Hercules Furens*, see Michael Putnam, *Virgil's Aeneid: Interpretation and Influence* (Chapel Hill: The Univer-

sity of North Carolina Press, 1995), 154–58; and Riley, *The Reception and Performance of Euripides' "Herakles,"* 69–70. On the Cacus episode, see also Karl Galinsky, "The Hercules-Cacus Episode in *Aeneid* VIII," *American Journal of Philology* 87.1 (January 1966): 18–51; Philip Hardie, *Virgil's Aeneid: Cosmos and Imperium* (Oxford: Oxford University Press, 1986), 110–18; and Lee Fratantuono, *Madness Unchained: A Reading of Virgil's Aeneid* (Lanham, MD: Lexington Books, 2007), 236–40.

62. Cf. Augustine, *City of God* 19.12.

63. "Nam maximus ultor / tergemini nece Geryonae spoliisque superbus / Alcides aderat taurosque hac victor agebat / ingentis, vallemque boves amnemque tenebant. / At furiis Caci mens effera, ne quid inausum / aut intractatum scelerisve dolive fuisset, / quattuor a stabulis praestanti corpore tauros / avertit, totidem forma superante iuvencas [. . .] Reddidit una boum vocem vastoque sub antro / mugiit et Caci spem custodita fefellit. / Hic vero Alcides furiis exarserat atro / felle dolor."

64. On *melancholia* in classical and early modern physiological theories, see above n18.

65. Cf. the above-cited passage from *Orlando Innamorato* (1.26.2), in which Orlando gnashes his teeth like Hercules while he waits to resume battle against his cousin Ranaldo.

66. See Virgil, *Aeneid* 6.752–853, where Anchises foretells the history of Rome from its Trojan roots to Augustus's empire. See in particular lines 791–807, where Virgil compares Augustus's empire to Hercules's and Bacchus's journeys around the world. See also Horace, *Carmina* III, 3, 9–16; and *Epistles* II, 1, 1–17. On Hercules as predecessor of Aeneas, Romulus, and Augustus, see Brooks Otis, *Virgil: A Study in Civilized Poetry* (Oxford: Oxford University Press, 1963), 330–38; Galinsky, "The Hercules-Cacus Episode in *Aeneid* VIII," especially 25–26, 46–48, and 41, where he argues that Virgil depicts a "furens" Hercules to foreshadow the identification between the Greek hero and Aeneas, and thus hint at the parallel between Cacus and Turnus. See also Galinsky, *The Herakles Theme*, 131–48; and Putnam, *Virgil's Aeneid*, 187–88. On Aeneas's shield, see Hardie, *Virgil's Aeneid*, 117–18, 135–36, and 346–66.

67. On the presence of *furor* in the *Aeneid*, see Hershowitz, *The Madness of Epic*, 68–124; and Fratantuono, *Madness Unchained*.

68. "Ille [Aeneas], oculis postquam saevi monumenta doloris / exuviasque hausit, furiis accensus et ira / terribilis: 'tune hinc spoliis indute meorum / eripiare mihi? Pallas te hoc vulnere, Pallas / immolat et poenam scelerato ex sanguine sumit.' / Hoc dicens ferrum adverso sub pectore condit / fervidus; ast illi solvuntur frigore membra / vitaque cum gemitu fugit indignata sub umbras."

69. *Aeneid* 6.851–53: "you, Roman, be sure to rule the world (be these your arts), to crown peace with justice, to spare the vanquished and to crush the proud" ["tu regere imperio populos, Romane, memento / (hae tibi erunt artes), pacique imponere morem, / parcere subiectis et debellare superbos"].

70. Cf. Quint, *Epic and Empire*, especially 78–80; Putnam, *Virgil's Aeneid*, 202–4, 214–15; and Hershowitz, *The Madness of Epic*, 122–23.

71. Among the numerous studies on the last episode of the *Aeneid* and its ideological implications, see Otis, *Virgil*, 373–82; Hardie, *Virgil's Aeneid*, especially 147–54; Karl

Galinsky, "The Anger of Aeneas," *American Journal of Philology* 109.3 (Autumn 1988): 321–48; Quint, *Epic and Empire*, especially 50–53 and 65–83; Putnam, *Virgil's Aeneid*, 152–245; Fratantuono, *Madness Unchained*, 394–99; Walter Johnson, *Darkness Visible: A Study of Vergil's "Aeneid"* (Berkeley: University of California Press, 1976), 114–34; Leah Whittington, *Renaissance Suppliants: Poetry, Antiquity, Reconciliation* (Oxford: Oxford University Press, 2016), 46–81, especially 76–81; and Craig Kallendorf, *The Other Virgil: Pessimistic Readings of the Aeneid in Early Modern Culture* (Oxford: Oxford University Press, 2007), especially v-ix, where he recapitulates the terms of the debate on Aeneas's anger. On whether Aeneas corresponds to the ideal king, compare J. A. S. Evans, "The *Aeneid* and the Concept of the Ideal King: The Modification of an Archetype," in *The Worlds of the Poet: New Perspectives on Vergil*, eds. Robert Wilhelm and Howard Jones (Detroit: Wayne State University Press, 1992), 146–56; and Francis Cairns, *Virgil's Augustan Epic* (Cambridge: Cambridge University Press, 1989), especially 58–84 on the last scene of the poem. See also T. S. Eliot, "Virgil and the Christian World," in *On Poetry and Poets* (New York: Octagon Books, 1975), 135–48, where he describes Aeneas as "the prototype of a Christian hero."

72. See Maffeo Vegio, *Short Epics*, ed. and trans. Michael Putnam with James Hankins (Cambridge, MA: Harvard University Press, 2004). On Renaissance critical interpretations of the *Aeneid*, including Filelfo, and on Aeneas's slayings of Tarquitus (10.550–60) and Mezentius (10.897–906), see Kallendorf, *The Other Virgil*, 17–66. See also Vito Giustiniani, "Il Filelfo, l'interpretazione allegorica di Virgilio e la tripartizione platonica dell'anima," in *Umanesimo e Rinascimento: studi offerti a Paul Oskar Kristeller* (Florence: Olschki Editore, 1980), 33–44.

73. See Joseph Sitterson, "Allusive and Elusive Meanings: Reading Ariosto's Vergilian Endings," *Renaissance Quarterly* 45.1 (Spring 1992): 1–19; and Kallendorf, *The Other Virgil*, 44–45. On the final canto of the *Furioso*, see also D. S. Carne-Ross, "The One and the Many: A Reading of the *Orlando Furioso*," *Arion* 3.2 (1976): 146–219, especially 205–9; David Quint, "The Figure of Atlante: Ariosto and Boiardo's Poem," *Modern Language Notes* 94.1 (January 1979): 77–91; Ascoli, *Ariosto's Bitter Harmony*, 376–93; Murrin, *History and Warfare in Renaissance Epic*, 200–1; Cavallo, *The Romance Epics of Boiardo, Ariosto, and Tasso*, 150–52; and Daniela Del Corno Branca, "La conclusione dell'*Orlando Furioso*: qualche osservazione" in *Boiardo, Ariosto e i libri di battaglia*, eds. Andrea Canova and Paola Vecchi Galli (Novara, Ita.: Interlinea Edizioni, 2007), 127–37.

74. For a comparison between Turnus and Rodomonte in relation to the siege of Paris, see also Marinelli, *Ariosto and Boiardo*, 210–13; and Sitterson, "Allusive and Elusive Meanings," 12–13.

75. On Saint John's remarks regarding the relationship between poetry and history, see Zatti, *Il Furioso tra epos e romanzo*, 142–48; Quint, *Origin and Originality in Renaissance Literature*, 82–92; Eleonora Stoppino, *Genealogies of Fiction: Women Warriors and the Dynastic Imagination in the "Orlando Furioso"* (New York: Fordham University Press, 2012), 131–35; Lene Waage Petersen, "Il poeta creatore del Principe," in *La corte di Ferrara e il suo mecenatismo*, 195–211; and Balzaretti, "L'*Orlando Furioso* in filigrana," especially 563–66. On Ariosto's ironic treatment of Ippolito d'Este, see Ascoli, *Ariosto's Bitter*

Harmony, especially 382–89. See also Ascoli, "Ariosto and the 'Fier Pastor,'" especially 502–5, on Pope Leo X as a "wolf in shepherd's clothing" (505). On Ariosto's relationship with his patrons, see also Richard McCabe, *'Ungainefull Arte': Poetry, Patronage, and Print in the Early Modern Era* (Oxford: Oxford University Press, 2016), 123–34.

76. He also repeatedly uses "Augusto" as a title for Leone (*OF* 44.56; 44.76; 44.89; 44.98; 46.71).

77. Cf. Virgil, *Eclogue* 4.4–10. On the idea of Astrea in relation to Charles V, see Frances Yates, *Astrea: The Imperial Theme in the Sixteenth Century* (London: Routledge and Kegan Paul, 1975), 22–23. On Charles V in the *Furioso*, see also Walter Moretti, "Carlo V e I suoi 'capitani invitti' nel 'Furioso' del 1532," in *Rinascimento meridionale e altri studi*, ed. Maria Cristina Cafisse, et al. (Naples: Società Editrice Napoletana, 1987), 321–31; Sergio Zatti, "Tasso e il nuovo mondo," *Italianistica* 24.2–3 (May-December 1995): 501–21, especially 504–08; and Ascoli, "Ariosto and the 'Fier Pastor,'" 517, none of whom considers this passage ironic. Cf. Theodore J. Cachey, who detects a possible polemical hint in Ariosto's praise in "Maps and Literature in Renaissance Italy," in *History of Cartography*, ed. David Woodward (Chicago: Chicago University Press, 2007), vol. 3, part 1, 450–60, especially 458. On the presence of *Eclogue* IV in Renaissance Humanism, see Annabel Patterson, *Pastoral and Ideology: Virgil to Valéry* (Berkeley: University of California Press, 1987), 60–132.

78. Aeneas Silvius Piccolomini (Pope Pius II), *On the Origin and Authority of the Roman Empire*, in *Three Tracts on Empire*, ed. and trans. Thomas Izbicki and Cary Nederman (Bristol, UK: Thoemmes Press, 2000), 95–112. Ficino's translation of the *Monarchia* into vernacular was recently published in Dante Alighieri, *Monarchia*, ed. Francesco Furlan (Milan: Mondadori, 2004). See Tommaso Campanella, *La Città del Sole: Dialogo Poetico*, ed. and trans. Daniel Donno (Berkeley: University of California Press, 1981).

79. On Gattinara and the idea of the Habsburg world empire, see John Headley, "The Habsburg World Empire and the Revival of Ghibellinism," *Medieval and Renaissance Studies* 7 (1975): 93–127; idem, *The Emperor and His Chancellor: A Study of the Imperial Chancellery Under Gattinara* (Cambridge: Cambridge University Press, 1983); Robert Finlay, "Prophecy and Politics in Istanbul: Charles V, Sultan Suleyman, and the Habsburg Embassy of 1533–1534," *Journal of Early Modern History* 2.1 (1998): 1–31, especially 20–22; Karl Brandi, *The Emperor Charles V: The Growth and Destiny of a Man and of a World-Empire*, trans. C.V. Wedgwood (London: Cape, 1963), 90–91 and 112–14, where Brandi underscores Gattinara's role as Charles's mentor; Fernand Braudel, *The Mediterranean and the Mediterranean World in the Age of Philip II*, trans. Sian Reynolds (New York: Harper & Row, 1973), 2:672–75; Carlo Bornate, "L'apogeo della casa di Asburgo e l'opera politica di un Gran Cancelliere di Carlo V," *Nuova Rivista Storica* 3 (1919): 396–439; and Rebecca Ard Boone, *Mercurino di Gattinara and the Creation of the Spanish Empire* (London: Pickering & Gatto, 2014), 1–72. Boone's book also includes the English translation of Gattinara's *Autobiography* (75–136). Gattinara was appointed Cardinal by Clement VII in 1529 for the efforts he made to mend the rift between Charles V and the Pope in the aftermath of the Sack of Rome. Cf. Ludwig von Pastor, *The History of the Popes from the Close of the Middle Ages*, ed. Frederick Ignatius Antrobus (Nendeln,

Lie.: Kraus Reprint, 1969), vol. 10:66–67. In addition to the above-cited essay by Finlay, on the prophecies of Charles V as a new World Emperor, see also Ottavia Niccoli, *Prophecy and People in Renaissance Italy*, trans. Lydia Cochrane (Princeton, NJ: Princeton University Press, 1990), 168–88; Marjorie Reeves, *The Influence of Prophecy in the Later Middle Ages: A Study in Joachimism* (Oxford: Clarendon Press, 1969), especially 258–74; and Marie Tanner, *The Last Descendant of Aeneas: The Hapsburgs and the Mythic Image of the Emperor* (New Haven, CT: Yale University Press, 1993), especially 119–30.

80. See Gattinara's epistle to Erasmus dated March 12, 1527 (just under two months before the Sack of Rome) in Desiderius Erasmus, *The Correspondence of Erasmus*, trans. R. A. B. Mynors and D. F. S. Thomson, in *Collected Works of Erasmus* (Toronto: University of Toronto Press, 1974–2009), letter no. 1790a, vol. 12:474–76. The editio princeps of Dante's *Monarchia* would eventually be published in 1559 in a collection of tracts on the Roman Empire: Andrea Alciati, *De formula romani Imperii libri duo* (Basel: Johannes Oporinus, 1559). On the relationship between Gattinara and Erasmus, see John Headley, "Gattinara, Erasmus, and the Imperial Configurations of Humanism," *Archiv für Reformationsgeschichte* 71 (1980): 64–98. On the cultural milieu of Charles V's empire, see also J. A. Fernandez-Santamaria, *The State, War and Peace: Spanish Political Thought in the Renaissance 1516–1559* (Cambridge: Cambridge University Press, 1996), 11–57.

81. The emblem was devised in 1516 by Bishop Ludovico Marliano, another Italian erudite serving at Charles's court and a friend of Gattinara's. On the emblem and the use of the passage from the Gospel of John, see Luigi Avonto, *Mercurino Arborio di Gattinara: documenti inediti per la storia delle Indie Nuove nell'archivio del gran cancelliere di Carlo V* (Vercelli, Ita.: S.E.T.C., 1981), 15–17; Brandi, *The Emperor Charles V*, 112–14; Headley, "The Habsburg World Empire and the Revival of Ghibellinism," 93–95; Yates, *Astrea*, 25–26; and Earl Rosenthal, "*Plus Ultra, Non plus Ultra*, and the Columnar Device of Emperor Charles V," *Journal of the Warburg and Courtauld Institutes* 34 (1971): 204–28.

82. For the 1519 memorandum, see Gattinara's autobiography in Carlo Bornate, ed., "Historia vitae et gestorum per dominum magnum canellarium, con note, aggiunte e documenti," *Miscellanea di storia e italiana* 48 (1915): 233–558, especially 278 and 405–13, which includes the text of the memorandum in the French original. Interestingly, in another document addressed to Charles in 1520, which arguably reflects the influence of Dante's *Monarchia*, Gattinara advises the Emperor to respect the local customs and laws of the various kingdoms under his authority. See Bornate, "*Historia vitae et gestorum per dominum magnum canellarium*, con note, aggiunte e documenti," 419.

83. See James Tracy, *Holland under Habsburg Rule, 1506–1566: The Formation of a Body Politic* (Berkeley: University California Press, 1990), 64–89.

84. Cf. Ascoli, *Ariosto's Bitter Harmony*, 385.

4. The Geography of the Enemy

1. See Sergio Zatti, *L'uniforme cristiano e il multiforme pagano* (Milan: Il Saggiatore, 1983), 36–37 (my translation); Sergio Zatti, "Tasso e il nuovo mondo," *Italianistica*

XXIV, 2–3 (May/December 1995): 501–21; and Zatti, "Dalla parte di Satana: sull'imperialismo cristiano nella 'Gerusalemme Liberata,'" in *La rappresentazione dell'altro nei testi del Rinascimento*, ed. Sergio Zatti (Lucca: Maria Pacini Fazzi Editore, 1998), 146–82; David Quint, *Epic and Empire: Politics and Generic Form from Virgil to Milton* (Princeton, NJ: Princeton University Press, 1993), 214–47; Franco Cardini, *L'invenzione del Nemico* (Palermo: Sellerio Editore, 2006), 186–94; Timothy Hampton, *Writing from History: The Rhetoric of Exemplarity in Renaissance Literature* (Ithaca, NY: Cornell University Press, 1990), 81–133; and Paul Larivaille, *Poesia e ideologia. Letture della "Gerusalemme Liberata"* (Naples: Liguori, 1987), 111–29.

2. All citations are from Torquato Tasso, *Gerusalemme liberata* (*GL*), ed. Bruno Maier (Milan: Rizzoli, 1995); all translations are from Torquato Tasso, *Jerusalem Delivered*, ed. and trans. Ralph Nash (Detroit: Wayne State University Press, 1987).

3. Among the scholars who express a more skeptical view of Tasso's purported efforts to suppress the romance component of the *Liberata* and to promote an unequivocal ideology of Christian imperialism, see: Marion Wells, *The Secret Wound: Love-Melancholy and Early Modern Romance* (Stanford, CA: Stanford University Press, 2007), 137–78; Barbara Fuchs, *Mimesis and Empire: The New World, Islam, and European Identities* (Cambridge: Cambridge University Press, 2001), 24–34; Jo Ann Cavallo, "Tasso's Armida and the Victory of Romance," in *Renaissance Transactions: Ariosto and Tasso*, ed. Valeria Finucci (Durham, NC: Duke University Press, 1999), 77–111; and Francesco Erspamer, "Il 'pensiero debole' di Torquato Tasso," in *La menzogna*, ed. Franco Cardini (Florence: Ponte alle Grazie, 1989), 120–36.

4. Ayesha Ramachandran, *The Worldmakers: Global Imagining in Early Modern Europe* (Chicago: The University of Chicago Press, 2015). On the construction of a European identity and the rise of a new world order in the Renaissance, see: Denis Cosgrove, *Apollo's Eye: A Cartographic Genealogy of the Earth in the Western Imagination* (Baltimore: The Johns Hopkins University Press, 2001); Carl Schmitt, *The Nomos of the Earth in the International Law of the Jus Publicum Europaeum*, trans. G. L. Ulmen (New York: Telos Press Publishing, 2006); Giuseppe Mazzotta, *Cosmopoiesis: The Renaissance Experiment* (Toronto: University of Toronto Press, 2001), especially 55–75; Roberto Dainotto, *Europe (in Theory)* (Durham, NC: Duke University Press, 2007), 11–51; John Headley, *The Europeanization of the World: On the Origins of Human Rights and Democracy* (Princeton, NJ: Princeton University Press, 2008); Anthony Pagden, "Europe: Conceptualizing a Continent," in *The Idea of Europe from Antiquity to the European Union*, ed. Anthony Pagden (Cambridge: Cambridge University Press, 2002), 33–54.

5. I am here referring to Samuel Huntington, *The Clash of Civilizations and the Remaking of World Order* (New York: Simon & Schuster, 1997).

6. See Isidore of Seville, *Etymologies* Book VIII, i, 6: "And in accordance with the future peace of the homeland it [the Church] is called Jerusalem, for 'Jerusalem' (*Hierusalem*) is translated as 'vision of peace.' There, when all hostility has been overwhelmed, one will possess peace, which is Christ, by gazing upon him face to face" ["Pro futura vero patriae pace Hierusalem vocatur. Nam Hierusalem pacis visio interpretatur. Ibi enim absorpta omni adversitate pacem, quae est Christus, praesenti possidebit obtutu"].

7. See Torquato Tasso, *Dialoghi*, ed. Giovanni Baffetti (Milan: Rizzoli, 1998), 2:1196 (my translation). Tasso also praises Charles V in *Gerusalemme conquistata* 20.103–7, and in various lyrical poems, including *Questa arca fu di preciosi odori*, *Di sostener qual novo Atlante il mondo*, and *Era meta la gloria*.

8. On Portugal and Spain's competing colonial interests, see Andrea Moudarres, "Islam e conflitti ispano-lusitani nella *Relazione del primo viaggio attorno al mondo* di Antonio Pigafetta," in *Storie del Grande Sud. Per Piero Boitani*, ed. Emilia Di Rocco (Bologna: Il Mulino, 2017), 139–52.

9. On Philip II, see Fernand Braudel, *The Mediterranean and the Mediterranean World in the Age of Philip II*, 2 vols., trans. S. Reynolds (New York: Harper & Row, 1973); and Marie Tanner, *The Last Descendant of Aeneas: The Hapsburgs and the Mystic Image of the Emperor* (New Haven, CT: Yale University Press, 1993), especially 131–45.

10. For an introduction to the history of the Ottoman Empire, especially between the fourteenth and sixteenth centuries, see Gilles Veinstein, "The Great Turk and Europe," in *Europe and the Islamic World: A History*, ed. John Tolan, et al. (Princeton, NJ: Princeton University Press, 2013), 111–253.

11. On the battle of Lepanto, see Palmira Brummett, "The Lepanto Paradigm Revisited: Knowing the Ottomans in the Sixteenth Century," in *The Renaissance and the Ottoman World*, eds. Anna Contadini and Claire Norton (Farnham, UK: Ashgate, 2013), 63–93.

12. Numerous sources are collected in *La caduta di Costantinopoli. L'eco nel mondo*, ed. Agostino Pertusi (Milan: Mondadori, 1976); and in *Testi inediti e poco conosciuti sulla caduta di Costantinopoli*, ed. Agostino Pertusi (Bologna: Pàtron Editore, 1983). On the siege of Constantinople, and for a reappraisal of the sources included in Pertusi's anthologies, see Marios Philippides and Walter Hanak, *The Siege and the Fall of Constantinople in 1453: Historiography, Topography, and Military Studies* (Farnham, UK: Ashgate, 2011). See also the collection of works on the wars against the Turks in the fourth volume of *Guerre in ottava rima*, ed. Marina Beer (Modena: Panini, 1988).

13. Aeneas Sylvius Piccolomini (Pope Pius II), *Reject Aeneas, Accept Pius: Selected Letters of Aeneas Sylvius Piccolomini*, ed. and trans. Thomas Izbicki, et al. (Washington, D.C.: The Catholic University of America Press, 2006), 311: "And so the monument to ancient wisdom has remained at Constantinople to this day, and it is as if the dwellings of letters was there [...] But now, with the victorious Turks possessing all which Greek potency had achieved, I wonder what will be done about Greek letters." For the Latin text, see Rudolf Wolkan, ed., *Der Briefwechsel des Eneas Silvius Piccolomini*, in *Fontes Rerum Austriacarum* (Vienna: A. Hölder, 1909–1918), ser. 2, vol. 68, 208–9: "Mansit usque in hanc diem vetuste sapientiae apud Constantinopolim monumentum, ac velut ibi domicilium litterarum esset [...] At nunc vincentibus Turchis et omnia possidentibus, quae Graeca potentia tenuit, actum esse de litteris Graecis arbitror."

14. Among the scholars who have discussed the transition toward a more secular depiction of the Turks, see Margaret Meserve, *Empires of Islam in Renaissance Historical Thought* (Cambridge, MA: Harvard University Press, 2008); Nancy Bisaha, *Creating East and West: Renaissance Humanists and the Ottoman Turks* (Philadelphia: University

of Pennsylvania Press, 2004), especially 135–73, dedicated to the religious aspect of the encounters between East and West; and James Hankins, "Renaissance Crusaders: Humanist Crusade Literature in the Age of Mehmed II," *Dumbarton Oaks Papers* 49 (1995): 111–207. See also Franco Cardini, *L'invenzione del Nemico*, especially 179–85; Richard Fletcher, *The Cross and the Crescent: Christianity and Islam from Muhammad to the Reformation* (New York: Allen Lane—The Penguin Press, 2003), 131–59; Norman Daniel, *Islam and the West: The Making of an Image* (Oxford: One World, 1993), 302–17; Robert Schwoebel, *The Shadow of the Crescent: The Renaissance Image of the Turk (1453–1517)* (New York: St. Martin's Press, 1967); and Steven Runciman, *The Fall of Constantinople 1453* (Cambridge: Cambridge University Press, 1965), 160–91. For an overview of a selection of studies on the issue of Islam in the Renaissance conducted between 2000 and 2010, see Francesca Trivellato, "Renaissance Italy and the Muslim Mediterranean in Recent Historical Work," *Journal of Modern History* 82 (March 2010): 127–55.

15. Piccolomini (Pope Pius II), *Reject Aeneas, Accept Pius: Selected Letters of Aeneas Sylvius Piccolomini*, 313; Wolkan, ed., *Der Briefwechsel des Eneas Silvius Piccolomini*, in *Fontes Rerum Austriacarum*, 68: 211.

16. On the *Cribatio*, see Jasper Jopkins, "The Role of *pia interpretatio* in Nicholas of Cusa's Hermeneutical Approach to the Koran," in *Concordia Discors. Studi su Niccolò Cusano e l'Umanesimo Europeo offerti a Giovanni Santinello*, ed. Gregorio Piaia (Padua: Editrice Antenore, 1993), 251–73.

17. Jasper Hopkins, ed. and trans., *Nicholas of Cusa's De Pace Fidei and Cribatio Alkorani* (Minneapolis: The Arthur J. Banning Press, 1994), 69. Nicholas of Cusa, *Opera omnia* (Hamburg: Felix Meier, 1932–2010), 7: 62.

18. *Nicholas of Cusa's De Pace Fidei and Cribatio Alkorani*, 181; Nicholas of Cusa, *Opera omnia*, 8: 177.

19. *Nicholas of Cusa's De Pace Fidei and Cribatio Alkorani*, 183; Nicholas of Cusa, *Opera omnia*, 8: 179–80.

20. On Pius's letter, see Franco Gaeta, "Sulla 'Lettera a Maometto' di Pio II," *Bullettino Istituto storico italiano per il Medio Evo* 77 (1965): 127–227; Paolo Brezzi, "La lettera di Pio II a Maometto II," in Luisa Rotondi Secchi Tarugi, ed., *Pio II e la cultura del suo tempo* (Milan: Guerini e Associati, 1991), 263–72; Luca D'Ascia's introduction to *Il Corano e la Tiara. L'epistola a Maometto di Enea Silvio Piccolomini (papa Pio II)* (Bologna: Pendragon, 2001), 13–149; and Bisaha, *Creating East and West*, 147–52 and 166–70.

21. Aeneas Silvius Piccolomini (Pope Pius II), *Epistola ad Mahomatem II (Epistle to Mohammed II)*, ed. and trans. Albert Baca (New York: Peter Lang, 1990), 11 [115].

22. Ibid., 17–18 [121–22]: "Si vis inter Christianos tuum imperium propagare et nomen tuum quam gloriosum efficere, non auro, non armis, non excercitibus, non classibus opus est. Parva res omnium qui hodie vivunt maximum et potentissimum et clarissimum te reddere potest [...] id est aquae pauxillum, quo baptizeris et ad Christianorum sacra te conferas et credas Evangelio. Haec si feceris, non erit in orbe princeps qui te Gloria superset aut aequare potential valeat. Nos te Graecorum et Orientis imperatorem appellabimus et quod modo vi occupas et cum iniuria tenes possidebis iure."

23. Ibid., 19 [123]: "O quanta esset abundantia pacis, quanta Christianae plebis exul-

tation, quanta iubilatio in omni terra: redirent Augusti tempora et quae poetae vocant aurea saecula renovarerunt! Habitaret pardus cum agno et vitulus cum leone; gladii verterentur in falces, in vomeres ac ligones [...] O quanta esset tua Gloria, qui pacem orbi reddidisses!" Cf. Isaiah 2:4 and 11:6.

24. As Hankins has suggested, Pius II may have hoped that the document would provoke European rulers to support his plans to launch a crusade. See Hankins, "Renaissance Crusaders," 130.

25. *La caduta di Costantinopoli. L'eco nel mondo*, 2, 132–33 (my translation).

26. Aeneas Silvius Piccolomini (Pius II), *Epistle to Mahomatem II*, 27 [132].

27. Marsilius of Padua, *Defensor Pacis*, ed. and trans. Alan Gewirth (New York: Arno Press, 1979), vol. 2, 310–13 (discourse 2 chapter 22), and 389–90 (discourse 2 chapter 28); and, among Dante's numerous attacks against the corruption of the Church, *Inferno* 19, *Inferno* 27, *Purgatorio* 16 and 32–33, and *Paradiso* 27.

28. Cf. Nicholas of Cusa, *The Catholic Concordance*, ed. and trans. Paul Sigmund (Cambridge: Cambridge University Press, 1991), especially 216–22 (book 3, chapter 2); and Lorenzo Valla, *On the Donation of Constantine*, trans. G. W. Bowersock (Cambridge, MA: Harvard University Press, 2007).

29. On Constantine, see Raymond Van Dam, "The Many Conversions of the Emperor Constantine," in *Conversion in Late Antiquity and the Early Middle Ages: Seeing and Believing*, ed. Kenneth Mills and Anthony Grafton (Rochester, NY: University of Rochester Press, 2003), 127–51.

30. See Aeneas Sylvius Piccolomini, *On the Origin and Authority of the Roman Empire*, in *Three Tracts on Empire*, eds. and trans. Thomas Izbicki and Cary Nederman (Bristol, UK: Thoemmes Press, 2000), 95–112. See also Pius's letter (September 1453) to Leonardo Benvoglienti, Siena's ambassador in Venice, in *Der Briefwechsel des Eneas Silvius Piccolomini*, in *Fontes Rerum Austriacarum*, vol. 68, 281: "The Italians ruled over the world, now the Empire of the Turks begins" ["Fuerunt Itali rerum domini, nunc Turchorum inchoatur imperium"].

31. Cf. Augustine, *City of God* 5.1 and 5.21; Dante, *Monarchia* 2.6 and 2.10.

32. Another humanist who emphasized the significance of Constantine's conversion was George of Trebizond, whose treatise *On the Eternal Glory of the Autocrat and his World-Dominion* begins and ends with references to Constantine's glory and universal monarchy. See George of Trebizond, *On the Eternal Glory of the Autocrat*, in *Collectanea Trapezuntiana: Texts, Documents, and Bibliographies of George of Trebizond*, ed. John Monfasani (Binghamton, NY: Medieval & Renaissance Texts & Studies), 493–95 and 524–25. Cf. Cosgrove, *Apollo's Eye*, 107. A similar view is expressed by Francesco Filelfo, who praised the sultan in a Greek ode written in 1454, offering his service if the Turkish sovereign decided to convert. Filelfo also states that if Mehmed became a Christian, he would rule over the entire world. See *Testi inediti e poco conosciuti sulla caduta di Costantinopoli*, 264–69.

33. On Lorenzo's gift of the *Geographia* to Mehmed II, see Sean Roberts, *Printing a Mediterranean World: Florence, Constantinople, and the Renaissance of Geography* (Cambridge, MA: Harvard University Press, 2013). On Bertoldo di Giovanni's medal for the

sultan, see James Draper, *Bertoldo di Giovanni, Sculptor of the Medici Household: Critical Reappraisal and Catalogue Raisonné* (Columbia: University of Missouri Press, 1992), 95–101. On the relationship between Lorenzo de' Medici's Florence and the Turkish Emperor, see Meserve, *Empires of Islam in Renaissance Historical Thought*, 131; Bisaha, *Creating East and West*, especially 74–75 and 116–17; Hankins, "Renaissance Crusaders," 124–27; Schwoebel, *The Shadow of the Crescent*, 161–65; Franz Babinger, *Mehmed the Conqueror and His Time*, trans. Ralph Manheim (Princeton, NJ: Princeton University Press, 1978), 384–87, 503–7; and idem, "Lorenzo de' Medici e la corte ottomana," *Archivio storico italiano* 121 (1963): 305–61.

34. See Anthony Pagden, *Worlds at War: The 2,500-Year Struggle between East and West* (New York: Random House, 2009), 156–292, especially 164–65. For a thought-provoking discussion of universalism in the three Abrahamic religions, see Peter Sloterdijk, *God's Zeal: The Battle of the Three Monotheisms*, trans. Wieland Hoban (Cambridge: Polity, 2009), especially 69–81 on Islam.

35. On the ideal of world domination in medieval and early modern Turkish history, see Kaya Şahin, *Empire and Power in the Reign of Süleyman: Narrating the Sixteenth-Century Ottoman World* (Cambridge: Cambridge University Press, 2013), 81–87; Robert Finlay, "Prophecy and Politics in Istanbul: Charles V, Sultan Suleyman, and the Habsburg Embassy of 1533–1534," *Journal of Early Modern History* 2.1 (1998): 1–31, especially 12 and 22–23; Kenneth Setton, *Western Hostility to Islam and Prophecies of Turkish Doom* (Philadelphia: American Philosophical Society, 1992), especially 29–46; Cornell Fleischer, "The Lawgiver as Messiah: The Making of the Imperial Image in the Reign of Süleymân," in *Soliman le Magnifique et son temps*, ed. Gilles Veinstein (Paris: Documentation Française, 1992), 159–77; Gülru Necipoğlu, "Süleyman the Magnificent and the Representation of Power in the Context of Ottoman-Hapsburg-Papal Rivalry," *The Art Bulletin* 71.3 (September 1989): 401–27, especially 407–17, who argues that Suleiman wanted to outdo Charles's 1530 coronation; and Osman Turan, "The Ideal of World Domination among the Medieval Turks," *Studia Islamica* 4 (1955): 77–90.

36. See Fleischer, "The Lawgiver as Messiah," 166.

37. On the interconnectedness between Western European states and the Ottoman Empire, see Claire Norton, "Blurring the Boundaries: Intellectual and Cultural Interactions between the Eastern and Western; Christian and Muslim Worlds," in *The Renaissance and the Ottoman World*, 3–21; Şahin, *Empire and Power in the Reign of Süleyman*, 6–10; and Carina L. Johnson, "Imperial Succession and Mirrors of Tyranny in the Houses of Habsburg and Osman," in *Representing Imperial Rivalry in the Early Modern Mediterranean*, eds. Barbara Fuchs and Emily Weissbourd (Toronto: University of Toronto Press, 2015), 80–100.

38. On the divisions within Christianity in the early modern age, see Carlos Eire, *Reformations: The Early Modern World, 1450–1650* (New Haven, CT: Yale University Press, 2016). On the Ottoman-Safavid conflicts, see Şahin, *Empire and Power in the Reign of Süleyman*, 205–13.

39. Desiderius Erasmus, *The Education of a Christian Prince*, trans. Neil M. Cheshire

and Michael J. Heath, ed. Lisa Jardine (Cambridge: Cambridge University Press, 1997), 108–9. The Latin text is from Desiderius Erasmus, *Institutio Principis Christiani*, ed. Otto Herding, in *Opera Omnia Desiderii Erasmi Roterodami* (Amsterdam: North-Holland Publishing Company, 1974), Vol. IV, Tome I, 95–219, especially 218.

40. See Cuart Moner's Introduction to *Cohortatio ad Carolum V*, ed. J. M. Rodríguez Peregrina, in *Obras Completas*, vol. 7, cccv-cccxvii (hereafter *Cohortatio*); and Luna Najera, "Myth and Prophecy in Juan Ginés de Sepúlveda's Crusading 'Exhortación,'" *Bulletin for Spanish and Portuguese Historical Studies* 35.1 (2011): 48–68.

41. Sepulveda, *Cohortatio*, especially 330–32.

42. Ibid., 334 (all translations from the *Cohortatio* are my own).

43. Ibid., 338.

44. See Martin Luther, *On War against the Turk*, in *Selected Political Writings*, ed. J. M. Porter (Philadelphia: Fortress Press, 1974), 121–31. Cf. Kenneth Setton, "Lutheranism and the Turkish Peril," *Balkan Studies* 3 (1962): 133–68.

45. See Desiderius Erasmus, *A Most Useful Discussion Concerning Proposals for War against the Turks*, trans. Michael Heath, in *Collected Works of Erasmus*, vol. LXIV, 201–66.

46. Sepulveda, *Cohortatio*, 345–46.

47. Ibid., 346.

48. Bartolomé de Las Casas, *In Defense of the Indians*, ed. and trans. S. Poole (DeKalb: Northern Illinois University Press, 1992), 155–67, 182–85. On the common elements between the representations of the American Indians and the Moors, see Fuchs, *Mimesis and Empire*, 1–8 and 72–78; and Stephen Clissold, *Conquistador: The Life of Don Pedro Sarmiento de Gamboa* (London: Derek Verschoyle, 1956), 62–65.

49. *The Battle of Lepanto*, ed. and trans. Elizabeth Wright, et al. (Cambridge, MA: Harvard University Press, 2014).

50. Ibid., xv.

51. On Juan Latino, see Elizabeth R. Wright, *The Epic of Juan Latino: Dilemmas of Race and Religion in Renaissance Spain* (Toronto: University of Toronto Press, 2016).

52. "Quin age surgamus genus omne et quicquid ubique est / gentis Romanae. Quicquid sub vindice mundi / candida signa sequi gaudet, properemus ad unum / hoc caput; hoc nobis est denique pervincendum. / Nec prius inceptum fas est dimittere cursum, / quam se perpetua solvent formidine terrae, / accipiantque iterum leges, melioraque iura" (lines 190–96).

53. Cf. Zatti, "Dalla parte di Satana," especially 146–48.

54. On the connection between *voto* (vow) and *voto* (empty), see Giuseppe Mazzotta, *Dante's Vision and the Circle of Knowledge* (Princeton, NJ: Princeton University Press, 1993), 38–39, with regard to the character of Piccarda Donati in cantos 3–5 of *Paradiso*; and Albert Ascoli, "Liberating the Tomb: Difference and Death in *Gerusalemme Liberata*," *Annali d'italianistica* 12 (1994): 159–80.

55. Torquato Tasso, *Giudicio sopra la Conquistata*, in *Prose diverse di Torquato Tasso*, ed. Cesare Guasti (Florence: Le Monnier, 1875), 458; translation mine. Cf. Franco Fari-

nelli, "La Gerusalemme catturata: ipotesi per una geografia del Tasso," in *Torquato Tasso tra letteratura, musica, teatro e arti figurative*, ed. Andrea Buzzoni (Bologna: Nuova Alfa Editoriale, 1985), 75–82, especially 78.

56. On these polarities, see Zatti, *L'uniforme cristiano e il multiforme pagano*, 9–44; and Ezio Raimondi, *Poesia come retorica* (Florence: Olschki Editore, 1980), 131–32. See also Bruscagli, *Stagioni della civiltà estense*, 187–222.

57. Zatti, *L'uniforme cristiano e il multiforme pagano*, 12. See also Jane Tylus, "Tasso's Trees: Epic and Local Culture," in *Epic Traditions in the Contemporary World: The Poetics of Community*, ed. Margaret Beissinger, et al. (Berkeley: University of California Press, 1999), 108–30, especially 117–23.

58. Quint, *Epic and Empire*, 214–34. On the reception of Tasso's works among Italian Protestants in exile, including the jurists Alberico and Scipione Gentili (originally, like Argillano, from the Marche region), see Diego Pirillo, "Tasso at the French Embassy: Epic, Diplomacy and the Law of Nations," in *Authority and Diplomacy from Dante to Shakespeare*, eds. Jason Powell and William Rossiter (Farnham, UK: Ashgate, 2013), 135–53.

59. Zatti, *L'uniforme cristiano e il multiforme pagano*, 118–21.

60. Quint, *Epic and Empire*, 243.

61. On Solimano as Lucifer, see Raimondi, *Poesia come retorica*, 116–17.

62. See, for instance, Aletto's exhortation in *Gerusalemme Liberata* 9.8–12. On Tasso's adaptation of Solimano as a historical figure, see F. David Wondrich, "The Crusade Within: 'L'Arabo imbelle' in Tasso's *Gerusalemme liberata*," *Mediterranean Studies* 7 (1998): 101–16, especially 110–16.

63. For a comparison of Solimano and Argante, see Giovanni Getto, *Nel mondo della Gerusalemme* (Rome: Bonacci Editore, 1977), 73–108. On the relationship between Tancredi and Argante, see Fredi Chiappelli, *Il conoscitore del caos. Una "vis abdita" nel linguaggio tassesco* (Rome: Bulzoni editore, 1981), 65–76. On the classical sources for the character of Argante, see Daniela Foltran, "Dalla 'Liberata' alla 'Conquistata.' Intertestualità virgiliana e omerica nel personaggio di Argante," *Studi Tassiani* 40–41 (1992–93): 89–134.

64. Tasso also compares Argante to Nimrod (*GL* 2.91) and Solimano to Anteus (20.108).

65. See also Dante's depiction of the heretic Farinata degli Uberti in *Inferno* 10.33.

66. Cf. Quint, *Epic and Empire*, 234–47. On the Copts' relationships with the Catholic Church and Western European countries, see Enrico Cerulli, *Eugenio IV e gli Etiopi al concilio di Firenze nel 1441* (Rome: Accademia Nazionale dei Lincei, 1933); and Alastair Hamilton, *The Copts and the West, 1439–1822: The European Discovery of the Egyptian Church* (Oxford: Oxford University Press, 2006), 9–82. On Clorinda's baptism and her newly discovered femininity, see Zatti, *L'uniforme cristiano e il multiforme pagano*, 142–43; and Chiappelli, *Il conoscitore del caos*, 56–64.

67. See Romans 6:6; Augustine, *Confessions* V, 16.

68. On Erminia, see Jane Tylus, "Imagining Narrative in Tasso: Revisiting Erminia," *Modern Language Notes* 127.1 (2012): 45–64, especially 59–60; Jonathan Combs-

Schilling, "Weaving the Crusades: Bodies of Interlace in Tasso's *Gerusalemme liberata*," *Modern Language Notes* 127.1 (2012): 1–22; Marilyn Migiel, "Tasso's Erminia: Telling an Alternate Story," *Italica* 64.1 (Spring 1987): 62–75; and Walter Stephens, "Trickster, Textor, Architect, Thief: Craft and Comedy in *Gerusalemme liberata*," in *Renaissance Transactions*, 146–77, especially 158–75.

69. On the use of the word "grembo" in the Armida and Erminia episodes, see Wells, *The Secret Wound*, 174.

70. The last battle depicted in the *Liberata*, in canto 20, would also see the Crusaders' victory at the expense of the large Egyptian army headed by the apostate Emireno, an Armenian Christian who converted to Islam. As noted above, some captains of the Ottoman fleet in the battle of Lepanto were also converts.

71. On the literary *topos* of the Fortunate Isles, see Theodore J. Cachey, *Le Isole Fortunate. Appunti di storia della letteratura italiana* (Rome: "L'Erma" di Bretschneider, 1995), especially 123–221, on sixteenth-century historiography, including the works of Pietro Martire, Oviedo, and Las Casas. On Armida's garden, see Angelo Bartlett Giamatti, *Earthly Paradise and Renaissance Epic* (Princeton, NJ: Princeton University Press, 1966), 179–210; Zatti, *L'uniforme cristiano e il multiforme pagano*, 45–90; and Chiappelli, *Il conoscitore del caos*, 182–97.

72. Cf. Dante, *Inferno* 26.90–142. On the presence of Dante's Ulysses in canto 15 of the *Liberata*, see Piero Boitani, *L'ombra di Ulisse. Figure di un mito* (Bologna: Il Mulino, 1992), 60–86; Matteo Residori, "Colombo e il volo d'Ulisse: una nota sul XV della *Liberata*," *Annali della Scuola Normale Superiore di Pisa*, ser. 3, vol. XXII, no. 3 (1992): 931–42; and Walter Stephens, "Tasso as Ulysses," in *Sparks and Seeds: Medieval Literature and Its Afterlife: Essays in Honor of John Freccero*, eds. Dana Stewart and Alison Cornish (Binghamton, NY: Medieval and Early Modern Studies, 2000), 209–39.

73. Cf. Theodore J. Cachey, "Tasso's *Navigazione del Mondo Nuovo* and the Origins of Columbus Encomium (GL, XV, 31–32)," *Italica* 69.3 (Autumn 1992): 326–44, especially 331–40. On the Este family's interest in geographical knowledge, see Cachey, "Maps and Literature in Renaissance Italy," 456–58.

74. Cf. Pietro Martire d'Anghiera, *De Orbe Novo Decades*, eds. Rosanna Mazzacane and Elisa Magioncalda (Genova: Dipartimento di Archeologia, Filologia classica e loro tradizioni, 2005); Giovanni Battista Ramusio, *Navigazioni e viaggi*, ed. Marica Milanesi (Turin: Einaudi, 1978–88); Geoffrey Symcox, ed., *Italian Reports on America 1493–1522: Letters, Dispatches, and Papal Bulls* (Turnhout, Bel.: Brepols, 2001); Geoffrey Symcox, ed., *Italian Reports on America 1493–1522: Accounts by Contemporary Observers* (Turnhout, Bel.: Brepols, 2002); Antonio Pigafetta, *The First Voyage around the World 1519–1522: An Account of Magellan's Expedition*, ed. and trans. Theodore J. Cachey (Toronto: University of Toronto Press, 2007); and Amerigo Vespucci, *Il mondo nuovo di Amerigo Vespucci*, ed. Mario Pozzi (Alessandria, Ita.: Edizioni dell'Orso, 1993). Among the numerous studies on Columbus's expeditions, see Nicolás Wey Gómez, *The Tropics of Empire: Why Columbus Sailed South to the Indies* (Cambridge, MA: MIT Press, 2008); David Abulafia, *The Discovery of Mankind: Atlantic Encounters in the Age of Columbus* (New Haven, CT: Yale University Press, 2008); Theodore J. Cachey, "Between Human-

ism and New Historicism: Rewriting the New World Encounter," *Annali d'Italianistica* 10 (1992): 28–46; Stephen Greenblatt, *Marvelous Possessions: The Wonder of the New World* (Chicago: The University of Chicago Press, 1991); Tzvetan Todorov, *The Conquest of America: The Question of the Other*, trans. Richard Howard (New York: Harper & Row, 1984); and the essays collected in *First Images of America: The Impact of the New World on the Old*, ed. Fredi Chiappelli (Berkeley: University of California Press, 1976).

75. See Cristóbal Colón, *Textos y documentos completos. Relaciones de viajes, cartas y memorials*, ed. C. Varela (Madrid: Allianza, 1982), 101: "Y [Columbus] dize qu'espera en Dios que, a la buelta que él entendía hazer de Castilla, avía de hallar un tonel de oro que avrín resgatado los que avía de dexar, y que avrían hallado la mina de oro y la espeçería, y aquello en tanta cantidad que los Reyes antes de tres años emprendiesen y adereçasen para ir a conquistar la Casa Sancta [Jerusalem]"; Christopher Columbus, *Journal of Christopher Columbus*, trans. C. Jane (New York: Clarkson N. Potter, Inc., 1960), 128: "And he says he trusts God that on his return, which he intended to make from Castile, he would find a barrel of gold, which those whom he had left there should have obtained by barter, and they would have found the gold mine and the spices, and in such quantity, that the Sovereigns, within three years, would undertake and prepare to go to the conquest of the Holy Places." On the "crusading" underpinnings of Columbus's motivations, see Abbas Hamdani, "Columbus and the Recovery of Jerusalem," *Journal of the American Oriental Society* 99.1 (January-March 1979): 39–48; and Paolo Emilio Taviani and Ilaria Caraci Luzzana's commentary in Ferdinand Columbus, *Historie Concerning the Life and Deeds of the Admiral Don Christopher Columbus*, ed. and trans. Luciano Farina (Rome: Istituto Poligrafico dello Stato, 1998), 2, 185–91.

76. Colón, *Textos y documentos completos*, 51; Columbus, *Journal of Christopher Columbus*, 52. See also Vespucci's letter to Lorenzo di Pierfrancesco de' Medici (1502) in Vespucci, *Il mondo nuovo di Amerigo Vespucci*, 87–89, and 115–17 and 167–68; Gaspare Contarini's report from Valladolid to the Doge of Venice (1522) in Symcox, ed., *Italian Reports on America 1493–1522: Letters, Dispatches, and Papal Bulls*, 84–87; and Michele da Cuneo, "News of the Islands of the Hesperian Ocean Discovered by Don Christopher Columbus of Genoa," in Symcox, ed., *Italian Reports on America 1493–1522: Accounts by Contemporary Observers*, 50–63.

77. See Michel de Montaigne, *Of Cannibals*, in *The Complete Works*, trans. D. Frame (New York: Everyman Library, 2003), 182–93.

78. Among the countless studies on the controversy between Sepulveda and Las Casas, see Rolena Adorno, *The Polemics of Possession in Spanish American Narrative* (New Haven, CT: Yale University Press, 2007); J.A. Fernandez-Santamaria, *The State, War and Peace: Spanish Political Thought in the Renaissance 1516–1559* (Cambridge: Cambridge University Press, 1996), 163–236; Anthony Pagden, "Ius et Factum: Text and Experience in the Writings of Bartolomé de las Casas," in *New World Encounters*, ed. Stephen Greenblatt (Berkeley: University of California Press, 1993), 85–100; idem, *The Fall of Natural Man: The Indian and the Origins of Comparative Ethnology* (Cambridge: Cambridge University Press, 1982), 109–45; Lewis Hanke, *All Mankind Is One: A Study of the Disputation Between Bartolomé de Las Casas and Juan Ginés de Sepulveda in 1550 on*

the Intellectual and Religious Capacity of the American Indians (DeKalb: Northern Illinois University Press, 1974); idem, *Aristotle and the American Indians: A Study in Race Prejudice in the Modern World* (Bloomington: Indiana University Press, 1970).

79. Juan Ginés de Sepúlveda, *Demócrates segundo; Apología en favor del libro sobre las justas causas de la guerra*, ed. A. Losada (Pozoblanco, Esp.: Exmco. Ayuntamento de Pozoblanco, 1997), 197 (my translation).

80. Las Casas, *In Defense of the Indians*, 325; Bartolomé de Las Casas, *Apologia*, in *Obras completas*, ed. Angel Losada (Madrid: Allianza Editorial, 1988), vol. 9, 598 (hereafter *Apologia*).

81. Las Casas, *In Defense of the Indians*, especially 151–52; Las Casas, *Apologia*, 300.

82. Las Casas, *In Defense of the Indians*, 153; Las Casas, *Apologia*, 302. On the use of the Roman Empire as a model for the colonization of the West Indies, see David Lupher, *Romans in a New World: Classical Models in Sixteenth-Century America* (Ann Arbor: The University of Michigan Press, 2003).

83. See Francisco de Vitoria, *On the American Indians*, in *Political Writings*, eds. and trans. Anthony Padgen and Jeremy Lawrence (Cambridge: Cambridge University Press, 1991), 282 and 288. On Vitoria, see Anthony Pagden, "Gentili, Vitoria, and the Fabrication of a 'Natural Law of Nations,'" in *The Roman Foundations of the Law of Nations: Alberico Gentili and the Justice of Empire*, eds. Benedict Kingsbury and Benjamin Straumann (Oxford: Oxford University Press, 2010), 340–61, especially 355–61; Fernandez-Santamaria, *The State, War and Peace*, 58–119; and Schmitt, *The Nomos of the Earth in the International Law of the Jus Publicum Europaeum*, 101–25.

84. Vitoria, *On the American Indians*, 285. The Latin text is from Francisco de Vitoria, *De Indis et De Iure Belli Relectiones*, ed. Ernest Nys (Buffalo: William S. Hein & Co., 1995), 263.

85. Tasso briefly discusses the status of the American Indians in his *Dialoghi*. See Tasso, *Il Nifo e De la dignità*, in *Dialoghi*, I, 266 and I, 456, respectively. On Tasso and the law of nations, see Pirillo, "Tasso at the French Embassy"; the chapter titled "Epic and the Law of Nations" in Timothy Hampton, *Fictions of Embassy: Literature and Diplomacy in Early Modern Europe* (Ithaca, NY: Cornell University Press, 2007), 78–96; and Christopher Warren, "Gentili, the Poets, and the Laws of War," in *The Roman Foundations of the Law of Nations*, 146–62, especially 155–59.

86. See Zatti, "Tasso e il nuovo mondo," 501–21, especially 514–17. Compare with Jane Tylus, "Reasoning Away Colonialism: Tasso and the Production of the *Gerusalemme Liberata*," *South Central Review* 10.2 (Summer 1993): 100–14, especially 106–8; and eadem, "Tasso's Trees," especially 117.

87. On the Magus of Ascalon, see David Quint, *Origin and Originality in Renaissance Literature* (New Haven, CT: Yale University Press, 1983), 92–117; and Matteo Residori, "Il Mago d'Ascalona e gli spazi del romanzo nella 'Liberata,'" *Italianistica* 24.2–3 (1995): 453–71.

88. This episode probably echoes a passage from book 6 (lines 285–94) of the *Aeneid* in which, as Aeneas enters Hades, he is tempted to use his sword against the shadows of various monsters, but he is stopped by the Cumaean Sybil.

89. Exceptionally, the translation of these lines is from Torquato Tasso, *The Liberation of Jerusalem*, trans. Max Wickert (Oxford: Oxford University Press, 2009).

90. Walter Stephens, "Saint Paul Among the Amazons: Gender and Authority in *Gerusalemme liberata*," in *Discourse of Authority in Medieval and Renaissance Literature*, eds. Kevin Brownlee and Walter Stephens (Hanover, NH: University Press of New England, 1989), 169–200, especially 198. See also Melinda Gough, "Tasso's Enchantress, Tasso's Captive Woman," *Renaissance Quarterly* 54.2 (Summer 2001): 523–52, especially 533–48; and Marilyn Migiel, *Gender and Genealogy in Tasso's "Gerusalemme Liberata"* (Lewiston, ME: The Edwin Mellen Press, 1993), 113–44.

91. Cavallo, "Tasso's Armida and the Victory of Romance," 96–109. Cf. Tylus, "Reasoning Away Colonialism," 108.

92. For a different reading of this passage, see Gough, "Tasso's Enchantress, Tasso's Captive Woman," 538.

93. On Goffredo's decision to spare Altamoro, see Walter Stephens, "Reading Tasso Reading Vergil Reading Homer: An Archeology of Andromache," *Comparative Literature Studies* 32.2 (1995): 296–319; and Lauren Scancarelli Seem, "The Limits of Chivalry: Tasso and the End of the *Aeneid*," *Comparative Literature* 42.2 (Spring 1990): 116–25.

94. Cf. David Quint, "Romance and History in Tasso's *Gerusalemme Liberata*," in *Romance and History: Imagining Time from the Medieval to the Early Modern Period*, ed. Jon Whitman (Cambridge: Cambridge University Press, 2015), 200–13, especially 203.

95. Tasso, *Giudicio sopra la Conquistata*, 458.

96. The allusion to Dante's thieves in relation to Goffredo's generosity is potentially deeply subversive, for it might fundamentally question the underlying motive of the Christian captain's mission. Such a thorough investigation, however, goes beyond the limits of this study.

97. Quint, *Epic and Empire*, 246.

98. On Goffredo's dream, see Quint, *Origin and Originality in Renaissance Literature*, 101–2; Giovanna Scianatico, *L'idea del perfetto principe. Utopia e storia nella scrittura del Torquato Tasso* (Naples: Edizioni Scientifiche Italiane, 1998), 29–63. See also Giovanna Scianatico, *L'arme pietose. Studio sulla* Gerusalemme Liberata (Venice: Marsilio, 1990), 193–225; and Erminia Ardissino, *"L'aspra tragedia." Poesia e sacro in Torquato Tasso* (Florence: Olschki Editore, 1996).

Epilogue

1. On the notion of *lyssa*, see Bruce Lincoln, "Homeric λύσσα: 'Wolfish Rage,'" *Indogermanische Forschungen* 80 (1975): 98–105.

2. Simone Weil, "The *Iliad*, or the Poem of Force," trans. Mary McCarthy, *Chicago Review* 18.2 (1965): 5–30, especially 6.

3. Ibid., 6.

4. See Miguel Herrero de Jáuregui, "Priam's Catabasis: Traces of the Epic Journey to Hades in 'Iliad' 24," *Transactions of the American Philological Association* 141.1 (Spring 2011): 37–68.

5. After sharing a meal, Priam and Achilles agree to an eleven-day truce to allow the Trojans to properly bury Hector's body (24.656–70).

6. Homer, *The Iliad*, trans. Richmond Lattimore (Chicago: The University of Chicago Press, 1951).

7. See Bruce Heiden, "The Simile of the Fugitive Homicide, *Iliad* 24.480–84: Analogy, Foiling, and Allusion," *American Journal of Philology* 119.1 (Spring 1998): 1–10.

8. Cf. Bernard Williams, *Shame and Necessity* (Berkeley: University of California Press, 1993), 39.

9. See Helen Cullyer, "Chrysippus on Achilles: The Evidence of Galen 'De Placitis Hippocratis et Platonis' 4.6–7," *The Classical Quarterly*, New Series 58.2 (2008): 537–46. On the Achilles-Priam encounter, see also Graham Zanker, *The Heart of Achilles: Characterization and Personal Ethics in the "Iliad"* (Ann Arbor: The University of Michigan Press, 1994), especially 115–25; and Dean Hammer, *The Iliad as Politics: The Performance of Political Thought* (Norman: University of Oklahoma Press, 2002), 182–97.

10. On the meaning of the name Achilles, see Gregory Nagy, *The Best of the Achaeans: Concepts of the Hero in Archaic Greek Poetry* (Baltimore: The Johns Hopkins University Press, 1999), 69–93.

11. On the concept of *philia*, see Martha Nussbaum, *The Fragility of Goodness: Luck and Ethics in Greek Tragedy and Philosophy* (Chicago: The University of Chicago Press, 1986), 343–72; on friendship in the Homeric poems, see David Konstan, *Friendship in the Classical World* (Cambridge: Cambridge University Press, 1991), 24–42.

Bibliography

Primary Sources

Acciaiuoli, Donato. *La "Vita Caroli" di Donato Acciaiuoli*. Edited by Daniela Gatti. Bologna: Paltron Editore, 1981.

Alan of Lille. *Literary Works*. Edited and translated by Winthrop Wetherbee. Cambridge, MA: Harvard University Press, 2013.

Alberti, Leon Battista. *Defunctus*. In *De commodis litterarum atque incommodis; Defunctus*, edited and translated by Giovanni Farris. Milan: Marzorati, 1971.

———. *Momus*. Edited by Virginia Brown and Sarah Knight. Translated by Sarah Knight. Cambridge, MA: Harvard University Press, 2003.

Albertus Magnus. *Alberti Magni Opera Omnia*. Edited by Auguste and Emil Borgnet. Paris: Ludovicum Vivès, 1891.

———. *On Animals: A Medieval* Summa Zoologica. Translated and annotated by Kenneth Kitchell and Irven Michael Resnick. 2 vols. Baltimore, MD: Johns Hopkins University Press, 1999.

Alighieri, Pietro. *Comentum super poema Comedie Dantis: A Critical Edition of the Third and Final Draft of Pietro Alighieri's "Commentary on Dante's 'Divine Comedy.'"* Edited by Massimiliano Chiamenti and Robert Hollander. Tempe, AZ: Arizona Center for Medieval and Renaissance Studies, 2002. As found in the Dartmouth Dante Project, https://dante.dartmouth.edu.

Aquinas, Thomas. *Summa Theologica*. 5 vols. Translated by the Fathers of the English Dominican Province. New York: Benziger Brothers, 1947.

———. *Summa Theologiae*. www.corpusthomisticum.org/iopera.html.

———. *Reasons for the Faith against Muslim Objections (and one Objection of the Greeks and Armenians) to the Cantor of Antioch*. Translated by Joseph Kenny. In *Islamochristiana* 22 (1996): 31–52.

———. *De rationibus fidei*. http://www.corpusthomisticum.org/ocg.html.

———. *Summa Contra Gentiles*. www.corpusthomisticum.org/iopera.html.

Ariosto, Ludovico. *Cinque Canti*. Translated and edited by Alexander Sheers and David Quint. Berkeley: University of California Press, 1996.

———. *Lettere*. Edited by Angelo Stella. Verona: Mondadori, 1965.

———. *Orlando Furioso*. Edited by Lanfranco Caretti. Turin: Einaudi, 1992.

———. *Orlando Furioso*. Translated by Guido Waldman. Oxford: Oxford University Press, 1998.

———. *Satire*. Edited by Cesare Segre. Turin: Einaudi, 1987.

Aristotle. *The Complete Works of Aristotle*. 2 vols. Edited by Jonathan C. Barnes. Princeton, NJ: Princeton University Press, 1984.

Augustine, Saint. *Confessions*. 2 vols. Translated by William Watts. Cambridge, MA: Harvard University Press, 1960.

———. *De Civitate Dei*. 7 vols. Translated by George E. McCracken, William M. Green, David S. Wiesen, Philip Levine, F. M. Sanford, and William Chase Green. Cambridge, MA: Harvard University Press, 1957–72.

Aurelius, Marcus. *The Meditations of Marcus Aurelius*. Translated by A. S. L. Farquharson. Oxford: Oxford University Press, 1989.

Avicenna, *The Canon of Medicine*. Adapted by Laleh Bakhtiar. Chicago, IL: Great Books of the Islamic World, 1999.

Baldi, Giovanni. *La disputa delle arti nel Quattrocento*. Edited by Eugenio Garin. Florence: Vallecchi, 1947.

Bandello, Matteo. *Tutte le opere di Matteo Bandello*. Edited by Francesco Flora. Milan: Mondadori, 1942.

Beer, Marina, ed. *Guerre in ottava rima*. 4 vols. Modena: Panini, 1988.

Benivieni, Antonio. *De abditis nonnullis ac mirandis morborum et sanationum causis*. Translated by Charles Singer. Springfield, IL: Charles C. Thomas Publisher, 1954.

———. *De abditis nonnullis ac mirandis morborum et sanationum causis*. Florence: Olschki, 1994.

Bertran de Born. *Liriche*. Edited and translated by Thomas G. Bergin. Varese: Magenta, 1964.

———. *Complete Works*. In G. Gourain, ed. *L'amour et la guerre. L'œuvre de Bertran de Born*. Aix-en-Provence: Université de Provence, 1985.

Biblia Sacra Vulgata. Stuttgart: Deutsche Bibelgesellschaft, 1994.

Boccaccio, Giovanni. *Corbaccio*. Edited by T. Nurmela. Helsinki: Suomalainen Tiedeakatemia, 1968.

———. *The Corbaccio*. Translated and edited by Anthony K. Cassell. Urbana: University of Illinois Press, 1975.

———. *Famous Women*. Edited and translated by Virginia Brown. Cambridge, MA: Harvard University Press, 2001.

———. *Ninfale fiesolano*. In *Tutte le opere*. 10 vols. Edited by Vittore Branca et al. Milan: Mondadori, 1964–94.

———. *Genealogia deorum gentilium*. In *Tutte le opere*. 10 vols. Edited by Vittore Branca et al. Milan: Mondadori, 1964–94.

Boethius. *Tractates: The Consolation of Philosophy*. Translated by H. F. Stewart, E. K. Rand, S. J. Tester. Cambridge, MA: Harvard University Press, 1989.

Boiardo, Matteo Maria. *Orlando innamorato*. Edited by Riccardo Bruscagli. Turin: Einaudi, 1995.

———. *Orlando Innamorato*. Translated by Charles S. Ross. Berkeley: University of

California Press, 1989. Boniface VIII. *Unam Sanctam*. Edited by W. Römer. Schaffhausen, 1889.

———. "Clericis Laicos." In *Corpus Juris Canonici*, edited by Emil Friedberg, 915. Tauchnitz: Leipzig, 1879–81.

Bornate, Carlo, ed., "*Historia vitae et gestorum per dominum magnum cancellarium*, con note, aggiunte e documenti," *Miscellanea di storia italiana* 48 (1915): 233–558.

Bruni, Leonardo. *History of the Florentine People*. 3 vols. Edited and translated by James Hankins with D.J.W. Bradley. Cambridge, MA: Harvard University Press, 2001–7.

Campanella, Tommaso. *La Città del Sole: Dialogo Poetico*. Edited and translated by Daniel Donno. Berkeley and Los Angeles: University of California Press, 1981.

Capellanus, Andreas. *The Art of Courtly Love*. Translated by J. J. Parry. New York: Columbia University Press, 1990.

———. *De Amore*. http://www.thelatinlibrary.com/capellanus.html.

Castellani, Francesco. *Ricordanze*. Edited by Giovanni Ciappelli. Florence: Olschki, 1992.

Cecco d'Ascoli. *L'Acerba*. Ascoli Piceno: Casa Editrice di Giuseppe Cesari, 1977.

Celsus. *De medicina*. 3 vols. Translated by W. G. Spencer. Cambridge, MA: Harvard University Press, 1989.

Chanson de Roland. Edited by Paulette Gabaudan. Paris: Nizet, 1994.

Cicero. *De officiis*. Translated by Walter Miller. Cambridge, MA: Harvard University Press, 1913.

———. *Tusculan Disputations*. Translated by J. E. King. Cambridge, MA: Harvard University Press, 2001.

———. *De finibus*. Translated by H. Rackham. Cambridge, MA: Harvard University Press, 1971.

———. *De Senectute; De amicitia; De Divinatione*. Translated by W. A. Falconer. Cambridge, MA: Harvard University Press, 1923.

———. *De natura deorum; Academica*. Translated by H. Rackham. Cambridge, MA: Harvard University Press, 1933.

———. *Philippics*. Edited and translated by D.R. Shackleton Bailey. Cambridge, MA: Harvard University Press, 2009.

Colón, Cristóbal (Christopher Columbus). *Textos y documentos completos. Relaciones de viajes, cartas y memoriales*. Edited by C. Varela. Madrid: Allianza, 1982.

———. *The Book of Prophecies Edited by Christopher Columbus*. Edited by Roberto Rusconi and translated by Blair Sullivan. Berkeley: University of California Press, 1997.

———. *The Journal of Christopher Columbus*. Translated by Cecil Jane. New York: Clarkson N. Potter, Inc., 1960.

———. *The Libro de las prophecías of Christopher Columbus*. Edited and translated by Delno C. West and August Kling. Gainesville: University of Florida Press, 1991.

Columbus, Ferdinand. *Historie Concerning the Life and Deeds of the Admiral Don Cristopher Columbus*. 2 vols. Edited and translated by Luciano F. Farina. Rome: Istituto poligrafico e Zecca dello Stato, 1998.

Cronica fiorentina compilata nel secolo XIII. In *Testi fiorentini del Dugento e dei primi del Trecento*, edited by Alfredo Schiaffini. Florence: Sansoni, 1926.

———. *Studi di critica e storia letteraria*. Bologna: Nicola Zanichelli, 1912.
Dante Alighieri. *La Commedia secondo l'antica vulgata*. 4 vols. Edited by Giorgio Petrocchi. Florence: Le Lettere, 1994.
———. *Il Convivio*. Edited and translated by Richard Lansing. New York: Garland, 1990.
———. *Dante's "Vita Nuova."* Translated by Mark Musa. Bloomington: Indiana University Press, 1973.
———. *The Divine Comedy of Dante Alighieri*. 3 vols. Translated by Robert Durling. Oxford: Oxford University Press, 1996–2011.
———. *Epistole*. In *Opere di Dante*. Vol. 3. Edited by Arsenio Frugoni and Giorgio Brugnoli. Milan: Ricciardi, 1996.
———. *Epistolae*. Edited and translated by Paget Toynbee. Oxford: Oxford University Press, 1966.
———. *Monarchia*. Translated by Richard Kay. Toronto: Pontifical Institute of Mediaeval Studies, 1998.
———. *Monarchia*. Edited by Francesco Furlan. Milan: Mondadori, 2004.
———. *Monarchia*. Edited by Prue Shaw. Florence: Le Lettere, 2009.
———. *Opere*. Edited by Gianfranco Fioravanti et al. Milan: Mondadori, 2014.
———. *Opere minori: Convivio*. Edited by Domenico De Robertis. Milan: Ricciardi 1995.
———. *Vita Nuova*. In *Le Opere di Dante*, Vol.1, edited by Michele Barbi. Florence, Società Dantesca Italiana, 1960.
———. *De Vulgari Eloquentia*. Translated by Steven Botterill. Cambridge: Cambridge University Press, 1996.
———. *De Vulgari Eloquentia*. Translated by Claire E. Honess. London: Modern Humanities Research Association, 2007.
Dati, Goro. *Istoria di Firenze dall'anno 1380 all'anno 1405*. Florence: Stamperia di Giuseppe Manni, 1735.
de' Bassi, Piero Andrea. *Le fatiche de Hercule*. Ferrara: Agostino Cameri, 1475.
Dies Irae. From the *Graduale Romano Serafico*, Ordinis Fratrum Minorum (Paris: Typis Societatis S. Joannis Evangelistae, Desclee & Socii, 1932), 97–100, in the sequence for the *Missa pro Defunctis*.
Dies Irae. Translated by William Josiah Irons. In *Seven Great Hymns of the Medieval Church*, edited by Charles C. Nott, 61. New York: Anson D. F. Randolph, 1870.
Diodorus of Sicily. *The Library of History*. 12 vols. Translated by C. H. Oldfather. Cambridge, MA: Harvard University Press, 1935.
Erasmus, Desiderius. *Collected Works of Erasmus*. 86 vols. Toronto: University of Toronto Press, 1974–2009.
———. *The Education of a Christian Prince*. Translated by Neil M. Cheshire and Michael J. Heath. Cambridge, MA: Cambridge University Press, 1997.
———. *Institutio Principis Christiani*. In *Opera Omnia Desiderii Erasmi Roterodami*, Vol. IV, Tome I, edited by Otto Herding. Amsterdam: North-Holland Publishing Company, 1974.

Ficino, Marsilio. *Commentarium in Phaedrum*. In *Marsilio Ficino and the Phaedran Charioteer*, edited by Michael Allen. Berkeley: University of California Press, 1981.

———. *Commentary on Plato's Symposium on Love*. Translated by Sears Jayne. Dallas: Spring Publications, 1985.

———. *The Letters of Marsilio Ficino*. 10 vols. Translated by members of the Language Department of the School of Economic Science. London: Shepheard-Walwyn, 1975–2015.

———. *Oratio de laudibus medicinae*. In *Svpplementvm ficianvm. Marcilii Ficini florentini philosophi platonici opvscvla inedita et dispersa*, edited by Paul Oskar Kristeller. Florence: Olschki, 1937.

———. *Platonic Theology*. Edited by James Hankins and William Bowen, and translated by Michael Allen and John Warden. 6 vols. Cambridge, MA: Harvard University Press, 2001–2006.

———. *Three Books on Life*. Edited and translated by Carol Kaske and John Clark. Binghamton: Center for Medieval and Early Renaissance Studies, State University of New York at Binghamton, 1989.

Galen. *Method of Medicine to Glaucon*. Edited and translated by Ian Johnston. Cambridge, MA: Harvard University Press, 2016.

———. *Translatio Libri Galieni De rigore et tremore et iectigatione et spasmo*. In *Arnaldi de Villanova Opera Medica Omnia*, Vol. 16, edited by Micheal McVaugh. Barcelona: Publicacions i Edicions de la Universitat de Barcelona, 1981.

George of Trebizond. *On the Eternal Glory of the Autocrat*. In *Collectanea Trapezuntiana: Texts, Documents, and Bibliographies of George of Trebizond*, edited by John Monfasani. Binghamton, NY: Medieval & Renaissance Texts & Studies, 1984.

Hartwig, Otto. *Quellen und Forschungen zur ältesten Geschichte der Stadt Florenz*. 2 vols. Marburg: Elvert, 1875.

Giles of Rome. *De ecclesiastica potestate*. Edited by R. W. Dyson. New York: Columbia University Press, 1994

Giraldi, Gregorio. *Vita Herculis*. Basilea: apud Mich. Ising., 1539.

Giraldi, Giovan Battista (Cinthio). *Dell'Hercole canti ventisei*. Modena: A. Gadaldini, 1557.

Hierocles the Stoic. *Hierocles the Stoic: Elements of Ethics, Fragments, and Excerpts*. Edited by Ilaria Ramelli. Translated by David Konstan. Atlanta, GA: Society of Biblical Literature, 2009.

Homer. *The Iliad*. Translated by Richmond Lattimore. Chicago, IL: University of Chicago Press, 1951.

Horace. *Carmina*. Translated by Niall Rudd. Cambridge, MA: Harvard University Press, 2004.

———. *Satires; Epistles; Ars Poetica*. Translated by H.R. Fairclough. Cambridge, MA: Harvard University Press, 1929.

Iacopo da Varazze. *Legenda Aurea*. Edited by Giovanni Paolo Maggioni. Florence: Sismel—Edizioni del Galluzzo, 1998.

Innocent III. "Letter to the Prefect of Acerbus and the nobles of Tuscany." In *Patrologia Latina* 214, edited by J. P. Migne. Col. 377.
Isidore of Seville. *Etymologies*. Edited and translated by Stephen A. Barney, et al. Cambridge, MA: Cambridge University Press, 2006.
———. *Etymologiarum Sive Originum*. www.thelatinlibrary.com/isidore.html.
James of Viterbo. *De Regimine Christiano*. Edited by R. W. Dyson. Leiden: Brill, 2009.
John of Damascus. *De Haeresibus*. In *John of Damascus on Islam. The "Heresy of the Ishmaelites,"* edited and translated by Daniel Sahas. Leiden: E. J. Brill, 1972.
John of Paris. *On Royal and Papal Power (Tractatus de Potestate Regia et Papali)*. Translated by John A. Watt. Toronto: Pontifical Institute of Mediaeval Studies, 1971.
John of Salisbury. *Policraticus: Of the Frivolities of Courtiers and the Footprints of Philosophers*. Edited and translated by Cary J. Nederman. Cambridge: Cambridge University Press, 1990.
Laertius, Diogenes. *Lives of Eminent Philosophers*. Vol. 1. Edited by Robert Drew Hicks. Cambridge, MA: Harvard University Press, 1925.
Landino, Cristoforo. *Comento sopra la Comedia*. In *I Commenti Danteschi dei Secoli XIV, XV e XVI*. Edited by Paolo Proacaccioli. Rome: Lexis Progetti Editoriali, 1999. As found in the Dartmouth Dante Project, https://dante.dartmouth.edu.
———. *Disputationes Camaldulenses*. Edited by Peter Lohe. Florence: Sansoni, 1980.
———. *De vera nobilitate*. Edited by Maria Teresa Liaci. Florence: Olschki, 1970.
Lanfranc of Milan. *Chirurgia magna*. In Tabanelli, Mario, ed. *La chirurgia italiana nell'Alto Medioevo*. Vol 2, 853–90. Florence: Olschki, 1965.
Las Casas, Bartolomé de. *In Defense of the Indians*. Edited and translated by Stafford Poole. DeKalb: Northern Illinois University Press, 1992.
———. *Obras completas*. 14 vols. Edited by Angel Losada. Madrid: Allianza Editorial, 1988–95.
Latini, Brunetto. *Tresor*. Edited by Pietro Beltrani. Turin: Einaudi, 2007.
———. *Il Tesoro di Brunetto Latini*. Edited by Alessandro D'Ancona. Rome: Tipografia della R. Accademia dei Lincei, 1888.
Livy. *Ab urbe condita*. 14 vols. Translated by F. G. Moore. Cambridge, MA: Harvard University Press, 1940.
Lullo, Raimondo. *Libro dell'ordine della cavalleria*. Translated into Italian by G. Allegra. Carmagnola: Edizioni Arktos, 1983.
Lucan. *The Civil War (Pharsalia)*. Translated by J. D. Duff. Cambridge, MA: Harvard University Press, 1997.
Luther, Martin. *Selected Political Writings*. Edited by J. M. Porter. Philadelphia: Fortress Press, 1974.
Machiavelli, Niccolò. *Opere*. Edited by Mario Bonfantini. Milan: Ricciardi, 1954.
Marsilius of Padua, *Defensor Pacis*. 2 vols. Translated by Alan Gewirth. New York: Arno Press, 1979.
Montaigne, Michel de. *Of Cannibals*. In *The Complete Works*, translated by Donald M. Frame, 182–93. New York: Everyman Library, 2003.
Nicholas of Cusa. *Opera omnia*. Hamburg: Felix Meier, 1932–2010.

———. *Nicholas of Cusa's De Pace Fidei and Cribatio Alkorani*. Minneapolis, MN: The Arthur J. Banning Press, 1994.

———. *The Catholic Concordance*. Edited and translated by Paul Sigmund. Cambridge: Cambridge University Press, 1991.

———. *Nicholas of Cusa's De Pace Fidei and Cribatio Alkorani*. Edited by Jasper Hopkins. Minneapolis, MN: The Arthur J. Banning Press, 1994.

Nott, Charles C., ed. *Seven Great Hymns of the Medieval Church*. New York: Anson D. F. Randolph, 1870.

Olivi, Pierre Jean. *Lectura super Apocalipsim*. In *Scritti scelti*, edited by Paolo Vian. Rome: Città Nuova, 1989.

———. *Quaestiones de Romano Pontifice*. Edited by Marco Bartoli. Grottaferrata: Editiones Collegii S. Bonaventurae ad Claras Aquas, 2002.

Orosius. *Adversus Paganos*. http://www.thelatinlibrary.com/orosius.html.

L'Ottimo Commento della Divina Commedia [Andrea Lancia]. Testo inedito d'un contemporaneo di Dante..., [ed. Alessandro Torri]. Pisa: N. Capurro, 1827–29. As found in the Dartmouth Dante Project, https://dante.dartmouth.edu.

Ovid. *Metamorphoses*. Translated by Frank Justus Miller. 2 vols. Cambridge, MA: Harvard University Press, 1977.

———. *Tristia. Ex Ponto*. Translated by Arthur Leslie Wheeler. Revised by G.P. Goold. Cambridge, MA: Harvard University Press, 1924.

Palmieri, Matteo. *Della vita civile*. Edited by Felice Battaglia. Bologna: Nicola Zanichelli Editore, 1944.

Pertusi, Agostino, ed. *La caduta di Costantinopoli. L'eco nel mondo*. Milan: Arnoldo Mondadori Editore, 1976.

———. *Testi inediti e poco conosciuti sulla caduta di Costantinopoli*. Bologna: Pàtron Editore, 1983.

Peter the Venerable. *Peter the Venerable and Islam*. Edited by James Kritzeck. Princeton, NJ: Princeton University Press, 1964.

Petrarca, Francesco. *Prose*. Edited by Giorgio Martellotti et al. Milan: Ricciardi, 1955.

———. *Canzoniere*. Edited by Marco Santagata. Milan: Mondadori, 2004.

Piccolomini, Aeneas Silvius (Pope Pius II). *Epistola ad Mahomatem II (Epistle to Mohammed II)*. Edited and translated by Albert R. Baca. New York: Peter Lang, 1990.

———. *On the Origin and Authority of the Roman Empire*. In *Three Tracts on the Empire*, edited by Thomas M. Izbicki and Cary J. Nederman. Bristol: Thoemmes Press, 2000.

———. *Letters*. In *Der Briefwechsel des Eneas Silvius Piccolomini*. Edited by Rudolf Wolkan. In *Fontes Rerum Austriacarum*. Series 2, Volume 68. Vienna: A. Hölder, 1909–18.

———. *Reject Aeneas, Accept Pius: Selected Letters of Aeneas Sylvius Piccolomini*. Edited and translated by Thomas M. Izbicki et al. Washington, DC: The Catholic University of America Press, 2006.

Pico della Mirandola. *Oration on the Dignity of Man*. Edited and translated by Francesco Borghesi et al. Cambridge: Cambridge University Press, 2013.

Pietro Martire d'Anghiera. *De Orbe Novo Decades*. 2 vols. Edited by Rosanna Mazzacane and Elisa Magioncalda. Genoa: Dipartimento di Archeologia, Filologia classica e loro tradizioni, 2005.

Pigafetta, Antonio. *The First Voyage around the World 1519–1522: An Account of Magellan's Expedition*. Edited and translated by Theodore J. Cachey. Toronto: University of Toronto Press, 2007.

Pigna, Giovan Battista. *I romanzi di M. Giouan Battista Pigna divisi in tre libri. Ne quali della poesia, & della vita dell'Ariosto con nuouo modo*. Venice: Valgrisi, 1554.

Plato. *The Collected Dialogues of Plato*. Edited by Edith Hamilton and Huntington Cairns. Princeton, NJ: Princeton University Press, 1989.

Poliziano, Agnolo, *Fabula di Orfeo*. In *Orfeo del Poliziano*, edited by Antonia Tissoni Benvenuti. Padua: Antenore, 1986.

———. *Prose volgari inedite e poesie latine e greche edite e inedite*. Edited by Isidoro del Lungo. Florence: Barbera Editore, 1867.

———. *Della congiura dei Pazzi (Coniurationis commentarium)*. Edited by Alessandro Perosa. Padova: Antenore, 1958.

———. *The Pazzi Conspiracy*. In *The Earthly Republic*, edited by Benjamin G. Kohl and Ronald G. Witt., 305–22. Philadelphia: University of Pennsylvania Press, 1978.

Prudentius. *Works*. 2 vols. Translated by Henry John Thompson. Cambridge, MA: Harvard University Press, 1949.

Ptolemy of Lucca. *De Regimine Principum*. Translated by James M. Blythe. Philadelphia: University of Pennsylvania Press, 1997.

Pulci, Luigi. *Morgante e le lettere*. Edited by Domenico De Robertis. Florence: Sansoni, 1984.

———. *Morgante*. Edited by Franca Ageno. Milan: Mondadori, 1994.

———. *Morgante: The Epic Adventures of Orlando and His Giant Friend Morgante*. Translated by Joseph Tusiani. Bloomington: Indiana University Press, 1998.

———. *Opere minori*. Edited by Paolo Orvieto. Milan: Mursia, 1986.

———. *Sonetti extravaganti*. Edited by Alessio Decaria. Florence: Società Editrice Fiorentina, 2013.

Ramusio, Giovanni Battista. *Navigazioni e viaggi*. 6 vols. Edited by Marica Milanesi. Turin: Einaudi, 1978–88.

Riccoldo da Montecroce. *Complete Latin Works*. http://www.e-theca.net/emiliopanella/riccoldo/index.htm.

———. *Contra legem Sarracenorum*. Edited by J.-M. Mérigoux, in "Fede e controversia nel '300 e '500," *Memorie domenicane* 17 (1986): 60–144.

———. *Epistole ad Ecclesiam triumphantem*. In *A Christian Pilgrim in Medieval Iraq: Riccoldo da Montecroce's Encounter with Islam*, translated by Rita George-Tvrtković. Turnhout: Brepols, 2012.

———. *Liber peregrinationis*. In *Riccold de Monte Croce: Pérégrination en Terre Sainte et au Proche-Orient et Lettres sur la chute de Saint-Jean d'Acre*, edited and translated by René Kappler. Paris: Champion, 1997.

———. *Liber peregrinationis*. In *A Christian Pilgrim in Medieval Iraq: Riccoldo da Monte-*

croce's Encounter with Islam, translated by Rita George-Tvrtković. Turnhout: Brepols, 2012.

———. *I Saraceni. Contra legem Sarracenorum*. Edited and translated by Giuseppe Rizzardi. Florence: Nardini Editore, 1992.

Rinuccini, Alamanno. *On Liberty*. In *Humanism and Liberty*, edited by Renée Neu Watkins, 185–224. Columbia: University of South Carolina Press 1978.

Sacchetti, Franco. *Il libro delle rime*. Edited by Alberto Chiari. Bari: Laterza, 1936.

Salutati, Coluccio. *De laboribus Herculis*. Edited by Berthold Louis Ullman. Zurich: Thesauri Mundi, 1951.

———. *De Tyranno*. In *Political Writings*, edited by Stefano U. Baldassarri and translated by Rolf Bagemihl. Cambridge, MA: Harvard University Press, 2014.

———. *Fabula de Vulpe et Cancro*. In Jensen, Richard C.; Babr-Volk, Marie. "The Fox and the Crab: Coluccio Salutati's Unpublished Fable." *Studies in Philology* 73, no. 2 (Apr., 1976): 170–75.

Santi, Giovanni. *La vita e le gesta di Federico da Montefeltro duca d'Urbino: poema in terza rima*. 2 vols. Edited by Luigi Michelini Tocci. Vatican City: Biblioteca Apostolica Vaticana, 1985.

Sanzanomis Gesta Florentinorum. In *Cronache dei secoli XIII e XIV*, 125–54. Florence: Tipi di M. Cellini, 1876.

Savonarola, Girolamo. *Prediche sopra Ezechiele*. 2 vols. Edited by Roberto Ridolfi. Rome: Belardetti, 1955.

Seneca, Lucius Anneus. *De beneficiis*. Translated by John W. Basore. In *Moral Essays*, Vol. 3. Cambridge, MA: Harvard University Press, 1989.

———. *De clementia*. Translated by John W. Basore. In *Moral Essays*, Vol. 1. Cambridge, MA: Harvard University Press, 1998.

———. *Seneca's "Hercules Furens."* A critical text with introduction and commentary by John G. Fitch. Ithaca, NY: Cornell University Press, 1987.

———. *Tragedies*. 2 vols. Translated by John G. Fitch. Cambridge, MA: Harvard University Press, 2002–4.

Sepúlveda, Juan Ginés de. *Obras Completas*. Edited by Ángel Losada García. Pozoblanco: Exmco. Ayuntamento de Pozoblanco, 1995–2003.

Silvestri, Domenico. *The Latin Poetry*. Edited by R. C. Jensen. Munich: Wilhelm Fink Verlag, 1973.

Silvestris, Bernardus. *Poetic Works*. Edited and translated by Winthrop Wetherbee. Cambridge, MA: Harvard University Press, 2015.

Statius. *Thebaid*. 2 vols. Edited and translated by D.R. Shackleton Bailey. Cambridge, MA: Harvard University Press, 2004.

Suetonius. *Life of Nero*. Translated by J. C. Rolfe. Cambridge, MA: Harvard University Press, 1914.

Symcox, Geoffrey, ed. *Italian Reports on America 1493–1522: Letters, Dispatches, and Papal Bulls*. Turnhout: Brepols, 2001.

———, ed. *Italian Reports on America 1493–1522: Accounts by Contemporary Observers*. Turnhout: Brepols, 2002.

Tasso, Torquato. *Dialoghi*. 2 vols. Edited by Giovanni Baffetti. Milan: Rizzoli, 1998.
———. *Gerusalemme liberata*. 2 vols. Edited by Bruno Maier. Milan: Rizzoli, 1995.
———. *Giudicio sopra la Conquistata*. In *Prose diverse di Torquato Tasso: nuovamente raccolte ed emendate*. 2 vols., edited by Cesare Guasti. Firenze: Le Monnier, 1875.
———. *Jerusalem Delivered*. Translated and edited by Ralph Nash. Detroit, MI: Wayne State University Press, 1987.
———. *The Liberation of Jerusalem*. Translated by Max Wickert. Oxford: Oxford University Press, 2009
———. *Opere*. 2 vols. Edited by Bruno Maier. Milan: Rizzoli, 1964.
Teodorico of Lucca. *Chirurgia*. In Tabanelli, Mario, ed. *La chirurgia italiana nell'Alto Medioevo*. Vol 1., 256–57. Florence: Olschki, 1965.
Uguccione da Pisa. *Derivationes*. 2 vols. Florence: Edizioni del Galluzzo, 2004.
Valla, Lorenzo. *On the Donation of Constantine*. Translated by G. W. Bowersock. Cambridge, MA: Harvard University Press, 2007.
Vegio, Maffeo. *Short Epics*. Edited and translated by Michael Putnam with James Hankins. Cambridge, MA: Harvard University Press, 2004.
Vespucci, Amerigo. *Il mondo nuovo di Amerigo Vespucci*. Edited by Mario Pozzi. Alessandria: Edizioni dell'Orso, 1993.
Villani, Giovanni. *Nuova cronica*. Edited by G. Porta. Parma: Ugo Guanda Editore, 1991.
Virgil. *Aeneid*. 2 vols. Translated by H. R. Fairclough. Cambridge, MA: Harvard University Press, 2000.
Vitoria, Francisco de. *De Indis et De Iure Belli* Relectiones. Edited by Ernest Nys. Buffalo, NY: William S. Hein & Co., 1995.
———. *Political Writings*. Edited and translated by Anthony Pagden and Jeremy Lawrance. Cambridge: Cambridge University Press, 1991.
William of Ockham. *Octo Quaestiones de Potestate Papae*. Edited by J. G. Sikes. Manchester: University Press, 1940.
Wright Elizabeth, et al (ed. and trans.). *The Battle of Lepanto*. Cambridge, MA: Harvard University Press, 2014.

Secondary Sources
Abulafia, David. *The Discovery of Mankind: Atlantic Encounters in the Age of Columbus*. New Haven, CT: Yale University Press, 2008.
Adorno, Rolena. *The Polemics of Possession in Spanish American Narrative*. New Haven, CT: Yale University Press, 2007.
Agamben, Giorgio. *Homo Sacer: Sovereign Power and Bare Life*. Translated by Daniel Heller-Roazen. Stanford, CA: Stanford University Press, 1998.
———. *Stasis: Civil War as a Political Paradigm (Homo Sacer II, 2)*. Translated by Nicholas Heron. Stanford, CA: Stanford University Press, 2015.
Ageno, Franca. "Ancora sui bestiari del 'Morgante.'" *Studi di filologia italiana*, 14 (1956): 485–93.
Ahl, Frederick. *Lucan: An Introduction*. Ithaca, NY: Cornell University Press, 1976.

Al Sabah, Rasha. "Inferno XXVIII: The Figure of Muhammad." *Yale Italian Studies*, I (Winter 1977): 147–61.
Allegretti, Paola. "Canto XXVIII." In *Inferno. Lectura Dantis Turicensis*, edited by Georges Güntert and Michelangelo Picone, 393–406. Florence: Franco Cesati Editore, 2000.
Allen, Michael J. B. "Homo ad Zodiacum: Marsilio Ficino and the Boethian Hercules." In *Plato's Third Eye: Studies in Marsilio Ficino's Metaphysics and its Sources*, 205–21. Aldershot: Variorum, 1995.
———. *The Platonism of Marsilio Ficino: A Study of His* Phaedrus *Commentary, Its Sources and Genesis*. Berkeley: University of California Press, 1984.
Annas, Julia. *An Introduction to Plato's* Republic. Oxford: Oxford University Press, 1981.
Appiah, Kwame. *Cosmopolitanism: Ethics in a World of Strangers*. New York: W.W. Norton, 2006.
Ardissino, Erminia. "*L'aspra tragedia.*" *Poesia e sacro in Torquato Tasso*. Florence: Olschki, 1996.
Armitage, David. "Cosmopolitanism and Civil War." In *Cosmopolitanism and the Enlightenment*, edited by Joan-Pau Rubiés and Neil Safier. Cambridge: Cambridge University Press, forthcoming.
Armour, Peter. "Dante's Contrapasso: Context and Texts." *Italian Studies* 55, no.1 (2000): 1–20.
Ascoli, Albert. *Ariosto's Bitter Harmony: Crisis and Evasion in the Italian Renaissance*. Princeton, NJ: Princeton University Press, 1987.
———. "Ariosto and the 'Fier Pastor': Form and History in Orlando Furioso." *Renaissance Quarterly* 54, no. 2 (Summer, 2001): 487–522.
———. *Dante and the Making of a Modern Author*. Cambridge: Cambridge University Press, 2008.
———. "Liberating the Tomb: Difference and Death in *Gerusalemme Liberata*." *Annali d'italianistica*, 12 (1994): 159–80.
Asín Palacios, Miguel. *Islam and the Divine Comedy*. Translated by Harold Sutherland. New York: Dutton, 1926.
Avonto, Luigi. *Mercurino Arborio di Gattinara: documenti inediti per la storia delle Indie Nuove nell'archivio del gran cancelliere di Carlo V.* Vercelli: S. E. T. C., 1981.
Babinger, Franz. "Lorenzo de' Medici e la corte ottomana." *Archivio storico italiano*, 121 (1963): 305–61.
———. *Mehmed the Conqueror and his Time*. Translated by Ralph Manheim. Princeton, NJ: Princeton University Press, 1978.
Balakrisnhan, Gopal. *Enemy: An Intellectual Portrait of Carl Schmitt*. London and New York: Verso, 2000.
Baldelli, Ignazio. "'Lo dolce piano che da Vercelli a Marcabò dichina': Inferno XXVIII, 74–75." *Lettere Italiane* 47 (1995): 193–202.
Balzaretti, Ugo. "L'Orlando Furioso' in filigrana: Ravenna, le armi da fuoco, la corte, l'ascesa negata di Ruggiero." *Aevum* 70, no. 3 (September–December 1996): 563–96.

Barański, Zygmunt G. *Dante e i segni: saggi per una storia intellettuale di Dante Alighieri*. Naples: Liguori, 2000.

———. "'E cominciare stormo': Notes on Dante's sieges." In *"Legato con amore in un volume": Essays in Honour of John A. Scott*, edited by John Kinder and Diana Glenn, 175–203. Florence: Olschki, 2013.

———. "Scatology and Obscenity in Dante." In *Dante for the New Millennium*, edited by Teodolinda Barolini and H. W. Storey, 259–73. New York: Fordham University Press, 2003.

———. "'Tres enim sunt manerie dicendi . . .': Some Observations on Medieval Literature, Dante, and 'Genre.'" In *"Libri poetarum in quattuor species dividuntur": Essays on Dante and 'Genre,'* edited by Zygmunt G. Barański. Supplement 2 of *The Italianist* 15 (1995): 9–60.

Barbi, Michele. *Problemi fondamentali per un nuovo commento della Divina Commedia*. Florence: Sansoni, 1956.

Barkan, Leonard. *Nature's Work of Art: The Human Body as Image of the World*. New Haven, CT: Yale University Press, 1975.

Barnes, John C. "Dante's Knowledge of Florentine History." In *Dante and his Precursors: Twelve Essays*, edited by J. C. Barnes and J. Petrie, 93–116. Dublin: Four Courts Press, 2007.

———. "'Guerre conviene surgere': Dante and War." In *War and Peace in Dante*, edited by John C. Barnes and Daragh O'Connell, 11–32. Dublin: Four Court Press, 2015.

———. "Storming the Barbican: A Military Reading of *Inferno* VIII-IX." In *War and Peace in Dante*, edited by John C. Barnes and Daragh O'Connell, 73–94. Dublin: Four Courts Press, 2015.

Barolini, Teodolinda. "*Amicus eius*: Dante and the Semantics of friendship." *Dante Studies* 133 (2015): 46–69.

———. *Dante's Poets: Textuality and Truth in the "Comedy."* Princeton, NJ: Princeton University Press, 1984.

Baron, Hans. *The Crisis of the Italian Renaissance: Civic Humanism and Republican Liberty in an Age of Classicism and Tyranny*. Princeton, NJ: Princeton University Press, 1966.

Bartoli, Vittorio. "Il midollo spinale 'principio' del 'cerebro' (*Inf*. XXVIII 140–41): un errore causato dalle scoperte scientifiche di fine Settecento." *La Cultura* 48, no. 2 (2010): 303–22.

Bartsch, Shadi. *Ideology in Cold Blood: A Reading of Lucan's Civil War*. Cambridge, MA: Harvard University Press, 1997.

———. *The Mirror of the Self: Sexuality, Self-Knowledge, and the Gaze in the Early Roman Empire*. Chicago, IL: The University of Chicago Press, 2006.

Baucom, Ian. "Cicero's Ghost: The Atlantic, the Enemy, and the Laws of War." In *States of Emergency: The Object of American Studies*, edited by Russ Castronovo and Susan Gillman, 124–42. Chapel Hill: University of North Carolina Press, 2009.

Bausi, Francesco. "'Paternae artis haeres'. Ritratto di Jacopo Bracciolini." *Interpres*, 8 (1988): 103–98.

Beer, Marina. *Romanzi di cavalleria. Il "Furioso" e il romanzo italiano del primo Cinquecento*. Rome: Bulzoni editore, 1987.
Beltrami, Pietro. "L'epica di Malebolge." *Studi Danteschi* 65 (2000): 119–52.
Benjamin, Walter. *The Origin of German Tragic Drama*. Translated by John Osborne. London: NLB, 1977.
Bernheimer, Richard. *Wild Men in the Middle Ages: A Study in Art, Sentiment, and Demonology*. Cambridge, MA: Harvard University Press, 1952.
Bertoni, Giulio. *La biblioteca estense e la coltura ferrarese*. Turin: Loescher, 1903.
Bessi, Rossella. "Luigi Pulci e Lorenzo Buonincontri." *Rinascimento* 14 (1974): 289–95.
———. "Santi, Leoni e Draghi nel 'Morgante' di Luigi Pulci." *Umanesimo volgare. Studi di letteratura fra Tre e Quattrocento*. Florence: Olschki, 2004. 103–36.
Bexley, Erica. "Replacing Rome: Geographic and Political Centrality in Lucan's *Pharsalia*." *Classical Philology* 104, no. 4 (October 2009): 459–75.
Biasin, Gian-Paolo. "'Messer Iacopo Giù Per Arno Se Ne Va . . .'" *MLN* 79, no. 1 (January 1964): 1–13.
Billerbeck, Margarethe. "Hercules Bound: A Note on Suetonius, Nero 21.3." *American Journal of Philology* 102, no. 1 (Spring 1981): 54–57.
Bisaha, Nancy. *Creating East and West: Renaissance Humanists and the Ottoman Turks*. Philadelphia: University of Pennsylvania Press, 2004.
Blössner, Norbert. "The City-Soul Analogy." In G. R. F. Ferrari, ed. *Cambridge Companion to Plato's "Republic."* Cambridge: Cambridge University Press, 2007.
Boccassini, Daniela. *Il volo della mente. Falconeria e Sofia nel mondo mediterraneo: Islam, Federico II, Dante*. Ravenna: Longo, 2003.
Boitani, Piero. *L'ombra di Ulisse. Figure di un mito*. Bologna: Il Mulino, 1992.
Bond, Christopher. "Lucan the Christian Monarchist: The Anti-Republicanism of the *De tyranno* and the *De bello civili*." *Renaissance Studies* 20, no. 4 (September 2006): 478–93.
Böninger, Lorenz. "Notes on the Last Years of Luigi Pulci." *Rinascimento* 27 (1987): 259–71.
Boone, Rebecca Ard. *Mercurino di Gattinara and the Creation of the Spanish Empire*. London: Pickering & Gatto, 2014.
Bornate, Carlo. "L'apogeo della casa di Asburgo e l'opera politica di un Gran Cancelliere di Carlo V." *Nuova Rivista Storica* 3 (1919): 396–439.
Bowsky, William. *Henry VII in Italy: The Conflict of Empire and City-State, 1310–1313*. Lincoln: University of Nebraska Press, 1960.
Brandi, Karl. *The Emperor Charles V: The Growth and Destiny of a Man and of a World Empire*. Translated by C. V. Wedgwood. London: Cape, 1963.
Braudel, Fernand. *The Mediterranean and the Mediterranean World in the Age of Philip II*. 2 vols. Translated by S. Reynolds. New York: Harper & Row, 1973.
Brezzi, Paolo. "La lettera di Pio II a Maometto II." In *Pio II e la cultura del suo tempo*. Edited by L. Rotondi Secchi Tarugi, 263–72. Milan: Guerini e Associati, 1991.
Brilli, Elisa. *Firenze e il profeta: Dante tra teologia e politica*. Rome: Carocci, 2012.

———. "Reminiscenze scritturali (e non) nelle epistole politiche dantesche." *La Cultura* 45, no. 3 (2007): 439–55.

Brown, Alison. "De-Masking Renaissance Republicanism." In *Renaissance Civic Humanism: Reappraisals and Reflections*, edited by James Hankins, 179–99. Cambridge: Cambridge University Press, 2000.

Brown, Eric. "The Stoic Invention of Cosmopolitan Politics," delivered as a lecture at "Cosmopolitan Politics: On the History and Future of a Controversial Idea." Frankfurt am Main, 2006 (accessed online at: https://pages.wustl.edu/files/pages/imce/ericbrown/invention.pdf on December 22, 2016).

Brugnoli, Giorgio. "Ut patet per Senecam in suis tragediis." *Rivista di cultura classica e medioevale* 5 (1963): 146–63.

Brummett, Palmira. "The Lepanto Paradigm Revisited: Knowing the Ottomans in the Sixteenth Century." In *The Renaissance and the Ottoman World*, edited by Anna Contadini and Claire Norton, 63–93. Farnham: Ashgate, 2013.

Bruni, Francesco. *La città divisa. Le parti e il bene comune da Dante a Guicciardini*. Bologna: Il Mulino, 2003.

Bruscagli, Riccardo. *Stagioni della civiltà estense*. Pisa: Nistri-Lischi, 1983.

———. *Studi cavallereschi*. Florence: Società Editrice Fiorentina, 2003.

Budelmann, Felix. "The Reception of Sophocles' Representation of Physical Pain." *American Journal of Philology* 128, no. 4 (Winter, 2007): 443–67.

Burckhardt, Jakob. *The Civilization of the Renaissance in Italy*. Translated by S. D. C. Middlemore. New York: The Modern Library, 2002.

Burman, Thomas. "How an Italian Friar Read His Arabic Qur'an." *Dante Studies* 125 (2007): 93–109.

———. *Reading the Qur'an in Latin Christendom*. Philadelphia: University of Pennsylvania Press, 2007.

Bynum, Caroline Walker. *Metamorphosis and Identity*. New York: Zone Books, 2001.

Cabani, Maria Cristina. *L'occhio di Polifemo. Studi su Pulci, Tasso e Marino*. Pisa: Edizioni ETS, 2005.

Cachey, Theodore J. "Between Humanism and New Historicism: Rewriting the New World Encounter." *Annali d'Italianistica* 10 (1992): 28–46.

———. "Cartographic Dante: A Note on Dante and the Greek Mediterranean." In *Dante and the Greeks*, edited by Jan Ziolkowski, 197–226. Washington, DC: Dumbarton Oaks Research Library and Collections, 2014.

———. *Le Isole Fortunate. Appunti di storia della letteratura italiana*. Rome: "L'Erma" di Bretschneider, 1995.

———. "Maps and Literature in Renaissance Italy." In *History of Cartography*, edited by David Woodward, Vol. III, part 1: 450–60. Chicago, IL: The University of Chicago Press, 2007.

———. "Tasso's *Navigazione del Nuovo Mondo* and the Origins of Columbus Encomium (GL, XV, 31–32)." *Italica* 69, no. 3 (Autumn 1992): 326–44.

Cairns, Francis. *Virgil's Augustan Epic*. Cambridge: Cambridge University Press, 1989.

Candido, Igor. *Boccaccio umanista. Studi sul Boccaccio e Apuleio*. Ravenna: Longo, 2014.

Canning, Joseph. *Ideas of Power in the Late Middle Ages, 1296–1417*. Cambridge: Cambridge University Press, 2011.
Cardini, Franco. *L'invenzione del Nemico*. Palermo: Sellerio Editore, 2006.
Carne-Ross, D. S. "The One and the Many: A Reading of the Orlando Furioso". *Arion* 3, no. 2 (1976): 146–219.
Carrai, Stefano. "La morte di Orlando nel *Morgante*." In *Luigi Pulci in Florence and Beyond: New Perspectives on his Poetry and Influence*, edited by James K. Coleman and Andrea Moudarres, 163–79. Turnhout: Brepols, 2017.
———. *Le muse dei Pulci*. Naples: Guida Editori, 1985.
———. "*Morgante* di Luigi Pulci." In *Letteratura italiana. Le Opere. Vol. 1: Dalle origini al cinquecento*, edited by Alberto Asor Rosa, 772–73. Turin: Einaudi, 1992.
Carroll, Clare. *The "Orlando Furioso": A Stoic Comedy*. Tempe, AZ: Medieval and Renaissance Texts and Studies, 1997.
Casadei, Alberto. *Dante oltre la "Commedia"*. Bologna: Il Mulino, 2013.
———. *Il percorso del "Furioso". Ricerche intorno alle redazioni del 1516 e del 1521*. Bologna: Il Mulino, 1993.
———. *La strategia delle varianti. Le correzioni storiche del terzo* Furioso. Lucca: Maria Pacini Fazzi, 1988.
Cassell, Anthony. "Il *Corbaccio* and the *Secundus* Tradition." *Comparative Literature* 25, no. 4 (Autumn 1973): 352–60.
———. *Dante's Fearful Art of Justice*. Toronto: University of Toronto Press, 1984.
———. "The Exiled Dante's Hope for Reconciliation: 'Monarchia' 3.16.16–18." *Annali d'Italianistica* 20 (2002): 425–49.
———. *The "Monarchia" Controversy*. Washington, DC: The Catholic University of America Press, 2004.
Cassirer, Ernst. *The Myth of the State*. New Haven, CT: Yale University Press, 1946.
Cavallo, Jo Ann. *The Romance Epics of Boiardo Ariosto, and Tasso: From Public Duty to Private Pleasure*. Toronto: Toronto University Press, 2004.
———. "Tasso's Armida and the Victory of Romance." In *Renaissance Transactions: Ariosto and Tasso*, edited by Valeria Finucci, 77–111. Durham, NC: Duke University Press, 1999.
———. *The World Beyond Europe in the Romance Epics of Boiardo and Ariosto*. Toronto: Toronto University Press, 2013.
Celli, Andrea. "'Cor per medium fidit.' Il canto XXVIII dell'*Inferno* alla luce di alcune fonti arabo-spagnole." *Lettere italiane* 65, no. 2 (2013): 171–92.
———. *Dante e l'Oriente. Le fonti islamiche nella storiografia novecentesca*. Rome: Carocci, 2013.
Ceron, Annalisa. *L'amicizia civile e gli amici del principe. Lo spazio politico dell'amicizia nel pensiero del Quattrocento*. Macerata: EUM, 2011.
Cerulli, Enrico. *Eugenio IV e gli Etiopi al concilio di Firenze nel 1441*. Rome: Accademia Nazionale dei Lincei, 1933.
———. *Nuove ricerche sul Libro della Scala e la conoscenza dell'Islam in Occidente*. Vatican City: Biblioteca Apostolica Vaticana, 1972.

Ceserani, Remo. "Due modelli culturali e narrativi nell'*Orlando Furioso*." *Giornale storico della letteratura italiana*, Vol. CLXI, Fasc. 516, (1984): 481–506.
Chance, Jane. "Monstra-naturalità distorte: Betram dal Bornio, Ecuba." In *I monstra nell'Inferno dantesco: tradizione e simbologie*, 235–75. Spoleto: Centro italiano di studi sull'alto Medioevo, 1997.
Chesney, Elizabeth. *The Countervoyage of Rabelais and Ariosto: A Comparative Reading of Two Renaissance Mock Epics*. Durham, NC: Duke University Press, 1982.
Chiappelli, Fredi. *Il conoscitore del caos. Una "vis abdita" nel linguaggio tassesco*. Rome: Bulzoni, 1981.
———, ed. *First Images of America: The Impact of the New World on the Old*. 2 vols. Berkeley: University of California Press, 1976.
Chiavacci Leonardi, Anna Maria. *Commentary to the "Commedia."* Milan: Arnoldo Mondadori Editore, 1991–97. As reproduced on dante.dartmouth.edu.
Chin, Tamara T. "What is Imperial Cosmopolitanism? Revisiting *Kosmpopolitēs* and *Mundanus*." In *Cosmopolitanism and Empire: Universal Rulers, Local Elites, and Cultural Integration in the Ancient Near East and Mediterranean*, edited by Myles Lavan et al, 129–51. Oxford: Oxford University Press, 2016.
Ciavolella, Massimo. "La licantropia d'Orlando." In *Il Rinascimento. Aspetti e problemi attuali*, edited by Vittore Branca et al., 311–23. Florence: Olschki, 1982.
———. *La "malattia d'amore" dall'Antichità al Medioevo*. Rome: Bulzoni Editore, 1976.
Clissold, Stephen. *Conquistador: The Life of Don Pedro Sarmiento de Gamboa*. London: Derek Verschoyle, 1956.
Coggeshall, Elizabeth. "Dante, Islam, and Edward Said." *Telos* 139 (Summer 2007): 133–51.
Combs-Schilling, Jonathan. "Weaving the Crusades: Bodies of Interlace in Tasso's *Gerusalemme liberata*." *MLN* 127, no. 1 (2012): 1–22.
Corti, Maria. "'La *Commedia* di Dante e l'oltretomba islamico." *Belfagor* 50 (1995): 301–14.
Cosgrove, Denis. *Apollo's Eye: A Cartographic Genealogy of the Earth in the Western Imagination*. Baltimore, MD: The Johns Hopkins University Press, 2001.
———. "Globalism and Tolerance in Early Modern Geography." *Annals of the Association of American Geographers* 93, no. 4 (2003): 852–70.
Costa, Antonio; Weber, Giorgio. *L'inizio dell'anatomia patologica nel Quattrocento fiorentino, sui testi di Antonio Benivieni, Bernardo Torni, Leonardo da Vinci*. Florence: Edizioni Riviste Mediche, 1963.
Cotton, Juliana Hill. "Materia medica del Poliziano." In *Il Poliziano e il suo tempo. Atti dei IV convegno internazionale di studi sul Rinascimento*, 237–45. Florence: Sansoni, 1957.
Courcelle, Pierre. *Connais-toi toi-même; de Socrate à saint Bernard*. Paris: Études augustiniennes, 1974–75.
Cullyer, Helen. "Chrysippus on Achilles: The Evidence of Galen 'De Placitis Hippocratis et Platonis' 4.6–7." *The Classical Quarterly* 58, no. 2 (2008): 537–46.
Cuttler, Simon. *The Law of Treason and Treason Trials in Later Medieval France*. Cambridge: Cambridge University Press, 1981.

Dainotto, Roberto. *Europe (in Theory)*. Durham, NC: Duke University Press, 2007.
D'Ancona, Alessandro. *Studi di critica e storia letteraria*. Bologna: Zanichelli, 1912.
Daniel, Norman. *Islam and the West: The Making of an Image*. Oxford: One World, 1993.
Daniels, Tobias. *La congiura dei Pazzi: i documenti del conflitto fra Lorenzo de' Medici e Sisto IV*. Florence: Edifir-Edizioni, 2013.
D'Ascia, Luca (ed.). *Il Corano e la Tiara. L'epistola a Maometto di Enea Silvio Piccolomini (papa Pio II)*. Bologna: Pendragon, 2001.
Davie, Mark. *Half-Serious Rhymes: The Narrative Poetry of Luigi Pulci*. Dublin: Irish Academic Press, 1998.
Davis, Charles T. *Dante and the Idea of Rome*. Oxford: Clarendon Press, 1957.
Debenedetti, Santorre. "Dante e Seneca filosofo." *Studi danteschi* 6 (1923): 5–24.
Decaria, Alessio. *Luigi Pulci and Francesco di Matteo Castellani: novità e testi inediti da uno zibaldone magliabechiano*. Florence: Società Editrice Fiorentina, 2009.
———. "Tra Marsilio e Pallante: una nuova ipotesi sugli ultimi cantari del *Morgante*." In *L'entusiasmo delle opere: studi in memoria di Domenico De Robertis*, edited by Isabella Becherucci et al., 299–339. Lecce: Pensa Multimedia, 2012.
Demaitre, Luke. "Medieval Notions of Cancer: Malignancy and Metaphor." *Bulletin of the History of Medicine* 72, no. 4 (1998): 609–37.
Del Corno Branca, Daniela. "La conclusione dell'*Orlando Furioso*: qualche osservazione." In *Boiardo, Aristo e i libri di battaglia*, edited by Andrea Canova and Paola Vecchi Galli, 127–37. Novara: Interlinea edizioni, 2007.
Della Palma, Giuseppe. "Una cifra per la pazzia d'Orlando." *Strumenti Critici* 9 (1975): 367–79.
De Robertis, Domenico. *Storia del Morgante*. Florence: Le Monnier, 1958.
De Vecchi, Bindo. "I libri di un medico umanista fiorentino del sec. XV dai 'Ricordi' di maestro Antonio Benivieni." *La Bibliofilia* 34 (1932): 293–302.
Derrida, Jacques. *The Beast and the Sovereign*. Edited by Michel Lisse et al., and translated by G. Bennington. Chicago, IL: The University of Chicago Press, 2009.
———. *Politics of Friendship*. Translated by G. Collins. London: Verso, 1997.
Di Fonzo, Claudia. *Dante e la tradizione giuridica*. Rome: Carocci, 2016.
Di Tommaso, Andrea. "'Insania' and 'Furor': A Diagnostic Note on Orlando's Malady." *Romance Notes* 14 (1972/73): 583–88.
Dinter, Martin. *Anatomizing "Civil War": Studies in Lucan's Epic Technique*. Ann Arbor: The University of Michigan Press, 2012.
Donato, Eugenio. "'Per selve e boscherecci labirinti': Desire and Narrative Structure in Ariosto's *Orlando Furioso*." In *Literary Theory/Renaissance Texts*, edited by Patricia Parker and David Quint, 33–62. Baltimore, MD: The Johns Hopkins University Press, 1986.
Donato, Maria Monica. "Hercules and David in the Early Decoration of the Palazzo Vecchio: Manuscript Evidence." *Jounal of the Warburg and Courtauld Institutes* 54 (1991): 83–98.
Doob, Penelope. *Nebuchadnezzar's Children: Conventions of Madness in Middle English Literature*. New Haven, CT: Yale University Press, 1974.

Dorter, Kenneth. "Weakness and Will in Plato's *Republic*." In *Weakness of Will from Plato to the Present*. Edited by Tobias Hoffmann, 1–21. Washington, DC: The Catholic University of America Press, 2008.
Dotti, Ugo. *La Divina Commedia e la città dell'uomo*. Rome: Donzelli, 1996.
Draper, James. *Bertoldo di Giovanni, Sculptor of the Medici Household: Critical Reappraisal and Catalogue Raisonné*. Columbia: University of Missouri Press, 1992.
Dronke, Peter. *Dante and Medieval Latin Traditions*. Cambridge: Cambridge University Press, 1986.
Dumézil, Georges. *The Destiny of the Warrior*. Translated by Alf Hiltebeitel. Chicago, IL: The University of Chicago Press, 1970.
Dusebury, David Lloyd. "Carl Schmitt on *Hostis* and *Inimicus*: A Veneer for Bloody-Mindedness." *Ratio Juris* 28, no. 3 (September 2015): 431–39.
Durling, Robert. *Figure of the Poet in Renaissance Epic*. Cambridge, MA: Harvard University Press, 1965.
Eire, Carlos. *Reformations: The Early Modern World, 1450–1650*. New Haven, CT: Yale University Press, 2016.
Eliot, Thomas Stearns. "Virgil and the Christian World". In *On Poetry and Poets*, 135–48. New York: Octagon Books, 1975.
Ercole, Francesco. *Il pensiero politico di Dante*. Milan: Edizioni Alpes, 1928.
Erspamer, Francesco. "Il 'pensiero debole' di Torquato Tasso." In *La menzogna*, edited by Franco Cardini, 120–36. Florence: Ponte alle Grazie, 1989.
Esposito Frank, Maria. "Dante's Muhammad: Parallels between Islam and Arianism." *Dante Studies* 125 (2007): 185–206.
Ettlinger, Leopold. "Hercules Florentinus." *Mitteilungen des Kunsthistorischen Institutes in Florenz* 16, no. 2 (1972): 119–42.
Evans, J. A. S. "The Aeneid and the Concept of the Ideal King: The Modification of an Archetype." In *The Worlds of the Poet: New Perspectives on Vergil*, edited by Robert Wilhelm and Howard Jones. Detroit, MI: Wayne State University Press, 1992.
Everson, Jane. *The Italian Romance Epic in the Age of Humanism: The Matter of Italy and the World of Rome*. Oxford: Oxford University Press, 2001.
Evrigenis, Ioannis. "The Psychology of Politics: The City-Soul Analogy in Plato's Republic." *History of Political Thought* 23, no. 4 (Winter 2002): 590–610.
Fabre, Cécile. *Cosmopolitan Peace*. Oxford: Oxford University Press, 2016.
———. *Cosmopolitan War*. Oxford: Oxford University Press, 2012.
Fantham, Elaine. "*Discordia Fratrum*: Aspects of Lucan's Conception of Civil War." In *Citizens of Discord: Rome and Its Civil Wars*, edited by Brian W. Breed et al, 207–20. Oxford: Oxford University Press, 2010.
Farinelli, Franco. "La Gerusalemme catturata: ipotesi per una geografia del Tasso." In *Torquato Tasso tra letteratura, teatro, musica e arti figurative*, edited by Andrea Buzzoni, 75–82. Bologna: Nuova Alfa, 1985.
Feder, Lillian. *Madness in Literature*. Princeton, NJ: Princeton University Press, 1980.
Fernandez-Santamaria, J. A. *The State, War and Peace: Spanish Political Thought in the Renaissance 1516–1559*. Cambridge: Cambridge University Press, 1996.

Ferrari, Giovanni R. F. *City and Soul in Plato's "Republic."* Sankt Augustin: Academia Verlag, 2003.

Ferroni, Giulio. "L'Ariosto e la concezione umanistica della follia." In *Atti del convegno internazionale "Ludovico Ariosto."* Rome: Accademia Nazionale dei Lincei, 1975.

Filosa, Elsa; Flora, Luisa. "Ancora su Seneca (e Giovenale) nel *Decameron*," *Giornale storico della letteratura italiana* 115 (1998): 210–19.

Finucci, Valeria. *The Lady Vanishes: Subjectivity and Representation in Castiglione and Ariosto.* Stanford, CA: Stanford University Press, 1992.

Fiocchi, Claudio. *Mala Potestas. La Tirannia nel Pensiero Politico Medioevale.* Bergamo: Lubrina Editore, 2004.

Finlay, Robert. "Prophecy and Politics in Istanbul: Charles V, Sultan Suleyman, and the Habsburg Embassy of 1533–1534." *Journal of Early Modern History* 2, no. 1 (1998): 1–31.

Fleischer, Cornell. "The Lawgiver as Messiah: The Making of the Imperial Image in the Reign of Süleymân." In *Soliman le Magnifique et son temps*, edited by Gilles Veinstein, 159–77. Paris: Documentation Française, 1992.

Fletcher, Catherine. *The Black Prince of Florence: The Spectacular Life and Treacherous World of Alessandro de' Medici.* London: The Bodley Head, 2016.

Fletcher, Richard. *The Cross and the Crescent: Christianity and Islam from Muhammad to the Reformation.* New York: Allen Lane—The Penguin Press, 2003.

Foltran, Daniela. "Dalla 'Liberata' alla 'Conquistata'. Intertestualità virgiliana e omerica nel personaggio di Argante." *Studi Tassiani*, XL-XLI (1992–93): 89–134.

Fosca, Nicola. *Commentary on the "Commedia."* The Dartmouth Dante Project. 2003–15. dante.dartmouth.edu.

Fratantuono, Lee. *Madness Unchained: A Reading of Virgil's Aeneid.* Lanham: Lexington Books, 2007.

Freccero, John. "The Eternal Image of the Father." In *The Poetry of Allusion: Virgil and Ovid in Dante's "Commedia,"* edited by Rachel Jacoff and Jeffrey Schnapp, 62–76. Stanford, CA: Stanford University Press, 1991.

Fubini, Mario. "Canto XXVIII." In *Lectura Dantis Scaligera. Inferno*, 997–1021. Florence: Le Monnier, 1967.

Fuchs, Barbara. *Mimesis and Empire: The New World, Islam, and European Identities.* Cambridge: Cambridge University Press, 2001.

Gaeta, Franco. "L'avventura di Ercole." *Rinascimento* 5 (December 1954): 227–60.

———. "Sulla 'Lettera a Maometto' di Pio II." *Bullettino Istituto storico italiano per il Medio Evo* 77 (1965): 127–227.

Galinsky, Karl. "The Anger of Aeneas." *American Journal of Philology* 109, no. 3 (Autumn, 1988): 321–48.

———. *The Herakles Theme: The Adaptations of the Hero in Literature from Homer to the Twentieth Century.* Totowa: Rowman and Littlefield, 1972.

———. "The Hercules-Cacus Episode in Aeneid VIII." *American Journal of Philology* 87, no. 1 (Jan., 1966): 18–51.

Ganz, Margery. "Perceived insults and their consequences: Acciaiuoli, Neroni, and

Medici relationships in the 1460's." In *Society and Individual in Renaissance Florence*, edited by William Connell, 155–72. Berkeley: University of California Press, 2002.

Gareffi, Andrea. *L'ombra dell'eroe: "Il Morgante."* Urbino: Quattroventi, 1986.

Garin, Eugenio. *Medioevo e Rinascimento*. Bari: Laterza, 1984.

———. *Rinascite e rivoluzioni. Movimenti culturali dal XIV al XVIII secolo*. Bari: Laterza, 1975.

George-Tvrtković, Rita. *A Christian Pilgrim in Medieval Iraq: Riccoldo da Montecroce's Encounter with Islam*. Turnhout: Brepols, 2012.

Getto, Giovanni. *Nel mondo della "Gerusalemme."* Rome: Bonacci, 1977. Giamatti, A. Bartlett. *Earthly Paradise and the Renaissance Epic*. Princeton, NJ: Princeton University Press, 1966.

Gierke, Otto. *Political Theories of the Middle Age*. Translated by F. W. Maitland. Cambridge: Cambridge University Press, 1927.

Gilson, Etienne. *Dante the Philosopher*. Translated by David Moore. London: Sheed & Ward, 1948.

Gilson, Simon. "Human Anatomy and Physiology in Dante." In *Dante and the Human Body*, edited by John C. Barnes and Jennifer Petrie, 11–42. Dublin: Four Court Press, 2007.

Ginsberg, Warren. *Dante's Aesthetics of Being*. Ann Arbor: University of Michigan Press, 1999.

Giustiniani, Vito. "Il Filelfo, l'interpretazione allegorica di Virgilio e la tripartizione platonica dell'anima." In *Umanesimo e Rinascimento: studi offerti a Paul Oskar Kristeller*, 33–44. Florence: Olschki, 1980.

Goudet, Jacques. "La 'parte per se stesso' e l'impegno politico di Dante." In *Nuove Letture Dantesche* 7 (1974): 289–316.

Gough, Melinda. "Tasso's Enchantress, Tasso's Captive Woman." *Renaissance Quarterly* 54, no. 2 (Summer, 2001): 523–52.

Grassi, Ernesto; Lorch, Maristella. *Folly and Insanity in Renaissance Literature*. Binghamton: Medieval and Renaissance Texts and Studies, 1986.

Greenblatt, Stephen. *Marvelous Possessions: The Wonder of the New World*. Chicago, IL: The University of Chicago Press, 1991.

Gregory, Tobias. *From Many Gods to One: Divine Action in Renaissance Epic*. Chicago, IL: The University of Chicago Press, 2006.

Griffin, Miriam. *Seneca: A Philosopher in Politics*. Oxford: Oxford University Press, 1976.

Habermas, Jürgen. *The Postnational Constellation: Political Essays*. Edited and translated by M. Pensky. Cambridge: Polity, 2001.

Hamdani, Abbas. "Columbus and the Recovery of Jerusalem." *Journal of the American Oriental Society* 99, no. 1 (January–March 1979): 39–48.

Hamill, Graham; Lupton, Julia Reinhard, eds. *Political Theology and Early Modernity*. Chicago, IL: The University of Chicago Press, 2012.

———. "Political Theology and Renaissance Literature." Special issue, *Religion & Literature* 38, no. 3 (Autumn 2006).

Hamilton, Alastair. *The Copts and the West, 1439–1822: The European Discovery of the EgyptianChurch.* Oxford: Oxford University Press, 2006.
Hammer, Dean. *The Iliad as Politics: The Performance of Political Thought.* Norman: University of Oklahoma Press, 2002.
Hampton, Timothy. *Fictions of Embassy: Literature and Diplomacy in Early Modern Europe.* Ithaca, NY: Cornell University Press, 2007.
———. *Writing from History: The Rhetoric of Exemplarity in Renaissance Literature.* Ithaca, NY: Cornell University Press, 1990.
Hanke, Lewis. *All Mankind Is One: A Study of the Disputation Between Bartolomé de Las Casas and Juan Giné de Sepulveda in 1550 on the Intellectual and Religious Capacity of the American Indians.* DeKalb: Northern Illinois University Press, 1974.
———. *Aristotle and the Amercian Indians: A Study in Race Prejudice in the Modern World.* Bloomington: Indiana University Press, 1970.
Hankey, Teresa. "Dante and Statius." In *Dante and his Literary Precursors*, edited by John C. Barnes and Jennifer Petrie, 37–50. Dublin: Four Courts Press, 2007.
Hankins, James. *Plato in the Italian Renaissance.* 2 vols. Leiden: Brill, 1990.
———. "Renaissance Crusaders: Humanist Crusade Literature in the Age of Mehmed II." *Dumbarton Oaks Papers* 49 (1995): 111–207.
Hanzer, Donuta. "The Punishment of Bertram de Born." *Yearbook of Italian Studies* VIII (1989): 95–97.
Hardie, Philip. *Virgil's Aeneid: Cosmos and Imperium.* Oxford: Oxford University Press, 1986.
Headley, John. *The Emperor and His Chancellor: A Study of the Imperial Chancellery Under Gattinara.* Cambridge: Cambridge University Press, 1983.
———. *The Europeanization of the World: On the Origins of Human Rights and Democracy.* Princeton, NJ: Princeton University Press, 2008.
———. "Gattinara, Erasmus, and the Imperial Configurations of Humanism." *Archiv für Reformationsgeschichte* 71 (1980): 64–98.
———. "The Hapsburg World Empire and the Revival of Ghibellinism." *Medieval and Renaissance Studies* 7 (1975): 93–127.
Heiden, Bruce. "The Simile of the Fugitive Homicide, *Iliad* 24.480–84: Analogy, Foiling, and Allusion." *American Journal of Philology* 119, no.1 (Spring, 1998): 1–10.
Hershowitz, Debra. *The Madness of Epic: Reading Insanity from Homer to Statius.* Oxford: Oxford University Press, 1998.
Hollander, Robert. "Dante and the Martial Epic." *Mediaevalia* 12 (1986): 67–91.
———. "The Lucanian Source of Dante's Ulysses," *Studi Danteschi* 63 (1997): 1–52.
Honess, Claire. "Dante and Political Poetry of the Vernacular." In *Dante and his Literary Precursors*, edited by John C. Barnes and Jennifer Petrie, 117–51. Dublin: Four Courts Press, 2007.
———. *From Florence to the Heavenly City: The Poetry of Citizenship in Dante.* London: Legenda, 2006.
Huntington, Samuel. *The Clash of Civilizations and the Remaking of World Oder.* New York: Simon & Schuster, 1997.

Jopkins, Jasper. "The Role of *pia interpretatio* in Nicholas of Cusa's Hermeneutical Approach to the Koran." In *Concordia Discors. Studi su Niccolò Cusano e l'Umanesimo Europeo offerti a Giovanni Santinello*, edited by Gregorio Piaia, 251–73. Padua: Editrice Antenore, 1993.

Irwin, Elizabeth. *Solon and Early Greek Poetry: The Politics of Exhortation*. Cambridge: Cambridge University Press, 2005.

Jáuregui, Miguel Herrero de. "Priam's Catabasis: Traces of the Epic Journey to Hades in 'Iliad' 24." *Transactions of the American Philological Association* 141, no. 1 (Spring 2011): 37–68.

Javitch, Daniel. "The Grafting of Virgilian Epic in *Orlando furioso*." In *Renaissance Transactions: Ariosto and Tasso*, edited by Valeria Finucci, 56–76. Durham, NC: Duke University Press, 1999.

Jensen, Richard C.; Babr-Volk, Marie. "The Fox and the Crab: Coluccio Salutati's Unpublished Fable." *Studies in Philology* 73, no. 2 (Apr., 1976): 162–68, 170–75.

Johnson, Carina L. "Imperial Succession and Mirrors of Tyranny in the Houses of Habsburg and Osman." In *Representing Imperial Rivalry in the Early Modern Mediterranean*, edited by Barbara Fuchs and Emily Weissbourd, 80–100. Toronto: University of Toronto Press, 2015.

Johnson, Walter Ralph. *Darkness Visible: A Study of Vergil's "Aeneid."* Los Angeles: University of California Press, 1976.

Jones, Philip. *The Italian City-State: From Commune to Signoria*. Oxford: Clarendon Press, 1997.

Jordan, Constance. *Pulci's "Morgante": Poetry and History in Fifteenth Century Florence*. Washington, DC: The Folger Shakespeare Library, 1986.

Jossa, Stefano. *Ariosto*. Bologna: Il Mulino, 2009.

Julian, John, ed. *A Dictionary of Hymnology: Setting forth the Origin and History of Christian Hymns of all Ages and Nations*. New York: Dover Publications, 1907.

Kahn, Victoria. *The Future of Illusion: Political Theology and Early Modern Texts*. Chicago, IL: The University of Chicago Press, 2014.

Kallendorf, Craig. *The Other Virgil: 'Pessimistic' Readings of the Aeneid in Early Modern Culture*. Oxford: Oxford University Press, 2007.

Kantorowicz, Ernst H. *The King's Two Bodies*. Princeton, NJ: Princeton University Press, 1957.

Katinis, Teodoro. *Medicina e filosofia in Marsilio Ficino*. Rome: Edizioni di Storia e Letteratura, 2007.

Kay, Richard. *Dante's Swift and Strong*. Lawrence: Regent Press of Kansas, 1978.

Kempshall, Matthew. "Accidental Perfection: Ecclesiology and Political Thought in *Monarchia*." In *Dante and the Church: Literary and Historical Essays*, edited by Paolo Acquaviva and Jennifer Petrie, 127–71. Dublin: Four Court Press, 2007.

———. "The Utility of Peace in 'Monarchia.'" In *War and Peace in Dante*, edited by John C. Barnes and Daragh O'Connell, 141–72. Dublin: Four Courts Press, 2015.

Kent, Dale. *Friendship, Love, and Trust in Renaissance Florence*. Cambridge, MA: Harvard University Press, 2009.

———. *The Rise of the Medici: Faction in Florence 1426–1434*. Oxford: Oxford University Press, 1978.
Kim, David D. *Cosmopolitan Parables: Trauma and Responsibility in Contemporary Germany*. Evanston, IL: Northwestern University Press, 2017.
Klibansky, Raymond, Erwin Panofsky, and Fritz Saxl. *Saturn and Melancholy: Studies in the History of Natural Philosophy, Religion, and Art*. Nendeln: Klaus Reprint, 1979.
Klinsman, Robert. "Folly, Melancholy and Madness: A Study in Shifting Styles of Medical Analysis and Treatment." In *The Darker Vision of the Renaissance: Beyond the Fields of Reason*, edited by Robert Klinsman, 273–320. Berkeley: University of California Press, 1974.
Konstan, David. *Friendship in the Classical World*. Cambridge: Cambridge University Press, 1991.
Kristeller, Paul Oskar. *The Philosophy of Marsilio Ficino*. Translated into English by V. Conant. New York: Columbia University Press, 1943.
———, ed. *Svpplementvm ficinianum. Marcilii Ficini florentini philosophi platonici opvscvla inedita et dispersa*. Florence: Olschki, 1937.
Lapidge, Michael. "Lucan's Imagery of Cosmic Dissolution." *Hermes* 107, no. 3 (1979): 344–70.
Larivaille, Paul. *Poesia e ideologia. Letture della "Gerusalemme Liberata."* Naples: Liguori, 1987.
Lee, Michelle V. *Paul, the Stoics, and the Body of Christ*. Cambridge: Cambridge University Press, 2006.
Lezra, Jacques. *Wild Materialism: The Ethic of Terror and the Modern Republic*. New York: Fordham University Press, 2010.
Lincoln, Bruce. "Homeric λύσσα: 'Wolfish Rage.'" *Indogermanische Forschungen* 80 (1975): 98–105.
Long, Alex. "Lucan and Moral Luck." *The Classical Quarterly* 57, no. 1 (May 2007): 183–97.
Longhi, Silvia. *Forme di mostri. Creature fantastiche e corpi vulnerati da Ariosto a Giudici*. Verona: Edizioni Fiorini, 2005.
Looney, Dennis. *Compromising the Classics: Romance Epic Narrative in the Italian Renaissance*. Detroit, MI: Wayne State University Press, 1996.
Loraux, Nicole. "*Oikeios polemos*: La guerra nella famiglia." *Studi Storici* 28, no.1 (Jan.–Mar. 1987): 5–35.
Lorenz, Hendrik. *The Brute Within: Appetitive Desire in Plato and Aristotle*. Oxford: Oxford University Press, 2006.
Lubac, Henri de. *Corpus Mysticum: The Eucharist and the Church in the Middle Ages*. Translated by G. Simmonds et al. London: SCM Press, 2006.
Lupher, David. *Romans in a New World: Classical Models in Sixteenth-Century America*. Ann Arbor: The University of Michigan Press, 2003.
Lupton, Julia Reinhard. *Citizen-Saints: Shakespeare and Political Theology*. Chicago, IL: The University of Chicago Press, 2005.
Mac Carty, Ita. "Olimpia: Faithful or Foolhardy?". *Olifant* 22 (2003): 103–18.

Maccarone, Michele. "Il terzo Libro della 'Monarchia.'" *Studi danteschi* XXXIII, no.1, (1955): 5–142.

Mallett, Michael; Shaw, Christine. *The Italian Wars, 1494–1559: War, State and Society in Early Modern Europe.* Harlow: Pearson, 2012.

Mallette, Karla. "Dante e l'Islam: sul canto III del *Purgatorio.*" *Rivista di Storia e Letteratura Religiosa* 41 (2005): 39–62.

———. "Muhammad in Hell." *Dante Studies* 125 (2007): 207–24.

Mancusi-Ungaro, Donna. *Dante and the Empire.* New York: Peter Lang, 1987.

Mantovanelli, Paolo. *Patologia del potere. Studi sulle tragedie di Seneca.* Bologna: Pàtron Editore, 2014.

Marcucci, Silvia. *Analisi e interpretazione dell'*Hercules Oetaeus. Pisa: Istituti Editoriali e Poligrafici Internazionali, 1997.

Marinelli, Peter. *Ariosto and Boiardo: The Origins of "Orlando Furioso."* Columbia: University of Missouri Press, 1987.

Martin, Dale. "The Promise of Teleology, the Constraints of Epistemology, and Universal Vision in Paul." In *St. Paul among the Philosophers*, edited by John Caputo and Linda Martin Alcoff, 91–108. Bloomington: Indiana University Press, 2009.

Martindale, Charles. "The Politician Lucan." *Greece & Rome* 31, no. 1 (April 1984): 64–79.

Martines, Lauro. *April Blood. Florence and the Plot against the Medici.* Oxford: Oxford University Press, 2003.

Masciandaro, Franco. *La conoscenza viva. Letture fenomenologiche da Dante a Machiavelli.* Ravenna: Longo, 1998.

Matarrese, Tina. "Il mito di Ercole a Ferrara nel Quattrocento tra letteratura e arti figurative." In *L'ideale classico a Ferrara e in Italia nel Rinascimento*, edited by Patrizia Castelli, 191–203. Florence: Olschki, 1998.

Mazzoli, Giancarlo. "Ricerche sulla tradizione medievale del *De beneficiis* e del *De clementia* di Seneca." *Bollettino del comitato per la preparazione dell'edizione nazionale dei classici greci e latini* 2, no. 26 (1978): 85–109.

———. "Ricerche sulla tradizione medievale del *De beneficiis* e del *De clementia* di Seneca. III Storia della tradizione manoscritta." *Bollettino dei Classici* 3, no. 3 (1982): 165–223.

Mazzoni, Francesco. "Le epistole di Dante." In *Conferenze aretine 1965.* Bibbiena: Società Dantesca Casentinese, 1966. 47–100.

Mazzotta, Giuseppe. *Cosmopoiesis: The Renaissance Experiment.* Toronto: Toronto University Press, 2001.

———. *Dante, Poet of the Desert: History and Allegory in the Divine Comedy.* Princeton, NJ: Princeton University Press, 1979.

———. *Dante's Vision and the Circle of Knowledge.* Princeton, NJ: Princeton University Press, 1993.

———. "Modern and Ancient Italy in Don Quijote." *Poetica* 38 (2006): 91–106.

Maxson, B. Jeffrey. "Kings and Tyrants: Leonardo Bruni's Translation of Xenophon's *Hiero.*" *Renaissance Studies* 24, no. 2 (April 2010): 188–206.

McCabe, Richard. *"Ungainefull Arte": Poetry, Patronage, and Print in the Early Modern Era*. Oxford: Oxford University Press, 2016.
McCormick, John. "Addressing the Political Exception: Machiavelli's 'Accidents' and the Mixed Regime." *American Political Science Review* 87, no. 4 (1993): 888–900.
Menocal, Maria Rosa. *The Arabic Role in Medieval Literary History*. Philadelphia: University of Pennsylvania Press, 1987.
Menzinger, Sara. "Law." In *Dante in Context*, edited by Zygmunt G. Barański and Lino Pertile, 47–58. Cambridge: Cambridge University Press, 2015.
Meserve, Margaret. *Empires of Islam in Renaissance Historical Thought*. Cambridge, MA: Harvard University Press, 2008.
Metzger, Nadine. "Battling Demons with Medical Authority: Werewolves, Physicians and Rationalization." *History of Psychiatry* 24, no. 3 (2013): 341–55.
Mezzadroli, Giuseppina. *Seneca in Dante. Dalla tradizione medievale all'officina dell'autore*. Florence: Le Lettere, 1990.
Mickel, Emanuel J. *Ganelon, Treason, and the "Chanson de Roland."* University Park: The Pennsylvania State University Press, 1989.
Migliorini, Paola. *Scienza e terminologia nella letteratura latina di età neroniana. Seneca, Lucano, Persio, Petronio*. Frankfurt: Peter Lang, 1997.
Migiel, Marilyn. *Gender and Genealogy in Tasso's "Gerusalemme Liberata."* Lewiston: The Edwin Mellen Press, 1993.
———. "Tasso's Erminia: Telling an Alternate Story." *Italica* 64, no. 1 (Spring, 1987): 62–75.
Miller, Nichole E. *Violence and Grace: Exceptional Life between Shakespeare and Modernity*. Evanston, IL: Northwestern University Press, 2014.
Mineo, Nicolò. *Profetismo e apocalittica in Dante. Strutture e temi profetico-apocalittici in Dante: dalla "Vita nuova" alla "Divina commedia."* Catania: Università di Catania, Facoltà di lettere e filosofia, 1968.
Mommsen, Theodor E. "Petrarch and the Story of the Choice of Hercules." *Journal of the Warburg and Courtauld Institutes* 16, no. 3/4 (1953): 178–92.
Monneret de Villard, Ugo. *Il libro della peregrinazione nelle parti d'oriente di Frate Ricoldo da Montecroce*. Rome: Institutm historicum fratrum predicatorum, 1948.
Monorchio, Giuseppe. *Lo specchio del cavaliere*. Ottawa: Canadian Society for Italian Studies, 1998.
Montemaggi, Vittorio. "'E 'n sua volontade è nostra pace': Peace, Justice and the Trinity in the *Commedia*." In *War and Peace in Dante*, edited by John C. Barnes and Daragh O'Connell, 195–225. Dublin: Four Courts Press, 2015.
Monti, Carla Maria; Pasut, Francesca. "Episodi della fortuna di Seneca tragico nel Trecento." *Aevum* 73, no. 2 (Maggio-Agosto 1999): 513–47.
Morani, Moreno; et al. *Amicus (Inimicus) Hostis. Le radici concettuali della conflittualità 'privata' e della conflittualità politica*. Milan: Giuffrè, 1992.
Moretti, Walter. "Carlo V e I suoi 'capitani invitti nel 'Furioso' del 1532." In *Rinascimento meridionale e altri studi*, edited by Maria Cristina Cafisse et al., 321–31. Naples: Società Editrice Napoletana, 1987.

———. *L'ultimo Ariosto*. Bologna: Pàtron Editore, 1977.

Most, Glenn. "*Disiecti membra poetae*: The Rhetoric of Dismemberment in Neronian Poetry." In *Innovations of Antiquity*, edited by Ralph Exeter and Daniel Selden, 391–419. New York: Routledge, 1992.

Moudarres, Andrea. "Crusade and Conversion: Islam as Schism in Pius II and Nicholas of Cusa." *MLN* 128, no. 1 (2013): 40–52.

———. "The Giant's Heel: Pride and Treachery in Pulci's *Morgante*." *MLN* 127, no.1 (2012): 164–72.

———. "Islam e conflitti ispano-lusitani nella *Relazione del primo viaggio attorno al mondo* di Antonio Pigafetta." In *Storie del Grande Sud. Per Piero Boitani*, edited by Emilia Di Rocco, 139–52. Bologna: Il Mulino, 2017.

———. "On the Threshold of Law: Dictatorship and Exception in Machiavelli and Schmitt." *I Tatti Studies* 18, no. 2 (Fall 2015): 349–70.

Mozzillo-Howell, Elizabeth. "*Divina Anatomia*: Laying Bare Body and Soul in the *Commedia*." In *Dante and the Human Body*, edited by John C. Barnes and Jennifer Petrie, 139–57. Dublin: Four Courts Press, 2007.

Mula, Stefano. "Muhammad and the Saints: The History of the Prophet in the *Golden Legend*." *Modern Philology* 101, no. 2 (2003): 175–88.

Murrin, Michael. *Allegorical Epic: Essays in its Rise and Decline*. Chicago, IL: The University of Chicago Press, 1980.

———. *History and Warfare in Renaissance Epic*. Chicago, IL: The University of Chicago Press, 1994.

Nagy, Gregory. *The Best of the Achaeans: Concepts of the Hero in Archaic Greek Poetry*. Baltimore, MD: The Johns Hopkins University Press, 1999.

Najemy, John. "Dante and Florence." In *The Cambridge Companion to Dante*, edited by Rachel Jacoff, 80–99. Cambridge: Cambridge University Press, 1993.

———. *A History of Florence 1200–1575*. Malden: Blackwell Publishing, 2006.

Najera, Luna. "Myth and Prophecy in Juan Ginés de Sepúlveda's Crusading 'Exhortación.'" *Bulletin for Spanish and Portuguese Historical Studies* 35, no. 1 (2011): 48–68.

Nardi, Bruno. *Dal "Convivio" alla "Commedia."* Roma: Nella sede dell'Istituto, 1960.

———. *Dante e la cultura medievale*. Bari: Laterza, 1983.

———. *Nel mondo di Dante*. Rome: Edizioni di Storia e Letteratura, 1944.

———. *Saggi di filosofia dantesca*. Florence: La Nuova Italia, 1967.

Nardo, Dante. "Sulle fonti classiche del 'Corbaccio.'" In *Medioevo e Rinascimento Veneto*, Vol. 1, 245–54. Padua: Antenore, 1979.

Nasti, Paola. *Favole d'amore e "saver profondo": la tradizione salomonica in Dante*. Ravenna: Longo, 2007.

Necipoğlu, Gülru. "Süleyman the Magnificent and the Representation of Power in the Context of Ottoman-Hapsburg-Papal Rivalry." *The Art Bulletin* 71, no. 3 (September 1989): 401–27.

Neutel, Karin B. *A Cosmopolitan Ideal: Paul's Declaration "Neither Jew Nor Greek, Neither Slave Nor Free, Nor Male and Female" in the Context of First-Century Thought*. London: Bloomsbury, 2015.

Newell, Waller. *Tyranny: A New Interpretation*. Cambridge: Cambridge University Press, 2013.
Niccoli, Ottavia. *Prophecy and People in Renaissance Italy*. Translated by Lydia Cochrane. Princeton, NJ: Princeton University Press, 1990.
Nigro, Salvatore S. *Pulci e la cultura medicea*. Bari: Laterza, 1972.
Nirenberg, David. *Neighboring Faiths: Christianity, Islam, and Judaism in the Middle Ages and Today*. Chicago, IL: The University of Chicago Press, 2014.
Norton, Claire. "Blurring the Boundaries: Intellectual and Cultural Interactions between the Eastern and Western; Christian and Muslim Worlds." In *The Renaissance and the Ottoman World*, edited by Anna Contadini and Claire Norton, 3–21. Farnham: Ashgate, 2013.
Nussbaum, Martha. *The Fragility of Goodness: Luck and Ethics in Greek Tragedy and Philosophy*. Chicago, IL: The University of Chicago Press, 1986.
———. "Kant and Stoic Cosmopolitanism." In *Perpetual Peace: Essays on Kant's Cosmopolitan Ideal*, edited by James Bohman and Matthias Lutz-Bachmann, 25–57. Cambridge, MA: The MIT Press, 1997.
———. "Patriotism and Cosmopolitanism." In *For Love of Country: Debating the Limits of Patriotism*, edited by Joshua Cohen, 3–17. Boston: Beacon Press, 1996.
Orvieto, Paolo. *Pulci medievale*. Rome: Salerno Editrice, 1978.
Otis, Brooks. *Virgil: A Study in Civilized Poetry*. Oxford: Oxford University Press, 1963.
Paden, William Jr. "Bertran de Born in Italy". In *Italian Literature: Roots and Branches. Essays in Honor Thomas Goddard Bergin*, edited by Giose Rimanelli and Kenneth John Atchity, 39–66. New Haven, CT: Yale University Press, 1976.
Pagden, Anthony. *The Fall of Natural Man: The Indian and the Origins of Comparative Ethnology*. Cambridge: Cambridge University Press, 1982.
———. "Europe: Conceptualizing a Continent." In *The Idea of Europe from Antiquity to the European Union*, edited by Anthony Pagden, 33–54. Cambridge: Cambridge University Press, 2002.
———. "Gentili, Vitoria, and the Fabrication of a 'Natural Law of Nations.'" In *The Roman Foundations of the Law of Nations: Alberico Gentili and the Justice of Empire*, edited by Benedict Kingsbury and Benjamin Straumann, 340–61. Oxford: Oxford University Press, 2010.
———. "*Ius et Factum*: Text and Experience in the Writings of Bartolomé de las Casas." In *New World Encounters*, edited by Stephen Greenblatt, 85–100. Berkeley: University of California Press, 1993.
———. "Stoicism, Cosmopolitanism, and the Legacy of European Imperialism." *Constellations* 7, no. 1 (2000): 3–22.
———. *Worlds at War: The 2,500-Year Struggle between East and West*. New York: Random House, 2009.
Panofsky, Erwin. *Hercules am Scheidewege und andere anitike Bildstoffe inder neueren Kunst*. Leipzig: B. G. Teubner, 1930.
Papadopoulou, Thalia. "Herakles and Hercules: The Hero's Ambivalence in Euripides and Seneca." *Mnemosyne* 57, no. 3 (2004): 257–83.

Paratore, Ettore. *Antico e nuovo*. Caltanissetta: Salvatore Sciascia Editore, 1965.
———. "Il Canto XXVIII." In *Inferno*, edited by Silvio Zennaro, 683–704. Rome: Bonacci, 1977.
Park, Katharine. *Doctors and Medicine in Early Renaissance Florence*. Princeton, NJ: Princeton University Press, 1985.
Parker, Patricia. *Inescapable Romance: Studies in the Poetics of a Mode*. Princeton, NJ: Princeton University Press, 1979.
Parry, Richard. "The Unhappy Tyrant and the Craft of Inner Ruler." In *Cambridge Companion to Plato's "Republic,"* edited by G. R. F. Ferrari, 386–414. Cambridge: Cambridge University Press, 2007.
Passerin d'Entrèves, Alessandro. *Dante as a Political Thinker*. Oxford: Oxford University Press, 1952.
Pastor, Ludwig von. *The History of the Popes from the Close of the Middle Ages*. 40 vols. Edited by F. I. Antrobus. Nendeln: Kraus Reprint, 1969.
Patterson, Annabel. *Pastoral and Ideology: Virgil to Valéry*. Berkeley: University of California Press, 1987.
Pavlock, Barbara. *Eros, Imitation, and the Epic Tradition*. Ithaca, NY: Cornell University Press, 1990.
Pedullà, Gabriele. "Una 'tirannide elettiva'. Ovvero: ciò che gli umanisti e Machiavelli possono insegnarci sulla dittatura e lo 'stato d'eccezione.'" In *Il governo dell'emergenza. Poteri straordinari e di guerra in Europa tra XVI e XX secolo*, edited by Francesco Benigno, 35–73. Rome: Viella, 2007.
Pelikan, Jaroslav. *The Growth of Medieval Theology*. Chicago, IL: University of Chicago Press, 1978.
Pellegrini, Carlo. *Luigi Pulci. L'uomo e l'artista*. Pisa: Nistri, 1912.
Pellegrini, Silvio. *Studi rolandiani e trobadorici*. Bari: Adriatica Editrice, 1964.
Perosa, Alessandro. "Codici di Galeno postillati dal Poliziano." In *Umanesimo e Rinascimento. Studi offerti a Paul Oskar Kristeller*. Florence: Olschki, 1980. 75–109.
———. "*Febris*: A Poetic Myth Created by Poliziano." *Journal of the Warburg and Courtauld Institutes* 9 (1946): 74–95.
Perrotta, Annalisa. "Lo spazio della corte: la rappresentazione del potere politico nel *Morgante* di Luigi Pulci." *The Italianist* 24 (2004): 141–68.
Pertile, Lino. "Dante Looks Forward and Back: Political Allegory in the Epistles." *Dante Studies* 115 (1997): 1–17.
Peters, Edward. "Pars, Parte: Dante and an Urban Contribution to Political Thought." In *The Medieval City*, edited by Harry A. Miskimin et al., 113–40. New Haven, CT: Yale University Press, 1977.
Petersen, Lene Waage. "Il poeta creatore del Principe". In *La corte di Ferrara e il suo mecenatismo*, edited by Marianne Pade et al., 195–211. Modena: Panini, 1990.
Philippides, Marios, and Walter Hanak. *The Siege and the Fall of Constantinople in 1453: Historiography, Topography, and Military Studies*. Farnham: Ashgate, 2011.
Picchio, Franco. *Ariosto e Bacco. I codici del sacro nell'Orlando Furioso*. Turin: Paravia, 1999.

Picone, Michelangelo. "I trovatori di Dante: Bertran de Born." *Studi e problemi di critica testuale* 19 (1979): 71–94.
Pieri, Piero. *La crisi militare italiana nel Rinascimento nelle sue relazioni con la crisi politica ed economica.* Naples: Ricciardi, 1934.
Pirillo, Diego. "Tasso at the French Embassy: Epic, Diplomacy and the Law of Nations." In *Authority and Diplomacy from Dante to Shakespeare*, edited by Jason Powell and William Rossiter, 135–53. Farnham: Ashgate, 2013.
Polcri, Alessandro. *Luigi Pulci e la Chimera. Studi sull'allegoria nel* Morgante. Florence: Società Editrice Fiorentina, 2010.
Putnam, Michael. *Virgil's Aeneid: Interpretation and Influence.* Chapel Hill and London: The University of North Carolina Press, 1995.
Quaglioni, Diego. "Un nuovo testimone per l'edizione della 'Monarchia' di Dante: il Ms. Add. 6891 della British Library." *Laboratoire italien* 11 (2011): 231–79.
Quinones, Ricardo. *Foundation Sacrifice in Dante's "Commedia."* University Park: Pennsylvania State University Press, 1994.
Quint, David. *Epic and Empire: Politics and Generic Form from Virgil to Milton.* Princeton, NJ: Princeton University Press, 1993.
———. "The Figure of Atlante: Ariosto and Boiardo's Poem." *MLN* 94, no. 1 (Jan. 1979): 77–91.
———. *Origin and Originality in Renaissance Literature.* New Haven, CT: Yale University Press, 1983.
———. "Romance and History in Tasso's *Gerusalemme Liberata*." In *Romance and History: Imagining Time from the Medieval to the Early Modern Period*, edited by Jon Whitman, 200–213. Cambridge: Cambridge University Press, 2015.
Raffa, Guy. "Enigmatic 56's: Cicero's Scipio and Dante's Cacciaguida." *Dante Studies* 110 (1992): 121–34.
Raimondi, Ezio. *Poesia come retorica.* Florence: Olschki, 1980.
Rajna, Pio. *Le fonti dell'Orlando furioso.* Florence: Sansoni, 1975.
Ramachandran, Ayesha. *The Worldmakers: Global Imagining in Early Modern Europe.* Chicago, IL: The University of Chicago Press, 2015.
Rayborn, Tim. *The Violent Pilgrimage: Christians, Muslims and Holy Conflicts, 850–1150.* Jefferson: MacFarland & Company, 2012.
Reed, Joseph. "The *Bellum Civile* as a Roman Epic." In *Brill's Companion to Lucan*, edited by Paolo Asso, 21–31. Leiden: Brill, 2011.
Reeves, Marjorie. *The Influence of Prophecy in the Later Middle Ages: A Study in Joachimism.* Oxford: Clarendon Press, 1969.
———. "Marsiglio da Padova and Dante Alighieri." In *Trends in Medieval Political Thought*, edited by Beryl Smalley, 86–104. Oxford: Blackwell, 1965.
Residori, Matteo. "Colombo e il volo d'Ulisse: una nota sul XV della *Liberata*." *Annali della Scuola Normale Superiore di Pisa*, III, Vol. XXII, 3 (1992): 931–42.
———. "Il Mago d'Ascalona e gli spazi del romanzo nella *Liberata*." *Italianistica* XXIV, 2–3 (May/December 1995): 453–71.

Retief, Francois Pieter and Louise Cilliers. "Tumours and Cancers in Graeco-Roman Times." *South African Medical Journal* 91, no. 4 (2001): 344–48.
Reynolds, Leighton Durham, ed. *Text and Transmission: A Survey of the Latin Classics.* Oxford: Clarendon Press, 1983.
Richter, Daniel S. *Cosmopolis: Imagining Community in Late Classical and the Early Roman Empire.* Oxford: Oxford University Press, 2011.
Riley, Kathleen. *The Reception and Performance of Euripides' "Herakles": Reasoning Madness.* Oxford: Oxford University Press, 2008.
Rinaldi, Rinaldo. *Le imprese imperfette. Studi sul Rinascimento.* Turin: Tirrenia, 1997.
Roberts, Sean. *Printing a Mediterranean World: Florence, Constantinople, and the Renaissance of Geography.* Cambridge, MA: Harvard University Press, 2013.
Robinson, Victor. *The Story of Medicine.* New York: The New Home Library, 1943.
Roche, Paul. *Commentary to Lucan, De bello ciuili.* Oxford: Oxford University Press, 2009.
Rose, Amy. "Seneca's HF: A Politico-Didactic Reading." *The Classical Journal* 75, no. 2 (December 1979–January 1980): 135–42.
Rosenthal, Earl. "*Plus Ultra, Non plus Ultra*, and the Columnar Device of Emperor Charles V." *Journal of the Warburg and Courtauld Institutes* 34 (1971): 204–28.
Rubinstein, Nicolai. "The Beginnings of Political Thought in Florence: A Study in Medieval Historiography." *Journal of the Warburg and Courtauld Institutes* 5 (1942): 198–227.
———. *The Government of Florence under the Medici (1434–1494).* Oxford: Clarendon Press, 1997.
Ruggieri, Ruggero. *Il processo di Gano nella "Chanson de Roland."* Florence: Sansoni, 1936.
———. *L'umanesimo cavalleresco italiano da Dante all'Ariosto.* Naples: Fratelli Conte, 1977.
Runciman, Steven. *The Fall of Constantinople 1453.* Cambridge: Cambridge University Press, 1965.
Russell, Frederick. *The Just War in the Middle Ages.* Cambridge: Cambridge University Press, 1975.
Saccone, Eduardo. *Il "soggetto" del Furioso.* Naples: Liguori, 1974.
———. "Prospettive sull'ultimo Ariosto." *MLN* 98, no. 1 (January 1983): 55–69.
Şahin, Kaya. *Empire and Power in the Reign of Süleyman: Narrating the Sixteenth-Century Ottoman World.* Cambridge: Cambridge University Press, 2013.
Said, Edward. *Orientalism.* London: Penguin Books, 1978.
Santoro, Mario. *Ariosto e il Rinascimento.* Napoli: Liguori, 1989.
———. *Letture Ariostesche.* Naples: Liguori, 1973.
Sarolli, Gian Roberto. *Prolegomena alla "Divina Commedia."* Florence: Olschki, 1971.
Savage, John. "Virgilian Echoes in the 'Dies Irae.'" *Traditio* 13 (1957): 443–51.
Savarese, Gennaro. *La Cultura a Roma tra umanesimo ed ermetismo: (1480–1540).* Anzio: De Rubeis, 1993.
Saylor, Charles. "Curio and Antaeus: The African Episode of Lucan *Pharsalia* IV." *Transactions of the American Philological Association* 112 (1982): 169–77.

Scancarelli Seem, Lauren. "The Limits of Chivalry: Tasso and the End of the *Aeneid*." *Comparative Literature* 42, no. 2 (Spring 1990): 116–25.

Schiesaro, Alessandro. *The Passions in Play: Thyestes and the Dynamics of Senecan Drama*. Cambridge: Cambridge University Press, 2003.

Schildgen, Brenda. *Dante and the Orient*. Urbana: University of Illinois Press, 2002.

Schmitt, Carl. *The Concept of the Political*. Translated by George Schwab. Chicago, IL: The University of Chicago Press, 2007.

———. *Glossario*. Translated into Italian by Petra Dal Santo. Milan: Giuffè, 2001.

———. *The Nomos of the Earth in the International Law of the Jus Publicum Europaeum*. Translated and annotated by G. L. Ulmen. New York: Telos Press Publishing 2006.

———. *Theory of the Partisan*. Translated by G. L. Ulmen. New York: Telos Press, 2007.

Schnapp, Jeffrey. *The Transfiguration of History at the Center of Dante's Paradise*. Princeton, NJ: Princeton University Press, 1984.

Schwoebel, Robert. *The Shadow of the Crescent: The Renaissance Image of the Turk (1453–1517)*. New York: St. Martin's Press, 1967.

Scianatico, Giovanna. *L'arme pietose. Studio sulla Gerusalemme Liberata*. Venice: Marsilio, 1990.

———. *L'idea del perfetto principe: utopia e storia nella scrittura del Tasso*. Napoli: Edizioni scientifiche italiane, 1998.

Sclavi, Susanna. "La biblioteca di Antonio Benivieni." *Physis* 17 (1975): 255–68.

Scott, John A. "Treachery in Dante." In *Studies in the Italian Renaissance. Essays in Memory of Arnoldo B. Ferruolo*, edited by Gian Paolo Biasin et al., 27–42. Naples: Società Editrice Napoletana, 1985.

———. *Understanding Dante*. Notre Dame, IN: University of Notre Dame Press, 2004.

Segre, Cesare. *Eperienze ariostesche*. Pisa: Nistri—Lischi, 1966.

———. *Fuori del mondo. I modelli nella follia e nelle immagini dell'aldilà*. Turin: Einaudi, 1990.

———. *La tradizione della "Chanson de Roland."* Milan: Ricciardi, 1974.

Setton, Kenneth. "Lutheranism and the Turkish Peril." *Balkan Studies* 3 (1962): 133–68.

———. *Western Hostility to Islam and Prophecies of Turkish Doom*. Philadelphia: American Philosophical Society, 1992.

Shapiro, Marianne. "The Fictionalization of Bertran de Born (*Inf*. XXVIII)." *Dante Studies* 92 (1974): 107–16.

Shaw, Christine. *Popular Government and Oligarchy in Renaissance Italy*. Leiden: Brill, 2006.

———. *The Poetics of Ariosto*. Detroit, MI: Wayne State University Press, 1988.

Shulters, John Raymond. *Luigi Pulci and the Animal Kingdom*. Baltimore, MD: J. H. Furst Company, 1920.

Sider, David; McVaugh, Michael. "Galen *On tremor, Palpitation, Spasm, and Rigor*." *Transactions and Studies of the College of Physicians of Philadelphia* 1, no. 3 (1979): 183–210.

Simon, Bennett. *Mind and Madness in Ancient Greece: The Classical Roots of Modern Psychiatry*. Ithaca, NY: Cornell University Press, 1978.

Simon, Marcel. *Hercule et le Christianisme*. Paris: Les Belles Lettres, 1955.
Simonetta, Marcello. *The Montefeltro Conspiracy: A Renaissance Mystery Decoded*. New York: Doubleday, 2008.
———. *Rinascimento segreto. Il mondo del Segretario da Petrarca a Machiavelli*. Milan: Franco Angeli, 2004.
Siraisi, Nancy. *The Clock and the Mirror: Girolamo Cardano and Renaissance Medicine*. Princeton, NJ: Princeton University Press, 1997.
———. *Medicine and the Italian Universities 1250–1600*. Leiden: Brill, 2001.
———. *Medieval and Early Renaissance Medicine*. Chicago, IL: The University of Chicago Press, 1990.
———. *Taddeo Alderotti and His Pupils: Two Generations of Italian Medical Learning*. Princeton, NJ: Princeton University Press, 1981.
Sitterson, Joseph. "Allusive and Elusive Meanings: Reading Ariosto's Vergilian Endings." *Renaissance Quarterly* 45, 1 (Spring, 1992): 1–19.
Skinner, Quentin. *The Foundations of Modern Political Thought*. 2 vols. Cambridge: Cambridge University Press, 1978.
Sloterdijk, Peter. *God's Zeal: The Battle of the Three Monotheisms*. Translated by W. Hoban. Cambridge: Polity, 2009.
Southern, R. W. *Western Views of Islam in the Middle Ages*. Cambridge, MA: Harvard University Press, 1962.
Stacey, Peter. *Roman Monarchy and the Renaissance Prince*. Cambridge: Cambridge University Press, 2007.
———. "Senecan Political Thought from the Middle Ages to Early Modernity." In *The Cambridge Companion to Seneca*, edited by Shadi Bartsch and Alessandro Schiesaro, 289–302. Cambridge: Cambridge University Press, 2015.
Steinberg, Justin. *Dante and the Limits of the Law*. Chicago, IL: University of Chicago Press, 2013.
Stephens, Walter. "Reading Tasso Reading Vergil Reading Homer: An Archeology of Andromache." *Comparative Literature Studies* 32, no. 2 (1995): 296–319.
———. "Saint Paul Among the Amazons: Gender and Authority in *Gerusalemme liberata*." In *Discourse of Authority in Medieval and Renaissance Literature*, edited by Kevin Brownlee and Walter Stephens, 169–200. Hanover: University Press of New England, 1989.
———. "Tasso as Ulysses." In *Sparks and Seeds: Medieval Literature and Its Afterlife: Essays in Honor of John Freccero*, edited by Dana Stewart and Alison Cornish, 209–39. Binghamton, NY: Medieval and Early Modern Studies, 2000.
———. "Trickster, *Textor*, Architect, Thief: Craft and Comedy in *Gerusalemme liberata*," in *Renaissance Transactions: Ariosto and Tasso*, edited by Valeria Finucci, 146–77. Durham, NC: Duke University Press, 1999.
Stok, Fabio. "Celso in Seneca?". *Orpheus* 6 (1985): 417–21.
Stone, Gregory. *Dante's Pluralism and the Islamic Philosophy of Religion*. New York: Palgrave MacMillan, 2006.

———. "Sodomy, Diversity, and Cosmopolitanism: Dante and the Limits of the Polis." *Dante Studies* 123 (2005): 89–132.
Stoppino, Eleonora. *Genealogies of Fiction: Women Warriors and the Dynastic Imagination in the "Orlando Furioso."* New York: Fordham University Press, 2012.
Stull, William; Hollander, Robert "The Lucanian Source of Dante's Ulysses." *Studi danteschi* 63 (1997): 1–52.
Tanner, Marie. *The Last Descendant of Aeneas: The Hapsburgs and the Mythic Image of the Emperor.* New Haven, CT: Yale University Press, 1993.
Tarrant, Richard J. "Greek and Roman in Seneca's Tragedies." *Harvard Studies in Classical Philology* 97 (1995): 215–30.
Taylor, Charles. *Sources of the Self: The Making of the Modern Identity.* Cambridge: Cambridge University Press, 1989.
Tierney, Brian. *The Crisis of Church and State 1050–1300.* Englewood Cliffs: Prentice-Hall, 1964.
Tissoni Benvenuti, Antonia. "Il mito di Ercole. Aspetti della ricezione dell'antico alla corte estense nel primo Quattrocento." In *Omaggio a Gianfranco Folena.* 3 vols. Padua: Programma, 1993: I: 773–92.
Todorov, Tzvetan. *The Conquest of America.* Translated by R. Howard. New York: Harper and Row, 1984.
Tolan, John. *Saracens: Islam in the Medieval European Imagination.* New York: Columbia University Press, 2002.
———. *Sons of Ishamel: Muslims through European Eyes in the Middle Ages.* Gainesville: University Press of Florida Press, 2008.
Tracy, James. *Holland under Habsburg Rule, 1506–1566: The Formation of a Body Politic.* Berkeley: University California Press, 1990.
Trivellato, Francesca. "Renaissance Italy and the Muslim Mediterranean in Recent Historical Work." *Journal of Modern History*, 82 (March 2010): 127–55.
Tuohy, Thomas. *Herculean Ferrara: Ercole d'Este, 1471–1505, and the Invention of a Ducal Capital.* Cambridge: Cambridge University Press, 1996.
Turan, Osman. "The Ideal of World Domination among the Medieval Turks." *Studia Islamica* 4 (1955): 77–90.
Tylus, Jane. "Imagining Narrative in Tasso: Revisiting Erminia." *MLN* 127, no. 1 (2012): 45–64.
———. "Reasoning Away Colonialism: Tasso and the Production of the Gerusalemme Liberata." *South Central Review* 10, no. 2 (Summer, 1993): 100–114.
———. "Tasso's Trees: Epic and Local Culture." In *Epic Traditions in the Contemporary World: The Poetics of Community,* edited by Margaret Beissinger et al., 108–30. Berkeley: University of California Press, 1999.
Ullman, Berthold L.; Stadter, Philip A. *The Public Library of Renaissance Florence: Niccolò Niccoli, Cosimo de' Medici and the Library of San Marco.* Padua: Antenore, 1972.
Ullmann, Walter. *Growth of Papal Government in the Middle Ages.* London: Metheun, 1955.

Usher, Jonathan. "Apicius, Seneca, and Surfeit: Boccaccio's Sonnet 95." *MLN* 118, no. 1 (January 2003): 46–59.
Valesio, Paolo. "The Language of Madness in the Renaissance." *Yearbook of Italian Studies* (1971): 199–234.
Valterza, Lorenzo. "Dante's Justinian, Cino's Corpus." *Medievalia et Humanistica* 37 (2011): 89–110.
Van Dam, Raymond. "The Many Conversions of the Emperor Constantine." In *Conversion in Late Antiquity and the Early Middle Ages: Seeing and Believing*, edited by Kenneth Mills and Anthony Grafton, 127–51. Rochester, NY: University of Rochester Press, 2003.
Veenstra, Jan. "The Ever-Changing Nature of the Beast: Cultural Change, Lycanthropy and the Question of Substantial Transformation (from Petronius to Del Rio)." In *The Metamorphosis of Magic from Late Antiquity to the Early Modern Period*, edited by Jan Bremmer and Jan Veenstra, 133–66. Leuven: Peeters, 2002.
Veinstein, Gilles. "The Great Turk and Europe." In *Europe and the Islamic World: A History*, edited by John Tolan et al., 111–253. Princeton, NJ: Princeton University Press, 2013.
Villa, Claudia. "Le tragedie di Seneca nel Trecento." In *Seneca e il suo tempo*, edited by Piergiorgio Parroni, 469–80. Rome: Salerno Editrice, 2000.
Vogt, Katja Maria. *Law, Reason, and the Cosmic City: Political Philosophy in the Early Stoa*. Oxford: Oxford University Press, 2008.
Volpi, Guglielmo. "Pulci contro i medici." *Rassegna* ser. III, vol. 1 (1916): 181–85.
Warren, Christopher. "Gentili, the Poets, and the Laws of War." In *The Roman Foundations of the Law of Nations: Alberico Gentili and the Justice of Empire*, edited by Benedict Kingsbury and Benjamin Straumann, 146–62. Oxford: Oxford University Press, 2010.
Wdzieczny, Gilbert. "The Life and Works of Thomas of Celano." *Franciscan Studies*, New Series, 5, no. 1 (March 1945): 55–68.
Weaver, Elissa. "A Reading of the Interlaced Plot of the *Orlando Furioso*: The Three Cases of Love Madness." In *Ariosto Today: Contemporary Perspectives*, edited by Donald Beecher et al., 126–53. Toronto: University of Toronto Press, 2003.
Weil, Simone. "The *Iliad*, or the Poem of Force." Translated by Mary McCarthy. *Chicago Review* 18, no. 2 (1965): 5–30.
Wells, Marion. *The Secret Wound: Love-Melancholy and Early Modern Romance*. Stanford, CA: Stanford University Press, 2007.
Wey Gómez, Nicolás. *The Tropics of Empire: Why Columbus Salied South to the Indies*. Cambridge, MA: MIT Press, 2008.
White, Hayden. "The Forms of Wildness: Archaeology of an Idea." In *The Wild Man Within: An Image in Western Thought from the Renaissance to Romanticism*, edited by Edward Dudley and Maximilian Novak, 3–38. Pittsburgh: University of Pittsburgh Press, 1972.
Whittington, Leah. *Renaissance Suppliants: Poetry, Antiquity, Reconciliation*. Oxford: Oxford University Press, 2016.

Williams, Bernard. "The Analogy of City and Soul in Plato's *Republic*." In *Plato's Republic. Critical Essays*, edited by Richard Kraut, 49–59. Lanham: Rowman and Littlefield Publishers, 1997.
———. *Shame and Necessity*. Berkeley: University of California Press, 1993.
Wilkins, Ernest H. "On the Dates of Composition of the *Morgante* of Luigi Pulci." *PMLA* 66, no.2 (March, 1951): 244–50.
———. "On the Earliest Editions of the 'Morgante' of Luigi Pulci." *The Papers of the Bibliographical Society of America* 45, no. 1 (First Quarter, 1951): 1–22.
Wilson, Robert. *Prophecies and Prophecy in Dante's "Commedia."* Florence: Olshki, 2008.
Witt, Ronald. *Hercules at the Crossroads: The Life, Works, and Thought of Coluccio Salutati*. Durham, NC: Duke University Press, 1983.
Wondrich, F. David. "The Crusade Within: 'L'Arabo imbelle' in Tasso's *Gerusalemme liberata*." *Mediterranean Studies* 7 (1998): 101–16.
Wright, Alison. "The Myth of Hercules." In *Lorenzo il Magnifico e il suo mondo*. Edited by Gian Carlo Garfagnini. Florence: Olschki, 1994. 323–39.
Wright, Elizabeth R. *The Epic of Juan Latino: Dilemmas of Race and Religion in Renaissance Spain*. Toronto: University of Toronto Press, 2016.
Yates, Frances. *Astrea: The Imperial Theme in the Sixteenth Century*. London and Boston: Routledge and Kegan Paul, 1975.
Zanato, Tiziano. "*Inferno* XXVIII." In *Lectura Dantis Bononiensis*, Vol. 4, edited by Emilio Pasquini and Carlo Galli, 157–81. Bologna: Bononia University Press, 2014.
Zanini-Cordi, Irene. "The Seduction of Ariosto's Olimpia: Mythopoetic Rescue of an Abandoned Woman." *Pacific Coast Philology* 42, no. 1 (2007): 37–53.
Zanker, Graham. *The Heart of Achilles: Characterization and Personal Ethics in the "Iliad."* Ann Arbor: The University of Michigan Press, 1994.
Zatti, Sergio. "Dalla parte di Satana: sull'imperialismo cristiano nella Gerusalemme Liberata." In *La Rappresentazione dell'Altro nei testi del Rinascimento*, edited by Sergio Zatti, 146–82. Lucca: Maria Pacini Fazzi, 1998.
———. *Il Furioso tra epos e romanzo*. Lucca: Maria Pacini Fazzi, 1990.
———. "Tasso e il nuovo mondo." *Italianistica* XXIV, 2–3 (May/December 1995): 501–21.
———. *Uniforme cristiano e multiforme pagano*. Milan: Il Saggiatore, 1983.
Zipes, Jack, ed. *The Trials and Tribulations of Little Red Riding Hood*. New York: Routledge, 1993.

Index

Abrahamic religions: split among, 26; universalism in, 8, 12, 114–15, 140, 194n34. *See also* specific religions
Acciaiuoli, Donato, *De vita Caroli,* 65
Accursius, 36
Achilles, 14, 143–46, 201n5
Actium, Battle of (31 BCE), 117
Aeneid (Virgil): Cacus, battle with Hercules, 93, 186n61, 186n66; compared to *Gerusalemme Liberata,* 139; compared to Lucan's *Civil War,* 32; Cumaean Sibyl predicting Aeneas's future in, 38; *Furioso* and, 93–99, 185n60; gnashing of teeth in, 80, 186n65; Hades encounter of Aeneas with his father who prophesizes Rome's future, 1–2; Hercules as predecessor of Aeneas, 186n66; inevitable battles of Aeneas, 38; internal turmoil and furor of Aeneas, 89, 93–100, 186n67, 186–87n71; Mercury exhorting Aeneas to leave Africa and Queen Dido, 33; Roman Empire's depiction in, 10, 186n66; Ruggiero as new version of Aeneas, 76, 77, 93, 98–99; Statius acknowledging influence of, 37; Turnus, Aeneas's slaying of, 6, 77, 98, 124, 186n66, 187n74
Aeschylus, 5; *Prometheus,* 148n12
African mission, of Curio, 32
Agamemnon and Achaean force, 143–45
Ageno, Franca, 61, 165n4
Alan of Lille, 16; *Anticlaudianus,* 36
Albert the Great (Albertus Magnus), 53; *On Animals* (*De animalibus*), 47, 50–51

Alberti, Leon Battista, 7, 86, 181–82n34; *Momus,* 7
Alcides, 6. *See also* Hercules
Alexander the Great, 86, 112
Alfonso V (king of Aragon), 113
Alì (Muhammad's cousin and son-in-law), 24–25, 157n32
Allen, Michael, 183n45
Ambrose, *Hexaemeron,* 47
American Indians. *See* colonization
Amidei clan, 34
Anchises (father of Aeneas), 1, 38
Annunciation, 106, 137
Antaeus, 90
Antichrist, 25, 26, 157–58n33
apostasy, 155n19. *See also* heresy
Aquinas, Thomas: commentary on Aristotle's *Ethics,* 62; compared to Dante, 21; comparing charity to other virtues, 20, 155n21; *De rationibus fidei,* 27; on heresy vs. sect, 20; on inner harmony, 75; on Muslims and Muhammad, 158n39; on peace, 20–21; quoting from Book of Proverbs, 155n19; on sins contrary to peace, 21; *Summa contra gentiles,* 27, 158n39; *Summa Theologiae,* 16, 20–21, 155n20, 175n1, 183n41
Arendt, Hannah, 13
Arianism, 26, 28, 154–55n17
Ariosto, Ludovico: *Cinque Canti,* 176–77n10; Este patronage of, 76, 88, 89, 100, 103, 183n47, 188n75; Ficino and, 179n22. *See also Orlando Furioso*

Aristotle: ancient physiology of, 40, 50, 163n76; on greed, 32; *Nicomachean Ethics*, 62, 80, 181n32; *Poetics*, 106; *Politics*, 16, 84, 86, 181n32; *Problems* (Pseudo-Aristotle), 81, 178n18, 180n26; on tyranny, 86, 181n32
Armitage, David, 9
Arnald of Villanova, 51, 53
Ascoli, Albert, *Ariosto's Bitter Harmony*, 76, 103
Augustine, Saint, 20, 54, 75, 114; *Confessiones*, 175n1; *De trinitate*, 28
Augustus, 1–2, 95, 99, 113; compared to Charles V, 100; compared to Hercules, 186n66; empire's origins in Trojan roots in *Aeneid*, 186n66; Octavian's defeat of Mark Antony and Cleopatra, 117; representing Este patrons of Ariosto, 100
Aurelius, Marcus, *Meditations*, 9
Averroës, 25
Avicenna, 25, 53; *Canon of Medicine*, 50, 166–67n17

Bandello, Matteo, 51
Bandini, Bernardo, 114
Barbi, Michele, 41
Basil the Great, *Hexaemeron*, 47
Beer, Marina, 88
Belgrade, Ottoman conquest of (1521), 123
Bellerophon, 84
Benivieni, Antonio, *De abditis*, 53
Benjamin, Walter, 13
Berlinghieri, Francesco, 114
Bernard of Clairvaux, 22
Bernardus Silvestris, 16
Bertoldo di Giovanni, 67, 114
Bertran de Born: compared to Virgil, 37–38; fostering enmity between Henry II and his son, 11, 36, 38, 40; in *Inferno* 28, 2, 17, 18, 27, 33, 35–40; "Si tuit li dol," 20, 38
Beyazid II (Ottoman ruler), 114
Boccaccino, Piero di, 62
Boccaccio, Giovanni, 7, 171n63; *Corbaccio*, 62, 171n61; *Famous Women*, 7; *Genealogia deorum gentilium*, 54
Bodin, Jean, 14

body politic imagery, 2–3, 11, 16, 18, 40, 152n3
Boethius, 183n45
Boiardo, Matteo Maria, *Orlando Innamorato*, 44, 79–80, 177n14, 186n65
Boniface VIII (pope), 158n43
Bracciolini, Jacopo, 66–67, 173n78
Bracciolini, Poggio, *History of Florence*, 66
Brutus, 44, 62, 164n1
Buondelmonti clan, 34
burial rites, importance of, 97, 144, 201n5

Cachey, Ted, 129
Campanella, Tommaso, 102
cancer: in medico-political writing, 48–53, 73, 166n10; treachery as, 11, 45–46, 49–53, 57, 105
Cancer constellation, 55
cannibalism, 131
Capellanus, 179n19
Carrai, Stefano, 45, 48, 56
Cassell, Anthony, 41
Cassius, 44, 62
Castellani, Francesco, 53, 62
Catiline, 6, 28
"catholic" and "church," etymology of, 149n24
Catholic Church. *See* Roman Catholic Church
Cato, 32
Cavallo, Jo Ann, 13, 137
Cecco d'Ascoli, *L'Acerba*, 47
Celsus, Cornelius, *De medicina*, 51–53, 167n28
Chance, Jane, 16–17
Chanson de Roland, 71, 174n86, 174n90
charitas, 11, 16, 20, 153n8, 155n21
Charlemagne. *See Morgante*
Charles V (Holy Roman emperor), 115–17; Ariosto's critique on, 12, 77, 100–104, 188n77; compared to Augustus, 100; compared to Hercules, 103, 109; emblem featuring Pillars of Hercules with saying "*Plus Ultra*," 103, 109, 189n81; Frisia origins of, 88; imperial realm and universal empire ambitions of, 11, 74, 102–4, 108–9, 188–89n79; Italian city-states vs. empire of, 99
Charles VIII (king of France), 73, 99

INDEX

Christian Crusaders. See *Gerusalemme Liberata*
Christianity. *See* conversion to Christianity; Coptic Christianity; Roman Catholic Church
Christian vs. Islamic forces: geography of the enemy and, 120, 127–28; as internal hostility due to shared religious origins, 2, 8; as justifiable war, 116; mirror images as enemies, 3, 115. See also *Gerusalemme Liberata*; Islam and Muslims; *Orlando Furioso*; Muhammad
Chrysippus of Soli, 9, 146
Ciavolella, Massimo, 88
Cicero: on common body of humanity, 16; cosmopolitanism and, 9; *De officiis*, 5–6, 16, 43, 54, 71, 90, 143, 149n14, 169n39; on "Hercules at the crossroads," 54; on justice's importance, 43; on madness, 179n19; *Tusculan Disputations*, 56, 179n19
civil discord: Caesar and Pompey engaging in civil war, 1–2, 7, 11, 18, 28–33, 96; cosmopolitanism and, 9; Dante on, 37; foreign intervention triggering, 4; *Iliad* and, 143; internal, as *psychomachia*, 75–76; Plato's description of, 5. See also *Inferno* 28
Clement VII (pope), 74, 104, 188n79
Cleopatra, 117
colonization of New World and indigenous American populations, 12, 108, 109, 116, 131
Columbus, Christopher, 105, 108, 121, 130–31, 133
Commedia (Dante): compared to *Gerusalemme Liberata*, 124, 142; giants' role in, 124; *Inferno* 8–9, 38; *Inferno* 9–11, 22; *Inferno* 12, 56, 86; *Inferno* 20, 97; *Inferno* 21–22, 38; *Inferno* 26, 140–41, 162n69; *Inferno* 27, 18, 77–78; *Inferno* 31, 64–65, 124; *Inferno* 34, 62–63; influence on Pulci, 59; Limbo in, 25, 37; Muhammad placed among sowers of discord in, 18–28, 155n17; Nessus in seventh circle of Hell, 56, 64; *Purgatorio*, 32, 36–37, 72; traitors and treachery in, 44, 45, 62–63; wolf imagery in, 86. See also *Inferno* 28

concentric circles of affiliation, 4–5, 10
Constantine (Roman emperor), 30, 113
Constantinople, 109; fall of (1453), 12, 65, 108, 109–10, 113, 114
conversion to Christianity: of American Indians, 116, 132–33; of Armida in *Gerusalemme Liberata*, 135–39, 141; of Clorinda in *Gerusalemme Liberata*, 124–26, 139; of Constantine, 113; of Erminia in *Gerusalemme Liberata*, 126–28, 139; of female characters in *Gerusalemme Liberata*, 106, 108, 122; of Longinus, 60; of Mehmed, as possibility that would bring peace to a unified world, 110, 114; of Statius, 37
Coptic Christianity, 124, 126, 139, 196n66
corpus mysticum imagery, 25, 27, 158n34
Cortés, Hernán, 102
cosmopolitanism, 4, 8–10, 75, 102, 150n26
crab's reputation and fatal bite, 3, 46–49, 166n13
Crucifixion, 8, 29, 72
Crusaders. See *Gerusalemme Liberata*
Curio, Gaius Scribonius, 11, 18, 28–33, 40

Dante: compared to Aquinas, 21; *Convivio*, 17, 20, 62; criticizing Constantine for putting Roman *De Vulgari Eloquentia*, 10, 35; Empire under papal control, 113; *Epistle* 5, 171n61; *Epistle* 7, 33, 40; *Epistle* 11, 158n36; *Epistle to Cangrande*, 38; father figures in, 154n14; martial genre and, 35, 38, 163n73; as poet of peace, 11, 17–18, 40–42; political environment depicted by, 10, 75, 77–78; possible sources of, 62; Riccoldo's and Peter the Venerable's description of Islam and, 22–23; scatological language used by, 20, 24, 157n29; on vengeance, 34, 161n61; *Vita Nova*, 75–76. See also *Commedia*; *Inferno* 28; *Monarchia*
Dante Studies (2007), 20
Decaria, Alessio, 45
Demaitre, Luke, 51
Derrida, Jacques, 13
Dies Irae (hymn), 61–62, 171n61
Diogenes, 9

Diomedes, 29, 162n69
discord. *See* civil discord; enmity; internal turmoil; internecine hostilities; madness
dismemberment, 2, 17–18, 72–74, 174n92

Elijah (prophet), 177n11
Emmaus, Christ's encounter with disciples at, 36
emperor: ability to create universal peace, 16; relationship with pope, 18, 33, 40–41, 163n77. *See also* Augustus; Charles V
enemy: concept of, 3–5, 14; cosmopolitan viewpoint and concept in Middle Ages and Renaissance, 10; as distorted mirror-image of protagonist, 3; geography of the enemy, 120, 127–28; *hostis* vs. *inimicus*, 4, 5–8, 10, 90; in Roman texts, 5–6
enmity: among Christian rulers, 109–10; circles of, 10–13; epic and, 13–14; exemplified in *Inferno* 28, 28–29, 42; Muhammad as embodiment of enmity against Catholic Church, 25; within political or religious entities, 2–3, 10; within self, 10; as violation of bonds of humanity, 144, 146; "war breeds war," 115; within world, 10. *See also* civil discord; internal turmoil; internecine hostilities
epic genre, 14
Erasmus, Desiderius, 103, 189n80; *Complaint of Peace*, 115; *Education of a Christian Prince*, 103, 115; rejecting crusade concept and preferring peaceful approach, 115, 132; *Utilissima consultatio de bello Turcis inferendo*, 116
Ercole I (duke), 89
Este, Alfonso d', 99, 100, 104
Este, Ippolito d', 89, 92, 99, 100, 103
Este family and patronage, 76, 77, 88, 89, 100, 103, 106, 183n47, 188n75
Eteocles, 37
ethics, relationship with poetry, 36–37, 162n67
Ethiopia, 124
Euripides: *Heracles*, 90, 179n19, 180n27, 184n52, 185n58; *Phoenician Women*, 174n88
Ezzelino da Romano, 78, 86

father-son relationships, 11, 17, 18, 30, 36, 40
Federico da Montefeltro (Duke of Urbino), 66
Ferdinand of Aragon, 66
Ferrara, 76, 89, 183nn46–47; in parallel foundational narrative to Rome, 99, 100
Ficino, Marsilio, 53, 66, 102, 167n28, 173n77, 178n18, 179n19, 179nn22–24, 183n45
fidelity. *See* trust
Filelfo, Francesco, 97
firearms, growing use of, 88, 103, 183n44
Florence, 11, 28, 34, 44–45, 53, 55; conspiracy and treason in, 66–67; Dante on reputation of, 140–41; France, links to, 63, 65; Hercules and, 54, 58, 89, 169n41, 169n44; Ottomans and, 114. *See also* Pazzi conspiracy
Fonzio, Bartolomeo, 52
force, definition of, 144
friendship: celebrated in conjunction with poetry, 37; *philia* concept, 146, 201n111; and politics in Florence, 165–66n8
Frisia, 88, 103
Furioso. See *Orlando Furioso*

Galatians, 8
Galen of Pergamon: ancient physiology of, 50, 51, 53, 163n76; *Method of Medicine to Glaucon*, 49; *On Tremor, Palpitation, Spasm, and Rigor*, 51
Gattinara, Mercurino di, 102–3, 108, 121, 130, 188n79, 189nn80–82
generosity, 43, 62, 200n96
geography, concept of. *See Gerusalemme Liberata*
Gerusalemme Liberata (Tasso), 12–13, 105–8, 118–42; Adrasto in, 134–35, 137; Altamoro spared from death, 108, 139–40; Argante, Solimano, and Clorinda, deaths of, 123–26; Armida's conversion to Christianity in, 135–39, 141; Armida's reconciliation with Rinaldo in, 128–31, 135–38; artists' depictions of Armida, 128; background to development of, 118; Carlo and Ubaldo's journey across the Atlantic in, 128–31, 133–34; Christian vs. Islamic forces in, 2–3, 12–13, 105, 107; Clorinda's conversion to

Christianity in, 124–26, 139; compared to *Aeneid*, 139; compared to *Commedia*, 124, 142; compared to *Inferno* 26, 140; compared to *Furioso*, 124; compared to *Iliad*, 126, 139, 143; conversion of female characters to Christianity in, 106, 108, 122, 139, 141; disunity of Crusaders in, 121; Erminia's conversion to Christianity in, 126–28, 139, 141; Eurocentric vision of power in, 106, 140; First Crusade in, 107, 118, 122, 140, 143; geography of the enemy in, 120, 127–28; good vs. evil and Muslim enemy in, 105; myth of Roman Empire in, 12; new geographic discoveries, Tasso's interest in, 129–31; "Other," representation of, 106; political-religious interplay in, 120–21, 129–30, 136; Protestant Reformation references in, 121; rapidly changing and diverse Europe in, 13, 105–7; revisions by Tasso to, 129; Rinaldo-Adrasto mirroring relationship in, 137; Rinaldo as future founder of Este House in, 106; Rinaldo as hero in, 106, 123; romance genre and, 127, 137; Satan's geopolitics and, 118–23; universal empire acknowledged as impossibility in, 106, 123, 139, 141
Ghibellines, 34
gnashing of teeth, 80, 186n65
God and generosity, in Dante, 62
Golden Age, prediction of, 37, 112
Gonzaga, Scipione, 121, 122
good shepherd imagery, 81–84, 87, 105, 182nn35–36
Gospels. *See* scriptural references
greed, 30–32
Gregory, Tobias, 13
Guelphs, 34
Guido da Montefeltro, 18
Guido da Pisa, 62

Habsburg rulers, 8, 12–13, 88, 102, 108–9, 115, 132. *See also* Charles V
Heaven of Jupiter, 30
Hector, 5, 93, 97, 99, 100, 144–45
Helen of Troy, 126, 143
Hellenes vs. Barbarians, 5

Henry II (king of England), relationship with Henry, the Young King, 11, 36, 38, 40
Henry VII (Holy Roman Emperor), Dante's letter to, 29–30, 33, 159n50
Hercules: Alberti on, 7; ambivalence in classical depictions of, 90; as benefactor of humanity, 184n50; Boccaccio on, 54; centaur Nessus and, 56, 57–58, 64, 170n46, 184n50; as Christ figure, 54; compared to Augustus, 186n66; compared to Charles V, 103, 109; depictions in works of art, 183n46; as epitome of human virtue, 54, 172n67; as epitome of reason, 89, 183n45; evolution of use of story of in ancient and medieval times, 169nn40–41; *Hercules Furens* (Seneca the Younger), 6, 12, 76, 77, 82, 89, 90–94, 179n19, 184n52, 185n61; Hydra and, 55, 57; Iole and, 56; Lucan on, 32; Lycus and, 6, 91; madness of, 81, 90–92, 143, 178–79n19, 180n27; parallel with Morgante, 45, 54–58, 169n37; parallel with Orlando, 76–77, 89–95, 184n49; as popular subject in fifteenth and sixteenth centuries, 183n46; *topos* of "Hercules at the crossroads," 54, 169n38
heresy, 20–21, 25, 28. *See also* Arianism
Hierocles, 9, 10
Hippocrates of Cos, *Aphorisms*, 51
Hobbes, Thomas, 14
Holy League, 108, 116–18
Homer: "enemy" defined by, 5; *Iliad*, 5, 14, 84, 126, 139, 143–46; *Odyssey*, 5
humanity amid horror of war, 145–46, 184n50

Ibrahim Pasha, 114
Inferno 28 (Dante's *Commedia*), 2, 10–11, 15–42; civil conflict in, 18, 28–33, 40, 105; cohesiveness based on its movement from macro- to micro-political structures, 17; compared to *Iliad*, 143; compared to *Monarchia*, 11, 75; enmity punished in, 42; father-son conflicts in, 11, 17, 18, 30, 40; on Islam in Europe, 11, 18–28; Mosca in, 34; Muhammad in, 17, 18–28, 105; sowers of discord in, 17, 18, 22–27, 29, 32–33, 36, 42, 43; vision of global empire in, 11, 16

inheritance, law of, 36, 161n65
internal turmoil: as enmity within self, 10; furor of Aeneas, 89, 93–100, 186n67, 186–87n71; "know thyself" injunction and, 3, 148n4; as *psychomachia*, 75–76; within sovereign's own self, 104. *See also* madness
internecine hostilities: in Florence, 58; in *Iliad*, 143; in *Inferno* 28, 11, 17, 18, 30, 40; kindred-fighting-kindred leitmotiv, 2; in *Monarchia*, 11, 40–41; in *Morgante*, 48
Iraq War, 4
Isidore of Seville, 20, 73; *Etymologies*, 25, 47, 49, 51
Islam and Muslims, 12; Christians seeking to convert Muslims, 110, 114, 157–58n33; in *Furioso*, Angelica's love for Muslim foot soldier, Medoro, 76, 81–82, 177n16; hostility with Christianity deemed internal dispute with heretical sect, 2, 8, 20, 22, 117, 121, 157n32; humanist critiques of, 110; rejection of Trinity and Eucharist by, 17, 22, 24, 26–27, 40, 111; Shia and Sunni rift, 24; Shiite Safavid Empire, 115; terms used for Muslims, 26; as universal faith, 114. *See also* Christian vs. Islamic forces; *Gerusalemme Liberata*; Muhammad; *Orlando Furioso*
Italian city-states: Charles V's empire vs., 99; familial ties and political authority intertwined in, 3. *See also* Florence; Medici regime

Jacobus de Voragine, *Legenda Aurea*, 60, 171n61
Jerome, Saint, 20
Jerusalem, 12–13, 25, 61, 107, 109
Jesus: injunction to love one's enemies, 7–8, 146; prophecy of Jerusalem's destruction, 61
John (saint), 78, 100, 102, 103, 187n75
John (son of Henry VII), 33
John of Austria, 109, 117
John of Damascus, 110, 158n36; *De Haeresibus*, 26
John of Salisbury, 16
Juba (African king), 32
Judaism, 26; Old Testament, 177n12
Judas, 29, 62, 63, 67, 69, 71, 72, 174n89

Julius Caesar, 1–2, 11, 29–31, 38, 40, 44, 65, 71, 112
Juno and Jove, 86, 87, 89–93, 95, 96
justice, importance of, 43–44, 172n72
Justinian, *Institutiones*, 36, 161n65
just war, 116, 159n48

Kahn, Victoria, 13, 152n39
Kant, Immanuel, 6
Kantorowicz, Ernst, 152nn39–40; *The King's Two Bodies*, 36
Kilij Arslan, 123
king-prince relationship, 11, 36, 38, 40. *See also* internecine hostilities
"know thyself" injunction, 3, 148n4
Kristeller, Paul Oskar, 167n28

Lactantius, 54
Lampognano, Andrea, 58
Landino, Cristoforo: *Comento sopra la comedia*, 55, 77, 86–87, 184n50; *Disputationes Camaldulenes*, 55, 66, 169n44; on Pliny, 47
Lanfranc of Milan, 51, 52
Las Casas, Bartolomé de, 116; *In Defense of the Indians*, 132–34
Latini, Brunetto, *Tresor*, 28, 34, 155n22, 159n51
Latino, Juan, *Song on the Victory of the Christian Fleet*, 117
Leo X (pope), 100, 188n75
Lepanto, Battle of (1571), 108, 109, 116–17
Lezra, Jacques, 13
Liberata. See *Gerusalemme Liberata*
literary scholarship, 14
Livy, 16, 19; *Ab urbe condita*, 20, 95
Llull, Ramon, 174n86
Longinus, 60
Looney, Dennis, 13
Lorenzo the Magnificent. *See* Medici, Lorenzo de
Louis XI (French king), 65
love, charity as, 11, 20, 155n21
Lucan: *Civil War*, 1–2, 7, 10, 11, 29, 30–33; cosmopolitanism and, 9, 10; on Curio, 11; suicide of, 3
Lupton, Julia Reinhard, 13, 152n39; *Citizen-Saints*, 14

Luther, Martin, 12, 107, 116. *See also* Protestant Reformation
Lutheranism, 109, 121. *See also* Protestant Reformation
lycanthropy, 85–89. *See also* tyranny
Lycaon, turned into a wolf, 87
Lycus, 6, 90–91

Machiavelli, Niccolò: compared to Schmitt, 151n37; critique of theories of power of, 76; *Mandragola*, 51
macrocosm-microcosm analogy, 16, 17, 75, 85, 152n3
madness: Cicero on, 179n19; of Hercules, 81, 90–92, 143, 178–79n19, 180n27; in *Iliad*, 143; wolf imagery and, 143. *See also Orlando Furioso*
Magellan, Ferdinand, 129, 131
Malatesta, Paolo, 29
Manini, Ottaviano, "The Long-Desired Day" (poem), 117
Mark Antony, 6, 117
Mark of Toledo (translator of Qur'an), 157n30
Marliano, Ludovico (bishop), 189n81
Marlowe, Christopher, 14
Marsilio. *See Morgante*
Marsilius of Padua, 113
Mazzotta, Giuseppe, 17, 76
Medici, Bianca de, 66
Medici, Cosimo de, 55, 65–66, 173n74
Medici, Giuliano de, 45, 48, 58, 66, 67, 74, 114
Medici, Giulio de (later Pope Clement VII), 74
Medici, Lorenzo de, 53, 58, 66–67, 72, 114, 164n1, 174n90
Medici regime/Medici Duchy, 44, 48, 55, 66, 73–74, 165n8, 175n94. *See also* Florence
medico-political writing. *See* cancer; *Morgante*
Medusa, myth of, 82
Mehmed II, 108–14
melancholy, 77, 81, 85, 88, 94, 178n18
Miller, Nichole, 13, 152n39
mirror image: Christian and Islamic enemies, 13, 115; in civil war between Caesar and Pompey, 2; enmity in Italian Renaissance shown through use of, 3, 18; in *Gerusalemme Liberata*, 106, 120; in *Hercules Furens*, 94; in *Morgante*, 65; Priam and Achilles in *Iliad*, 145–46; Rinaldo-Adrasto relationship, 137; Seneca offering his work to Nero as, 3, 92–93, 185n58; between tyrant and martyr, 92, 185n56
Monarchia (Dante), 15–18; compared to *Inferno* 28, 11, 75; Ficino's translation into vernacular, 102; friendship and trust in, 43–44; influence of, 189n82; internecine strife's destructive nature in, 11, 40–41; later revision suggested by Nardi, 41, 164n78; peace concept in, 105, 153n8; quest for ideal world government in, 15–18; on Roman Empire's rise, 29, 114, 171n61, 189n80; vision of global empire in, 10, 11
Montaigne, Michel de, *Des Cannibales*, 131
Montemaggi, Vittorio, 17
Morani, Moreno, 5
Morgante (Pulci), 11–12, 43–74, 105; apocalyptic motif in, 61; cancer analogy with treachery in, 49–53; Charlemagne in, 44, 58–62, 64, 65, 68–70, 72, 172n73; Christological subtext in, 68–71, 174n91; civic discord in, 2–3, 10, 44; commissioned by Lucrezia Tornabuoni, 65; compared to *Iliad*, 143; crab as symbol of treachery, 48; crab bite leading to death of Morgante in, 45, 46–47, 57–58; Dante's influence in, 63–64, 172n68; dismembering the enemy in, 72–74; doctrinal orthodoxy vs. sacrilegious parody in, 48; Falserone in, 68–69; Giudecca in, 63; Judas in, 62, 63; Lucifer in, 60–64, 69; madness of Orlando depicted in, 79–80; Margutte in, 44–45, 47–48; medico-political perspective on, 45, 48–53; nemesis of Morgante in, 3; Orlando's ambush by Ganelon (with Marsilio) in, 11, 45, 58–59, 63–72; parallel between Morgante's and Hercules's death in, 45, 54–58, 169n37; passion of Astolfo in, 58–65; plots and vengeance, 54, 65–72; possible sources for, 50–53, 56, 59, 62; pride in, 11, 45, 58, 60, 64, 65, 171n57; punishments in, 72–73, 171n61; relationship to contemporary political events, 48; treachery in, 11–12, 43–46, 48–53, 58, 105

Mosca dei Lamberti, 28, 34
Muhammad (prophet): in *Inferno* 28, 17, 18–28, 155n17, 155n21; journey from Mecca to Medina, 114; as renegade who turned against the Church, 2, 10, 22, 25, 40, 110–11, 117, 157n30; traditional medieval view of, 11, 12, 22, 24, 156n22
Murrin, Michael, 13
Muslims. *See* Islam and Muslims
mythology, 54, 55, 82, 117, 171n58. *See also specific mythological figures*

Naaman the Syrian, 177n12
Nardi, Bruno, 41, 164n78
Nebuchadnezzar, 78–79, 177n11
Nero, 3, 78, 92–93, 185n58
Nestorianism, 26
New Testament, 177n12. *See also* scriptural references
New World. *See* colonization
Niccoli, Niccolò, 52, 167n28
Nicene Creed, 44
Nicholas of Cusa (cardinal), 108, 121; *The Catholic Concordance*, 113; *Cribatio Alkorani*, 110, 111; *De pace fidei*, 110–11
Nimrod, 65
Nussbaum, Martha, 9

Odysseus, 5
Old Testament, 177n12. *See also* scriptural references
Orlando Furioso (Ariosto), 2–3, 75–104, 105; *Aeneid* (Virgil) and, 93–99, 185n60; Angelica's love for Muslim foot soldier, Medoro, in, 76, 81–82, 177n16; Christological subtext in, 87; Cimosco and Marganorre episodes in, 88, 89–91, 103, 185n55; compared to *Gerusalemme Liberata*, 124; cure of Orlando's madness, 177n11; desire in, 80–81, 85–86, 177n16; *Eclogue* 4 and Book of Isaiah evoked in, 102, 112; firearms, condemnation of use of, 88, 103, 183n44; historico-political implications of, 76; later additions to 1532 edition, 76, 88, 97, 99, 102, 183n43; madness as allusion to tyranny, 77; Mandricardo's duel and brawl in, 81; Marganorre in, 87–88; melancholy in, 77, 81, 85, 88, 94, 178n18; *Morgante*'s depiction of Orlando's madness and, 79; Nebuchadnezzar, comparison with Orlando, 78–79, 177n11; parallel of Orlando with Hercules, 76–77, 89–95, 184n49; Plato's city-soul analogy and, 76, 85, 180–81n30; Plato's influence on, 81–87; Plato's tripartite soul and, 76, 83–84; presented by author to Charles V, 104; psychological manifestations of Orlando's madness in, 80–85, 143, 176n4, 176n8, 180n29; Rodomonte in, 77, 97–99, 124; Ruggiero as Orlando's alter ego in, 77, 93, 98–99; self-enmity and loss of reason in, 3, 10, 12, 54, 76; Seneca as influence for, 86, 89–94; traitors and treason in, 44; tyranny in, 77–79, 85–89, 105; undeserving receiving fame from poets and, 100
Orlando's ambush by Ganelon. *See Morgante*
Otranto (Italian town), Turkish occupation of, 114
Ottoman rulers, 8, 12–13, 108–14, 132
Ovid: *Metamorphoses*, 56, 87, 185n55; *Tristia*, 20

Palmieri, Matteo, *De vita civile*, 55
parody, 44, 45, 48, 173n77
Patroklos, death in *Iliad* of, 143–44
Paul, Saint, 21–22, 177n12; 1 Corinthians, 21, 22, 25, 27, 137; Galatians, 8; letters from, 16, 25, 27, 137
Pazzi, Francesco de, 66, 73
Pazzi, Guglielmo de, 66
Pazzi, Jacopo de, 66, 73
Pazzi conspiracy (1478), 45, 48, 59, 66–67, 73–74, 114
Pazzi family, 66, 164n1
peace: in *Aeneid*, 97; Aquinas on, 20–21; Bertran's reputation as warmonger opposing, 38; Dante as poet of, 11, 17–18, 40–42, 153n8, 162n70; Erasmus as proponent of peace over war, 115, 132; in *Iliad*, peaceful reconciliation between Priam and Achilles, 144, 146; Jerusalem becoming city of peace, 107, 190n6; only possible under unity of

one ruler, 16, 108, 109, 141; Pius II extolling, 112; Renaissance political discourse on, 102; Rome as universal empire offering global unity and peace, 108, 118; universal peace as vision of Tasso, 141
Peleus (father of Achilles), 145
Peter the Venerable, 8, 20, 149n23; on Arian heresy, 28; as critic of Islam, 110; on Muhammad's religious education, 22–23; *Summa totius haeresis Saracenorum*, 22–23, 26–27; as translator of Qur'an, 157n30
Petrarch: *Canzoniere*, 137; *De vita solitaria*, 169n39; *Triumph of Fame*, 66
Pharsalia, Battle of (48 BC), 2
philia (friendship), 146, 201n11
Philip II (1527–1598), 109
Piccolomini, Aeneas Silvius. *See* Pius II
Pico della Mirandola, *Oration on the Dignity of Man*, 76
Pier da Medicina, 28
Pietro Martire d'Anghiera, 130
Pigafetta, Antonio, 129
Pigna, Giovan Battista, *I Romanzi*, 89
Pilate, 68
Pillars of Hercules, 12, 100, 103, 109, 119, 128, 131, 189n91
Pitti conspiracy (1466), 66
pity, in *Iliad*, 144
Pius II (pope, formerly Aeneas Silvius Piccolomini), 8, 102, 108, 113; *De ortu et auctoritate imperii romani*, 102; *Epistle to Mohammed II*, 110–14; letter to Nicholas of Cusa (1453), 110, 149n23
Plato: city-soul analogy of, 76, 85; on furor's various types, 179n23; influence on *Furioso*, 81–87; on inner harmony, 75, 179–80n24; melancholy and, 81; *Mexenus*, 5; *Phaedrus*, 12, 83, 181n31; *Republic*, 4, 5, 12, 75–77, 83, 85, 87, 181n30; *Timaeus*, 83; tripartite soul described by, 76, 83–84; tyrant as wolf imagery in, 77, 85, 87
Pliny, *Natural History*, 47
Poliziano, Angelo, 53, 69, 168n36; *Pactianae Historia Coniurationis*, 66, 67, 174n92
Pollaiuolo, Antonio, 55, 170n46

Polynices, 37
Pompey, 1–2, 11, 29, 38, 40
Pomponius, Sextus, *Digest*, 4
Pope-Emperor relationship, 18, 33, 40–41, 163n77
Portugal's colonies, 109, 191n8
Poussin, Nicolas, 128
Priam, 5, 14, 144–46, 201n5
pride, 11, 45, 58, 60, 64, 65, 171n57
Prodicus, 54
Protestant Reformation (1517), 12, 107, 109, 115, 121
Prudentius, 75, 175n1
psychomachia (battle within the soul), 75–76
Ptolemy, *Geographia*, 114
Ptolemy XIII (pharaoh), 2, 29
Pulci, Luigi: background of, 53, 168n35, 170n53; "E' c'è venuto un medico Rosato" (sonnet), 50; Ficino and, 173n77; *Giostra*, 67; pro-Medicean party of, 44. *See also Morgante*

Quint, David, 13, 92, 121, 124, 141
Qur'an, 22, 27, 110–11, 155n17, 157n30

Ramachandran, Ayesha, 107
Ramusio, Giovan Battista, 130–31
Reeves, Marjorie, 41
Renaissance Italy: fluid state alliances in, 66; historical and intellectual dynamics of, 14; political power in, 13; revival of Augustan Roman empire and, 102; tyranny in, 77
Reni, Guido, 128
Rhodes, Ottoman conquest of (1522), 123
Riccoldo da Montecroce, 20, 26–28; *Contra legem Sarracenorum*, 22–23, 27, 110, 157n32; *Epistole*, 27; *Liber peregrinationis*, 156n28, 157n32
Rinaldo degli Albizzi, 66
Rinuccini, Alamanno, 164n1
Rodomonte, 124
Romagna region, 28
Roman Catholic Church: criticized for political meddling, 113; division with Lutheranism, 121; Islam as offshoot from, 108

Roman Empire: *Aeneid*'s depiction of, 10; Augustus's empire's origins in Trojan roots, 186n66; Dante criticizing Constantine for allowing papal control, 113; *Gerusalemme Liberata* telling myth of, 12; *Monarchia* on rise of, 29, 114, 171n61, 189n80; Renaissance Italy as revival of, 102; vision of global empire and, 10, 11, 132

Roman-Florentine rivalry, 28

Roman foundational myths, 77, 89, 93

Rome-Ferrara foundational parallel, 99, 100

Roncesvalles, Battle of (778), 58, 64, 66–70, 72–73, 165n3

Rosati, Giovanni, 168n31

Ruggieri, Archbishop, 29

Sacchetti, Franco, 54–55, 169n42

Sack of Rome (1527), 99, 103, 188n79

Safavid Empire, 115, 139

Sagundino, Nicola, 112–13

Said, Edward, 155n17

Saladin, 25, 140

Salutati, Coluccio, 7, 86, 165n6; *De laboribus Herculis*, 7, 55, 57–58; *Fabula de Vulpe et Cancro*, 47–48

Salviati, Francesco (Archbishop of Pisa), 73

Satan, 25, 70, 108, 118–23

Savonarola, Girolamo, 73

schism, Muhammad's responsibility for, 18–28, 40, 105. *See also* Muhammad

Schmitt, Carl: compared to Machiavelli, 151n37; *The Concept of the Political*, 3–5, 7–8, 13; on difference between *inimicus* and *hostis*, 7–8; on enmity in political life, 13, 14, 146; *Glossarium*, 8; other critics and thinkers in dialogue with, 13–14; *Theory of the Partisan*, 148n7

Scipio, 32, 65

scriptural references: 1 Corinthians, 137; 1 Corinthians 11:3, 27; 1 Corinthians 12:13–14, 25; 1 Corinthians 12:27, 21, 25; 1 Corinthians 13:13, 22; Daniel 4:12–34, 78; Ezekiel 22:27, 87; Ezekiel 34:1–31, 182n36; Galatians 3:8, 8; Galatians 3:28, 8; Genesis 11:1–9, 65; Genesis 16, 26; Genesis 21, 26; Isaiah 14:12–13, 61; John 10:11, 182n36; John 10:12, 103; John 10:16, 102, 105, 121; John 10:30, 28; John 19:19–22, 68; Judges 13–16, 177n12; Judith 13, 71; 2 Kings 5, 177n12; Luke 2:14, 68, 174n84; Luke 6:27, 8, 146; Luke 21:6, 61; Luke 22:45, 174n89; Luke 24:13–15, 36; Mark 13:2, 61; Mark 15:38, 174n89; Matthew 5:43–48, 111; Matthew 5:44, 8, 146; Matthew 24:37–25:2, 61; Matthew 26:49, 174n85; Matthew 26:50, 69; Matthew 27:46, 72; Matthew 27:51–54, 174n89; Psalm 113, 72

Seneca the Younger: *Aeneid*'s influence on, 185n61; *Apocolocyntosis*, 92; cosmopolitanism and, 9; *De beneficiis*, 54, 62, 171n64; *De Clementia*, 3, 62, 86, 90, 92, 104, 181n33, 185n59; *Epistles*, 62; Erasmus as editor of, 103; *Hercules Furens*, 6, 12, 76, 77, 82, 89, 90–94, 179n19, 184n52, 185n61; *Hercules on Oeta* (attributed to Pseudo-Seneca), 56–57, 170n47, 170n49; on Hercules's virtuous nature, 54; *hostis* and *adversarius* usage by, 6–7, 90; influence of, 86, 89–94, 181n33; Nero and, 3, 92–93, 185n58; suicide of, 3; tyranny as subject of, 86, 90–91, 104, 185n54

Sepulveda, Juan Ginés de, 8; *Apologia en favor del libro sobre las justas causas de la guerra*, 131–34; career of, 115–16; *Cohortatio ad Carolum V*, 115–16

Sergius (monk), 26, 110, 111, 156n22

Sforza, Galeazzo Maria, 58

Shakespeare, William, 14

Siege of Vienna (1529), 108, 109, 115, 123

Silvestri, Domenico, 165n6; *Cancer*, 48

Sixtus IV (pope), 66

Socrates, 81, 83

Sophocles, 5; *Ajax*, 81, 180n28; *Antigone*, 148n11; *Philoctetes*, 148n12; *Women of Trachis*, 57, 170n49

soul, battle within. *See* internal turmoil

Spanish colonies, 109, 116, 132–33, 191n8

speculum principis (mirror of the prince), 3

Spinoza, Baruch, 14

Statius, 36–37, 162n68; *Achilleid*, 37; *Thebaid*, 37

Stephens, Walter, 137, 139

Stoic thinkers, 4–7; on Achilles's conduct, 146; on cosmopolitanism, 9–10, 16, 75; Orlando's madness and, 76. *See also* Seneca the Younger
Strozzi, Palla, 66
Suetonius, *Lives of the Caesars*, 92
Suleiman the Magnificent, 108, 109, 114, 123
Sulla, 78
Sylvester (pope), 30, 113
Syria, 4, 25, 26, 177

Tasso, Torquato: *De la dignità*, 121–22, 141; *Giudicio sopra la Conquistata*, 120, 140. See also *Gerusalemme Liberata*
Teodorico of Lucca, 51, 52
Thebes, 37, 162n68
Thomas of Celano, 61
tongue, as instrument of discord, 159n51
Tonielli, Dolcino, 28
Tornabuoni, Lucrezia, 65
treachery: cancer imagery and, 11, 45–46, 49–53, 57, 105; in *Commedia*, 44, 45, 62–63; in *Iliad*, 143; as violation of trust, 43. See also *Morgante*
Trinity, 17–18, 26–27, 40, 111, 158n39, 158n43
Trojans, 19, 38, 89, 95–97, 100, 186. *See also* Hector; Priam
trust: justice linked with, 44, 172n72; in *Monarchia*, 43–44; in *Morgante*, 12, 44; treachery as violation of, 43
Turnus. See *Aeneid*
tyranny: Aristotle's description of tyrant, 86, 181n32; in *Furioso*, 77–79, 85–89, 105; internal turmoil within sovereign's own self and, 104; in medieval and Renaissance Italy, 77; mirrored relationship between tyrant and martyr, 92, 185n56; Plato's description of tyrant, 77, 85, 87, 105, 181n31;

Seneca's focus on, 86, 90–91, 104, 185n54; Spanish tyranny over American Indians, 132; tyrant as wolf imagery, 77, 84–85, 87, 182n35, 182nn37–38

Uguccione da Pisa, *Derivationes*, 47
Ulysses, 162n69
universalism, 3, 8, 10, 108, 114–15, 132–33, 140, 146. *See also* cosmopolitanism

Valla, Lorenzo, *Oration on the Donation of Constantine*, 113
Vegio, Maffeo, *Aeneidos liber*, 97
Vienna. See Siege of Vienna
Villani, Giovanni, *Cronica*, 51
Vincent of Beauvais, *Speculum Naturale*, 47
Virgil: compared to Bertran de Born, 37–38; in Dante's *Purgatorio*, 36–37; *Eclogue 4*, 37, 102, 112; Statius and, 36–37. *See also Aeneid*
Virgin Mary, 106, 137
Vitoria, Francisco de: *On the American Indians*, 133–34; *On the Evangelization of the Unbelievers*, 132
Vogt, Katja Maria, 9

Weil, Simone, 14, 144, 146
West Indies, 102, 103, 108, 116, 131
wild man, in Western culture, 84, 180n29
wolf imagery: madness and, 143; tyranny and, 77, 84–85, 87, 182n35, 182nn37–38

Xenophon: *Cyropaedia*, 66; *Memorabilia*, 54, 169n44

Zatti, Sergio, 106, 120–21
Zeno of Citium, 9

www.ingramcontent.com/pod-product-compliance
Lightning Source LLC
Chambersburg PA
CBHW030438300426
44112CB00009B/1055